A PRACTICAL GUIDE
TO CONDUCTING EMPIRICAL RESEARCH

A PRACTICAL GUIDE TO CONDUCTING EMPIRICAL RESEARCH

R. BARKER BAUSELL
University of Maryland

1817

HARPER & ROW, PUBLISHERS
New York, Cambridge, Philadelphia, San Francisco, London, Mexico City, São Paulo, Singapore, Sydney

Sponsoring Editor: Susan Mackey
Project Editor: Ellen MacElree
Cover Design: Miriam Recio
Text Art: Vantage Art, Inc.
Production: Willie Lane
Compositor: Progressive Typographers
Printer and Binder: The Maple-Vail Book Manufacturing Group

A Practical Guide to Conducting Empirical Research

Library of Congress Cataloging-in-Publication Data

Bausell, R. Barker
  A practical guide to conducting empirical research.

  Includes bibliographies and index.
  1. Psychology—Research.   2. Human experimentation
in psychology.   I. Title.
BF76.5.B388   1986   300′.72   85-24935
ISBN 0-06-040542-2

86 87 88 89 9 8 7 6 5 4 3 2

To Carole, my wife and partner.

CONTENTS

PREFACE

This book is designed to teach all the concepts needed to conduct empirical research involving the behavioral attributes of human subjects. As such, it is not targeted solely to aspiring psychologists, but to all the behavioral, educational, health, and helping professions that deal with people.

The philosophy guiding this endeavor is eminently pragmatic. Only content essential to the actual conduct of empirical research is included. Furthermore, when two or more options exist for accomplishing the same objective, I almost inevitably opt for simplicity rather than esoterica.

The book's primary reason for existence is completely reflected in its title. It is *a practical guide to conducting empirical research.* Its sole purpose is to enable the practitioner to conduct competent research addressing the well-being of human subjects with as little additional preparation as possible. To the extent that it succeeds in this far from modest objective, its author is indebted to five remarkable professionals.

I am grateful to the many people at Harper & Row who worked on this project, but especially to my former editor George A. Middendorf. From the inception of this project to its completion, and despite a great personal loss, he provided guidance, experience, and leadership. Appreciation is also extended to his extremely competent and conscientious reviewers: Douglas K. Candland of Bucknell University; Alfred Hall of the College of Wooster; and Michael H. Siegel of the State University of New York at Oneonta. Finally, I would like to thank William B. Moody of the University of Delaware, who introduced me to research and gave me the opportunity to conduct it.

R. Barker Bausell

A PRACTICAL GUIDE
TO CONDUCTING EMPIRICAL RESEARCH

one

INTRODUCTORY CONCEPTS

chapter *1*

An Overview of the Research Process

The creation of new knowledge is the primary means by which people attempt to understand their universe. It is also their primary, long-term strategy for improving their lot in that universe. There are many ways of attempting to obtain knowledge. Some of these methods, such as intuition, revelation, authority, logical manipulation of basic assumptions, informed guesses, observation, and reasoning by analogy, are of ancient and highly revered lineage. This book is concerned with another, relatively newer approach. It is an extremely goal-oriented technique called *empirical research.*

Empirical research is a term used to signify a method by which numbers are assigned to phenomena in order to make specific *comparisons* of some sort. Like science itself, though, empirical research eludes any really satisfactory attempts to arrive at a truly useful definition. Perhaps this is because empirical research is both a process and a product. As a process, it can be described in terms of a discrete, relatively small set of behaviors that basically constitute the tools of scientific inquiry. As a product it can be viewed either as a specific answer to a specific question or as a 10- to 20-page report describing both the genesis of the question and the means by which that question was answered.

There are many ways to categorize both empirical research (for example, basic versus applied, laboratory versus field, theory versus evaluative) and the genre of questions it addresses (such as psychological, educational, medical, physiological). In reality, however, the process and its product are completely generic to all such categorizations. The author's sole concession in this regard will thus be that the present book will largely confine itself to discussing research involving *human subjects* because of the specialized knowledge and skill required to assign numbers to things such as particles or forces (as in a discipline such as physics), tissues or specimens (as in physiological and biological research), solutions (as in chemistry), and so forth.

The basic principles and concepts certainly still apply to all types of empirical research; it is just that a book of this size cannot deal with topics as diverse as vagaries in the use of electron microscopes or special problems encountered in the dissection of rat livers. When the condition of the human animal as a *whole* is being studied, however, the commonalities are sufficiently strong to permit ample explanation of the specific behaviors necessary to the conduct of most scientific inquiry, regardless of any other categorization scheme. *This book is therefore designed to teach the reader the basic concepts underlying these behaviors.*

THREE DISTINGUISHING CHARACTERISTICS OF EMPIRICAL RESEARCH

Although empirical research differs from other methods of obtaining knowledge in a number of ways, three of its most important distinguishing characteristics are:

1. Its verifiable nature.
2. Its cumulative nature.
3. The finite nature of the resulting product.

Verification (or Replicability)

The research process involves a discrete series of steps that can be repeated, not only by the researcher who first performs them, but also by an independent colleague. This allows for independent corroboration of answers obtained to specific questions and it is perhaps the single characteristic that most uniquely separates the research process from the more introspective ways of obtaining knowledge. A mystic, for example, might very well come up with a specific answer to a specific question. Independent corroboration of this answer and the process by which it was generated would be, to say the least, most tenuous.

The Cumulative Nature of Empirical Knowledge

The genre of questions, sometimes called hypotheses, that are addressed by empirical researchers are *very* specific. They are of the form: is X greater than Y or is X related to Y? Empirical researchers cannot address big issues such as the meaning of life or the best way to interact with one's environment. Others, such as philosophers, can address these problems, perhaps even satisfactorily. *The problem is again that unlike empirical research their results are not subject to independent corroboration, thus no one ever knows for sure whether or not their solutions are correct.*

The Finiteness of Empirical Research

Because research studies address small, specific questions and because the steps taken to arrive at answers to these questions must be capable of replication by other researchers, the research process itself comprises small, discrete, almost ritualistic components. The final product accruing from a research study can thus be visualized as an answer to a very specific question accompanied by a detailed description of exactly how this answer was generated. In operational terms, what this amounts to is a written research report composed of certain clearly identifiable components that, in combination, are often no longer than 10 typed (double-spaced) pages. Though some scholars may object to the reduction of something as sacrosanct as the research process to such mundane terms, these research reports are the basic building blocks of many entire disciplines. They are the end product to which researchers aspire and they are a most *finite* product. Basically, the next fifteen chapters of this book can be visualized as designed to teach the reader how to effect each of the components of this final written research report while the last chapter discusses its evaluation and presentation.

THE COMPONENTS OF EMPIRICAL RESEARCH

The basic steps in the empirical research process are quite straightforward. Briefly they are:

1. *Identifying and composing a research question.* This step entails being familiar with past research studies in the chosen area of inquiry and, based on that familiarity, being able to construct an important, answerable question of the form:

    Is X greater than Y or is X related to Y?

2. *Selecting the subjects to be used to answer the research question.* Several things must be considered here, including:
    (a) that the prospective subjects' safety, dignity, and right to refuse to participate are protected,
    (b) that the types of subjects available for the study are representative of the types of people for whom the research question is most relevant, and
    (c) that sufficient numbers of subjects are available to provide a reliable answer to the research question.
    The first two issues will be discussed in Chapter 3, the third in Chapter 4.

3. *Deciding how to use the subjects to answer the research question.* Besides the obvious ethical considerations of protecting the subjects' safety, dignity, and right both to refuse participation and to withdraw from the study at any time (see Chapter 3), this step requires a number of very crucial procedural decisions including:
    (a) what attributes or reactions of subjects to address,

(b) how numbers will be assigned to these attributes or reactions, and

(c) how these measures will be used to form the basis of the comparison that will answer the research question. (For example, will some subjects be given an experimental treatment and then compared to a comparison group of some sort? Will one type of subject be compared to another type on the chosen attribute or reaction?)

Issues related to the first two decisions will be discussed in the measurement section (Part Three) of this book. Issues related to the third problem will be covered in the design section (Part Two).

4. *Analyzing the results.* This is perhaps the most straightforward component of the entire process. Here, the numbers resulting from the immediately preceding step are submitted to a statistical analysis with the express purpose of providing a "yes" or "no" answer to the research question. Chapters 13 through 16 are devoted to this very specific task.

5. *Interpreting and communicating the results.* Once the investigator has answered the research questions, the next step is to evaluate steps 1 through 4 as critically as possible to determine if the results obtained were valid. Should they be valid, then the following steps should be taken:

(a) probable reasons for the obtained results are advanced (primarily by tying them into previous research in the area),

(b) implications for theory, practice, or research are suggested,

(c) a suitable publishing medium (usually a journal or conference) is selected, and

(d) a report is written and submitted to that medium for peer review and possible publication.

These then are the basic components involved in the successful conduct of empirical research. The specific issues and behaviors associated with the actual performance of each step comprise the remainder of this book.

THE BOOK'S PURPOSE

Since its basic purpose is to attempt to explain all the concepts actually needed to conduct empirical research involving human subjects, this is an extremely ambitious little book. This is especially true since there are larger books dedicated to a single statistical procedure or a single methodological technique. What is unique about this book, however, is that it contains *only* that content necessary to conduct basic empirical research involving human subjects. What makes the achievement of its primary objective feasible is that the actual conduct of empirical research does not need to be a particularly formidable task. It does not require the internalization of an inordinately large number of intricate behaviors. What it does entail is a thorough understanding of a relatively small number of procedures, many of which are unfortunately mainly outside the realm of common sense human experience.

Thus, while this book may be brief, some of its contents are not necessarily easily mastered. Certain sections will require serious, uninterrupted study, for there is very little between its covers that the practitioner does not truly *need* to know. It is my opinion, in fact, that at least 95 percent of all published studies in the human sciences were either conducted using the techniques and concepts presented in this book or would have produced the same results had they been.

This is not to say, of course, that the conduct of any single study will require knowledge of every concept in this book, or that there are not several equally appropriate alternatives for each strategy presented here. Certainly there are also a great many more elegant, useful, and sophisticated procedures in use today than can (or should) be presented in an introductory text such as this. Multivariate statistical procedures are not covered, for example, nor are single-subject research models treated in any real depth. Such absences certainly do not reflect a bias against these procedures on the part of the author. Instead, they reflect a belief that more simple strategies are better suited for beginning researchers without either advanced training or access to an experienced mentor.

This book is therefore not intended for those who have the luxury of studying advanced methods and applied statistics prior to actually *conducting* their research. It is also, however, not intended solely for students taking their first-level research course. *A practical guide to conducting empirical research* is specifically designed for anyone who aspires to begin conducting good, clean, useful research into the human condition as *quickly* as possible. Toward this end, it is therefore dedicated to teaching *only* the basic, generic mechanisms required for actually doing research to address those important questions that remain unanswered in every discipline touching the well-being of human subjects.

chapter 2

Generating the Research Question

The formulation of an important, answerable question is undoubtedly the most crucial step in the research process. The ability to accomplish this step presupposes a basic core of knowledge within a discipline, for empirical research is not conducted in a vacuum. This knowledge, of course, is what chiefly differentiates a psychologist from an educator, or a sociologist from a health professional. It also is of inestimable value in enabling a professional to judge what is important and what is trivial, or in differentiating between what is needed and what is not.

Since anyone reading this book almost certainly has either obtained this fundamental background knowledge (or is in the very active pursuit thereof), this chapter will concentrate on the specific behaviors entailed in arriving at an answerable question, in assessing its importance, and in translating it into a testable hypothesis. Prerequisite to the first two objectives is a thorough *review of the literature* relative to the topic under consideration.

THE LITERATURE REVIEW

Although a general idea for a research study may come prior to a formal literature review, I believe that the final formulation of the research question should always follow such a review. There are a number of reasons for this advice, the most important of which is that a thorough conversance with a discrete body of research is perhaps the most fertile single source of good, answerable, research questions. Experienced investigators very often generate their research questions directly from perceived gaps in what has already been accomplished or from perceived shortcomings in specific studies. Although it is time consuming, there are a number of other reasons why acquiring a thorough knowledge of a literature is an efficient use of a beginning researcher's time. Among these are:

1. Occasionally the study being planned has already been executed, sometimes on a larger scale. Finding this out ahead of time can save both time and embarrassment.
2. Knowledge of other studies in the area often suggests additional variables or procedural changes that can strengthen the study being planned.
3. Since successful researchers normally conduct more than one study in a given area, familiarity with that area can be used over and over again in planning, report writing, and generating new research ideas. Once the past literature is assimilated, updating this knowledge is a relatively simple matter.
4. Research not published is effort wasted. Extensive knowledge of a literature enhances the probability of a manuscript being accepted for publication, both because of an improved introductory literature review (which is mandatory) and the possibility of a more coherent, thoughtful interpretation and discussion of one's results.
5. A thorough knowledge of a literature is useful for many extra-research purposes, including teaching, consulting, and nonempirical writing.

Thorough literature reviews can be relatively extensive undertakings. In most cases it is patently impossible to read all of the studies conducted in an area because their numbers may literally run into the thousands. Fortunately, it is seldom necessary to read an entire literature of this sort, since much of it will not be relevant to the problem at hand and since there will be a certain amount of duplication with the same study (or tiny parts thereof) by the same authors appearing in several different journals.

Although there are no hard and fast rules for conducting a literature review, there are some general, common sense guidelines that usually render the task quite manageable. Some of these include:

1. *Search for published literature reviews.* Some journals specialize in such pieces, including the *Sociological Review, Review of Educational Research,* and the *Psychological Bulletin.* Certain scholarly books of the sort typically published by university presses have long literature reviews as well. They may be used to get a feel for the type of research accomplished in a particular area as well as sources of key studies. Their conclusions should not be taken at face value, however, since independent reviewers often disagree about the same evidence. When available, seek *meta-analyses** of topics. These are empirical treat-

---

* For the most definitive (and readable) account of this methodology, see Glass, G. V., McGraw, B., and Smith, M. L. *Meta-Analysis in Social Research.* Beverly Hills, Calif.: Sage Publications, 1981.

ments of completed research studies and as such give a much more systematic assessment of a literature. (Unfortunately, relatively few have been completed to date.)

2. *Employ all the relevant abstracting and citation services available.* Possibilities include:

> *Child Development Abstracts and Bibliography*
> *Current Index to Journals in Education*
> *Dissertation Abstracts International*
> *Education Index*
> *Government Reports Announcements & Index*
> *Index Medicus*
> *Index of Economic Articles*
> *Interagency Panel Information System*
> *International Bibliography of Economics*
> *International Bibliography of Political Science*
> *International Political Science Abstracts*
> *Journal of Economic Literature*
> *Library of Congress Catalog*
> *Medical Literature and Retrieval System*
> *National Clearinghouse for Mental Health Information*
> *National Institute for Mental Health Grants and Contracts Information System*
> *National Technical Information Service*
> *Psychological Abstracts*
> *Research in Education*
> *Smithsonian Science Information Exchange*
> *Sociological Abstracts**

3. *Use computerized retrieval systems as gross screens.* Too much should not be expected of computerized literature searches since they are only as good as their cataloguers. Some systems are better than others, although all are probably in their infancy as compared to their eventual potential. In general, regardless of the system used, such searches produce only a fraction of the relevant literature and should *never* constitute the only method used.

4. *Concentrate on major journals in any given area.* Anyone unfamiliar with academic publishing would be astonished at the sheer number of scholarly journals available. Every discipline does have relatively *few* high prestige journals, however, and, although there are exceptions, most major studies are published in them simply because of this prestige and the fact that their circulations tend to be so much greater than that of minor journals. The *quality* of the research published in these major journals tends to be higher as well. (They are most often published by major professional societies, such as the American Psychological Association, the American Educational Research Association, the American Sociological Association, and so forth.) For a selected few journals, actually reading the yearly title index of recent volumes may yield an otherwise missed study.

---

* Borrowed largely from Glass et al., p. 62.

5. *Ask for help.* Reference librarians are often excellent sources of ideas. So are college professors and researchers who have published in an area. A long-distance telephone call to a recognized authority is often an excellent investment, although some people are harder to reach than others. (If this strategy is used, it is helpful to make one's questions as brief and focused as possible. Also, it is unrealistic to expect busy professionals to return calls when it is they who are being asked for a favor.)

6. *Read the key studies* (that is, the ones most often cited) *in the area.* There is often a good reason for their popularity.

7. *Employ the Social Sciences Citation Index as a systematic extension of item 6.* If a few truly landmark studies can be located in a particular area, then chances are that most subsequent research will cite them. This service provides bibliographic information on authors who do subsequently cite the keyed studies.

8. *Use the reference lists of published studies as sources of additional references.* Their authors had to do literature reviews too and there is nothing wrong with using the fruits of these labors. Dissertations are especially productive in this regard, since they usually contain long, thorough literature reviews. (All such references used should of course be read, not simply lifted from the secondary source, since different researchers sometimes interpret the same findings quite differently.)

9. Regardless of the strategies used, *always record and categorize one's efforts in some systematic way.* Memory will not suffice after a certain number of studies have been read. Use of tried and trusted index cards detailing full bibliographic information as well as a synopsis of selected procedures and results remains as good a technique as any. One should also keep in mind the reasons the literature review is being conducted in the first place. Each study should be read with an eye toward gleaning procedural ideas for the study under consideration *as well as* the generation of additional (or alternative) research questions. One should not rely on memory here either, but instead keep a list of all brainstorms (and even minor squalls).

OTHER SOURCES OF RESEARCH QUESTIONS

Previously published research is certainly not the only source of new research questions. Some very credible authors, in fact, contend that all research should be generated from existing *theory,* that the purpose of science itself is to test (and thereby generate) theory and *nothing else.*

Although such an extreme position may place too heavy a burden on some of the younger human sciences whose theories tend to be a bit too diffuse to predict something as specific as phenomenon *A* occurring under conditions *B, C,* and *D,** there is no question that theory can be another fertile source of research questions for beginning and experienced researchers alike. It is therefore wise for all researchers to be conversant with the major theories in their

* In the way, for example, that Einstein's work was able to predict the effect of gravity on light.

fields. (If such a familiarity does not lead to specific, testable predictions, then there is certainly nothing wrong with even beginning researchers' formulating their own theories and testing them.*)

Another potentially profitable source of research questions emanate from exclusively *practical* considerations. These questions are based on a desire or a need either to know if an existing program or practice works or to solve a pressing clinical problem. For example:

1. Is the drug abuse therapy supplied by clinic *X* effective in reducing recidivism?
2. Does the master's degree offered by program *Y* produce more effective teachers?
3. Is antacid *Z* more effective than antacid *Y* in reducing heartburn?
4. Will reducing class size facilitate learning?

In many cases the primary audience for such studies is restricted to the institution in which they are conducted, although the investigators undertaking them usually aspire to generalize their results to other settings and situations. This type of research is sometimes called *evaluation* (or *evaluation research*) and its main distinction (which admittedly has a degree of arbitrariness about it) is that its questions are pretty much preexisting, being of the "Does it work?" genre. Although fraught with their own special difficulties, evaluation research can serve as an excellent starting point for beginning researchers who have difficulty in generating other types of questions.

RESEARCH QUESTIONS AS COMPARISONS

Regardless of their source, research questions always reduce to comparisons between two or more things. These comparisons in turn always take the form either of differences or of relationships.

Differences

In research, differences are usually assessed between groups (for example, subjects who received an experimental treatment versus those who did not), different types of people (for example, males versus females), or different periods of time. These entities are compared on a specific measure of some sort, such as scores on a test, perceptual or sensory reactions to a stimulus, physiological state, and so forth. All four of the hypothetical research questions presented above would probably be answered in terms of such a difference.

Relationships

Relationships are assessed between measures themselves. If they exist, they are either positive, negative, or curvilinear in nature. A positive relationship re-

---

* To be credible, of course, a theory must be both consonant with (i.e., not contradicted by) previous research findings and capable of being invalidated by the study it is being used to justify.

flects a situation in which a person who scores high on measure X would be expected to also score high on measure Y. An example of such a relationship might be the relationship between intelligence and school achievement, where students with higher IQ scores also tend to score higher on standardized achievement tests. A negative relationship reflects the scenario in which people who score high on one measure tend to score low on the other measure. As an example, individuals with higher incomes might be expected to be less liberal than those with moderate and lower incomes. An example of a curvilinear relationship might be the association between age and physical strength. Here the two measures would be expected initially to bear a positive relationship with one another as individuals' physical strength increases from childhood well into adulthood. Following a leveling off period the relationship then changes direction with physical strength decreasing with advanced age.

EVALUATING THE IMPORTANCE OF A RESEARCH QUESTION

Ironically, the requirement that an empirical research question must be answerable in terms of a specific comparison of some sort can invite triviality. Although judgments as to which research questions are important and which trivial are undeniably subjective, I would counsel all beginning investigators to at least address this issue by taking the following steps:

1. Construct (preferably in writing) all the conceivable outcomes that can accrue from a given study. (It is important to remember that these answers will be in terms of a comparison of some sort, namely that a difference or relationship exists between two or more entities. The answers will *not* be of the form: "the meaning of life is" or "the best way to teach young children mathematics is. . . .")
2. Judge the probability of each of these answers occurring as realistically as possible. (Some outcomes may be much more likely than others. Some outcomes are almost always more exciting or interesting than others.)
3. Attempt to judge exactly what effect each of the possible outcomes is likely to have. If the study is clinical in nature, what effect (if any) will each answer have on clinical *practice?* If the study is theoretical in nature, can any of the answers substantively challenge the credibility of the theory being tested? If the study is an empirical extension of other research, can any of the answers explain previously unexplained phenomena? (In other words, to what use can the answers to the research questions be put?)
4. Connect the probabilities assigned in step 2 with any positive answers accruing from step 3 and decide whether or not the study is worth conducting. If there are no definitely positive answers to step 3, then the research question is probably of questionable significance.

CONVERTING RESEARCH QUESTIONS INTO HYPOTHESES

Once an important research question has been formulated, it is often a good idea for a beginning researcher to convert it into an operational definition of the exact comparison that comprises what the study is all about. Traditionally framed as declarative sentences, these operational distillations of a study's purpose are called *hypotheses.*

A formally written hypothesis has a number of merits. Among these are its ability:

1. To delineate to the reader exactly what the comparison is that comprises the purpose of the study.
2. To force the researcher to come to grips with exactly what is being tested.
3. To underline for both the reader and the researcher the relatively mundane fact that, regardless of how important a study seems, it is really nothing more than a tool for providing a simple "yes" or "no" answer to a relatively simple question.

These are all important points, for it is far too easy to view a study as more than it is and to forget that empirical research is little more than a series of maddeningly tiny steps. Once this basic realization is obtained, the actual writing of a hypothesis becomes a relatively simple matter. There are certain rules that should be kept in mind, however. Five of the important of these follow:

1. *The hypothesis must be testable.* This means that it must specify a relationship or difference to which a single probability level can be assigned. It also means that words such as "good," "best," or "right" have no place. "A combination of exercise and diet is the best way to lose weight" is not a testable hypothesis. Research can only *compare.* To determine the best possible method of doing something would necessitate the empirical comparison of all *possible* treatments, which is an obvious impossibility. "A combined program of exercise and diet results in greater weight loss than diet alone" does involve an empirical comparison:

Exercise + diet   versus   diet alone

2. *The hypothesis must state exactly what variables make up this relationship or difference.* This does not mean that the exact title of a particular measure need be given or that the procedural differences between groups need be specified, but it does mean that an unfamiliar reader should be able to glean what the study is generally about by reading its hypothesis(es). Thus, "Intelligence is positively related to achievement" is not specific enough. "Lorge-Thorndike IQ scores are positively related to California Achievement Test scores" is probably too cumbersome (although there is nothing logically wrong with such specificity). "Intelligence is positively related to standardized mathematics test scores among fifth grade students"* is probably a happy medium, although large individual differences are possible (and permissible).

---

* I suggest the inclusion of at least a cursory description of the types of subjects being employed, since this sheds further light on the nature of the variables being studied.

3. *Without specifying actual statistical procedures to be used, the hypothesis must convey the nature of the relationship or difference being tested.* To begin with, it is helpful to specify whether it is a relationship between measures or a difference between groups (or types of subjects) that is being tested. Thus, for a study in which one group receives a manipulation of some sort and the other does not, the hypothesis should be stated in terms of differences or effects. For example:

> *Longer fifth-grade math classes result in higher scores on a standardized mathematics exam.*

or, more explicitly

> *Fifth-grade students taught mathematics for 60 minutes per day will achieve higher scores on a standardized mathematics test than comparable students receiving 30 minutes of mathematics instruction per day.*

or, if the researcher prefers not to specify a direction to the difference:

> *There will be a difference in fifth-grade standardized mathematics scores between students receiving 30-minute and those receiving 60-minute mathematics classes.*

Note that, although all of these formulations are perfectly acceptable, there is considerable variation in their wording. It is hoped that this highlights the fact that there is no single correct way to write a hypothesis. Hypotheses, after all, are a means of prose communication and anyone familiar with literature realizes the extremely wide variations in style between equally effective writers. Note also that these hypotheses are capable of communicating a great deal in a single sentence about the study being conducted. In the immediately preceding examples, the second two formulations are a bit more helpful in this regard than the first. All serve notice, however, that class length is being manipulated to ascertain its effect on mathematics achievement.

4. *Without going into excruciating detail, the hypothesis must reflect all of the variables (or categories of variables) of interest.* For the relatively simple examples used so far, this rule is self-explanatory and obvious. A hypothesis such as "Longer mathematics classes are superior to shorter ones" would tell the reader very little about the purpose of the study. (Superior with respect to what would be the obvious question.) For studies involving more than two variables, however, it is important that the attendant hypothesis reflect all of the relevant variables. For example, the hypothesis

> *Fifth-grade, standardized mathematics scores are a function of (or are related to or can be predicted by) intelligence, socioeconomic status, sex, and previous mathematics grades.*

heralds a study in which a number of measures are to be correlated with standardized mathematics scores. If a large number of such variables were to be employed, the hypothesis would simply list the categories to which they belong:

> *Fifth-grade, standardized mathematics scores are related to intelligence, previous achievement measures, and selected demographic characteristics of the students and their families.*

Sometimes authors eschew formal hypotheses altogether for studies employing complex relationships, but it remains a good idea for beginning investigators to write out their hypotheses formally, even if these formulations do not find their way into the final research report.

5. *Hypotheses are formulated prior to the conduct of a study.* Explicitly formulating hypotheses prior to a study can help avoid inadvertently capitalizing on spurious results. In most present-day research, a great deal more data are collected than are needed to test a study's primary hypotheses. Thus, while none of these primary relationships may pan out, one or more incidental variables may be found to be related to *something.* Given the ubiquitous power of hindsight, it is then sometimes tempting to ignore completely one's original predictions (hypotheses) in favor of the incidental findings. The problem with such a strategy is that if enough relationships are tested, some of them will pan out by chance alone. Hypotheses are thus not only a form of communication, they are also a means of forcing researchers to make their choice and pay their money rather than betting on the horse after the race has been run.

Types of Hypotheses

There are two basic types of hypotheses that will be discussed in this book. These are *null* hypotheses and *research* hypotheses. The main difference between the two is that a null hypothesis explicitly states that there is *no* difference or relationship between the groups or measures being studied while a research hypothesis states that such a difference or relationship *does* exist. Which form a hypothesis takes makes very little difference since they are really simply different sides of the same coin.

All the examples presented so far have been written as research hypotheses. To change any of them to the null form it is simply necessary to insert a negative disclaimer at an appropriate point. Hence the null form of:

> *There will be a difference in average fifth-grade standardized mathematics scores between students receiving 30-minute and those receiving 60-minute classes.*

becomes

There will be no difference in average fifth-grade standardized mathematics scores between students receiving 30-minute and those receiving 60-minute classes.

HYPOTHESIS TESTING

The chief function of a hypothesis is to distill a study's purpose into a testable comparison. This comparison, be it a relationship or a difference, is then subjected to statistical analysis that in effect is used to assign a probability level to the study's results. If the resulting probability is below a predetermined value (usually .05, which means that the actually obtained difference would occur by chance alone *less* than 5 times out of a 100), then the result is said to be *statistically significant* and the null hypothesis is rejected. (Since it is the other side of the coin, the research hypothesis is then said to be supported, although strictly speaking it is the null hypothesis that is considered to be tested by statistical analysis.) If the analysis does not result in statistical significance, then the null hypothesis is *not* rejected (and the research hypothesis is obviously not supported).*

Although the logic of hypothesis testing will be considered in much more detail in Chapter 4, this is really all there is to the basic process. In many ways it is an appealing process because there are no maybes involved. A hypothesis is either rejected or not rejected (in the case of the null), supported or not supported (in the case of the research hypothesis).

SUMMARY

The three most common sources of important, testable hypotheses are:

1. Previous research literature.
2. Theory.
3. Practical problems within a particular discipline.

The most important points to remember when formulating a hypothesis are:

1. *Communicate the essence of what is being studied.* The reader should be able to obtain a good sense of what a study is all about by simply reading its hypotheses. This includes specifying what the variables are and the general manner in which they will be compared to one another (for example, whether differences between groups or relationships between the measures administered to the same subjects are of interest).
2. *Make sure that the hypothesis, via the procedures actually employed in*

---

* The usage of this terminology occasionally varies from discipline to discipline. Some investigators prefer "accept as probably true" or "reject as probably false," for example. Others object to the use of the word "accept" at all, especially with respect to the null hypothesis. The beginning researcher is therefore advised to adopt the most common usage in his or her field.

the study, can either be rejected as probably false or accepted as probably true. Said another way, if a single probability cannot be assigned to a discrete comparison, the hypothesis is not testable. A hypothesis that is not testable is not a hypothesis as far as empirical research is concerned.

Thus, "A combination of diet and exercise is an effective way to lose weight" is not an empirically testable hypothesis simply because no discrete *comparison* was specified. The word "effective" has no meaning without a definition of some sort, and this definition *is* the thing, condition, standard, or group to which a "combination of diet and exercise" is to be compared.

"Intelligence is strongly correlated to fifth-grade standardized mathematics scores" is not testable because "strongly correlated" has no empirical definition. "Measure x is reliable" is not a testable hypothesis, because reliability standards are left undefined. *Empirical research, by definition, demands a comparison of some sort.* There is no more important rule than this, both for writing hypotheses and for actually conducting research.

The basic logic behind testing a hypothesis involves:

1. *Assigning a probability level to the specific comparison with which it is associated.* This is done via statistical analysis.
2. *Comparing this obtained probability with a predetermined value* (usually .05).
3. *If the obtained probability level is below the predetermined value, then the results are said to be statistically significant, the null hypothesis is rejected, and the research hypothesis is said to be supported.*

chapter 3

Selecting Subjects

Once an answerable research question or testable hypothesis has been formulated, the next step is to decide what types of people will be employed in the study at hand. This decision is usually dictated by two factors: the types of subjects available for study and the types of subjects to whom the researcher wishes to generalize the study results.

PROTECTING SUBJECTS' RIGHTS

It is natural for researchers to confine their efforts to populations with whom they are most familiar and to whom they have the most free access. Clinical psychologists thus employ patients in the facilities in which they have privileges; educational researchers work with students; college instructors conduct experiments on students enrolled in their courses. Exceptions certainly exist, but the use of large groups of subjects who are representative of the total population of the country as a whole is rare.

Given the vulnerable nature of many of these groups, coupled with the unfortunate fact of life that some researchers (albeit a very small minority) can be insensitive to the rights and safety of others, the first priority in selecting subjects must be the insurance of their rights. Most institutions have committees dedicated to protecting the rights of human subjects. In addition, thesis and dissertation students must typically receive permission from an academic committee as well. If the researcher is conducting the study in an institution other than his or her own, the chances are excellent that still another source of permission must be obtained. One of the first steps that a researcher must take, therefore, is to find out from whom formal permission to approach subjects must be obtained and the way in which this permission must be obtained. (In most cases a written proposal of some sort is required that details the purpose of the study and exactly how it will be carried out.)

The responsibility of researchers to their subjects extends beyond compliance with any committee guidelines, however. Most major professional associations and funding agencies have published extensive ethical guidelines dealing both with institutional and individual responsibilities in this regard.

In general, most suggest the following minimum set of behaviors on the part of the investigator:

1. *List in detail everything that research participation entails.* This includes the amount of time required, possible embarrassment, pain, physical or emotional discomfort, and, of course, risk to the subject of any sort. None of these should be minimized in order to encourage participation. In general, I do not believe that beginning researchers should be allowed to employ procedures that are *capable* of resulting in any sort of physical or emotional risk to subjects. I am not even sure that they should be permitted to conduct physically unsupervised research on very ill or emotionally damaged subjects. Part of the process of learning to do research is making mistakes. These mistakes are best made in settings in which the consequences are less severe.

2. *Ensure that the subject is capable of understanding what participation entails.* Obviously, if children are to be used, participation (if it involves any conceivable physical or emotional risk) should be solicited both from them (if they are old enough to understand the situation) and from their parents. If the subjects are mentally incompetent, participation should be solicited from a competent family member or guardian whether the institutional guidelines require this or not. Regardless of the type of subject used, the language must be explicit and simple enough so that subjects can understand what they are agreeing to. This does not mean that the researcher needs to explain all the intricacies involved in a study or to go into a great deal of detail concerning how the study is designed. It is enough to tell subjects the general topic area of the research and exactly what will be required of them (or done to them).

3. *Assure the subject that participation is totally voluntary and that no adverse consequences will accrue as a result of refusing to participate.* This should be spelled out and not assumed. Children must know that their teachers won't frown on their nonparticipation. Patients must be assured that their care will in no way be affected by their refusal to participate. If feasible, subjects should be assured that no one but the researcher will even know whether or not they participate. If such anonymity is not possible, the researcher should take pains to communicate to whomever deals with these subjects that it is all right if people do refuse to participate. The researcher has an obligation to protect his or her subjects, even after the study is over.

4. *Give the subject the right to withdraw from the study at any time.* Withdrawals during the course of a study can be a bitter pill for a

researcher to swallow, since enough of them can completely invalidate the entire effort. However, subjects must feel they have this right. On the positive side, few are likely to do so if the procedures are reasonable. Furthermore, assurance that withdrawal without penalty of *any* sort is an option will probably increase initial participation.

5. *Whenever possible, preserve the subject's anonymity. Confidentiality should always be maintained.* Steps should be taken to ensure that no one except the researcher (or research staff) can identify an individual subject's responses or behaviors in the experimental setting. Further, subjects should be apprised of the identity of those persons who will have access to their records as well as any possible exceptions to this stated degree of confidentiality. People are often quite sensitive about their personal performance. Since grouped data are usually of primary interest in most research anyway, there is seldom a need to examine any one person's responses. If the subject is institutionalized, requests by clinicians to review subjects' research performance should be tactfully refused. If names are not necessary for study purposes, they should not even be collected. If individual identification is necessary (such as for matching a pretest with a posttest), special numbers should be employed when the data are recorded with a code book containing the matching names kept separately. When the study has been completed, this code book should be destroyed.

6. *Since time is a valuable resource for both subjects and researchers, conserve it by performing only clean and worthwhile research.* (Assurance of which is the purpose of this book.)

GENERALIZING FROM A SAMPLE TO THE POPULATION

The group of subjects the investigator actually studies (or collects data on) is called the research *sample.* Researchers, of course, almost always aspire to generalize the results of their studies to larger numbers of people than comprise a single sample. This larger group, of which the sample is a subset, is called the research *population.*

The cleanest example of the relationship between the research sample and its attendant population is found in large-scale survey research in which a pollster attempts to estimate the proportion of the people in the country as a whole who, say, indicate an intent to vote for candidate X. Since it is patently impossible to ask the entire voting population of the United States whom they intend to vote for, the pollster interviews a representative subset (or sample) of this population instead and *generalizes* the resulting answers to this total population. Here, the absolute representativeness of the sample to the population as a whole is of crucial importance. Should a sample of educational psychology students be polled instead, for example, the survey's results would probably be seriously biased, given the number of ways that psychology students differ from the general voting population (such as education, socioeconomic status, age, and so forth).

For the types of studies dealt with in this book, the relationship between the research sample and the population to whom the results can be generalized is seldom so clear-cut. For the vast majority of these studies, there are really two populations: the one actually available to the researcher (and from which a sample is drawn) and the one to which the researcher aspires to generalize the study results. Thus, the educational researcher who studies students in middle school X because he or she is friendly with its principal really wishes to generalize the findings to all school children of this approximate age group; the psychologist conducting research in the drug abuse clinic in which he or she works hopes the findings will be relevant to all patients undergoing drug abuse therapy.

Such inferential leaps are, of course, often quite hazardous. Fortunately, for research involving relationships or differences (which is the primary focus of this book) the issue of absolute representativeness of a sample to its population is not so crucial as it is for a study whose purpose is only to arrive at a precise description, such as that 48 percent of the population indicate an intent to vote for candidate A, 46 percent for candidate B, and 6 percent undecided.

Thus, the relative effectiveness of drug A versus drug B in preventing colds might very well be ascertainable by employing educational psychology students, since a *relative* answer would be sought (that is, A is more effective, less effective, or no different than B).* If longer classes are shown to result in greater learning in middle school X, it may be quite reasonable to expect the same relationship to occur in other middle schools (1) *as long as the study in question was competently performed* and (2) *as long as middle school* X *is not very different in some way from most other middle schools.* This entire book is dedicated to ensuring the first point. The second point is best addressed by

1. Collecting as much descriptive data on an available population and its resulting sample as possible.
2. Evaluating that data objectively.
3. Communicating both the descriptive data and their evaluation in the final research report in order to enable other researchers to form an informed opinion regarding just how far the study's results can be generalized.

DESCRIBING A SAMPLE

There are many ways of effectively describing a sample, depending on the nature of the variables involved. In this book, variables and the numbers associated with them will be divided into two basic camps: one whose primary purpose is to *categorize* subjects, the second to *order* subjects in some way along a continuum.

Categorical Variables

Examples of categorical descriptors are marital status, sex, personality type, diagnosis, profession, religion, and so forth. Here, if numbers are assigned to

---

* The issue of differential effectiveness of an intervention is referred to as aptitude-treatment interactions (Bracht, 1970). In my opinion they occur very rarely and seldom replicate when they do occur.

Table 3-1   A TYPICAL FREQUENCY DIS-
                TRIBUTION

Marital status	Frequency	Percentage (%)
Single	241	33
Married	421	58
Divorced	42	6
Widowed	24	3

categories at all, their only function is to label those categories; the particular numbers used are completely arbitrary, imply no order whatever, and are interchangeable. Thus, for coding purposes married persons might be assigned a 1, unmarried people a 2, divorced people a 3, and widows or widowers a 4. These numbers imply no order between categories: widow/widowers are neither more or less than single people, they could have just as easily been assigned either a 1, a 2, or a 3.

Samples are usually described on variables such as this via simple frequency distributions, where the numbers of subjects (or frequencies) and perhaps percentages of the total are given for each category. The marital status of a research sample might therefore be presented as shown in Table 3-1.

Variables Involving an Intrinsic Order

Here the assignment of particular numbers is not arbitrary but reflects subjects' relative possession of an attribute or their relative reaction to a stimulus. Such numbers can also be used to place individual subjects on a continuum from low to high, lesser to greater, or fewer to more.*

Examples of such variables are performance of almost any kind, scores on tests, attitudes, physiological characteristics (for example, height, weight, age, body temperature, reaction time), and so forth. Samples are usually described on such variables in terms of an average score (referred to as a measure of *central tendency*) and a statistic that describes the spread of scores (or *dispersion*) within the group.

Although there are several methods of describing a sample's *central tendency* and *dispersion* on a measure, only two will be recommended here, the *arithmetic mean* and the *standard deviation.*

The Arithmetic Mean   The mean or average of a group of scores is undoubtedly the most widely used descriptive statistic in existence. All students use it to compute their grades and grade point average. Whenever the average value or amount of something is desired, it is the mean that is usually used to compute it.

The mean is arrived at by simply adding up all the scores contained in a group and dividing by the number of scores involved. In other words:

---

* As will be discussed in Chapter 10, I do not recommend the use of pure *ranks* except for descriptive purposes.

$$\overline{X} = \frac{\Sigma X}{n} \tag{3-1}$$

where $\overline{X}$ designates the mean

Σ indicates sum of

X represents any given individual's score

n designates the number of subjects (or scores) involved

(These symbols will be used throughout this book, thus the reader should attempt to become familiar with them.)

Thus, to compute the mean of a hypothetical sample's body weights, one would simply add up the scores involved and divide by the actual number of scores. If a sample were composed of the following five weights (110, 140, 150, 160, and 190), then, its mean body weight would be computed as follows:

$$\overline{X} = \frac{110 + 140 + 150 + 160 + 190}{5} = \frac{750}{5} = 150$$

The Standard Deviation   Although extremely useful, the mean has one serious descriptive limitation. It tells the reader very little about individual differences *within* the sample. A mean of 150, for example, could just as easily describe the following set of scores in which there is much less variability or range than the five previous scores: 145, 148, 150, 152, and 155.

What is obviously needed, therefore, is some single number like the arithmetic mean capable of describing variability among subjects in a sample. One possibility would simply be the *range* of the scores (that is, 110 to 190 in the present case). A better descriptor (since it takes all the numbers into account instead of just two) is a statistic called the *standard deviation.* (Actually, it is sometimes helpful to report both the range of scores *and* the standard deviation.)

To understand how the standard deviation functions, it is most helpful to first look at its parent concept, suitably named the *variance.* (In reality the two can be visualized as the same entity, since the square root of the variance is equal to the standard deviation: $\sqrt{\text{variance}} = \text{S.D.}$ or $\text{S.D.}^2 = \text{variance}$.)

In statistics, the variance of a *set* of scores is defined as the *average squared difference of those scores from the set's arithmetic mean.* (Thus, the standard deviation of a set of scores could be defined as *the square root* of the average squared difference of those scores from the set's arithmetic mean.) It is, in other words, possible to generate *one* number that represents the variance in a set of scores. This number represents how divergent the scores are from the average or mean score. The larger this number, the greater the difference among individual scores.

Symbolically, this variance can be represented as follows:

$$\text{Var} = \frac{\Sigma(X - \overline{X})^2}{n - 1} \tag{3-2}$$

where it will be remembered that

Σ means sum of
X stands for any given individual's score
$\overline{X}$ = the arithmetic mean
n = the number of scores in the set
Var = the variance

or, alternately,

$$\text{S.D.} = \sqrt{\frac{\Sigma(X - \overline{X})^2}{n - 1}} \tag{3-3}$$

To illustrate the computational aspects of this formula, the variance of the hypothetical sample's body weights will be computed. The standard deviation will simply be the square root of this figure. In actual practice, researchers seldom compute such statistics themselves, relying on computers (and, in some cases, inexpensive calculators) to do it for them. To rely on such aids without understanding the computational and conceptual underpinning of this integral statistic is not wise.

Variance

$$= \frac{(110 - 150)^2 + (140 - 150)^2 + \cdots + (190 - 150)^2}{5 - 1}$$

$$= \frac{(-40)^2 + (-10)^2 + (0)^2 + (10)^2 + (40)^2}{5 - 1}$$

$$= \frac{1600 + 100 + 0 + 100 + 1600}{5 - 1}$$

$$= \frac{3400}{4} = 850$$

and thus the standard deviation equals $\sqrt{850} = 29.15$.

The Normal Bell-Shaped Curve

Although it is not obvious with numbers of this size, the standard deviation is the more useful formulation from a descriptive perspective, even though the standard deviation and the variance of a set of scores are *the same basic entity*. The standard deviation is a reflection of the amount of dispersion within a set of scores based on the actual scale of measurement being used, pounds in the present case. The standard deviation, in conjunction with the arithmetic mean, has an even more interesting characteristic, however. It is part and parcel of the most successful mathematical model in the human sciences: *the normal bell-shaped curve.*

For reasons that are not entirely clear, scientists have learned that the scores on most human attributes (for example, intelligence, height, body weight) are dispersed in remarkably similar ways. Approximately the same number of people fall above the mean as below it (which is not tautological since the mean is heavily influenced by extreme scores) and, much more remarkably, approximately 68 percent of these scores fall between one standard deviation above and one standard deviation below the mean.

Furthermore, approximately 95 percent of the population falls between *two* standard deviations above and below the mean, 99.7 percent within plus and minus three standard deviations, and so forth (Figure 3-1).

Obviously, this model cannot be interpreted literally for very small samples such as the one illustrated above. Suppose, however, that our sample had consisted of 1,000 subjects. Chances are that the resulting distribution would *approximate* a normal curve. To the extent that it did, it would be predicted that 68 percent, or 680 of the subjects, would weigh somewhere between 120.85 (that is, the mean minus one standard deviation: $150 - 29.15$) and 179.15 ($150 + 29.15$) pounds. Furthermore, 950 of the scores would fall between 91.70 and 208.30 (plus and minus two standard deviations from the mean).

There is, of course, no guarantee that any set of scores will conform so nicely to the mathematical model represented by the normal curve. The smaller the sample employed, the more probable that the actual distribution will not so conform, although this of course also depends on the sample's representativeness to the population from which it was drawn. The normal curve, after all, is a theoretical construction assuming an infinite number of scores on a measure that has no upward or lower limit.

A sample of, say, 30 scores on a 10-item test can thus only very grossly approximate a normal curve. The concept remains helpful in a conceptual way,

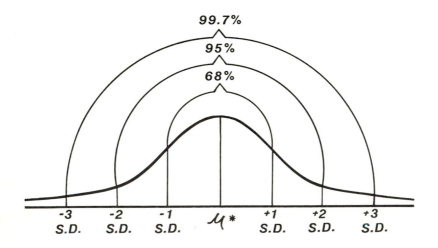

* This symbol is used to denote the mean of a population.

Figure 3-1   The normal curve.

however, since it can usually be assumed that if the test were to be administered to a *very* large sample the distribution would *approximate* a normal curve. This assumption then lends some meaning to the absolute size of the standard deviation: it allows the researcher to perform the quick mental calculation of adding and subtracting the value from the mean. This conceptual aid constitutes a very important use for the standard deviation in and of itself. And, when coupled with the arithmetic mean (and possibly the range of scores), it allows a sample to be described quite succinctly within the text of a research report. In the present case, this description might take the following form:

> *Body weights were approximately normally distributed and ranged from 110 to 190 with a mean of 150 and a standard deviation of 29.15.*

or

> *Body weights were approximately normally distributed and ranged from 110 to 190 ($\overline{X} = 150$, S.D. = 29.15).*

If several means and standard deviations are to be used to describe a sample, the researcher may, of course, opt to place them all in a table (Table 3-2). (Note that the total number of subjects involved is always presented along with the other descriptive statistics.)

Limitations of Sample Descriptions

Regardless of how carefully a sample is described for research in which a relationship or difference is to be generalized, there is always a danger in unintentionally winding up with a group of research subjects who are not demonstratively similar to any other known group of people (not even of the specific, available population of the institution or setting from which they were chosen). If this is allowed to happen, *the particular results achieved by the study may be specific to the types of subjects selected rather than the actual procedures employed.*

Given the myriad ways in which groups of people can differ from one another, a natural question thus becomes:

> *How can researchers ever be sure of arriving at a completely representative group of subjects, given the fact that all the relevant variables needed to ensure representativeness may not even be known?*

Table 3-2 DESCRIPTIVE STATISTICS FOR
SAMPLE X (*n* = 5)

Variable	$\overline{X}$	S.D.
Body weight	150.00	29.15
Age	42.11	10.24
IQ	110.42	9.40

The answer lies in one of the most powerful and intriguing procedures in research, a procedure called *random sampling.*

RANDOM SAMPLING

Implicit in the discussion that follows is the assumption that all the available subjects in a given setting cannot be employed in the study itself. This is usually the case, for even if it is theoretically possible to employ a large number of subjects it is seldom cost effective to do so.

When more subjects exist than can be employed (or than are needed) the researcher's task becomes the selection of a group or *sample* of predetermined size* that is representative in all relevant dimensions of the larger available *population* from which it is drawn. Given that individuals or groups of individuals are capable of differing on far more factors than researchers are able to identify, much less measure, this task may, at first glance, take on awesome dimensions.

In actuality, what researchers do is freely admit their limitations and simply give every member of the population to which they have access *an equal chance of being in their research sample.* By so doing, they greatly minimize the possibility of all the brightest students or the patients with the best prognoses (indeed of the most, least, best, or worst of anything) being selected for the study. If *all* subjects (which includes the best, worst, and everyone in between) have an equal chance of being selected it can usually be assumed that the resulting sample will be representative.

An Example

Suppose that a researcher had access to all the patients from a given hospital and that all these patients were appropriate for the study under consideration. Suppose further that time, money, and statistical considerations dictated that 50 patients was the optimal sample size to be employed.

The first step would entail generating a list of the total patient population. This is almost always already available in some form, regardless of the institution. The names comprising this list would then be numbered sequentially, regardless of the way in which they appear (for example, alphabetically or chronologically with respect to date of admission) (Table 3-3).

Next, a list of random numbers would be obtained, either via a computer† or a table such as contained in most standard statistical texts. The requisite amount of numbers, corresponding to the size of the desired sample (50 in the present case), is then generated, with those names corresponding to the selected numbers constituting the study subjects.

* The optimal sample size is most often determined by estimating the number of subjects needed to enable the rejection of the null hypothesis. This is discussed under the concept of *statistical power* in Chapter 4.

† Many computers have programs that require that the user only specify the number of subjects in the population and the desired number for the sample before automatically generating a list of random numbers.

Table 3-3 HYPOTHETICAL LISTING FOR RANDOM
                         SAMPLING

1. B. Smith	6. T. Quincy
2. C. Jones	7. A. Bedford
3. L. Jones	8. G. Goodhartz
4. Q. Williams	9. M. Moody
5. A. Bobrow	10. B. Jenkins

Table 3-4 A PORTION OF A RANDOM NUMBER TABLE

5	1	2	5	0	4	8	9	4	8	0	2	8	4	5	9	1	2
6	6	1	8	2	8	6	4	5	1	6	9	4	4	1	2	8	6
8	0	4	4	1	3	5	6	0	3	3	6	4	8	0	2	4	8
9	0	1	0	4	7	7	8	1	4	4	4	3	9	2	4	1	5
0	3	4	0	6	6	9	8	4	9	2	7	3	9	1	2	4	1
3	4	1	3	4	2	8	1	4	5	6	7	8	4	3	3	6	7
1	0	2	4	0	5	6	8	4	6	4	0	5	0	3	7	4	8
5	4	6	3	8	2	9	1	0	2	3	5	1	9	4	5	3	2
0	5	6	3	4	7	2	8	1	9	1	2	3	3	0	5	4	2
1	4	2	1	9	4	3	5	8	6	5	2	0	4	0	5	3	5

For example, consider the portion of a hypothetical table of random numbers shown in Table 3-4. (Tables of random numbers are laid out in many different formats, with the above five-row configuration being only one example.) All such tables should consist of several pages of numbers, hence allowing the researcher the option of beginning on any page and on any part of any page as long as the numbers are not examined first.

Suppose our researcher chose to begin with the above portion simply by blindly pointing. Suppose further that the hospital in question had a total of 380 eligible patients available for the study. This would mean that only three-digit numbers were needed (if there were over a 1,000 patients, then four-digit numbers would be required), so the researcher again blindly chooses which three rows in each set of five will be employed. Let us assume that rows three, four, and five of each five-line paragraph were selected.

The researcher would now search for 50 different numbers with a value of 380 or less. In the first paragraph, this would be 003, 146, 376, 014, 349, 342, 021, and 242 (Table 3-5). The numbers 890, 414, 400, 579, 688, 647, 433, 899, 414, and 851 are all larger than 380 and thus of no use. This process would be continued until 50 numbers between 001 and 381 were selected. (If the same number appeared twice, its second manifestation would simply be ignored.) The patients associated with each number would then comprise the research sample. (L. Jones from the partial list in Table 3-3 would be one of the 50, since 003 was selected.) There are as many different ways to use a table of random numbers as there are researchers. The procedure itself doesn't really matter as long as it is consistently employed and as long as the researcher does not look at the number configuration first *and* abides by the results. (L. Jones, for example, must be included in the study whether it is convenient to use this particular subject or not.)

Table 3-5   USING A TABLE OF RANDOM NUMBERS

5	1	2	5	0	4	8	9	4	8	0	2	8	4	5	9	1	2
6	6	1	8	2	8	6	4	5	1	6	9	4	4	1	2	8	6
8	(0)	4	4	(1)	(3)	5	6	(0)	(3)	(3)	6	4	8	(0)	(2)	4	8
9	(0)	1	0	(4)	(7)	7	8	(1)	(4)	(4)	4	3	9	(2)	(4)	1	5
0	(3)	4	0	(6)	(6)	9	8	(4)	(9)	(2)	7	3	9	(1)	(2)	4	1

There are also many other procedures for drawing a random sample, such as flipping a coin if exactly half of the population is to be used, rolling a die if one-sixth or one-third of the population is to be used (for thirds, each third can be represented by two sides of the die instead of one), mixing the names up thoroughly in a hat and blindly drawing the required number, and so forth. Again, the procedure is not important as long as it is not purposeful in some manner. (Taking the first 50 names on the above hospital list would not constitute a random procedure, since the list itself could be ordered in some systematic way.)

Stratified Random Sampling

Although simple random sampling might be described as a means of capitalizing on ignorance, there is a variation on its theme that combines what is known about important dimensions along which subjects can vary with what is not known. If male patients are known to differ from female patients with respect to their reactions (or scores on) the variables under consideration in our hospital study, for example, the researcher can capitalize on this knowledge by *forcing* the sample to have the same ratio of male to female patients as the entire hospital population. This strategy, called *stratified random sampling,* in turn will force the sample to be more representative than it would be via a simple random selection technique if the stratifying variable (in this case sex) is indeed related to the study's variables. (If sex bears no relationship to the other study variables, then it should not be so employed.)

To illustrate how this would work, suppose the hospital census revealed that 60 percent of the patients were female and 40 percent were male. A simple random selection of patients as described in the previous section would result in proportions very similar to this, but probably not in an exact 60–40 split. Should the researcher wish both to achieve exact representativeness with respect to sex and to avoid incurring unrepresentativeness with respect to any other (possibly unknown) variables, the following strategy could be employed (assuming a sample size of 50 were still desired):

1. The overall patient list for the hospital would be separated into two separate lists, one male, one female.
2. Each list would then be sequentially numbered separately.
3. Thirty random numbers would be generated for the female list in the same manner as described above (50 × 60 percent = 30).

4. Twenty random numbers would be generated for the male list (50 ×
   40 percent = 20).
5. The names corresponding to the numbers would then comprise the
   new sample.

Note that because this technique (which is more commonly used in large-scale descriptive surveys than in correlational or experimental research) still gives each subject in the population an equal chance of being selected for the study, it qualifies as a random sampling technique. For purely descriptive studies, it allows researchers to use smaller sample sizes to achieve equal precision, but it is seldom used for other types of research where the use of equal numbers of males and females, for example, afford more analytic options (see Chapter 15).

Cluster Sampling

A variation on this theme is to begin the process by randomly selecting clearly defined units from the whole and then randomly selecting subjects from these smaller units. This strategy is most helpful in descriptive research when subjects must be interviewed in person, since traveling costs and time are reduced. Thus, a pollster might randomly select several states, then randomly select certain communities or geographic units within those states, and only then randomly select subjects from within these smaller units.

OTHER APPLICATIONS OF RANDOM SAMPLING

Subjects are not the only entities in empirical research that sometimes need to be selected from a larger pool. Suppose, for example, that a study involved observing client-therapist interactions. Suppose further that practical concerns limited the number of these interactions and the amount of time that could be devoted to any given session.

Since the researcher would certainly not wish inadvertently to observe either unrepresentative sessions or unrepresentative interactions within those sessions, the wisest strategy would probably be to use a random selection procedure of some sort to avoid these possibilities altogether. One possibility would be to select a random sample of the total number of sessions occurring over the study interval and then randomly select one 15-minute block of time from each of these sessions. A stratified procedure such as this would certainly be superior to, say, observing the first 15 minutes of the first 20 sessions administered after the start of the study since both the sessions and the time intervals so selected might be unrepresentative of typical client-therapist interactions.

An even more precise strategy might be to employ a stratified random selection procedure. Here, the researcher would select an equal number of sessions from each available therapist and an equal number of time periods from the employed sessions. Thus, if 40 sessions were to be observed, if 10 therapists were available, and if each session lasted an hour, the researcher might randomly select four sessions from each therapist's case load and ensure that a different 15-minute interval within the hour was observed for each therapist. The order in which these different intervals (that is, 0–15 minutes, 16–30 minutes, 31–45 minutes, and 46–60 minutes) is observed would of course also be randomly selected.

In general, any time a limited number of *anything* must be selected for research purposes, a random selection procedure is preferable, since it reduces the possibility of bias. (When practical, a stratified procedure usually adds precision to the process.) Thus, if more items exist for a test than can be employed practically, a random (or stratified random) sample can be selected. If more tests themselves exist than can be handled (or scored) practically (such as with a very large data set), then these entities too can be randomly sampled. In other words, as a general rule of thumb: *when in doubt, select randomly.*

LIMITATIONS OF RANDOM SAMPLING

Although it is unquestionably one of the most powerful tools available to researchers, random sampling is not a panacea in all situations. Some of the procedure's limitations follow:

1. *Regardless of how it is selected, a sample is only an approximation of the population from which it is drawn.* Even when random sampling is employed, there is almost always a certain amount of sampling error present. The extent of this error can be estimated via a statistic called the standard error of the mean and it can be relatively large for small samples or for measures that possess a large amount of variability.* Still, when a smaller set of entities must be chosen from a larger one, a random sampling procedure of some sort remains the best strategy available to the researcher in the vast majority of situations.
2. *If only one or two entities may be selected from a larger pool, random sampling is not always the best procedure.* If, for example, a city has four hospitals in which a researcher can conduct a study and if practical constraints dictate that only one can actually be used in the study, then random selection of that single hospital might be unwise if, say, two of the four hospitals were extremely small and one was attempting to weather a protracted nursing strike. If the remaining institution appeared to be a fairly representative community hospital, then the

---

* As an example of how this statistic might be used, suppose that a researcher wished to know how representative a random sample of 100 subjects were to a much larger population with respect to their mean score on an intelligence test. If the sample IQ mean were 106.2 with a standard deviation of 10.0, then the standard error of the mean would be computed as follows:

$$\text{S.E.}_{\text{mean}} = \frac{\text{Standard deviation of the sample}}{\sqrt{\text{Number in sample}}} = \frac{10.0}{\sqrt{100}} = 1.0$$

This figure is then interpreted very similarly to a standard deviation, only it is applied to the range that the population mean is most likely to take. In other words, approximately 95 percent of the time the sample mean would be expected to be within two standard errors above or below the population mean or somewhere between 104.2 and 108.2.

best strategy would probably be to collect as much descriptive data on this hospital as possible (in order to help other professionals decide the extent to which the setting employed is representative of their setting) and to go ahead and use it for the study. When nothing is known about what constitutes an important characteristic and what does not, on the other hand, random sampling remains the best insurance available against bias.

3. *Random sampling protects against bias only if all subjects have an equal chance of being selected.* Thus if a sizable number of subjects decline to participate in a study, this may in itself result in an unrepresentative sample simply because the people who refuse to participate may be systematically different from those who do not. The fact that people who volunteered were randomly selected can do nothing to ameliorate the situation. The best protection against this possibility is to attempt to minimize the refusal rate as much as possible by:

   (a) Requiring as little as possible of the subject with respect to time, effort, and personal inconvenience.

   (b) Being as open as possible with potential subjects regarding the importance of the study and exactly what is to be required of them.

   (c) Setting up a mechanism by which the results of the study can be shared with participants. (This lets people know that they are considered something more than human guinea pigs and that their participation is valued.)

   Even if a study's refusal rate remains high after these steps, random sampling remains the procedure of choice since it at least helps ensure that the sample will be representative of those members of the population who would have volunteered to participate.

4. *Random selection protects the representativeness of the sample only as far as the available population is concerned; it does not ensure representativeness to the aspired population.* Strictly speaking, the only population for which a randomly selected sample can be assumed to be representative is that population from which names (or other entities) were listed and physically selected. If this available population is itself unrepresentative of the population to which a researcher aspires to generalize a study's results, then any random sample drawn from it will probably also be unrepresentative of the aspired population. Still, it is better for a sample to be representative of the available population than of nothing, so random sampling is still indicated whenever it is feasible.

TECHNICAL ASPECTS OF SAMPLING

This chapter has treated the selection of human subjects in a very general, nontechnical way. For the vast majority of research situations, this discussion will suffice. The reader should be aware, however, that sampling is practically a discipline in and of itself. For a relatively thorough (and thoroughly understandable) treatise on the subject, the present author recommends Levy and Lemeshow's *Sampling for Health Professionals* (1980).

SUMMARY

Protecting the rights of human subjects, including their right to refuse participation in a research study, is the first step in selecting subjects. Although more detailed guidelines are almost universally available within the researcher's primary professional association, most suggest the following steps:

1. Obtain all appropriate formal institutional permissions.
2. Inform potential subjects of everything participation involves (including what will be required of them).
3. Ensure that subjects understand what will be required of them.
4. Assure subjects that participation is voluntary and that they have the right to withdraw from the study at any time.
5. Preserve subject anonymity when possible.
6. Preserve subject confidentiality.
7. Conduct good, useful research to ensure that subjects' time is not wasted.

Researchers almost always aspire to generalize their results to larger groups of people than they can practically employ in a study. There are really two populations involved in this process, the *available* population from which subjects are actually selected and the population to which the researcher *aspires* to generalize. *Random sampling,* or the process of giving all subjects an equal chance of being in the research sample, is the best strategy for ensuring representativeness of the employed sample to the available population. Thorough statistical description, the avoidance of obviously biased samples, and cleanly conducted research are among the best strategies for enabling other researchers to judge the limits to which a study can be generalized outside of the available population.

REFERENCES

Bracht, G. H. Experimental factors related to aptitude-treatment interactions. *Review of Educational Research,* 1970, *40,* 629–645.

Levy, P. S., and Lemeshow, S. *Sampling for Health Professionals.* Belmont, Calif.: Lifetime Learning Publications, 1980.

chapter *4*

Testing Hypotheses

So far we have discussed the steps involved in formulating a hypothesis and in selecting the subjects that will be used to test this hypothesis. The purpose of the present chapter is to discuss the *logic* behind hypothesis testing, especially behind the actual decision as to whether or not to accept a hypothesis as tenable or reject it as false.

To facilitate this discussion, let us assume that we have already completed a hypothetical study designed to facilitate weight loss among overweight, postoperative cardiovascular patients involving two groups of subjects: one that received a weight loss program consisting of both dietary information and an exercise regimen, and another that received no formal weight loss help at all. Let us further pretend that these two groups are to be compared with respect to the amount of weight they were able to lose within a month's time following their surgeries.

A null hypothesis written for this study might be:

There is no difference between overweight, postoperative cardiovascular patients who receive a program of dietary information coupled with an exercise regimen and those who do not receive such a program with respect to the average amount of weight they lose.

The group of patients who received the experimental program is aptly enough called the *experimental* group. It will often be abbreviated in this book as *E*. The program itself is variously called the treatment, the intervention, the experimental treatment, and so forth. The group who did not receive the experi-

Table 4-1 HYPOTHETICAL NUMBER OF POUNDS LOST OF SUB-
JECTS WHO RECEIVED THE WEIGHT LOSS TREATMENT
(E) VERSUS THOSE WHO DID NOT (C)

E		C	
Subject	Number pounds lost	Subject	Number pounds lost
1	4	5	3
2	6	6	2
3	8	7	1
4	7	8	5
	25		11

mental program is called either the *control* or the *comparison* group. It will be
abbreviated here as *C*.

Let us pretend that Table 4-1 represents the actual data collected to test
the above hypothesis. (Obviously a real study would employ considerably more
than four subjects per group, but small numbers will aid the explanations that
follow.) In examining Table 4-1, it is obvious that the experimental group did
lose more weight overall than the control group: 14 pounds to be exact (25
versus 11).

Since it is highly improbable that the four experimental subjects would
have lost *exactly* the same number of pounds as the four control subjects, any
obtained difference must be evaluated in terms of its *statistical significance*.
This is done by first setting a probability level that must be met before the above
hypothesis can be rejected (usually .05), assigning a probability to the observed
difference (14 pounds in the present case), and comparing the two. If the
observed probability is below .05 (or whatever the a priori probability was
chosen to be), then the null hypothesis is rejected. If the observed probability is
above its a priori counterpart, then the null hypothesis is not rejected. The
question thus becomes: How can a single probability be assigned to a particular
configuration of numbers?

There are a number of possibilities. In actual practice, the researcher
would choose an appropriate statistical procedure and enter the eight numbers
listed above (that is, each subject's weight loss) into a computer. The computer
in turn would (1) substitute the chosen statistic (most likely a *t*) for the observed
difference (14 pounds) and (2) compare said statistic to a distribution of other
statistical values to ascertain how likely such a value (and hence the difference it
represents) would be to occur by chance alone. If said statistic were larger than
95 percent of the other statistics in the distribution, then it would be assumed
that a difference of the size obtained would *not* have occurred by chance alone
and that the null hypothesis was probably false. If the statistic were not larger
than 95 percent of the other statistics in the distribution, then the null hypothesis would be considered tenable. (This is one of the beauties of hypothesis
testing. Regardless of what happens, a hypothesis will either be rejected or not
rejected. There are no maybes.)

Although permitting the computer to do all the work once a study's data
have been collected is definitely recommended, it is helpful to have at least an

intuitive grasp of how a probability *could* be assigned to a unique group of numbers such as those presented in Table 4-1 without the use of statistics, statistical distributions, and computers. Although no one ever computes such a probability without their use, working through such a process should enhance the reader's understanding of the conceptual basis behind hypothesis testing.

Returning to the data in Table 4-1, then, the task at hand is to decide whether the null hypothesis should be rejected or not. Basically, this task becomes nothing more than the determination of whether or not a difference of 14 total pounds is *statistically significant.* This task can be rephrased as a relatively simple question: Given the eight records of weight loss observed in this study (that is, 4, 6, 8, 7, 3, 2, 1, and 5), is the actual probability of a difference as large as 14 pounds or greater occurring *less than* the probability level selected to determine whether or not the null hypothesis can be rejected?

The real difficulty involved in answering this question lies in determining the exact probability of this particular event occurring (that is, a difference of 14 occurring given the set of eight numbers involved). One way of computing such a probability would be to write the numbers 4, 6, 8, 7, 3, 2, 1, and 5 on separate slips of paper, mix them thoroughly in a hat, and draw two groups of four numbers from the hat without looking. Each group of four numbers could then be totaled and the difference between these totals could be recorded. If this were repeated perhaps a thousand times, the number of differences 14 or greater could then be divided by the total number of drawings to yield the estimated probability of a difference of this magnitude actually occurring. If this figure were less than our researcher's a priori value of .05, then the null hypothesis would be rejected. If it were larger, the null hypothesis would not be rejected.

Although the significance level of any experiment could certainly be determined in this manner, no one would have the patience to construct a unique distribution of findings for each study they completed and research would go the way of marathon dancing. Actually a much more direct, accurate method of constructing a definition of chance occurrence exists, one which bears many similarities (although it is not identical) to the way in which statistical significance is determined in actual practice.

Thus, instead of drawing large numbers of four subjects from a hat, the total number of possible combinations of two groups of four numbers each could be calculated mathematically. Starting with the eight numbers listed in Table 4-1, for example, it is possible to construct 70 different combinations, of which having the numbers 3, 2, 1, and 5 in *E* and 4, 6, 8, and 7 in *C* is only one.* Table 4-2 shows a few of these combinations.

The researcher could then compute differences between these 70 unique combinations (that is, subtract the total for the control group from that of the experimental) and construct a distribution of such differences as illustrated in Table 4-3. (Note that although there are 70 different combinations of four numbers possible, there are not 70 unique *differences* between the groups. A

---

* The number of possible combinations increase drastically as the number of subjects increases. Ten scores possess 252 possible combinations of five-subject groups; twenty scores can be divided into halves 184,756 ways.

Table 4-2   SELECTED POSSIBILITIES FOR DIVIDING EIGHT SCORES INTO TWO GROUPS OF FOUR

(1)		(2)		(3)			(68)		(69)		(70)	
E	C	E	C	E	C		E	C	E	C	E	C
5	1	4	1	4	1	. . .	1	4	1	4	1	5
6	2	6	2	5	2		2	5	2	6	2	6
7	3	7	3	7	3		3	7	3	7	3	7
8	4	8	5	8	6		6	8	5	8	4	8
26	10	25	11	24	12	. . .	12	24	11	25	10	26
+16		+14		+12			−12		−14		−16	

Table 4-3   DISTRIBUTION OF POSSIBLE GROUP DIFFERENCES OF TWO GROUPS OF FOUR BASED ON THE EIGHT SCORES PRESENTED IN TABLE 4-1

Absolute differences between E and C totals	Total number of unique combinations that can produce these differences
16	2
14	2
12	4
10	6
8	10
6	10
4	14
2	14
0	8
	70

difference of 0 can be obtained, for example, when E versus C scores are 1, 3, 6, 8 — 2, 4, 5, 7 and 2, 3, 6, 7 — 1, 4, 5, 8.)

This particular distribution represents all the possible ways that two groups of four can differ from one another (based on the eight numbers presented in Table 4-1). Once constructed, all the researcher need do is: (1) divide the total number of ways that a difference of 14 or more *could* occur, (i.e., *four;* the two for 14 plus the two for 16) by 70 and (2) compare this value (.057) with the a priori definitive of statistical significance (.05).

Since .057 (the obtained probability) is greater than .05, this particular result would be deemed not statistically significant and the null hypothesis would not be rejected, which means that the researcher would be forced to conclude that the results do not support the conclusion that a program of dietary information and an exercise regimen is an effective way for overweight, postoperative cardiac patients to lose weight. It does not matter that the results came close.* Empirical research is not like a game of horseshoes; it is more akin to a horse race. If you bet on a horse to win and it loses by a whisker you still lose your money. This is also an advantage to the logic of hypothesis testing; one way or another the researcher knows that a definitive answer to the advanced hypothesis will be obtained. (Note that if a difference between E and C groups of 16 had been obtained the null hypothesis would have been rejected, since $2/70 = .029$.)

DIRECTIONALITY (OR ONE- VERSUS TWO-TAILED HYPOTHESIS TESTS)

The above discussion assumes that the researcher did not wish to specify the direction of the hypothesized relationship before conducting the study. Now certainly the experimental program was expected to result in greater weight loss than the control condition. In fact, the researcher would have probably been quite shocked if control subjects had lost significantly *more* weight than their experimental counterparts (which would have indicated that the experimental condition was actually *detrimental*). Still, the vast majority of hypotheses are tested from a nondirectional perspective.

Framed as a research hypothesis, the investigator tested the following formulation:

> *There is a difference in the average amount of weight lost between over-weight, postoperative cardiac patients exposed to a program consisting of dietary information and an exercise regimen and patients who do not receive such a program.*

Given this hypothesis, a difference of 14 favoring the control group would receive the same treatment as the observed difference of 14 favoring the experimental group. A very different situation would exist, however, if the researcher had posited a direction to the relationship.

Suppose the following research hypothesis had been framed instead:

> *Overweight, postoperative cardiac patients exposed to a program consisting of dietary information and an exercise regimen will lose more weight, on the average, than patients who do not receive such a program.*

In this scenario, unlike the previous one, a difference of 14 favoring the control group would not receive the same treatment as the observed difference of 14 favoring the experimental group. The reason for this is probably obvious. The second hypothesis posited a statistically significant difference between the groups *favoring* the experimental group, hence any difference (no matter how great) favoring the control group would be considered supportive of the null

---

* It should be noted that opinions differ on this point, although certainly the majority of empirical researchers adhere to the view presented in this book.

hypothesis, not the research hypothesis. Interestingly enough, the null hypothesis for the second scenario changes as well. It is really:

> *Overweight, postoperative cardiac patients exposed to a program consisting of dietary information and an exercise regimen will not lose more weight on the average than patients who do not receive such a program.*

Usually, researchers do not go to the trouble of changing the way they formally present their hypotheses when they choose to conduct a directional test thereof. They simply state their intentions, usually by saying that they plan to use a *one-tailed* test (as opposed to a *two-tailed,* nondirectional test, which is assumed if not stated). The term *tail* comes from the way in which statistical distributions are normally graphed (Figure 4-1), where the large center portion represents the differences (in statistics) that would be expected to occur by chance alone and the two tails as those differences/statistics that are larger in absolute value than 95 percent of the rest of the distribution. [Note that a *one*-tailed test applies the same logic to one side of the distribution only. (Figure 4-2)]

This distinction between directional and nondirectional hypotheses will probably be clearer if it is considered in light of the eight hypothetical scores first introduced in Table 4-1. The task then becomes to redefine chance occurrence from a directional perspective and then to determine the statistical significance of a difference as large as 14 favoring the experimental group.

Obviously, the distribution presented in Table 4-3 can no longer be used, since no distinctions were made between the direction of the differences between *E* and *C*. Referring to that distribution indicates, for example, that from the total of 70 unique combinations of groups of four numbers, two could be expected to produce differences as large as 16 and two produce differences as large as 14.

In reality, only one combination was capable of producing a difference of 16 favoring the experimental group (that is, *E*, containing scores of 5, 6, 7, and 8 and *C* scores of 1, 2, 3, and 4), the other difference of 16 favored the control group as illustrated in Table 4-2. The same situation held for differences of 14;

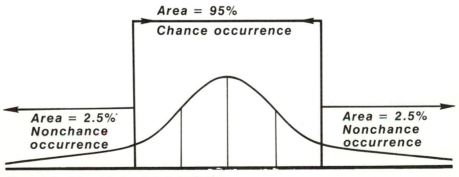

Figure 4-1   A two-tailed statistical distribution.

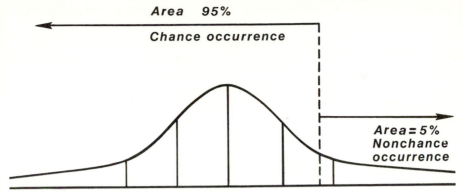

Figure 4-2   A one-tailed statistical distribution.

only one combination of the 70 possible favored the experimental group (#2 in Table 4-2); the other (#69 in the same table) favored the control group.

To ascertain the probability of a difference as great as 14 favoring the experimental group occurring by chance alone, then, only the single difference of 16 and the single difference of 14 would be included in the numerator. Thus, instead of dividing 4 (two differences of 16 and two of 14) by 70, 2 would be divided by 70 instead, producing a significance level of .029. The directional research hypothesis would therefore be considered tenable (since .029 is less than .05) and the attendant null hypothesis rejected as probably false. Note that the numerator is exactly halved in a directional hypothesis test. This means that, everything else being equal, the same difference is half as likely to occur by chance in a directional hypothesis as in a nondirectional one *if that difference occurs in the proper direction.*

Naturally, no one uses so cumbersome a procedure for ascertaining the significance level of an obtained set of data. All researchers translate their observed relationships/differences into a statistic and then compare that to an appropriate statistical distribution. In the vast majority of cases, both these steps are done via computers. In either case, provisions for directional and nondirectional hypothesis tests are built in. When a particular distribution does not contain such an option, the researcher using a directional hypothesis can compensate by simply halving the probability (significance level) actually obtained, providing of course that it is in the proper direction. Thus if a two-tailed significance level of .10 is obtained, the one-tailed level is .05; if the two-tailed level is .02, the one-tailed value is .01.

As mentioned above, most researchers employ a nondirectional test in their studies, possibly because this has traditionally been the case, possibly because many journals require a sound rationale or theoretical basis before they will accept a directional test. In my opinion, there is no good reason why a directional hypothesis should not be used if the researcher (1) is truly interested only in a relationship or difference manifesting itself in one direction and is willing to throw away results in the other direction no matter how impressive they may be, (2) has a sound theoretical or empirical rationale (over and above a simple hunch) for specifying said direction, and (3) specifies the direction *before* collecting any data. If these three criteria can be met, there is absolutely nothing wrong with using a directional or one-tailed hypothesis, because in reality a one-tailed null hypothesis is just as difficult to reject as its two-tailed counterpart *if* it is indeed posited a priori. The chief disadvantage of this practice is the difficulty of fulfilling the first criterion listed above. If the control condition were found to be statistically superior to E in our hypothetical weight loss study, for example, there would be a great temptation on the part of the researcher to warn clinicians about the possible *detrimental* effects of the experimental program. The logic of hypothesis testing prohibits this, however, since in reality all that can be said was that there was no statistically significant difference between the two groups.

STATISTICAL ANALYSIS

The preceding discussion was designed solely to give the reader a conceptual grasp of what is meant by declaring that a given difference between two groups is or is not statistically significant. In reality, it would of course be extremely unwieldy to compute a mathematical definition of statistical significance for every possible combination of unique numbers.

Instead such a difference is always represented by a statistic and that statistic is compared to its own distribution. If the significance level is set at .05, then the absolute value of the obtained statistic must be greater than 95 percent of its peers in that distribution for it to be considered statistically significant.

For a single statistic to be capable of representing an infinite number of unique combinations of numbers, however, these numbers must be described in some standard, manageable way. The numbers associated with two different groups of subjects, for example, can differ from study to study in three distinct ways:

1. They may differ with respect to the actual number of subjects per group.
2. They may differ with respect to the average score possessed by the subjects within each group.
3. They may differ with respect to how much the subjects within each group differ from one another (that is, in the amount of spread in subjects' scores, or their homogeneity/variability).

The statistics recommended in this book, whether dealing with a difference between groups or a relationship between variables, all approach this problem in the same way. They take into consideration the number of subjects in the actual computation of the statistic itself. They employ a measure of central tendency (that is, the arithmetic *mean,* which takes into consideration the number of subjects involved) to describe the subjects' average score on each

Table 4-4 DESCRIPTIVE STATISTICS FOR
THE DATA IN TABLE 4-1

	Experimental group (n = 4)	Control group (n = 4)
Mean	6.25	2.75
S.D.	1.71	1.71

variable employed. Finally, they employ a measure of dispersion (the standard deviation, which takes into consideration both the number of subjects involved and their average score). In other words, they conveniently employ the same statistics recommended for use in sample description (Table 4-4).

A Statistical Example

As useful as the mean and standard deviation (or variance) are to *describe* empirical results, their true strength lies in their statistical applications. We have already discussed some mechanistic and mathematical ways of determining whether or not there is a statistically significant difference between the two groups of numbers presented in Table 4-1. Let us now see how this could be done statistically.

The discussion in Part Four of this book will facilitate the reader's selection of an appropriate statistical procedure for most empirical situations. At this point, the reader may accept on faith that the appropriate statistic to represent a difference between two groups on a variable *for which the mean and standard deviation are appropriate descriptors* is the *t*-test for independent samples.

The formula for the *t*-test used for groups containing different, unrelated subjects is given as follows.*

$$t = \frac{\overline{X}_E - \overline{X}_C}{\sqrt{\dfrac{\mathrm{Var}_E}{n_E} + \dfrac{\mathrm{Var}_C}{n_C}}} \tag{4-1}$$

where $\overline{X}_E$ = mean of the experimental group
$\overline{X}_C$ = mean of the control group
Var_E = variance of the experimental group
Var_C = variance of the control group
n_E = number of subjects in E
n_C = number of subjects in C

---

* This formula makes no assumptions regarding the population variances and was chosen because of its computational simplicity.

Plugging in the descriptive values from Table 4-4, we have:

$$t = \frac{6.25 - 2.75}{\sqrt{\dfrac{2.92}{4} + \dfrac{2.92}{4}}} \qquad (Note: 2.92 = 1.71^2; \text{Var} = \text{S.D.}^2)$$

$$= \frac{3.50}{\sqrt{1.46}} = \frac{3.50}{1.21} = 2.89$$

Comparing this statistic to a distribution of t-statistics and using the relatively more powerful parametric statistic as opposed to the actual mathematical probability, we would find that the obtained value of 2.89 for eight subjects is statistically significant at the .05 level, hence the difference it represents is large enough to allow the null hypothesis to be rejected.

Certainly, most people would agree that determining statistical significance via this procedure is far easier than constructing a distribution of all the possible outcomes for a particular set of data as was done earlier in this chapter. For present purposes, the important point to grasp is that any relationship or difference can be represented by a statistic to which a single probability can be assigned. That probability automatically dictates one of two decisions: the null hypothesis will either be rejected or not rejected.

STATISTICAL POWER

Regardless of folklore and stereotypes to the contrary, *the true objective of every research study is, and should be, the rejection of the null hypothesis.* Every *legitimate* effort should be aimed at this end because:

1. *By definition it is more difficult to reject the null hypothesis than it is not to reject it.* Setting the significance level at .05 ensures this. To reiterate, this level means that if nothing *but* chance were operating the null hypothesis would be rejected only one time in twenty. (If the significance level were set at .50, it would be just as easy to reject the null hypothesis as it would be not to reject it.)
2. *Sloppily conducted research is less likely to result in a rejection of the null hypothesis than is a cleanly run study.* So much is made of the possibility of obtaining statistically significant results by chance alone that many beginning researchers assume that poorly executed procedures will enhance the probability of such an occurrence. This is true only of procedural errors that *systematically* increase the difference between groups. Error is usually more or less random, however, and random error tends to increase the heterogeneity of subjects' scores in general, which requires *even greater* differences between groups for statistical significance to be achieved.

At the risk of oversimplification, suppose that the eight scores in Table 4-1 had been 1, 5, 10, 15, 20, 25, 30, and 35 instead of 1, 2, 3, 4, 5, 6, 7, and 8. If we were to construct a distribution of all the mathematically possible combinations, there would still be 70 possibilities, but to achieve nondirectional statistical significance a group difference of 71 instead of the original 16 would be required. Similarly, a much larger mean difference would also be required to achieve statistical significance with a *t*-test.

What this means is that researchers must not only worry about obtaining statistical significance by chance alone; not achieving statistical significance when true differences or relationships exist should be of *equal,* if not greater concern. There are therefore two separate (but not independent) types of error possible in every hypothesis test. The first, titled *Type I error,* deals with the possibility that statistical significance can be obtained when it should not be. The second type of error (called *Type II error*) involves the possibility that statistical significance may *not* be obtained when it should. *Type I error is thus defined as the error that occurs when the null hypothesis is falsely rejected; Type II error is defined as the error that occurs when a false null hypothesis is not rejected.*

That Type I error is considered a virulent problem is illustrated by the fact that levels of significance are set so relatively low (that is, .05 or below). The possibility of Type II error should be considered an equally serious problem, however, since the personal/professional rewards are usually far greater for those who find statistical significance than for those who do not. Fortunately a statistical procedure exists that enables investigators to predict how likely they are to achieve statistical significance if a true difference or relationship exists prior to ever conducting a study. This resulting probability is called the statistical *power* of the hypothesis test.

Power, which is alternately defined as the probability of rejecting the null hypothesis when it should be rejected (that is, when in reality it is false), is a function of four parameters:

1. The significance level (also called the *alpha* level) set by the researcher (the more stringent the alpha level, the lower the power).
2. The relative size of the hypothesized difference or relationship (the greater the difference/relationship that is likely to occur, the greater the power).
3. The precision with which the study's data is collected and analyzed (some statistical procedures result in statistical significance more readily than others and some procedural techniques result in more precision, hence power, than others).
4. The number of subjects participating in the study (the more subjects, the greater the power).

If this definition is kept in mind (that is, *the probability of obtaining statistical significance when a real difference/relationship exists*), the reasons that these four parameters are related to power are relatively straightforward. The relationship of the significance level (alpha level) to power may be the most obvious. The more stringently it is defined, the more difficult will be the rejection of the null hypothesis. By definition, a significance level of .01 is more difficult to obtain than .05; .001 is even more difficult to obtain. The significance level set by the researcher prior to the study definitely influences the likelihood of achieving statistical significance and therefore power. Since the .05 level is so commonly used, however, the stringency of the alpha level is not normally a consideration.

To understand the relationship between the relative size of the hypothesized difference/relationship expected in a study (also called the *effect size*), it is necessary to remember that power is normally estimated *prior to* a study being conducted. This means, of course, that the researcher has no foolproof way of knowing the size of the effect, if any, that is likely to be generated. Table 4-2 clearly indicates, however, that the largest differences between groups are the ones *least* likely to occur by chance alone, or the ones most difficult to attain. If the researcher has a good reason to expect that one of these large differences is likely to occur as a *function* of the study variables, then said differences will almost certainly be statistically significant.

The final two determinants of power are a function of the logic of establishing statistical significance. Most statistical techniques used to assess a mean difference between groups can be visualized as a ratio between the mean difference as the numerator and error as the denominator. This error (or denominator) is a function of both the number of subjects involved and the unexplained variation between those subjects. The *more* subjects, the smaller this error, the larger the statistic, and the more likely statistical significance is of being obtained. Similarly, the *smaller* the unexplained variance between subjects, the smaller the error, and the more likely statistical significance is of being obtained. Many of the techniques discussed in the latter half of this book are dedicated to reducing unexplained variations between subjects.*

TYPE I VERSUS TYPE II ERROR

The binary nature of hypothesis testing leads to two possible types of error. One occurs when statistical significance is obtained (and the null hypothesis is rejected) and the other when statistical significance is not obtained (and the null hypothesis is not rejected). As mentioned above, the first genre of error is called Type I error; the second is called Type II error.

From an a priori perspective, then, there are two and only two possible *outcomes* with respect to testing a null hypothesis: statistical significance will either be obtained or it will not be obtained. In each case, there are two possibilities: statistical significance *should* have been obtained (that is, the null hypoth-

---

* To illustrate, suppose that the number of subjects represented in the computation of the *t*-test on pages 43–44 were doubled and the unexplained variation between those subjects was halved. The *t* statistic would thus increase in size from 2.89 to 5.83 even if the mean difference were to remain the same:

$$t = \frac{6.25 - 2.75}{\sqrt{\dfrac{1.46}{8} + \dfrac{1.46}{8}}} = \frac{3.50}{.60} = 5.83$$

esis was in reality false) or it *should not* have been obtained (the null hypothesis was really true).

Unfortunately, empirical researchers never know anything absolutely, thus they never know what is really true or false. This means that they never know for *sure* whether their decision to reject a hypothesis was correct or incorrect. They are in the enviable position of being able to estimate the probability of any given decision being correct, however, and this process is where the concepts of Type I and Type II error, power, and statistical significance all merge into one unified whole.

To illustrate, consider the four possibilities for a hypothesis test:

1. The null hypothesis will be rejected *(that is, statistical significance will be obtained)* when in reality it should be rejected *(that is, when it truly was false and there was a real difference or relationship).*

The probability of this scenario (which represents a *correct* decision) is given by the *statistical power* of the test, which will range from .00 (no possibility at all of obtaining statistical significance, even when a real difference exists) to 1.00 (absolute certainty that statistical significance will be obtained when it should be obtained). Generally speaking, a value of .80 (which is interpreted as an 80 percent chance of obtaining statistical significance when the null hypothesis is in reality false) is considered an acceptable level of statistical power. If this value is indeed obtained, then the probability of the above scenario would be .80 (Cohen, 1977). (Note, however, that this has nothing to do with the probability of the null hypothesis being false, only of rejecting it *if* it is false. There is no way of estimating how likely a hypothesized difference or relationship is to exist. If there were, there would be no need to conduct empirical research.)

2. The null hypothesis will be rejected *(statistical significance will be obtained)* when in reality it should not be rejected *(there was no real difference or relationship to be observed).*

This is Type I error. It represents an incorrect decision and the probability of its occurrence is nothing more than the a priori set alpha level, which is usually .05 (that is, there are five chances in a hundred of its occurrence).

3. The null hypothesis will not be rejected *(statistical significance will not be obtained)* when it should be rejected *(that is, when a real relationship or difference actually exists).*

This, of course, is Type II error. The probability of this incorrect decision is one minus the power of the test. It is the reverse of the first scenario.

4. The null hypothesis will not be rejected *(statistical significance will not be obtained)* when in reality it should not be rejected.

What is true in Reality

What occurs:	The null hypothesis is false.	The null hypothesis is true.
The null hypothesis is rejected.	(1) Correct decision (power)	(2) Incorrect decision (Type I error) probability = alpha (.05)
The null hypothesis is not rejected.	(3) Incorrect decision (Type II error) probability = 1-power	(4) Correct decision (1-alpha)

Figure 4-3 Possible outcomes for a hypothesis test.

The probability of this *correct* decision is simply one minus the a priori set alpha level (which is usually $1 - .05 = .95$) *if* the null hypothesis is in reality true.

Diagrammatically these four scenarios are often summarized as shown in Figure 4-3.

Applications

It is important to remember that all of the above probabilities are based on something that is never known for sure. Thus, since we never know whether or not a hypothesis is really true or false, we never really know the probability that we are correct or incorrect with respect to our decision to reject or not to reject that hypothesis.

The utility of the concept behind statistical power comes from the fact that researchers believe that the null hypothesis is really false prior to conducting their studies. (If they did not believe so, chances are that they would not bother to conduct them.) Given this belief, statistical power is thus very helpful in estimating how likely a researcher is to be successful in rejecting the null hypothesis (assuming the absence of some procedural error in the conduct of the study).

Since it can usually be assumed that (1) the significance level for a study is fixed (usually at .05), (2) the effect size will be maximized as much as the purposes of the study will permit, and (3) the researcher will employ the most sensitive procedural and statistical techniques available, the chief uses of statistical power are either to:

1. Estimate the number of subjects that will be needed to achieve a given level of power.
2. Estimate the power (or alternately, the probability of incurring a Type II error, which it will be remembered is $1 -$ power) of a given hypothesis test when a fixed number of subjects are available for a study.

The first application assumes some flexibility with respect to the resources available and thus is a definite aid in designing a study that has a reasonable chance of rejecting its null hypothesis. The second use assumes no flexibility and thus is chiefly used to determine whether or not the study is worth conducting in the first place.

The first step in either application involves estimating the most likely effect size for the study at hand. Admittedly, this is a tenuous affair since the researcher really does not know whether any difference exists at all between the two groups employed. The task is made somewhat easier, however, by defining the size of the effect in terms of standard deviation units, with a large effect being defined as a mean difference that is 80 percent as large as the standard deviation of the dependent variable, a medium effect size as 50 percent of the standard deviation, and a small effect size as 20 percent of the standard deviation.

Let us assume that the researcher decides that a medium effect size is the most likely outcome for a study. This means that if the standard deviation is 10, the experimental and control groups will differ from one another by 5 points or more. If the standard deviation turns out to be 8, the two groups would then be expected to differ by 4 or more points, regardless of what these points are. (Actually a medium effect size is a fairly reasonable target for most research purposes.)

Tables exist, most notably in Jacob Cohen's *Statistical Power Analysis for the Behavioral Sciences* (1977), that allow the researcher to estimate quite precisely how many subjects will be required to achieve a given level of statistical power (or how much power a given number of subjects will afford).* To find the number of subjects required to achieve a statistical power of .80 at a .05 level of significance, for example, it would be discovered that 50 subjects per group would be needed. If only 20 subjects per group were actually available, the statistical power would only be .46, which means that the probability of a real difference not being judged statistically significant (Type II error) would be .54. Such a figure might seriously question the wisdom of conducting the study at all. If 15 subjects per group were employed, the probability of Type II error would jump to .62. If 100 subjects were available per group, however, the probability of a Type II error would be reduced to .02!

To achieve a power estimate of .80 for a smaller effect size (that is, a mean difference of only 20 percent of the dependent variable's standard deviation), slightly more than 300 subjects per group would be needed, while the 50 subjects that yielded a power of .80 for a medium effect result in a power estimate of only .16. For a large effect size, on the other hand, only 20 subjects per group would be needed to achieve a probability of Type II error of .20 (power = .80).

---

* This discussion assumes an appropriate sampling method. If the sample is systematically biased in some important way, increasing the number of subjects may do nothing more than increase the size of this error.

The situation is much the same when a relationship between two variables (rather than a difference between two groups) is hypothesized. Here, however, the researcher simply makes an educated guess with respect to the probable size of the relationship (which usually ranges in value from -1.00 to 1.00) rather than for the relative size of a mean difference. Thus if a relationship of .30 is the best guess for a given relationship, 84 subjects would be required to achieve a power estimate of .80.* If a relationship of .50 were expected, only 28 subjects would be needed. These same 28 subjects would result in a power estimate of only .35 for a projected relationship of .30, however, again questioning the wisdom of conducting the study at all if more subjects were not available.

Recommendations

I make the following recommendations with respect to the issue of statistical power:

1. *The most powerful, appropriate statistical and procedural techniques available should always be employed in a study.* For example, if statistical control is appropriate via some of the more sophisticated techniques discussed in Chapters 15 and 16, it should be employed. Similarly, the more precise models for collecting data (see Chapters 7 and 8) are always preferable if they are feasible.
2. *If the number of subjects available to the researcher is fixed, then the study's statistical power should be estimated prior to conducting the study.* If said power is much below .80 (which means that the probability of a Type II error will be greater than .20), then the wisdom of conducting the study is seriously in doubt. The researcher might consider the option of reformulating groups (or redefining variables) in such a way that the expected effect size would be greater. (Such a reformulation must, of course, be interesting scientifically.)
3. *If there is some flexibility with respect to the number of available subjects, then the minimum number necessary to achieve an acceptable level of power should be estimated.* For most effects, two group studies should employ a minimum of 50 subjects per group in the absence of statistical control (see Chapter 14), perhaps 40 per group if statistical control is present. For three or more groups, even more subjects per group are required if individual comparisons between all the groups are desired. For most studies involving simple correlations between two variables, the researcher would be wise to employ from 50 to 85 subjects. For more than two variables the reader is referred to Chapter 16. All of this assumes that resources are limited, of course, and that it is not feasible to employ more subjects. In general, as long as they are representative of the population from which they are drawn, the more subjects the better. Some methodologists argue that when power is *too* great, spurious relationships can be found to be statistically significant.

---

* These estimates are based on the assumption that the Pearson r (see Chapter 5) will be used as the statistic of choice.

Since the strength of a relationship can be ascertained independently of the number of subjects involved, however, I would argue that the only consideration of importance in defining the upper limits of sample size is economics (in terms of both resources and time), which leads to the final recommendation.

4. *When in doubt use as many subjects as possible.* And if there is one thing that is omnipresent in empirical research, it is doubt.

SUMMARY

The logic of hypothesis testing involves the assignment of a probability level to the difference or relationship actually obtained from the data collected for a study. This probability is obtained via statistical analysis and is directly compared to an a priori probability that reflects the amount of error the researcher is willing to risk in rejecting the null hypothesis when it is true (usually .05). If the obtained probability is less than the a priori probability, then the results are said to be statistically significant and the null hypothesis is rejected. If the obtained probability is greater than the a priori probability, the results are said not to be statistically significant and the null hypothesis is not rejected.

When the null hypothesis is rejected, there are two possibilities: either the decision to reject was correct or incorrect. The error made when the null hypothesis is rejected when it in reality should not have been is called *Type I error.* The probability of this type of error occurring is equal to the a priori probability level selected by the researcher (usually .05).

When the null hypothesis is not rejected, there are also two possibilities: either the decision not to reject was correct or incorrect. The error made when the null hypothesis is not rejected when in reality it should have been is called *Type II error.* The probability of this type of error occurring is a function of the study's statistical power. The greater the statistical power, the less the probability of a Type II error.

All legitimate steps possible should thus be taken to maximize statistical power. The most effective of these strategies include:

1. Employing a sufficiently large number of subjects.
2. Employing the most precise statistical and procedural techniques that are appropriate to the study at hand.
3. Conducting the study carefully and cleanly.

REFERENCE

Cohen, J. *Statistical Power Analysis for the Behavioral Sciences.* New York: Academic, 1977.

chapter 5

Correlation

The contents of this chapter should probably logically be located in the statistical analysis section (Part Four). The correlational concept permeates so many aspects of the research process, however, that a thorough understanding of the Pearson *r* and its two primary applications, partial and multiple correlation, are best attained early.

In my opinion, the Pearson *r* is the single most important statistical application of the standard deviation (or variance) and the arithmetic mean in empirical research. It can be visualized as both a descriptive and an inferential statistic (that is, a statistic which can be used to test a hypothesis).

In its descriptive guise, a correlation coefficient describes how two different measures available on the same sample *vary* together. In other words, are those subjects with high scores (that is, high in relationship to the sample's mean) on the first measure also the subjects with high scores on the second? In its inferential guise, the correlation coefficient is convertible (or expandable) to a host of seemingly diverse statistical procedures (for example, the *t*-test, ANOVA, multiple regression) discussed later in this volume.

As with all statistical procedures, today's researchers rarely compute correlation coefficients themselves. Instead, they rely on computers to do it for them. The concept of correlation is such an integral one to the entire research process, however, that it is essential for all practicing researchers to understand it *thoroughly.* One way to achieve such an understanding is to examine the concept via a numerical example, but prior to this, two of the more important assumptions regarding the use of the Pearson *r* must be explored in some detail.

MINIMAL ASSUMPTIONS REGARDING THE USE OF THE PEARSON PRODUCT MOMENT CORRELATION COEFFICIENT *r*

1. The arithmetic mean must be an appropriate descriptive statistic for the two measures on which the Pearson *r* is to be computed. This issue is often discussed under the concept of levels of measurement, where classically the Pearson *r* has been considered appropriate only for situations in which the intervals between the scales for both measures employed are considered equal. Since very few measures can satisfy a strict interpretation of this concept (for a more thorough discussion of interval scales, see Chapter 10) and since recent research has shown that such interpretation is usually not a necessary condition for the employment of the Pearson *r* or the other types of statistics discussed in this book,* I recommend the more relaxed rule given above.

Basically, as discussed in Chapter 3, the arithmetic mean can be an appropriate descriptive statistic for any set of numbers that reflect a basic order of some sort. Thus, the members of a sample's ages, scores on a test of some sort, or even affective responses on a scale that has a built-in intrinsic order (for example, strongly disagree → strongly agree; poor → excellent) all qualify.

The only types of numbers that usually do not qualify are those associated with measures that place subjects into categories without any intrinsic order of any kind. Thus, a demographic item such as race, where numbers are arbitrarily assigned to categories (for example, 1 = white; 2 = black; 3 = Hispanic; 4 = Oriental, and so forth) cannot be appropriately described by an arithmetic mean.† To explore this concept in a little more detail, let us examine a numerical example as reflected in the hypothetical frequency distribution shown in Table 5-1. A mean computed on this data would result in a figure of 1.50, that is,

$$\frac{(215 \times 1) + (150 \times 2) + (15 \times 3) + (4 \times 4)}{215 + 150 + 15 + 4}$$

---

* The issue of what types of statistics should be used on what types of data is at least a century old (Tractman, Giambalvo, and Dippner, 1978). I base my position on work accomplished by researchers classified by Baggaley and Hull (1983) as empirical liberals who have systematically manipulated scalar properties of measures and basically demonstrated no radical interpretive problems as a result. For a more thorough defense of this position the reader may refer to the following citations:

Baker, B. O., Hardyck, C. D., and Petrinovich, L. J. Weak measurement versus strong statistics: an empirical critique of S. S. Steven's prescriptions on statistics. *Educational and Psychological Measurement,* 1966, *26,* 291–309.

Baggaley, A. R., and Hull, A. L. The effect of nonlinear transformations on a Likert scale. *Evaluation and the Health Professions,* 1983, *6,* 483–491.

Gaito, J. Measurement scales and statistics: resurgence of an old misconception. *Psychological Bulletin,* 1980, *87,* 564–567.

Lord, F. M. On the statistical treatment of football numbers. *American Psychologist,* 1953, *8,* 750–751.

Nunnally, J. C. *Psychometric Theory.* New York: McGraw-Hill, 1978.

Tractman, J. J., Giambalvo, V., and Dippner, R. S. On the assumptions concerning the assumptions of a t test. *Journal of General Psychology,* 1978, *99,* 107–116.

† Other examples of categorical data might be marital status (married, single, widowed, divorced), diagnosis, personality type, academic discipline (for example, psychology, sociology, education, medicine), treatment modality, and so forth.

Table 5-1   HYPOTHETICAL FREQUENCY DISTRIBUTION

Category	Numerical code	Frequency	Percentage (%)
White	1	215	56
Black	2	150	39
Hispanic	3	15	4
Oriental	4	4	1

Table 5-2   ANOTHER HYPOTHETICAL FREQUENCY
DISTRIBUTION

Category	Numerical code	Frequency	Percentage (%)
White	1	316	82
Black	2	4	1
Hispanic	3	4	1
Oriental	4	60	16

Unfortunately, the next very different distribution (in which, among other things, there were 26 percent more whites and 38 percent fewer blacks) would also result in a mean of 1.50, as shown in Table 5-2.

Obviously, reliance on a mean to describe categorical data such as these would be most misleading. Even more telling, since the assignment of numbers as codes to this type of data is completely arbitrary, very different means would result from the same distribution if different numbers were assigned to the categories (for example, "1" to black and "2" to white). *Such classification schemes are often referred to as nominal and their use with a Pearson r can be just as misleading as the use of a mean to describe their distributions.*

An Exception

The one exception to this rule occurs when only two categories are involved. Here, regardless of the numbers assigned to these categories, the arithmetic mean describes the distribution quite accurately. As an example, consider the distribution shown in Table 5-3.

Here the mean will reflect the percentage of the sample that falls into each of the two categories. When whites are coded "1" and blacks "2," the mean for the above distribution is equal to 1.44 (which reflects the fact that 44 percent of this sample was black or was coded the higher number). If blacks were coded "1" and whites "2" (which would be just as reasonable, since the assignment of numbers is completely arbitrary for such measures), then the mean would have been 1.56 (since 56 percent of the sample would now be coded the higher number). If blacks were coded "0" and whites "1", then the mean would be 0.56. The arithmetic mean is therefore a completely appropriate descriptor of a dichotomously coded measure, and thus a Pearson *r* can also be used to describe

Table 5-3   A DICHOTOMOUS FREQUENCY DISTRIBUTION

Category	Numerical code	Frequency	Percentage (%)
White	1	215	56
Black	2	169	44

such a measure's relationship with any other appropriately scaled set of numbers.

2. The relationship being investigated must not be curvilinear. Many researchers do not test this assumption, since the only harm that will accrue from the use of a linear procedure, such as the Pearson r, for a nonlinear relationship between two variables will be the conclusion that no relationship exists at all when, in reality, a very strong curvilinear relationship may be present. It is usually a good idea to check this assumption when the possibility of a curvilinear relationship does exist, however, since a simple graph is often enough to lay the issue to rest.

To understand what a curvilinear relationship might look like, it is helpful first to review what is meant by a positive or negative linear relationship. It will be remembered from Chapter 2 that a positive relationship reflects a situation in which persons who score high on measure X are also the people who score high on measure Y; a negative relationship is one in which people who score high on one measure are expected to score low on the other. (By implication, no relationship at all reflects the situation in which peoples' scores on X have *nothing at all* to do with their scores on Y.)

As an example of the difference between a linear relationship and a curvilinear one, let us reconsider the example used in Chapter 2 employing the relationship between age and physical strength. If the sample consisted of subjects ranging in age from, say 2 to 25 years, the resulting r would probably be statistically significant. The older subjects would generally be stronger than their younger counterparts, reflecting a positive, linear relationship. If the age range were extended to age 65, on the other hand, the relationship would be curvilinear with physical strength increasing to a certain point and then beginning to decrease as the subjects became older. A Pearson r computed on the latter set of data might well result in a near zero correlation coefficient, while a curvilinear coefficient (such as eta) might prove statistically significant.

One relatively simple method of determining the overall nature of a relationship is to graph scores of the two measures involved. For the age versus physical strength example, the simplest way to construct such a graph would probably be to group subjects into age ranges and compute the mean strength levels for each of these ranges. (Many computer programs exist that will accomplish this task automatically.) Four scenarios reflecting (a) a positive linear relationship, (b) a negative linear relationship, (c) a curvilinear relationship, and (d) no relationship at all are shown in Figure 5-1.

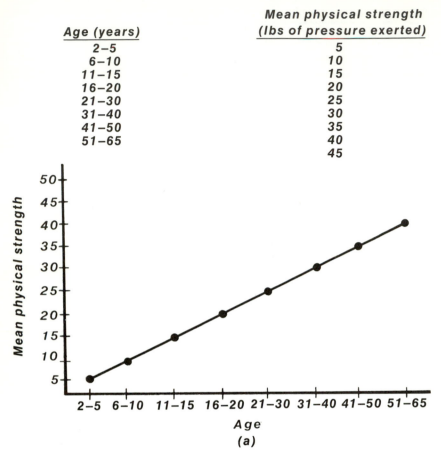

| | Mean physical strength |
Age (years)	(lbs of pressure exerted)
2–5	5
6–10	10
11–15	15
16–20	20
21–30	25
31–40	30
41–50	35
51–65	40
	45

Figure 5-1 Four different types of relationships. (a) A positive, linear relationship. (b) A negative, linear relationship. (c) A curvilinear relationship. (d) No relationship at all.

A HYPOTHETICAL EXAMPLE

To explore the correlation concept in more detail it will be necessary to employ some hypothetical data. Let us therefore examine a set of data consisting of two pieces of information collected on a sample of five subjects:* their ages and their responses to the following question:

In general, I believe that mentally incompetent people can best be cared for in an institutional setting.

1	2	3	4	5
Strongly Disagree				Strongly Agree

* This small number of subjects was selected solely for computational ease. Obviously a larger sample size would be employed in practice.

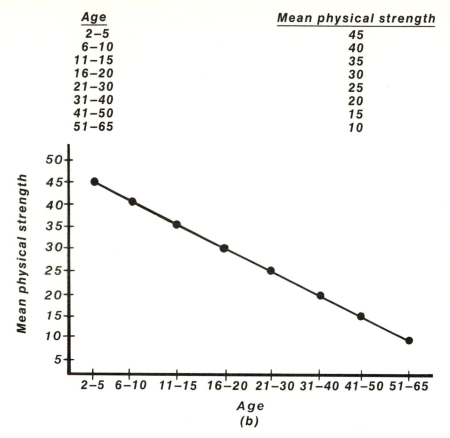

Age	Mean physical strength
2–5	45
6–10	40
11–15	35
16–20	30
21–30	25
31–40	20
41–50	15
51–65	10

(b)

Figure 5-1   *(Continued)*

Suppose further that the sample's ages and responses to this item are shown in Table 5-4.

Note that these data conform to our two assumptions regarding the use of the Pearson *r*:

1. *The arithmetic mean could be used appropriately to describe scores on both measures.* Said another way, the numbers assigned to both measures (age and attitudes) are not simply arbitrary category labels; they have a definite intrinsic order (that is, 80 is older than 18 and "5" reflects more agreement with the statement than "1").
2. *The relationship between the two measures does not appear to be curvilinear in nature* (Figure 5-2).

Since the numbers assigned to these two measures are on such different scales—that is, age is given in years ($\overline{X} = 43.8$); attitudes are on a five-point continuum ($\overline{X} = 3.0$)—it will be helpful in the discussion that follows to convert both sets of numbers to a common metric. One way to do this would be to convert each person's score on each measure to a standard scale with a mean of 0 and a standard deviation of 1.

Age	Mean physical strength
2–5	5
6–10	10
11–15	15
16–20	20
21–30	20
31–40	15
41–50	10
51–65	5

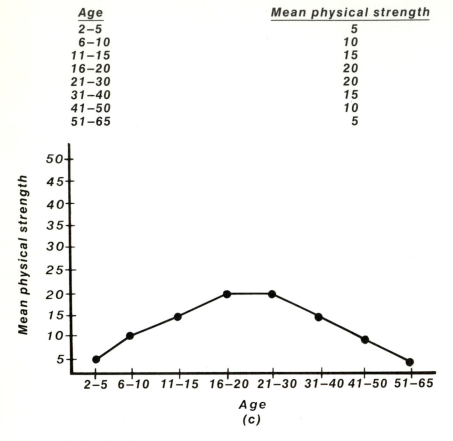

Figure 5-1 *(Continued)*

Called *z*-scores, this task is accomplished by simply dividing the difference between each score and its mean by the sample's standard deviation.

$$z\text{-score} = \frac{X - \overline{X}}{\text{S.D.}} \tag{5-1}$$

where X = any subject's score
$\overline{X}$ = the sample's mean
S.D. = the sample's standard deviation

Table 5-4 **HYPOTHETICAL CORRELA-TIONAL DATA**

Subject I.D.	Age	Attitudinal response
1	18	1
2	26	2
3	40	4
4	55	3
5	80	5

Age	Mean physical strength
2–5	5
6–10	20
11–15	15
16–20	20
21–30	5
31–40	10
41–50	10
51–65	15

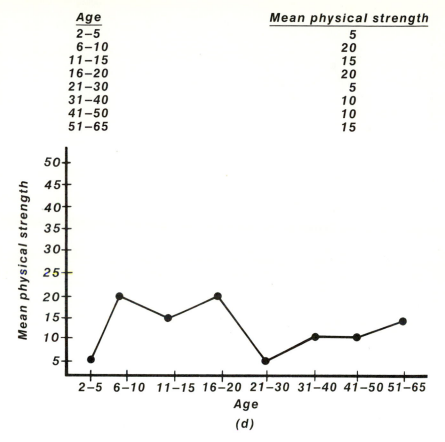

Figure 5-1 *(Continued)*

The first step in this process would be to compute the mean and the standard deviation for both age and attitudes*:

Age: $\bar{X} = \dfrac{\Sigma X}{n}$

$$= \frac{18 + 26 + 40 + 55 + 80}{5}$$

$$= 43.80$$

S.D. $= \sqrt{\dfrac{\Sigma(X - \bar{X})^2}{n - 1}}$

$$= \sqrt{\frac{(18 - 43.80)^2 + (26 - 43.80)^2 + \cdots + (80 - 43.80)^2}{5 - 1}}$$

$$= 24.66$$

* If the sample were larger, these individual statistics would give the researcher (and the professionals who read the final research report) an idea about the average age and opinions regarding the care of mentally incompetent people in the sample employed *and* the amount of variability therein with respect to each measure.

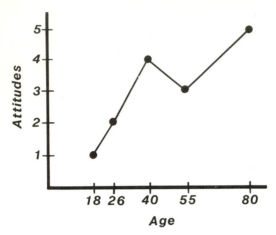

Figure 5-2   A graphic representation of the data presented in Table 5-4.

$$\text{Opinions:} \quad \bar{X} = \frac{1 + 2 + 4 + 3 + 5}{5}$$

$$= 3.00$$

$$\text{S.D.} = \sqrt{\frac{(1 - 3)^2 + (2 - 3)^2 + (4 - 3)^2 + (3 - 3)^2 + (5 - 3)^2}{5 - 1}}$$

$$= 1.58$$

Next, each subject's age and attitudinal z-score could be computed using Equation 5-1, as shown in Table 5-5.

Now the question of how age and opinions are related to one another becomes somewhat easier to visualize, even without a graph. One need only to compare each subject's two z-scores to get a general answer to questions such as:

Do they vary together?

Do older people tend to differ from younger people with respect to their opinions about the care of mental patients?

Such questions address the relationship between the two variables and are answered by the computation of a correlation coefficient that ranges in value from -1.00 (which is called a perfect negative relationship and, in the present case, would indicate that the older subjects *disagreed* with the statement in question) to $+1.00$ (which would indicate that older subjects agreed with said statement).* A value of 0.00 would indicate absolutely no relationship between age and opinions or that there was no difference between older and younger

---

* This assumes a relatively normal distribution for each measure and that the variability between individual scores for either measure is not severely restricted. Should either not be the case, the range that the Pearson r is likely to take will probably be reduced.

Table 5-5 COMPUTATION OF AGE AND ATTITUDINAL z-SCORES

Subject	X (Age)	$z_x = \dfrac{X - 43.8}{24.66}$	Y (Opinion)	$z_Y = \dfrac{Y - 3.00}{1.58}$
1	18	$\dfrac{18 - 43.8}{24.66} = -1.05$	1	$\dfrac{1 - 3}{1.58} = -1.27$
2	26	$\dfrac{26 - 43.8}{24.66} = -.72$	2	$\dfrac{2 - 3}{1.58} = -.63$
3	40	$\dfrac{40 - 43.8}{24.66} = -.15$	4	$\dfrac{4 - 3}{1.58} = .63$
4	55	$\dfrac{55 - 43.8}{24.66} = .45$	3	$\dfrac{3 - 3}{1.58} = 0$
5	80	$\dfrac{80 - 43.8}{24.66} = 1.47$	5	$\dfrac{5 - 3}{1.58} = 1.27$

people with respect to their opinions regarding the care of mentally incompetent patients.

A PRIMITIVE FORM OF CORRELATION

The simplest possible type of correlation coefficient would address only the order between subjects with respect to their ages and opinions, and perhaps that is a good place to begin. In other words, given that S_2 was older than S_1 (26 years of age versus 18 or $-.72$ versus -1.05 in terms of z-scores), was S_2's opinion score also higher? The answer is yes, since S_2's opinion score was 2 and S_1's was 1 ($-.63$ versus -1.27 in z-scores). If this sort of relationship held for all the possible combinations of pairs of subjects, then certainly a positive relationship could be said to exist between the two variables. In fact, if we counted the number of yes answers to the above question, subtracted the number of no answers, and divided the difference by the total number of combinations of pairs, we would have the most elementary possible form of correlation coefficient, called *Gamma*.

$$\text{Gamma} = \frac{\text{Number of ``yes'' responses} - \text{number of ``no'' responses}}{\text{Number of possible pairs}} \quad (5\text{-}2)$$

For the present data, there are *10* possible combinations of pairs of subjects, 9 of which vary in the same direction with respect to the two variables ("yes") and 1 of which varies in the opposite direction ("no"). This indicates a positive relationship, thus the correlation coefficient would be expected to be closer to $+1.00$ than -1.00. As illustrated at the top of page 62, this is indeed the case.

Had the number of "no" responses predominated, then the correlation coefficient would have been negative, indicating a relationship in the opposite direction of the one above. Had there been no difference between the number of "yes" responses and "no" responses, the correlation would have been 0 — indicating no relationship between age and opinion.

Pairs	Do age and opinion vary in the same direction?
S_1 versus S_2	yes
S_1 versus S_3	yes
S_1 versus S_4	yes
S_1 versus S_5	yes
S_2 versus S_3	yes
S_2 versus S_4	yes
S_2 versus S_5	yes
S_3 versus S_4	no
S_3 versus S_5	yes
S_4 versus S_5	yes

$$\text{Gamma} = \frac{9-1}{10} = .89$$

A MORE IN-DEPTH LOOK AT THE PEARSON r

Although Gamma very nicely illustrates the logic behind the correlation concept (that is, the extent to which two scores vary together among the same sample of subjects), it has a severe limitation. It ignores the relative distance between scores—in other words, the difference between the ages of S_1 and S_2 (18 versus 26) is treated exactly the same as the age differential between S_1 and S_5 (18 versus 80).

What is obviously needed, then is a correlation coefficient that takes into account not only whether or not the *direction* of the two scores is the same for each pair of subjects but also whether or not the relative size of the difference is similar. Fortunately such a technique exists. It is called the Pearson product moment correlation coefficient, or more simply, the Pearson r. By using the z-scores presented in Table 5-5, the differences between the ages of S_1 and S_2 (−1.05 versus −.72) can be compared directly to the difference in opinions between S_1 and S_2 (−1.27 versus −.63).

This can be done for the entire sample be simply summing the product of each subject's z-scores and dividing by $n - 1$ and results in a Pearson r between attitudes and age. In the present example, this can be written as:

$$r = \frac{\Sigma(\text{standardized age scores} \times \text{standardized opinion scores})}{n - 1^*} \quad (5\text{-}3)$$

or, more generically,

$$r = \frac{\Sigma z_x z_y}{n - 1^*}$$

where x is the first variable
        y is the second variable

---

* n (instead of $n - 1$) is used if the standard deviation is computed with a denominator of n rather than $n - 1$.

Substituting the *z*-scores computed in Table 5-5, we have

$$r = \frac{(-1.05 \times -1.27) + (-.72 \times -.63) + \cdots + (1.47 \times 1.27)}{n - 1}$$

$$= \frac{1.33 + 0.45 + (-.09) + 0 + 1.87}{4}$$

$$= .89$$

which indicates a high positive relationship between the two variables.

Since most correlational coefficients are computed on at least 50 subjects, it is easy to see why researchers seldom compute a Pearson *r* by hand anymore. A cursory examination of Equation 5-3 and the subsequent computations should enable the reader to see, however, that in general, when the number of subjects is constant, the closer each pair of standard scores is to one another, the larger will be the numerator (that is, $\Sigma z_x z_y$) and consequently the larger will be the Pearson *r*. Thus, the standardized age and opinion scores for S_1, S_2, and S_5 contribute powerfully to the overall *r*, because in each case these subjects' ages and opinion scores are approximately the same distance (and of course in the same direction) from their respective means. S_3 and S_4, on the other hand, actually serve to decrease the *r*, since in the first case the person's two scores were on opposite sides of their respective means and in the second both scores were so close to the mean that their product added nothing to the numerator.

Although there are many equivalent formulas for computing the Pearson *r*, Equation 5-3 highlights three extremely important characteristics of the statistic. All three emanate from the fact that the size of the *r* is a function not of the size of the scores themselves, but of their relative *distance* from the sample mean. These characteristics are:

1. *The size of* r *is unrelated to the size of either mean of the two scores on which it is computed.* Thus, it makes no difference if the two variables in question have wildly different scales of measurement, as was the case in the example employed above. A corollary of the phenomenon is the fact that *a constant can be added to either (or both) set(s) of scores without affecting the* r. Thus, if everyone in the above study were exactly 20 years older (that is, S_1 was 38, S_2 was 46, and so forth), the correlation between age and opinions would still be .89, as long as each subject registered the same opinion score. To see why this is true it is only necessary to realize that adding a constant to each score will not change the size of the standard deviation. The mean will change from 43.8 and 63.8, but the standard deviation will remain at 24.66. This means that each subject's *z*-score will also remain the same.

2. *The size of the* r *is affected by the amount of variability in the two sets of scores.* Generally speaking, the more spread out both sets of scores are in the sample, the higher the *r* will be *if* the two sets of standardized scores match. Thus, if a sixth subject with an age of 14 and an opinion score of 1 had existed, both the standard deviations (and hence the

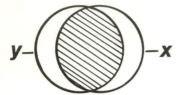

Figure 5-3   Venn diagram for a Pearson *r*.

amount of variability) would increase for both measures and the *r* would go up from .89 to .92.

3. *Since* r *is a sort of average product of each subject's standardized scores, and since standardized scores are the actual scores minus the mean corrected for by the size of the standard deviation, it follows that* r *is a sort of reflection of shared variability between two sets of scores. Actually, it is* r² (just as the variance is S.D.²) *that can be said to be a reflection of the amount of variance shared by two measures* administered to the same sample of subjects.

This is an extremely important concept in empirical research. It is most commonly represented in terms of Venn diagrams, where circles are used to represent a measure's variance for a given sample of subjects. Our original *r* of .89 would thus be represented as shown in Figure 5-3, with the shaded area indicating that exactly 79 percent (.89²) of the variance of the two measures is shared in this particular sample. This statistic (r^2), which varies from 0 to 1.00,* is also referred to as the *strength* of a relationship.

The Statistical Significance of a Pearson *r*

Should the researcher wish to know whether or not a given Pearson *r* represents a relationship greater than would be expected to occur by chance alone, most computer routines automatically print out a significance level when they compute the statistic itself. Thus, a Pearson *r* can be used as an inferential statistic to test a hypothesis. (An example of such a hypothesis was presented in Chapter 2.)

PARTIAL AND MULTIPLE CORRELATION

As important as the concepts of correlation (*r*) and shared variance (r^2) are to empirical research, it is two simple extensions of these concepts that truly give the Pearson *r* its great utility. These derivative statistics are called partial and multiple correlation coefficients.

---

* Note that a squared number cannot be negative, hence an *r* of −.89 also yields an r^2 of .79 and a shared variance of 79 percent.

Partial Correlation

The idea behind partial correlation is quite straightforward. If the variability shared between two measures can be expressed as the average product of two sets of standard scores squared, that is

$$r^2 = \left(\frac{\Sigma z_x z_y}{n-1}\right)^2$$

why couldn't a third variable be statistically controlled by subtracting or partialling out the variance that it shares with the two original variables?

The answer, of course, is that it can. Furthermore this truly useful strategy can be accomplished by computing three simple Pearson r's: one reflecting the correlation between the two original variables and one between the new controlling variable and each of these two variables.

To illustrate, let us suppose that it was expected that at least some of the shared variability between age and opinions toward the care of the mentally incompetent was due to the subjects' educational levels. To test this hypothesis, the researcher would need not only to compute a Pearson r between age and opinions, but also between educational level and age as well as between educational level and opinions.

Suppose that the five original subjects' educational levels (given in the number of years of education they had completed) broke down as shown in Table 5-6.

Computing the two additional r's between education and both age and opinion would yield coefficients of .92 and .79, respectively. With a little thought, it should be apparent that (1) education and opinion share almost as much variance ($r^2 = .79^2 = .62$) as age and opinion ($r^2 = .89^2 = .79$), and (2) even more of the subjects' variation in age and education is *shared* ($r^2 = .92^2 = .85$). Thus, subtracting out that part of the relationship between age and opinion that is shared with education will result in a weaker relationship than is reflected in the original r (.89).

When these values are plugged into the partial correlation formula, this supposition is indeed proved to be true:

$$r_{xy.z} = \frac{r_{xy} - r_{xz}r_{yz}}{\sqrt{1 - r_{xz}^2}\,\sqrt{1 - r_{yz}^2}} \tag{5-4}$$

Table 5-6 HYPOTHETICAL THREE-VARIABLE DISTRIBUTION

Subject	Age (X)	Opinion (Y)	Education (Z)
1	18	1	12
2	26	2	12
3	40	4	14
4	55	3	16
5	80	5	16

where x = age
y = opinions
z = education
$r_{xy.z}$ = the correlation between age and opinion with education partialled out
r_{xy} = the simple correlation between age and opinion
r_{xz} = the simple correlation between age and education
r_{yz} = the simple correlation between opinion and education

Thus:

$$r_{xy.z} = \frac{.89 - .92 \times .79}{\sqrt{1 - .92^2} \sqrt{1 - .79^2}}$$

$$= \frac{.16}{.39 \times .62} = \frac{.16}{.24} = .67$$

The original correlation was thus substantively reduced when the third variable (education) was partialled out *because* the correlation between this controlling variable and *both* the original variables was relatively high. If *either* or both of these correlations had been very low, the partial r would not have differed substantively from the original Pearson r.

In the vast majority of cases, a partial correlation will be lower than the original Pearson r. This does not have to be so, however, if the controlling variable is correlated positively with one of the original variables and negatively with the other. Although this is a relatively rare phenomenon, it has the effect of *adding to* the original correlation instead of subtracting therefrom.

As an example, consider the scenario in which opinions were correlated .40 with both age and education, but the latter two bore a negative correlation of $-.40$ with one another. Plugging these values into the partial correlation formula results in a partial r of .67, a considerably higher value than the Pearson r between age and opinions (.40).

$$r_{xy.z} = \frac{.40 - (-.40) \times (.40)}{\sqrt{1 - (-.40)^2} \sqrt{1 - .40^2}}$$

$$= \frac{.40 - (-.16)}{\sqrt{.84} \sqrt{.84}}$$

$$= \frac{.56}{.84} = .67$$

Perhaps the following rules will help the reader better visualize the partialling process:

1. The size of the original correlation (r_{xy}) is reduced if r_{xz} and r_{yz} are either both positive or both negative (for example, if $r_{xy} = .40$, $r_{yz} = .40$, and $r_{xz} = .40$, then $r_{xy.z} = .286$).
2. The size of the original correlation is increased in the rare event that r_{xz} is in the opposite direction from r_{yz} (see the example above).

3. The size of the original correlation is reduced the most when both r_{xz} and r_{yz} are relatively high (for example, if $r_{xy} = .30$, $r_{xz} = .50$, and $r_{yz} = .50$, then $r_{xy.z} = .067$).
4. The size of the original correlation is reduced the least when both r_{xz} and r_{yz} are extremely low (for example, if $r_{xy} = .40$, $r_{xz} = .04$, and $r_{yz} = .04$, then $r_{xy.z} = .399$).
5. The size of the original correlation is not much affected (but increased slightly) if one of the other correlations approaches 0 and the other is substantively higher (for example, if $r_{xy} = .40$, $r_{xz} = .02$, and $r_{yz} = .40$, then $r_{xy.z} = .427$).

Interpreting a partial correlation is very similar to interpreting a simple Pearson r. Its values vary from -1.00 to $+1.00$ and $r^2_{xy.z}$ is also an indicator of the percentage of variance that is shared between x and y; the only difference being that it reflects the percentage of unique shared variance (that is, variance that is not shared with z).

The partialling-out process can be visualized in a number of ways. It can be seen as a form of *statistical control* or as a means of taking into account the effect of a third variable on the relationship between two other variables. Although causation cannot be assumed, a researcher employing our example would probably at least subconsciously pose the question:

> *Is age really related to opinions regarding the treatment of the mentally incompetent or is education really what is related to said opinions?*

The partial correlation answers this question in a fashion by partialling out any of the relationship shared with education and seeing what is left. It is an extremely effective technique, since it is a means of testing rival hypotheses or of considering alternative explanations for phenomena, especially since more than one variable can be statistically controlled at a time. Researchers investigating the original relationship between cigarette smoking and heart disease, for example, have statistically controlled for many, many variables that are known to be related to both smoking and increased risk of heart disease. The technique is also an integral part of an even more commonly employed extension of the Pearson r: multiple correlation.

Multiple Correlation

Multiple correlation as a concept is in some ways easier to grasp than partial correlation. In this model, one variable is designated as the dependent variable (also called the criterion) and the others as the independent variables (sometimes called predictors). The dependent variable is normally considered either (1) to be causally affected (or capable of being causally affected) by the independent variables, (2) to occur later in time, or (3) occasionally, simply to be more important.

The multiple correlation (designated as $R_{y.x_1x_2}$ for the three-variable model) is the combined correlation between all the independent variables taken as a set and the single dependent variable. $R_{y.x_1x_2}$, unlike the partial correlation, will always be at least as high as either r_{xy_1} or r_{yx_2} (the singular correlations between each of the independent variables and the dependent variable), higher in more than 99.9 percent of the cases.

Venn diagrams can perhaps best illustrate the relationship between a simple Pearson r, a partial correlation, and a multiple correlation. Figure 5-4 thus represents the situation in which all three simple correlations (r_{yx_1}, r_{yx_2}, $r_{x_1x_2}$) are .40. This diagram can be interpreted as follows:

1. Since the y circle represents the total dependent variable variance, the entire shaded area (crossed, solid, and dotted) represents $R^2_{y.x_1x_2}$ which in turn represents the dependent variable variance that is shared with both independent variables (x_1 and x_2).
2. The dotted region represents unique shared variance between x_1 and y after any variance the two share with x_2 has been partialled out. In other words, $r^2_{yx_1.x_2}$.
3. The crossed portion represents the variance shared by y and x_2 with x_1 partialled out ($r^2_{yx_2.x_1}$).
4. The dotted plus the solid area represents the total variance shared by y and x_1 ($r^2_{yx_1}$).
5. The crossed plus the solid area represents the total variance shared by y and x_2 ($r^2_{yx_2}$).

The multiple correlation between the dependent variable (y) and the two independent variables (x_1 and x_2) can thus be visualized as a two-step process designed to ascertain the proportion of y that is shaded. The first step begins with a simple correlation being computed between y and either x_1 or x_2. If r_{yx_1} is chosen and squared, the resulting value is .16 (.40²), which means that 16 percent of the total y variance is shared by the first independent variable. In Figure 5-4, this represents the dotted and solid shadings.

This means that 84 percent of the y variance remains to be explained, of which a certain proportion corresponds to the shaded area. It so happens that the proportion of the remaining unexplained 84 percent that is so shaded is equivalent to the squared partial correlation between y and x_2 holding x_1 con-

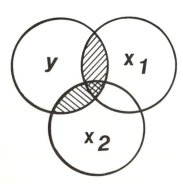

Figure 5-4 Venn diagram for a multiple correlation coefficient.

stant (because the original 16 percent took x_1 into account and it is obviously not reasonable to count it twice).

This partial correlation is computed as follows (see Equation 5-4):

$$r_{yx_2.x_1} = \frac{.40 - (.40 \times .40)}{\sqrt{1 - .40^2}\,\sqrt{1 - .40^2}}$$

$$= \frac{.24}{\sqrt{.84}\,\sqrt{.84}}$$

$$= .286$$

And, since it is *shared* variance that is of interest, this partial correlation coefficient is squared ($.286^2 = .082$) and multiplied by the remaining unexplained y variance ($.082 \times .84 = .069$).

This figure indicates that once the relationship between the first independent variable is removed (and it doesn't matter in the final analysis which variable is removed first and which second), 6.9 percent of the remaining variance is accounted for or shared with or explained by the second independent variable.

It therefore follows, that since $R^2_{y.x_1x_2}$ is equal to the total y variance shared by the combination of x_1 and x_2, $R^2_{y.x_1x_2}$ is thus equal to .16 (the total y variation shared with x_1) *plus* .069 (the additional or unique y variation shared with x_2), which equals .229 and not coincidentally is identical to the value yielded by the actual squared multiple correlation formula for two independent variables.

$$R^2_{y.x_1x_2} = \frac{r^2_{yx_1} + r^2_{yx_2} - 2r_{yx_1}r_{yx_2}r_{x_1x_2}}{1 - r^2_{x_1x_2}} \qquad (5\text{-}5)$$

$$= \frac{.40^2 + .40^2 - 2 \times .40 \times .40 \times .40}{1 - .40^2}$$

$$= \frac{.192}{.84}$$

$$= .229$$

and
$$R_{y.x_1x_2} = \sqrt{R^2_{y.x_1x_2}}$$

$$= \sqrt{.229}$$

$$= .479$$

Although the use of Equation 5-5 is not particularly burdensome, the formula can become unmanageably complicated when additional variables are employed, thus most researchers prefer to employ computers in such situations. In my opinion, even with the use of a computer, a conceptual grasp of (1) the Pearson r, (2) partial correlation, and (3) multiple correlation remains essential for anyone planning to engage in serious empirical research. It is recommended, therefore, that the past few pages be reviewed occasionally and certainly prior to tackling the very important chapter devoted to the multiple-regression model (Chapter 16).

SUMMARY

The Pearson r is the preferred statistic in describing a linear relationship between two measures that can both be appropriately described by the arithmetic mean. The resulting statistic, which ranges in value from -1.00 to $+1.00$, is useful both in testing hypotheses and, when squared (r^2), in describing the amount of variability shared between two measures.

The two most important extensions of the Pearson r are partial and multiple correlation. A partial correlation allows the researcher to assess the relationship between two measures when one or more additional variables are held constant (or partialled out). When squared, this statistic indicates the amount of unique variation shared (that is, variation that is not shared with the other variables involved) between the two original measures. A multiple correlation allows a researcher to assess the relationship between a single measure (variously called the criterion or the dependent variable) and two or more predictor or independent variables. A squared multiple correlation coefficient indicates the total amount of the dependent variable's variance that is shared with the multiple independent variables.

two

THE DESIGN OF
EMPIRICAL RESEARCH

chapter 6

Primitive Single-Group Research Models

Suppose a clinician who was confronted with the need for facilitating weight loss in overweight patients following cardiovascular surgery decided to design a research study to evaluate a promising procedure. Suppose further that this procedure entailed special dietary instruction coupled with a closely supervised exercise regimen.

At first glance this study may appear to be in a very rudimentary stage of development. Actually the researcher is well on the way to designing it, since the first tentative, prerequisite steps have already been taken:

1. *The general problem or research question* (Does a program of dietary instruction and exercise result in weight loss among overweight, postoperative cardiovascular patients?) *has been formulated.*
2. *The independent variable* (dietary instruction coupled with an exercise regimen) *and the dependent* (number of pounds of body weight lost) *variables have been identified.*
3. *The sample* (overweight, cardiovascular patients receiving postoperative care in the institution in which the clinician worked) *has been selected.*

Certainly each of these steps needs further delineation. The specifications for ascertaining the number of pounds lost, for example, might include:

1. The type of scale to be used to weigh subjects.
2. The definition of ideal body weight, a value that will be subtracted

from subjects' actual weights to obtain the number of ounces overweight.
3. The qualifications of the measurer(s).

The intervention (independent variable), which in this case involves a
dietary/exercise treatment, would also require extremely careful and detailed
definition. Exactly what would be said to patients under what conditions would
need to be delineated in minute detail. Finally, the sample itself would require
description with respect to:

1. How many pounds overweight patients must be to qualify for the
   study.
2. Types of cardiovascular surgical procedures to be included.
3. Minimum physical conditions of patients.
4. Procedures for obtaining subjects.
5. Salient characteristics of the final sample.
6. Characteristics of the institution from which the sample is to be drawn.

Once these preliminary decisions have been made, the researcher is confronted by a special genre of decisions found only in studies in which something
is actually done to subjects (that is, those that employ an intervention of some
sort). In our present example, this translates to questions such as:

*When will subjects be weighed? Before and after the dietary/exercise pro-
gram or afterward only? Will all subjects meeting the criteria receive the
program or will only a subsample be exposed to it?*

*If the latter is the case, how will this subsample be selected and what will
happen to subjects not receiving the program?*

Decisions such as these are the very heart of empirical research. Their
purpose is to enable the researcher to arrive at a single assessment of an intervention's effect(s). Collectively, they determine the *model* by which subjects are
studied and data collected. No more important issue exists in empirical research, because the selection of an inappropriate model will inevitably produce
alternative explanations for a study's final results. Since the existence of even
one plausible, alternative interpretation of an intervention's effect(s) can invalidate the noblest of efforts, it behooves the serious researcher to be familiar with
the strengths and weaknesses of the different available options.
   This chapter will focus on the most primitive of these models, those
involving the administration of a single treatment to a single group of subjects.
Although seemingly possessed of some very real practical advantages, a recur-
ring theme in empirical research will soon become apparent: what appears to be
the easiest, most economic course of action often turns out to be the most
costly.

THE ONE-GROUP—POSTTEST-ONLY MODEL

Certainly the easiest way to conduct our hypothetical study would be to administer the dietary/exercise intervention to the chosen sample and then measure its effects after a specified period of time. This method of data collection may be referred to as the *one-group–posttest*-only model* (Figure 6-1).

There is something very wrong with this model, however, and it involves interpretation of the results. Suppose the researcher found that, on the average, patients were 14.2 pounds overweight one month after the advent of the dietary/exercise intervention. Given the above design, this figure ($\overline{X} = 14.2$ pounds) must therefore constitute the program's effect.

What does the number 14.2 pounds mean, however? How is it to be interpreted? Can the researcher infer from this result that the dietary/exercise intervention was effective?

These questions underline the most fundamental tenet of empirical research:

> *Without a comparison of some sort, numbers cannot be evaluated, hypotheses cannot be tested, and causal or relational inferences cannot be made.*

The one-group–posttest-only model, therefore, does not qualify as a method of conducting empirical research as we have defined it.† Our investigator must first find something to which the 14.2 pounds can be compared in order to bring inferential meaning to the study. Two obvious solutions present themselves: the figure can be compared either to the average amount that subjects were overweight prior to the dietary/exercise intervention or to the weights of a similar group of subjects who did not receive the intervention. Let us save the second option for Chapter 7.

THE ONE-GROUP—PRETEST/POSTTEST MODEL

The easiest way to design the study at hand with a *meaningful* comparison is to ascertain how much subjects were overweight immediately before the intervention and then statistically contrast this figure to how much they were overweight

---

* In this book, any measurement performed on human subjects is referred to as a *test*.

† Some researchers argue that primitive models such as this can alert us to ideas worthy of more rigorous subsequent research. I do not recommend that the one-group–posttest-only model be considered as research, however, given its complete lack of a comparison of any sort.

Figure 6-1   The one-group–posttest-only model.

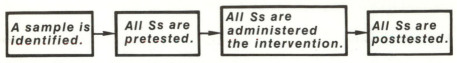

Figure 6-2   The one-group–pretest/posttest model.

afterward. If the second mean is significantly lower than the first, then at the very least the researcher knows that subjects lost weight *following* the dietary/ exercise program and that this change was probably not simply due to chance fluctuations (Figure 6-2).

The chief objection to the one-group–posttest-only model has now been eliminated. The investigator has an excellent standard by which to compare posttreatment means, thus the study would appear to meet the minimum requirement generating causal or relational inferences.

Would the researcher therefore be justified in concluding that, since it occurred after the intervention, the observed weight loss occurred *because* of the intervention? The answer, in the absence of additional information, is *no*. The *one-group–pretest/posttest model* permits the existence of too many plausible alternative explanations for its results. Unless they can be ruled out, the researcher will have been unsuccessful in providing a definitive answer to the original research question, and failure here constitutes failure of the entire effort.

FIVE COMMON ALTERNATIVE EXPLANATIONS

In science nothing should be taken on faith. Everything is subject to question. Given the above-described weight loss, therefore, the following premise would be advanced automatically:

> *The patients would have lost the weight anyway, with or without the intervention.*

There are a number of reasons why this statement is all too plausible. The five that follow are based on the Campbell and Stanley (1963) classic list of threats to internal validity.*

1. *External events, other than the intervention, occurring during the course of a study capable of influencing its outcome.* What, for example, if during the course of our research study one of the major television networks ran an extremely effective special dealing with the negative relationship between

---

* These authors' most succinct definition of internal validity is given in terms of the question: "Did the experimental treatments in fact make a difference in this specific experimental instance?" This they conceive as separate from the issue of generalizability, or: "To what populations, settings, treatment variables, and measurement variables can this effect be generalized?"

obesity and longevity in victims of heart attacks. If most of the subjects and their families watched the program (as they probably would if they knew about it), how could anyone ever be sure that the observed weight loss occurring in these subjects was solely due to the intervention? Taken one step further, how can a researcher (much less anyone else) ever be completely sure that all such potentially confounding occurrences are even recognized? Such an alternative explanation for a study's results is called *history,* because it encompasses everything that happens to the subjects during the course of the study. The *one-group–pretest/posttest model* offers no protection whatever against its potentially ruinous effects.

2. *An inborn propensity of the sample itself to change with regard to the dependent variable, irrespective of the intervention.* What if the patients who agreed to participate in the study were systematically different from those who did not? Perhaps these particular patients volunteered because they were more motivated to lose weight in the first place. Perhaps they were more afraid of the consequences of not doing so. It would not be unreasonable to assume that a large proportion of such a sample might try very hard to lose weight irrespective of the intervention: many individuals might succeed through personal effort alone. Consequently, the observed weight loss would be a function of the special type of subjects selected for the study and not the dietary/exercise treatment per se. This phenomenon, called *selection,* is not an easy explanation to rule out in single-group studies whose samples have not been *randomly* selected from a larger population as discussed in Chapter 3 and therefore may not be completely representative of that population. It, like *history,* can occur without the knowledge of the researcher, who may inadvertently choose a sample with a selective propensity to change on the dependent variable.

3. *A preexisting characteristic possessed by the study's subjects (or by their environment) that predisposes them to change on the dependent variable.* In other words, what if the study's sample were completely representative of the overall population of postoperative cardiovascular patients but part of the natural history of this type of patient involves a propensity to lose weight? (Perhaps such patients experience a temporary loss of appetite or other physiological problems associated with the healing process.) If this hypothetical propensity, called *maturation,* were not taken into account (and it will not be by the *one-group–pretest/posttest model*), the observed weight loss would be fallaciously attributed to the intervention instead. Many types of subjects change naturally over time: sick people get better (or sicker) and children develop. Researchers must therefore make provisions for these effects (or their possibility) in the way they design their studies.

4. *A statistically demonstrable tendency for subjects chosen, because they possessed extreme scores on a pretest, to exhibit less extreme scores on a posttest as a function of chance alone.* Called *regression toward the mean* (or *statistical regression*)—because the posttest scores tend to regress (or move closer) to the mean—this alternative explanation for a study's results is less obvious than its predecessors. It is an easily demonstrable statistical artifact that operates only when subjects are chosen *because* they possess either higher

or lower scores than average. To understand how this phenomenon occurs, it is necessary to realize that *all* measures contain a certain amount of random error. Because of this error component, a set of scores will fluctuate randomly from measurement to measurement, with some going up and some going down. Under normal circumstances this fluctuation averages out, with as many people going up on the posttest as going down. Our present situation represents a slightly different situation, however, since *all* subjects began the study already overweight. This means that any error present in these weights (and there is always some) is more likely to be on the positive than the negative side (the opposite would be true if subjects had been selected because they were underweight). Since error is random, there is no reason to assume that positive errors will predominate the second time these people are weighed, thus their scores will go down simply as a function of the disappearance of part of the original positive error.

   5. *Subjects were lost from the study that would have scored differently on the posttest from those who were actually measured.* It is an unfortunate fact of a researcher's life that few studies finish with the same number of subjects with which they begin. It is still more unfortunate that those subjects who drop out are often very different from those who do not. What if our hypothetical study sustained a substantial loss of subjects because of extreme reluctance on their parts to both diet and exercise? Even more damning, what if it were suspected that the lost subjects actually *gained* weight over the study interval and thus failed to show up for the final weigh-in *because* they were ashamed of their failure? Obviously the researcher's inference regarding the intervention's efficacy might be completely invalid; an overall weight loss would not have occurred if the entire sample had been measured. This problem, referred to as *experimental mortality* (or subject attrition), is an especially serious threat to the ability to interpret research employing one-group models.

TWO LESS-COMMON ALTERNATIVE EXPLANATIONS

The final two categories of alternative explanations to be discussed in this chapter could just as easily be held for the measurement section (Part Three), since they can be conceptualized as dealing primarily with the measurement of the dependent variable. Neither are likely to be serious considerations with a relatively precise, objective measure such as weight, although both are perfectly capable of totally invalidating studies employing other types of instruments.

   6. *Changes occurring in the measuring process (or in the way a measurement instrument is used) over the course of a study.* This is sometimes called *instrumentation* and is especially problematic where scores are assigned by observers or raters. As mentioned above, it would not be likely to occur in our ongoing research example, although the use of a different scale (or one whose accuracy deteriorated over time) weighing several pounds light for the posttest could quite easily result in an erroneous inference. As a more plausible example, let us suppose the dependent variable for a study dealing with group leadership dynamics involved having observers rate the type of directives initiated by designated subjects. Changes in instrumentation (in this case, observer performance) could occur in one of two ways: (a) if different observers were used for the pre- and posttests, or (b) if the same raters changed over time, becoming more careless, fatigued, skillful, or simply different as a function of practice (that is, sort of maturation effect for observers). Regardless of how instrumentation occurs, its presence in a one-group–pretest/posttest model can easily be mistaken for an effective intervention, unless specific steps are taken to avoid it.

7. *A tendency of subjects to score higher on their second exposure to a testing situation purely as a function of their first exposure.* This phenomenon, called *testing* (or simply a practice effect for some measures), is not likely to occur with a dependent variable such as weight (although some people have been known to learn to reduce their readings on bathroom scales solely as a function of leaning). It could easily be mistaken for a positive intervention effect in a one-group design employing a measure such as learning, however, where subjects may: (a) remember items and subsequently look up answers prior to the posttest, (b) remember mistakes made during the pretest and subsequently correct them, and/or (c) be more familiar with the items themselves the second time around and thus have more time to concentrate on their solution.

FALSE-POSITIVE VERSUS FALSE-NEGATIVE RESULTS

So far we have discussed the potentially crippling effects of seven alternative explanations for positive results (that is, pre-to-posttest changes in the dependent variable). Positive results, however, are not the only possible outcome for a research study. They are not even the most likely.

Therefore, a natural question arises concerning the roles of *history, selection, maturation, statistical regression, experimental mortality, instrumentation,* and *testing* when significant differences do *not* occur: Can we at least be assured of the quality of our inferences concerning the relative impotence of the evaluated treatment? Alas, the answer is *no.* Many of these same phenomena can just as easily conspire to produce means that should differ significantly from one another but do not (that is, false-negative results).

Returning to our dietary/exercise example, let us assume that no change in body weight was observed over the course of the study. The most obvious inference to make is that the results do not support the hypothesis that the evaluated treatment is effective in helping patients lose weight. Unfortunately, this conclusion could be as fallacious as the original.

Could not a counterproductive event (*history*) have occurred over the course of the research to invalidate the potentially positive effects of the intervention? Perhaps, for example, the study was scheduled over the Christmas vacation where most people exhibit a tendency to gain weight. If so, the fact that the research subjects did not do so may in itself have been positive. Perhaps postoperative patients have a natural tendency to gain weight as part of the recovery process (*maturation*); again, the fact that those exposed to the intervention did not gain weight could then be interpreted as positive. Perhaps only those obese subjects who had a previous history of failing to lose weight (and hence were less likely to succeed irrespective of the intervention) volunteered for the study (*selection*). Perhaps those subjects who were unusually successful in losing weight dropped out of the study (*experimental mortality*) because they no longer needed the very real help provided by the intervention (hence leaving those who had not lost weight for the final assessment).

Although it would be possible to continue enumerating alternative explanations for the failure of this (or any other) intervention to result in a significant effect, the point here is that *failure to remedy these potential flaws at the design stage will largely invalidate the results of a study regardless of outcome, be it positive or negative.* Researchers who fail in this quest pay a high personal price, for it is their personal labor and aspirations that are squandered. It is thus very much incumbent on the individual researcher to design studies as free from alternative explanations for their results as possible. The *one-group–pretest/ posttest model* is not a particularly good choice.

ATTACKING ALTERNATIVE EXPLANATIONS OF RESEARCH RESULTS

Rare occasions do exist where there is no choice but to use the *one-group– pretest/posttest model.* When this is the case, the researcher must try to invalidate the effects of all the alternative explanations of results possible within the limitations of this design. Though not capable of completely discrediting these potential problems, there are strategies that can at least serve to undermine their credibility. The remainder of this chapter is devoted to discussing the more useful of these strategies. Since these alternative explanations are potentially problematic with even the best research models (in contributing to false-negative findings if nothing else), the advice that follows really applies to any type of research.

1. History *or did some event, other than the intervention, occur during the course of the study that was capable of influencing the dependent variable?*

The most effective preventive step is to be thoroughly familiar with the clinical/research setting. In our ongoing example, this would include interviewing treatment staff to determine typical everyday procedures, both educational and medical. This would tip the researcher off to rival educational or exercise programs available in the setting and allow the sample's exclusion from them. Other steps that might be taken are:

(a) To plan the study with great care with respect to its timing (such as by avoiding major holidays or other unusual disruptions in either the clinical setting or the subjects' environment) and instructions to both subjects and auxiliary personnel (subjects might be warned not to engage in other educational or exercise programs, for example).

(b) To keep the time interval between pre- and posttests as brief as possible while still being consonant with the objectives of the study (the shorter this interval, the less time there will be for something to go wrong; it must be long enough, however, to permit a substantive reduction in body weight).

(c) To monitor events carefully during the study with a view to exerting as much control as possible; by doing so, the researcher might learn of a new effort being planned within the institution to encourage patients to lose weight, such as to join Weight Watchers, for example. Knowledge of this potentially confounding event might permit the researcher to persuade interested parties to delay it until after the posttest.

(d) To keep records of all unusual events occurring during the study, including perhaps actually interviewing subjects and staff following its completion to determine if anything happened of which the researcher was not aware. (Such a record can be used to evaluate the probable effects of history and, it is hoped, serve as documentation of its absence.)

2. Selection or was the final sample selected for the study biased in such a way that the subjects were more (or less) likely to change on the dependent variable than the population they were meant to represent?

The only completely foolproof way of avoiding this artifact is by randomly sampling from an available population that is itself not obviously biased in some way (see Chapter 3). Even here, however, a selection bias can accrue if substantial numbers of subjects decline participation.

Selectivity with respect to who does and does not elect to participate is best handled by:

(a) Persuasion, with respect to the importance of the research both to the subject and to scientific knowledge in general (if an effective case cannot be made, then the research is probably *not* worth doing).

(b) Making participation attractive (by offering payment, for example, or by requiring as little as possible of subjects).*

(c) Collecting as much relevant data as possible on both participants and nonparticipants to allow subsequent comparison of the two groups with respect to potential differences.†

As with all the alternative explanations of results discussed in this chapter, very little can be done to salvage a study if a selection bias is discovered. The

---

* Payment has the potential of introducing its own selection bias (it is less effective as an inducement for affluent and educated subjects), while decisions concerning how much to demand of subjects often must be dictated primarily by the research objectives.

† This sort of knowledge is of only limited value since it is really propensity to *change* on the dependent variable that is of interest.

researcher has the obligation of reporting it honestly and letting the consumer judge if the study is worth considering. Carefully looking and failing to find one, however, strengthens the generalizability of any study.

3. Maturation or is there some inherent characteristic associated with this type of subject or environment that will result in change on the dependent variable across time irrespective of any intervention?

The key to answering this question within a single-group model is to know as much as possible about the type of subject being used (postoperative cardiovascular patients in our example) and the area itself (cardiovascular surgery, patient care, diet, exercise, education, and weight loss) as possible. As discussed in Chapter 2, to have no prior knowledge of a research area is to invite disaster. To have such knowledge can often result in a priori awareness of potential artifacts such as maturation.

Other techniques for at least discovering the potential for maturation include:

(a) Interviewing professionals with direct experience involving the research setting and sample (this might include physicians, nurses, and physical therapists in our example).
(b) Being *thoroughly* conversant with the research and professional literature, since other studies have undoubtedly been conducted with similar subjects that may even describe their natural history (with respect to the dependent variable).

Prevention, of course, is preferable to documentation after it is too late to do anything about the problem. Unfortunately, about the only preventive options available to the researcher are to:

(a) Use subjects for whom maturation is not problematic.
(b) Restrict the treatment interval sufficiently to prevent any substantive maturation from occurring.

4. Statistical regression or can an observed pre-to-posttest shift in the dependent variable be explained by the tendency of extreme scores to move toward the mean irrespective of any intervention?

This phenomenon occurs *only* with the selection of subjects systematically above or below the population mean on the dependent variable. It can be avoided completely via the use of a heterogenous sample, although this and all such decisions must be made congruent with the study's overall purpose. In our hypothetical study, for example, it would make no sense at all to employ subjects who were overweight, underweight, or neither (that is, a heterogenous sample of patients with respect to body weight), since the treatment is exclusively aimed at overweight individuals. What the researcher might do is obtain two premeasures on each subject with enough time in between for the weights to fluctuate. If regression toward the mean occurred, the researcher could use the second premeasure as the initial point of comparison, with the knowledge that the posttest's regression would be even less (assuming a comparable time interval).* If regression toward the mean did not occur (or if it were minimal), then this artifact could be ruled out as an alternative explanation of the results.

5. Experimental mortality or can systematic differences between subjects who complete the study and those who do not explain its outcome?

Here as always, two aspects of the problem need consideration: documentation and prevention. The latter may be accomplished in a number of ways:

(a) By making the treatment as undemanding as possible (the more that is required of subjects, the greater will be their propensity to drop out).
(b) By restricting the time between the administrations of the pre- and posttests.
(c) By using captive subjects (for example, institutionalized individuals such as patients receiving ongoing treatment, schoolchildren, or workers at their jobs) where feasible.†
(d) By impressing on subjects the importance of completing all research protocols at the time they agree to participate.‡

All of these strategies are geared toward encouraging subjects not to drop out of a study. Obviously experimental mortality is not a problem in studies that do not lose their participants. It is not even necessarily a problem in those that do, unless those subjects who are lost differ systematically from those retained with respect to pre-to-posttest changes on the dependent variable. Unfortunately, the existence of such a systematic bias can seldom be categorically documented, since dropouts are not around for the posttest (and even if they were, they would not have had the full benefit of the intervention).

In keeping with the consciously conservative practices of scientific documentation, therefore, the burden of proof is placed on the researcher to demonstrate the *absence* of bias. In many ways, this is an impossible task; the best that can usually be done is to compare retainees and dropouts with respect to pretest scores (or any other measures known to be related to pre-to-posttest changes in retainees).

The presence of a systematic difference between the two types of subjects is very nearly fatal to a one-group – pretest/posttest model's interpretability.

---

* An even better strategy would be to continue the measurement process until the entire regression artifact was used up, a process that would closely approximate the *time-series models* discussed in Chapter 9.

† These first three strategies are viable only if they are consonant with the research objectives. Each has disadvantages. Making the treatment undemanding can reduce its potency, restricting the time it has to operate can have the same effect, and using institutionalized subjects can decrease the study's generalizability.

‡ There can be a fine line here between the advantages inherent in decreasing experimental mortality and the disadvantages accruing from increasing the obtrusiveness of the intervention.

The absence of such a problem at least affords indirect encouragement that an observed effect *may not be* a function of this particular alternative explanation.

6. Instrumentation *or did the way in which numbers were assigned to subjects change systematically over the course of the study?*

This is the most easily prevented of all the potentially invalidating factors discussed in this chapter. For many dependent variables it is not a problem at all (for example, objective paper-and-pencil and most physiological measures). For tests in which instrumentation is more likely, careful training of experimenters, constant monitoring of their performance, and the use of very *explicit* instructions usually suffices. (When multiple data collectors are used, the procedures outlined in Chapter 11 should ensure sufficient agreement to avoid measurement changes as an alternative explanation of results.)

7. Testing *or did subjects score differently on the posttest as a function of taking the pretest?*

Since the testing artifact implies improvement on the posttest, it is normally considered a problem only for positive results.* There is no easy way to avoid its presence in the one-group – pretest/posttest model for certain types of measures, although using more items or presenting those used less obtrusively (such as embedding them in other instruments) may prevent the occurrence of testing.† Like all the alternative explanations of results discussed in this chapter, if testing is considered a potential threat to the interpretability of the study then one of the more robust models presented in the next two chapters should be employed.

SUMMARY

No more important decisions affect the researcher than the model by which subjects are studied and data collected. The most primitive of these models, the *one-group – posttest-only model,* involves the administration of an experimental intervention to a single group of subjects prior to measuring them. For present purposes this strategy is not considered empirical research.

The *one-group – pretest/posttest model* constitutes a definite improvement over its more primitive counterpart, since it meets one of the primary conditions of empirical research (the existence of a comparison of some sort — in this case pretest versus posttest), although it is subject to a number of alternative explanations. These include the possibility that:

---

* Although testing can be conceptualized as disguising a truly *decremental* intervention effect, this situation is rarely encountered in actual practice.

† For cognitive tests, equivalent forms can be employed as the dependent variable (Gulliksen, 1950). This will prevent familiarization with individual items.

1. External events, other than the intervention, may occur during the course of the study to influence its outcome (*history*).
2. The sample itself may have been biased in such a way that it had an unusual propensity to change on the dependent variable (*selection*).
3. The study subjects may have had a preexisting characteristic that caused them to change on the dependent variable (called *maturation*).
4. The subjects, because they possessed extreme scores on the pretest, may have had an artifactual tendency to exhibit less extreme scores on the posttest (called *regression toward the mean*).
5. Subjects may have been lost from the study who would have scored differently on the posttest from those who were actually measured (called *experimental mortality*).
6. The measurement instrument or the way it was employed may have changed over the course of the study to influence the results (*instrumentation*).
7. The measure employed as both the pretest and the posttest was susceptible to a practice effect (also called *testing* effect).

These threats (or combinations thereof) to the model's validity can result in either false-positive (that is, a statistically significant result being obtained artifactually) or false-negative results (that is, no statistically significant results being obtained when the experimental intervention was indeed effective). Although common sense strategies exist to minimize the occurrence of these alternative explanations, the recommended course of action involves the selection of one of the research models discussed in Chapters 7 and 8.

REFERENCES

Campbell, D. T., and Stanley, J. C. *Experimental and Quasi-Experimental Designs for Research.* Chicago: Rand McNally, 1963.
Gulliksen, H. *Theory of Mental Tests.* New York: Wiley, 1950.

chapter 7

The Randomly Assigned Comparison Group

By now the severe limitations of the *one-group–pretest/posttest* model should be painfully apparent: we can never know exactly to what its results can be attributed. Certainly the intervention is one possibility. Unfortunately, so are a plethora of competing explanations. What seems to be needed, therefore, is some magical strategy, some *deus ex machina,* capable of neutralizing the more virulent of these explanations. Fortunately for us all, it actually exists.

The chief problem with the *one-group–pretest/posttest model* is that it contains only one comparison: the same subjects before and after the intervention. This setup is far too vulnerable to the occurrence of confounding, extraneous events that can operate in conjunction with the intervention and whose effects are subsequently indistinguishable from that intervention.

What is really needed here is another type of comparison relatively immune to these problems. One possibility is to bring in another entire group: a group identical to the original in *all* respects except that it does not experience the intervention; a group equally exposed to all the confounding, extraneous events to which the original is so vulnerable. If the group receiving the intervention then changes significantly more than the one that does not, *then said difference can be attributed to that intervention and only to that intervention.*

The logic here is unassailable. If two groups could be identified that were, for all practical purposes, *identical,* if following an intervention a difference existed between these groups where none existed previously, *and* if this difference met previously agreed on criteria that assured its statistical reliability, then to what could it be attributed other than the intervention?

Not *history,* for if the two groups were identical except for the intervention, then any extraneous, outside event would occur to, and have the same effect on, both. Not *selection,* because to be identical subjects must be chosen in the same way. Not *maturation,* because the natural history of subjects (and of their environments) would be identical. Not *statistical regression,* because even if subjects were selected on the basis of their extreme scores on the dependent variable, the resulting artifactual shift in scores would occur equally for both groups. Not *experimental mortality,* since subjects in one group would be as likely to drop out as subjects in the other.* Not *testing* or *instrumentation,* since all subjects would be administered the same tests in the same way.

Given the undeniable power of such a strategy, the crucial question becomes: How is it possible to create two groups that are identical in every sense except the intervention? The answer lies in:

1. Employing a special method by which subjects with congruent propensities to change on the dependent variable (or be affected by the independent variable) are assigned to the two groups.
2. Constructing a research environment that minimizes the possibility of any extraneous events occurring to invalidate the crucial treatment versus no treatment comparison.

The first part of this task is relatively simple; the second is a bit more involved. Let us begin with the easier of the two.

THE USE OF RANDOM ASSIGNMENT IN ASSURING COMPARABLE SUBJECTS BETWEEN GROUPS

Let us assume that a power analysis (see Chapter 4) has indicated a need for at least 25 subjects in each of the two planned groups in order to have an acceptable chance of demonstrating a statistically significant difference if such a difference actually exists. The task then becomes the division of an original pool of 50 subjects into identical samples of 25 each.

At first glance it might seem reasonable simply to match subjects with respect to their scores on the pretest or some related variable. There is a problem with this procedure, however, and it resides in the fact that it is not enough to ensure that two groups are initially equivalent on the dependent variable; *they must be equivalent with respect to their propensity to change on the dependent variable.*

The difficulty with ensuring this type of equivalence is that researchers seldom know much about propensities to change. In our ongoing dietary/exercise study, for example, a host of factors could be associated with a predetermined tendency to lose weight (such as motivation, fear, health status, work schedule, stress level, love of life, ad nauseam). Even more unpredictably, some

---

* As will be discussed later (see the section on differential experimental mortality) this statement may not be true if subjects are aware of which group they are in or if one group requires more effort than another.

subjects may possess a predetermined tendency to profit more from the intervention (such as those with higher educational levels, histories of prior involvement in athletics, and so forth). Even if all such variables were identifiable, it would not be feasible to measure the 50 subjects on them in order to construct two matched groups.*

What then is the solution? It is simplicity itself! Since there is no way of knowing which subjects are more or less likely to change as a function of the intervention, why not use this ignorance to our advantage? Why not give each of the 50 subjects an *equal* chance of becoming a member of either group? What better way of preventing systematic bias between groups than to eliminate the possibility entirely save for random chance?

Such a procedure is actually used. It is analogous to flipping a coin, where given enough flips similar numbers of heads and tails will be recorded. It is called *random assignment* of subjects to groups and it is one of the most powerful tools in research. The most common ways of effecting random assignment entail:

1. Actually flipping a coin (allowing heads to represent one group, tails the other) for each subject until half are in one group and half are in the other.†
2. Throwing the 50 names (or identification numbers) into a hat, *thoroughly* mixing them, and drawing the names (or numbers) one at a time, allowing even numbers to represent one group and odd numbers the other.‡
3. Employing a table of random numbers, the use of which is illustrated in Chapter 3.

At first glance, random assignment might appear to be rather risky, since it is always *possible* for all the subjects with the greatest propensity to change to be assigned to the same group. This is extremely unlikely, however, occurring on the average less than once in a million times. It is also very unlikely that even a sizable majority of any one type of subject would find its way into one of the groups.§

---

* Matching subjects from separate, intact samples is an even poorer strategy that can result in decidedly nonequivalent groups if the two samples themselves differ in some systematic way. This unacceptable alternative to random assignment is discussed in more detail in Chapter 9.

† Equal numbers of subjects assigned to groups are optimal statistically. Thus if two groups of 50 each are desired, the coin should be flipped until one of the two groups is filled. The remaining subjects may then be automatically assigned to the other group. This fits our definition of random assignment, since each subject had an equal chance of being assigned to each group prior to the first coin flip.

‡ If the numbers are mixed thoroughly enough, allowing the first 25 drawn to represent one group is acceptable. Using the "every other" procedure compensates for less energetic mixing.

§ The reader may want to confirm this personally by writing random numbers on 50 slips of paper, mixing them up, drawing two equal sized groups, and computing the arithmetic means based upon the random numbers for each group. Although the two means will seldom be identical, the difference between them will consistently be small in relationship to their standard deviations.

Random assignment, then, is a technique that very nearly assures equivalence between groups, not only with respect to propensity to profit from the intervention but also along any other dimension the researcher cares to specify. Its effectiveness is influenced by:

1. The number of subjects (the more subjects involved, the more likely random assignment is to produce equivalent groups).
2. The homogeneity of the overall sample with respect to the dependent variable (the more homogenous the better; as heterogeneity increases, the more subjects are needed for the study and the more helpful are the stratifying and covariance procedures discussed in this and the next chapter).
3. The shape of the distribution (normal is best).

In all but the most unusual circumstances (such as with very small sample sizes, say below 12 subjects per group, or very bizarre distributions involving extreme dependent variable scores) random assignment is a godsend for empirical research.

Disadvantages of Randomly Assigned Comparison Groups

It is an unfortunate fact of life that something as powerful as the random assignment of subjects almost always has a price. Some of its disadvantages are:

1. More subjects are needed to achieve comparable statistical power, probably twice as many as for a single-group study. This involves more time and expense on the part of researchers.
2. It is often necessary to isolate groups physically so that they do not contaminate one another. This can sometimes be both difficult and obtrusive, especially in an institutional setting, where a dramatic break in a well-established routine can highlight the fact that a research study is being conducted.
3. There are sometimes ethical and political objections to withholding an intervention from a comparison group. (Administrators especially are tempted to demand that either everyone or no one have the advantages of a new treatment.) In such instances, the following arguments and strategies might be considered:
    (a) *Logic.* The purpose of the research study is to find out if the intervention does indeed work. If it does not, comparison subjects miss nothing by not being exposed to it. (The intervention might even be inferior, although this is not a recommended argument.) If a comparison group is not used, moreover, the effectiveness (or lack thereof) of the intervention may never be determined.
    (b) *Delaying the intervention.* A group of subjects can often function as a comparison during the course of a study and then be administered the intervention following its completion. This normally answers all ethical problems (except for the very rare, special case of subjects degenerating beyond repair in the absence of treat-

ment) and most political ones, since a delay is more palatable than enforced abstinence. Administering the intervention later to the comparison group can actually be used to strengthen some studies, since the comparison group can be measured again following the delayed intervention as a sort of quasi-replication of the original study.*

(c) *Purposefully choosing too large a setting.* If a researcher cannot physically (or fiscally) administer an intervention to everyone eligible (or who volunteers), then pressure is considerably reduced to try to service everyone. What more equitable and democratic way of choosing who will and will not receive the intervention than by giving everyone an equal (random) chance? Obviously the researcher in need of such an argument should select the study's setting accordingly.

(d) *Making the comparison group more palatable.* Often, the most strident objections to a randomly assigned comparison group involves those situations in which subjects receive no treatment at all. As will be discussed shortly, such comparisons are seldom either desirable or necessary. If the comparison group can receive "treatment as usual," such as normal classroom instruction in a school or the standard medical protocol in a hospital, then ethical and political objections tend to dissipate.

As the above suggestions indicate, my position is that random assignment is usually feasible and almost always desirable. That it is sometimes difficult cannot be denied. That it is often not necessary simply is not true.

Although random assignment of subjects may not always appear necessary, especially when a plausible reason why an effect accruing from a *one-group–pretest/posttest model,* for example, cannot be advanced, the possibility always exists of a fatal flaw lurking just beneath the surface of such a study. Also, as our knowledge unfolds, inadequacies of previously acceptable studies become all too apparent. Random assignment is, and probably always will be, the best insurance against incorrect research conclusions.

RANDOM ASSIGNMENT VERSUS RANDOM SAMPLING

At first glance the random assignment of subjects to groups may appear identical to randomly selecting subjects for the study in the first place. There are distinct similarities, most notably that each strategy compensates for ignorance and unknown biases by treating each subject with absolutely blind equality.

However, there are also major differences between the two techniques. Random sampling ensures representativeness between a sample and the population from which it is drawn. Its use has little effect on any of the alternative explanations for research results discussed in this and the previous chapter

---

* That is, a quasi-replication conceptualizing the comparison group as a *one-group–pretest/ posttest model.* Advantages and disadvantages of the use of a delayed treatment (including temporal effects) will be discussed in Chapter 9.

except for selection. Thus, even though a sample is randomly selected for a study, the accruing results will remain extremely suspect if one of the single-group models outlined in Chapter 6 is employed. In other words, using our ongoing research example, we still won't know for sure whether our dietary/exercise intervention worked or not.

On the other hand, even if a sample is relatively unrepresentative of the population as a whole, we can have a good deal of confidence in any observed experimental/control difference if subjects were randomly assigned to the two groups (and the study was otherwise properly conducted), at least for this type of sample. Random selection is thus a factor in the external validity of a study, which could be defined as the extent to which a study's results (such as an observed experimental/control difference) can be generalized beyond the sample actually employed. Random assignment is related to a study's internal validity, which is defined here as the extent to which the study's conclusions are likely to be correct for the sample actually employed. The best of all possible worlds, of course, is the scenario in which subjects were both randomly selected for the study and randomly assigned to groups once they were so selected.* If I were forced to choose between the two concepts, I would without hesitation nominate random assignment of subjects as the more crucial strategy simply because a study cannot be generalized to other samples if its conclusions are not appropriate for its own sample. Internal validity is thus a necessary condition of external validity (although the opposite is not true).

FOUR RESEARCH MODELS EMPLOYING RANDOM ASSIGNMENT

The research models discussed in this and the next chapter (that is, research employing randomly assigned groups: some of which receive an intervention, some of which do not) are regarded as *true experiments.* For this reason, the group receiving the intervention is usually referred to as the *experimental* group while its counterpart is called the *control* (because its existence serves as a controlling influence on many of the confounding factors, or alternative explanations of results, normally attending less powerful designs).†

The Randomized-Experimental/Control-Group–Posttest-Only Model

Here, as depicted in Figure 7-1, subjects are randomly assigned to two groups, one of which receives the intervention while the other does not. Following completion of the intervention, subjects from both experimental and control groups are tested on the dependent variable.

* The two techniques do not differ in the rare instance when two samples of subjects are randomly selected from the same population: one to serve as the experimental group and one as the control group. In this scenario, random selection and random assignment have occurred in the same step, and hence are in effect identical.

† The discussion that follows will refer to two-group models, although there is no reason why it cannot be extended to the multiple-group models of Chapter 8.

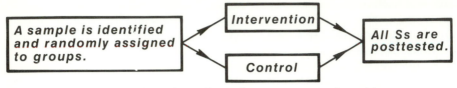

Figure 7-1   The randomized-experimental/control-group–posttest-only model.

At first glance, this model may appear to have an intrinsic disadvantage in comparison to the one-group–pretest/posttest alternative, since changes are not available before and after the intervention. Returning to our dietary/exercise study, use of this model would assume that for some reason it was not possible to weigh subjects prior to the advent of the experimental intervention. How then would the researcher be able to ascertain exactly how much weight subjects lost?

The answer is that the *randomized-experimental/control-group–posttest-only model* addresses an even more important question:

How much weight did subjects lose (or fail to gain) as a function of the dietary/exercise intervention.*

or

Did the dietary/exercise intervention result in superior weight control as compared to no such intervention.

The randomized-experimental/control-group–posttest-only model answers this particular question with much greater precision than its single-group counterpart because the control group's posttest mean is a measure of what would have happened without the intervention. The difference between this value and the experimental group's mean therefore represents the *functional* or *causative effect* of that intervention.

We have already seen that the same cannot be said for the difference between pretest and posttest means within the single-group model. A great many extraneous factors (such as the previously discussed alternative explanations of results) can intervene to influence this value. Even if the intervention can be assumed to be effective, there is no guarantee that one or more variables did not operate in conjunction with it, thus making the pretest/posttest difference a reflection of the intervention's effectiveness *plus* one or more unknown quantities. This is not a problem in the experimental/control group comparison, since the effect of any of the alternative explanations discussed so far will be

---

* Without a preintervention measure, it is not possible to ascertain whether a postintervention-experimental-group advantage over experimental subjects was due to their: (1) losing more weight than control subjects, (2) maintaining their weight while control subjects gained weight, or (3) gaining *less* weight than control subjects.

reflected in the means of both groups, *hence any statistically significant difference between those means should reflect only the effect of the intervention.* Obviously then the *experimental/control-group–posttest-only model* therefore represents a far better test of the hypothesis that a combined program of dietary instruction and an exercise regimen will result in greater weight control than no such intervention for overweight, postoperative cardiovascular patients.

Using Both Pre- and Posttests in Experimental Research

By employing the *experimental/control-group–posttest-only model,* the researcher has made a conscious decision for some reason not to administer a pretest. The advantages of this strategy are:

1. It is sometimes difficult to convene subjects for a pretest prior to a study.
2. Repeated measurement can often be expensive in terms of both time and resources.
3. Some tests are quite transparent and the researcher may wish to disguise the purpose(s) of a study or even the fact that a study is in progress, since it is sometimes problematic to explain to control subjects why they must take a test twice with nothing intervening in between.
4. It is possible (as discussed in Chapter 6) that in some studies the pretest may *cause* subjects to react differently to the treatment (this alternative explanation is sometimes called *pretest sensitization*).

There is, however, a major disadvantage in failing to obtain a preintervention measure for subjects. Since there is usually at least a moderate relationship between two administrations of the same measure, a pretest can be used to increase radically the probability of obtaining statistically significant results if a true difference between experimental and control groups does indeed exist. Viewed from another perspective, this can mean that the same statistical power can be maintained with a considerably reduced sample size, since the pretest itself is used as a controlling variable in either a repeated measures analysis of variance or an analysis of covariance (see Chapter 14).

The advantages and disadvantages of including a pretest in a design must be weighed for each study. In our ongoing example, the advantages would certainly outdistance the disadvantages due to the relative ease, inexpensiveness, and unobtrusiveness of obtaining subjects' body weights. When subjects are in limited supply, the use of a pretest is always recommended where appropriate to increase statistical power. When a measure is administered both before and after an experimental intervention to both the experimental and control groups, the resultant strategy is called a *randomized-experimental/control-group–pretest/posttest model.* Due to its greater statistical power and descriptive potential (for example, it allows the researcher to document pre- and postintervention gains or losses for both groups), this model is much more popular that its posttest only counterpart (Figure 7-2).

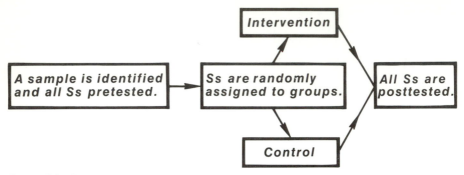

Figure 7-2   The randomized-experimental/control-group–pretest/posttest model.

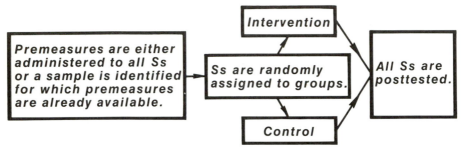

Figure 7-3   The randomized-experimental/control-group-with-covariates model.

The Covariate Model

Even when the disadvantages of employing a pretest outweigh its very considerable advantages, the *randomized-experimental/control-group – posttest-only model* remains a somewhat obsolete design for most research settings. This is because *any* premeasure can be used to increase a study's statistical power in the same way as an actual pretest if it too is related (or correlated) to the posttest. Since a little creativity can usually unearth such a variable (which can be in existence prior to the beginning of a study), this strategy, shown in Figure 7-3 as the *randomized-experimental/control-group-with-covariates model,* is usually also preferable to the *randomized-experimental/control-group – posttest-only model.*

It should be noted that a number of variations of this model exist. Some of these are:

1. More than one premeasure (called a covariate because the statistical analysis that will be used to analyze the results of the study is called analysis of covariance — see Chapter 14) can be used, although there are seldom any real statistical benefits to employing more than two.
2. One or more covariates can be used in addition to a pretest (which could be termed a *randomized-experimental/control-group – pretest-posttest/covariate model*).

3. The data to be used as the covariate(s) may be collected after the study begins if they are not capable of being influenced by the treatment and if they are temporally stable (for example, educational level, age, diagnosis).

The Randomized-Matched-Block Model

The randomized-experimental/control-group–posttest-only model relies solely on the considerable strength of random assignment to ensure initial equivalence between groups and thereby control most alternative explanations that can be plausibly advanced to attack a study's credibility. The randomized-experimental/control-group–pretest/posttest and the randomized-experimental/control-group-with-covariates models are able to facilitate (or supplement) the use of random assignment with statistical precision.

The *randomized-matched-block model* takes this logic one step further by *procedurally* (as opposed to statistically) facilitating the randomization process. Thus, instead of statistically adjusting any slight vagaries that occur by chance when randomly assigning subjects, the *randomized-block model* rules out the *possibility* of such an occurrence by first matching subjects and *then* randomly assigning them.

To illustrate how this is done, let us assume that the number of pounds that the subjects in our ongoing study were overweight prior to their surgeries was known to be related to how likely they were to lose weight following surgery. The first step would then be to rank order all subjects on the premeasure as illustrated below.*

Subject	No. pounds overweight prior to the study
John Smith	32
Paul Jones	31
Jim Turner	28
Mary Ragan	28
Bill Moody	24
Jerry Carter	21

Next, blocks of two subjects each are defined by simply calling the two most overweight subjects (John Smith and Paul Jones) block 1, the next two block 2, and so forth:

John Smith	32 ⎫	block 1
Paul Jones	31 ⎭	
Jim Turner	28 ⎫	block 2
Mary Ragan	28 ⎭	
Bill Moody	24 ⎫	block 3
Jerry Carter	21 ⎭	

* Note that here subjects were rank ordered from high to low. There is no reason that they could not be placed in ascending order.

The final step involves randomly assigning subjects within each block to either the experimental or control group. One means of doing this might be simply to designate the heads side of a coin to represent the experimental group and the tails side the control. The coin would then be flipped once (and only once) per block. In other words, let's say the coin turned up heads for the first flip: John Smith would then be assigned to the experimental group and Paul Jones would automatically go into the control group. The coin would next be flipped to see to which group Jim Turner would be assigned with Mary Ragan automatically going into the opposite group and so on until the entire sample had been so assigned:

E		C
John Smith	↔	Paul Jones
Jim Turner	↔	Mary Ragan
Jerry Carter	↔	Bill Moody

When procedurally feasible, I recommend this model over all others. For it to be feasible, the following conditions must be met with respect to the premeasure (also called the *blocking variable*):

1. As with the two previous models, *a premeasure must be available that is related to the dependent variable.* Unlike those models, however, this blocking variable must be *continuous.* In other words, there cannot be any substantial number of ties with different subjects achieving identical scores on the blocking variable. If sex, for example, were identified as a premeasure known to be related to the dependent variable, it could not be used as a matching variable, since everyone in the sample would possess either one of two scores, say 1 for maleness and 2 for femaleness. Similarly, a single 5-point Likert scale* also could not be used, since there would be many subjects sharing the same score (such as a 4 on the 5-point scale). Either of the two could function quite well as a covariate, however, or as a second independent variable in one of the factorial models discussed in the next chapter.

2. A slightly more restricting limitation to the widespread use of the randomized-matched-block model resides in the requirement that *scores on the blocking variable must be available on all subjects prior to the beginning of the study.* If this condition is not met, then subjects cannot be rank ordered, blocked, and randomly assigned to groups *prior* to the intervention. Since this is a necessary condition to the use of the randomized-matched-block model, settings in which subjects are limited and become available a few at a time (such as in a clinic or hospital) are not appropriate for the use of this model. In such circumstances, *premeasures may still be used as covariates since these values can be usually collected as access to subjects is obtained.*

---

* A Likert scale consists of a statement with which the respondent is asked to agree or disagree. See Chapter 10 for examples.

FALSE-NEGATIVE RESULTS

As was their one-group – pretest/posttest ancestor before them, true experimental models are relatively impotent with respect to preventing false-negative results. To see why this is true, let us return to our previous example of *history.*

We have seen why an unusually effective television show, broadcast during the course of the study, would not itself be likely to produce false-positive results: both experimental and control subjects would be exposed to it and both would be expected to profit equally unless it were plausible to assume that the televised program reinforced the dietary/exercise intervention and thus was *more* effective for experimental than control subjects. Although perhaps not likely, this could conceivably occur if the television program was helpful only if the viewer had access to an organized dietary/exercise program through which the program's content could be practically implemented. Given the *possibility* of such effects, it is a good idea for the researcher to be vigilant with respect to anything that can be differentially effective for one group, since the random assignment of subjects to groups does not provide a safeguard against this occurrence.

What if the television program induced control subjects to lose weight, however, but had no incremental effect on the already effective dietary/exercise intervention? In other words, what if both the experimental intervention *and* the television program were effective (but not additive)?

The answer is that the final experimental versus control group comparison would result in no statistically significant differences and the researcher would be forced to infer that the dietary/exercise intervention did not work. This inference would be *incorrect,* hence a false-negative result.

Additional examples using other alternative explanations of results could be offered, but the moral remains the same:

> *The random assignment of subjects to groups is largely ineffective in vitiating an entire class of alternative explanations related to the implementation of experimental procedures.*

It is therefore incumbent on the researcher to construct personally a sufficiently controlled research environment to avoid the occurrence of false-negative results in particular and incorrect inferences in general.

ASSURING A CONTROLLED RESEARCH ENVIRONMENT

Randomly assigning subjects within an appropriate research model is thus only a preliminary step in the conduct of an effective study. To permit attainment of the ultimate objective of all experimental research — correct inference — *it is necessary to structure (or control) the research environment in such a way that the experimental and control groups differ only along the predetermined, evaluative dimension.*

This is one of the most important tenets in empirical research because, regardless of an investigator's objectives, it is the manner in which experimental and control groups *actually* differ from one another that defines what is truly being studied. This difference involves the way in which groups are formulated (or operationally defined) as well as how competently these planned formulations are implemented.

This section is therefore dedicated to discussing strategies that enable the researcher to control extraneous variables and alternative explanations that can compromise experimental inferences. Unlike the previous chapter, these potential threats to inferential validity will not be categorized or labeled (although they too could easily be conceptualized as comprising alternative explanations of results). Instead, they will be subsumed under simple dicta, adherence to which are mandatory for quality research.

All the suggestions tendered beneath each dictum are not mandatory for all researchers. Experienced scientists incorporate most of them informally and unconsciously; simple studies often do not require some of the more elaborate precautions. Beginning researchers, however, may wish to give this section serious consideration.

Define the Experimental Intervention Carefully, Thoughtfully, and Operationally

The operational definition of exactly what is to be done to experimental subjects should be one of the most carefully planned aspects of any research effort. It flows directly from the study's objectives and it is a product of both expertise in the content area(s) involved and familiarity with its research literature.

Unlike the majority of the topics in this section, the skills that go into the formulation of a successful treatment are not primarily methodological in nature. They are, to a large extent, specific to the subject matter area in which the scientist is trained. In our ongoing dietary/exercise study, for example, it would be presumptuous, potentially disastrous, and almost certainly self-defeating for the investigator (or team of investigators as a whole) not to be conversant with both the research and clinical literatures involving cardiovascular surgery, nutrition, education, physical therapy, and patient care. (By the same token, an intervention involving the implementation of a new teaching strategy should be designed by an educational specialist, a new therapeutic regimen by a psychologist, and so forth.)

Based on this knowledge, and armed with a feel for the types of practices that would have the potential to be adopted if proven effective, the following steps might be taken:

1. A dietary educational script would be written with full cognizance of the reading level, vocabulary, attention span, and life-styles of the sample.

2. The modality of its delivery (for example, pamphlet, slide show, didactic presentation) would be specified.
3. The exercise regimen would be carefully constructed, including frequency of application and method of supervision based on the physical condition of the patients.
4. The length of the study as well as the order in which all its components take place (including their durations) would be specified.
5. A plethora of additional details would be worked out before anything was set in motion (for example, exactly what to say to subjects under different circumstances, how much to tell subjects about the study's design, what to do about absenteeism).

As will be discussed in the next chapter, when the construction of experimental groups is examined in more detail, each decision inexorably defines, delimits, and delineates the study's actual research objectives (and hence the specific inferences that are possible). It therefore follows that even the most minute of these decisions should be made only after careful consideration regarding all probable implications.

Define the Control Group Just as Carefully, Thoughtfully, and Operationally

Although seldom as involved, the formulation of a suitable control is equally important to that of the experimental group. It is, after all, the direct comparison of the two that will form the basis of the final research inference.

The first decision that must be made is between the use of a *pure* control group and some other form of comparison. Although no such distinctions are made in this book, a pure control is usually defined as the absence of any intervention or treatment whatever. Its use is relatively rare in most research involving human subjects, especially in applied research.

To see why, it is only necessary to think what a pure control group would be like in our dietary/exercise study; no dietary information, no exercise regimen, no intervention of any kind capable of effecting weight loss in obese patients. Such a procedure would be suspect on both ethical and practical grounds: it would be unethical because failing to warn such patients is potentially life threatening, and it would be impractical because all treatment settings dealing with this type of patient would at least attempt to persuade their clients to lose weight and would probably offer advice regarding a good method of doing so. Since our researcher would wish both to generalize the findings to as many clinical settings as possible and to have these findings widely adopted should they prove positive, it would be foolish to employ a control group that would never be encountered in clinical practice. To do so would be as damaging to the ultimate utility of the study as to employ an intervention so expensive or dangerous that no one would use it even if it proved effective. What our researcher would undoubtedly choose, therefore, is a comparison group employing the usual protocol for dealing with obese postoperative cardiovascular patients. It is almost always far more useful to be able to infer that an experimental intervention is better than conventionally accepted practice than that it is simply better than nothing.*

The same principle applies to most disciplines involving human subjects. The assessment of a new teaching method in education, for example, could use either a veridical comparison group (normal clinical instruction, for example) or a pure control (no instruction at all) depending on the study's objectives. To illustrate, consider the following research questions:

1. Can patients learn when instructed by method X?
2. Do patients learn more when instructed by method X than when instructed via conventional procedures?

The first question is best answered with the use of a noninstructed control group. A control group consisting of normal clinical instruction would be problematic, because patients would probably learn something via regular instruction; the contrast between experimental and control groups might thus not be statistically significant even if the answer to the first question was yes. The second question, on the other hand, can *only* be answered by the inclusion of a group consisting of conventional instruction. The use of a noninstructed control would not address the problem, since conventional instruction is almost surely better than nothing.

It is hoped that this discussion has driven home a crucial point: *the way in which groups are formulated inexorably dictates the research questions actually addressed. The researcher's aspirations are irrelevant if both experimental and control groups are not specifically designed to achieve them.*

The reader should not infer from this discussion that pure control groups are not quite useful on occasion. They are — especially in basic research and in research dealing with a dependent variable that cannot be manipulated by any known means (such as in the original tests of the Salk vaccine, where no other effective interventions existed). The reader should also not conclude that the utilization of standard operating procedures or conventional methods as control groups in any way absolves the researcher from formulating rigorous operational definitions. The operational definition of a comparison group is equally important to that of an intervention since, as has been said before, it is the direct contrast of the two that generates the final empirical inference.

Returning to the dietary/exercise study, then, it is not enough to know that our carefully designed intervention is superior to the way in which clinic X normally treats its overweight, postoperative cardiovascular patients. Such a statement will be effectively worthless both for anyone wishing to know just how effective the intervention was and for anyone trying to decide whether to implement the program in his or her setting.

What consumers of our study need to know is *exactly* to what the intervention was compared so that they can know to what it is superior. What does

---

* It is, of course, more difficult to achieve statistical significance using a treatment-as-usual comparison than a pure control group, since the former is, one hopes, more effective than the latter.

clinic X normally do for patients? How much dietary instruction and exercise advocacy is normally administered? What form do they take? What is their content? Who administers them? When? How? Only by precisely knowing the effective parameters by which both groups differ can the final inference be evaluated.

Since the control group is subject to such close scrutiny, it follows that more should go into its formulation than careful description. If clinic X employs a relatively unique protocol for the type of patient being considered, then the generalizability of any study employing it as a control is pretty much limited to clinic X. Consequently the investigator would be wise to either search for a new setting or persuade the current one to alter its standard operation procedures for the experimental interval (although this could introduce problems in and of itself). Regardless of specific strategies, the crucial point to grasp here is that a great deal of care must go into these decisions for they will ultimately decide the research's utility.

Once the Two Groups Have Been Formulated as Desired, Monitor Both Carefully to Ensure Their Integrity Throughout the Study

A great deal more care is customarily devoted to measuring the dependent than the independent variable. Given the importance of the latter, its neglect is a hard practice to justify.

Certainly, appropriate measurement of the dependent variable is a necessary condition for meeting any research objectives. It is equally important to monitor carefully what goes on in both the experimental and control groups throughout the treatment interval to ensure that originally planned distinctions are maintained. There are a number of ways in which the integrity of these groups can dissipate. The two most common are described below.

1. *Conscious or unconscious changes in the implementation of the intervention.* Here staff may find what they consider a better or easier way of dealing with subjects, thus allowing the implementation (and hence the definition) of the intervention to drift over the course of the study. This can be prevented by observations or informal interviewing of staff and subjects during the study. If caught in its early stages, a return to the original protocol can often be effected with *minimal* damage. If ongoing observation is not possible, then the researcher may administer a questionnaire to staff and participants after the study's completion to learn retrospectively exactly what occurred with a view to reporting the findings honestly. (Perfect procedures are rare in experimental research.) For studies conducted by a single investigator, frequent reference to the original *written* protocol should be enough to prevent the occurrence of this problem. (Notes taken during the course of the study, especially with respect to anything that goes wrong, are often helpful in evaluating how cleanly experimental procedures were implemented.)

2. *Imitation of the intervention by control staff or subjects.* This can occur in several ways, such as via conscious efforts on the part of staff to give control subjects the same opportunities as their experimental counterparts or communication between experimental and control subjects resulting in contamination of the latter. The possibility of the staff contaminating the intervention can often be minimized by giving the study as low a profile as possible and supervising the study as closely as possible. It is helpful for a researcher to remember that everyone will not have an equal commitment to the study. Clinicians, for example, by the nature of their jobs are more interested in effecting recovery any way they can than in the results of a research study, which means that they may very well choose to try out a promising new technique in the middle of an experiment if not persuaded otherwise. Subjects too should know as little as possible* about experimental/control differences as well as who is assigned to which. When possible, participants should be physically or temporally isolated. When none of these options is feasible, simply asking experimental subjects not to discuss what is being done to them may be better than nothing (although care should be taken that this does not increase the study's obtrusiveness).

Design the Study to Be as Unobtrusive as Possible

This dictum is especially important when dependent variables are employed over which the subject has any degree of control (as in affective, personality, and certain types of performance measures). In such situations, if the desired outcome is very obvious, subjects may attempt to oblige the researcher.

In other cases, even when subjects have no idea concerning a study's purpose, the obtrusiveness itself (or simply the break in routine) can produce atypical behavior irrespective of what the intervention happens to be. The classic example of this is the now famous Hawthorne effect, where factory workers increased their performance simply as a function of being studied, irrespective of the experimental intervention being tested. The resulting effect could probably have been relatively easily controlled either by employing a randomly assigned control group that received as much personal contact as the workers in the experimental group or by disguising the fact that a study was taking place.

Another frequently mentioned manifestation of experimental obtrusiveness is a hypothesized interaction between the dependent and independent variables in some studies. Previous methodologists have visualized the problem primarily in terms of obtrusive, self-manipulatable pretests, whose obvious connection with the intervention *combine* to produce an effect that would not occur if either were not present (such as with a randomized-experimental control-group–posttest-only model).

This phenomenon, called *pretest sensitization* or the *interactive effects of testing* (Lana, 1959; Campbell and Stanley, 1963), would not be a problem in our dietary/exercise study because of both the relative unobtrusiveness of weight as a dependent variable and the fact that it cannot be easily self-manipulated by the obese subjects. Consider instead, therefore, a hypothetical study in which the intervention is an educational unit designed to dispel myths about

---

* Within reasonable human rights guidelines of course.

homosexuality and the dependent variable is a scale designed to measure attitudes toward homosexuals. Here the *interactive effect of testing* would normally
be conceived in terms of exposure to the attitudinal scale, subsequently making
the intervention more (or less) effective than it would have been if the pretest
had been eliminated.

Unfortunately, this phenomenon can be viewed from another perspective. It may be more realistic, and certainly more worrisome, to conceptualize
the problem as a function of the *intervention sensitizing the subjects to experimenter expectations*. In the homosexuality study, this would operate by the
educational unit tipping subjects off as to how they were expected to (or how
they perceived themselves being expected to) respond to the attitudinal scale
regardless of whether or not they had been exposed to a pretest. Any observed
experimental versus control group difference accruing could be due solely to
experimental subjects wishing to please (or be kind to) the researcher. Control
subjects would not necessarily be less kind, they would simply not know the
purpose of the study. In other words, the observed effect would not be a real
change in attitudes toward homosexuality; it would only exist on the paper-
and-pencil measure employed. Therefore, what seemed like an effective educational unit might actually be completely impotent.

The classic conceptualization of the *interactive effects of testing* can be
documented in actual research only by employing both a randomized-
experimental/control-group–pretest/posttest and a posttest-only model in the
same study!* If significant differences occur for the pretest/posttest model and
not in the posttest-only version, then the classic conception of the *interactive
effects of testing* has occurred. Since it seldom does in practice (Campbell and
Stanley, 1963), the use of such an elaborate, laborious, and ultimately wasteful†
procedure is most definitely not recommended.

Although the *interactive effects of testing* can be ascertained, the existence
of the more generic phenomenon conceptualized as the intervention sensitizing
the subjects to experimenter expectations cannot really be assessed in any
practical sense. In some ways, this makes it even more potentially damaging in
studies designed to effect changes in obtrusive and subject-manipulatable dependent variables. The only known control is to reduce the obtrusion of both
the independent and dependent variables so that subjects are not able to perceive (or do not believe they perceive) so-called desired responses. Unfortunately, this is easier to say than to effect in practice,‡ so the best course of action

---

* This is also called a *Solomon four-group model* and is discussed in Campbell and Stanley
(1963).

† Wasteful because the design requires either that each model be analyzed separately (hence
resulting in a significant decrease in power) or that the pretests administered to half of the subjects
be ignored since either ANCOVA or repeated measures ANOVA (see Chapter 14) require a
premeasure on all subjects, hence again wasting both power and effort.

‡ In the homosexuality study, for example, reducing the obtrusiveness of the treatment
might make it less effective as an intervention. Given the probable sensitizing effect of the treatment, therefore, it would be necessary to change the dependent variable to some medium not
directly under the respondent's control.

is probably to avoid this type of research altogether unless unobtrusive measures can be obtained.*

Keep the Overt Differences Between Groups as Inconspicuous as Possible

The optimal experimental study is one employing some variation of the double-blind technique where neither investigators nor participants know to which groups the latter has been assigned. This avoids the potential biasing effects of both experimenter and participant expectations, two potentially serious threats to any study's internal validity.

The classic example of the potential power of participants' expectations is the medical study designed to test the effectiveness of a new drug in a field setting. First, patients are randomly assigned to either receive the drug (the experimental group) or not receive it (the control group), with the idea that the two sets of subjects will differ only with respect to this single factor.

By allowing patients to know the identity of the group to which they have been assigned, however, the researcher is planting the seed of a virulent alternative explanation for the study's future outcome. This is the phenomenon known as the placebo effect, where individuals can demonstrably reduce objective, physiologically measurable symptoms simply as a function of *believing* that they are receiving an effective treatment, even when they are in reality receiving nothing more than an inert substance (placebo). The phenomenon can be intensified if the physicians know who is receiving the drug and who is not by encouraging more confident behavior toward participants perceived to be receiving an effective treatment.

Although not as often documented, there is another side to this coin. It is at least conceptually possible that if patients feel they are not receiving effective treatment because they are in the control group, they may take things into their own hands and self-administer other medications or seek outside professional advice. The same relationship could manifest itself if physicians of control patients feel sorry for them and prescribe supplementary treatment. In either scenario, unplanned systematic differences would be introduced between groups by unnecessarily supplying too much information. In both cases the problem could have been avoided by keeping *both* subjects and staff as ignorant of the experimental procedures as possible.

There are so many corollaries of this admittedly medically oriented example that it is wise for any investigator, regardless of discipline, to guard the specifics of group membership as closely as possible.

Experimenter expectations   Individuals implementing a study's procedures or collecting/scoring its data often cannot avoid *expecting* differential subject behavior as a function of group membership. These expectations can then

---

* See Webb, Campbell, Schwartz, and Sechrest's (1972) *Unobtrusive Measures: Nonreactive Research in the Social Sciences* as an excellent source.

either be communicated to subjects or allowed to influence the assignment of scores on the dependent variable.

Anyone involved with the conceptual aspects of a study should thus *never* administer both experimental and control treatments in a situation in which the group membership of subjects is recognizable (such as by teaching the same materials to two intact groups via different instructional methods). Naive research assistants should be used instead: it is simply too easy to treat the groups differently in some unplanned, unconscious way. In a similar vein, the person collecting the data (or assigning scores to subjects) should also never know to which group individuals have been assigned. The possibility of bias is even greater here.

Subject expectations   There are many ways for subjects' reactions to the experimental milieu to bias a study's outcomes as well. What if, for example, control subjects either resented the lack of attention paid them or became demoralized at being measured (perhaps repeatedly) on a dependent variable on which they were receiving no help in improving their performance? It is quite conceivable that these individuals' performances might be depressed as a function of knowing that they were receiving substandard treatment. This could, in turn, result in a final experimental versus control group difference on the dependent variable that was a function of the perceived inferiority of the control group, not of the superiority of the intervention.

If this problem is severe enough, the attempt to maintain subjects' ignorance of their group memberships will not be enough. It may also be necessary to alter the control procedures to make them appear more reasonable in participants' eyes, such as by requiring more of them in the form of irrelevant (to the research objectives) but reasonable activities. Care must be taken, of course, that such a strategy does not subvert the contrast in which the researcher is primarily interested. (In our ongoing study, for example, the irrelevant activities should not include the opportunity to ask the clinician for hints on losing weight; some of the ones supplied might be the same ones used within the experimental group.)

Differential experimental mortality   This potential problem is related not to subject expectations but to expectations *of* subjects. Regardless of how much a researcher attempts to disguise group identity and membership, experimental and control groups *must* differ to a certain extent in order to provide a meaningful contrast. Part of this difference usually comprises unequal requirements for subjects' participation. Subjects, in turn, perceive the value of that participation differently. The combination may result in a greater dropout rate among the group for whom more is required.

This situation can be illustrated in our dietary/exercise example by a design that requires experimental subjects to attend twice weekly exercise classes while their control counterparts need return to the clinic only for routine monthly physicals. It would therefore not be particularly surprising if more experimental subjects dropped out of the study than controls. Also, since control subjects would hardly be aware that they were in an experiment, only patients with very unusual extenuating circumstances (for example, who moved, changed physicians, or suffered a relapse) would drop out of the study. Completely different categories of experimental subjects might be expected to leave, however, including those who were less conscientious, losing weight on their own (thus needing the treatment less), busier (hence more stressed), ashamed at their failure to profit from the program, or any number of other possibilities.

Whatever their reasons, the bottom line here is that subjects remaining in the experimental group may well be very different either from those experimental subjects who dropped out or from the control group as a whole. If this exodus is severe enough, either a false-positive or a false-negative inference could result from the primary experimental versus control comparisons.

As always, there are two ways to ameliorate the problem: prevention and documentation. The latter is most easily accomplished via one of three strategies:

1. In the experimental designs using either a pretest or a covariate,* dropouts can be compared to retainees with respect to these measures. If the two types of subjects do not differ, then an argument can be made that *differential experimental mortality* did not occur.† (If there is reason to suspect mortality a priori — or if the researcher is cautious by nature — additional information likely to be related to the dependent variable can be collected specifically for this purpose.)
2. If posttest scores are available on dropouts (which is rarely the case), then all experimental subjects can be compared to all control subjects. This results in a more conservative test, but one that precludes the possibility of false-positive results accruing as a function of *differential experimental mortality.*
3. Finally, if a considerable number of subjects have been lost from a study and no posttest scores are available, the researcher has the option of attempting to locate dropouts to ascertain (such as via a questionnaire) their reasons for leaving. Although not likely to be conclusive, such evidence can sometimes be marshaled to argue for or against the seriousness of *differential experimental mortality* as an alternative explanation of experimental results. (It can also be used to help avoid the problem in future studies.)

Prevention of a threat to a study's internal validity, of course, is preferable either to its documentation alone or to patchwork arguments regarding its

---

* Differential experimental mortality is partially controlled in the randomized-matched-block model, since loss of one subject in a block requires the dropping of the matched counterpart from the statistical analysis. This control is very tenuous, however, since the subject lost may well be different from the one retained in a way that is basically uncorrelated with the blocking variable.

† Again it must be remembered that the real issue is propensity to change (which is basically not capable of being tested if subjects drop out before that change) or lack thereof (which can be measured).

virulence. Impressing on subjects the importance of completing a study as well as soliciting agreement to do so as part of the initial requirements for participation can go a long way toward reducing the dropout rate. In addition, it is sometimes advantageous to ask as much of one group as another, even though the research question(s) may not specifically require it.* This is a dangerous procedure, however, and should be employed judiciously. The first choice is always to limit the demands placed on the experimental group as much as possible, especially for tasks such as physically attending meetings. *The more personal effort involved in research participation, the greater will be the experimental mortality; the more the mortality, the greater the chance that it will be differential.*

Choose the Research Sample as Representatively as Possible

This issue has already been discussed in detail, but it is important to remember that the sequence that 99 percent of all experimental researchers actually follow is to:

1. Identify an *accessible* sample.
2. Randomly assign it to experimental and control groups.

Since random selection from target populations is simply not a luxury normally available in research involving human subjects, the best that can be hoped for is that the intact, accessible sample employed will be as representative of the target population as possible.

If an experiment is conducted cleanly, with sufficient statistical power, with subjects that are not obviously atypical, and if the overall experimental effect holds for different subgroups within the studied sample (for example, for males versus females, highly educated versus less highly educated subjects), then chances are good that the results can be generalized. In any case, given the way the world is structured (which is not for the sole convenience of researchers), the individual investigator must leave the ultimate verdict concerning replicability to other scientists. If a study is important enough, it will eventually be repeated.

Use Common Sense

There is no way that all the potential problems that can, and probably will, crop up during the course of even the most straightforward of studies can be anticipated. There is thus no substitute for good judgment.

There are a thousand separate mistakes that a beginning researcher can make during the conduct of an empirical investigation. I have made a large proportion of these at least once myself. The best advice I can offer at this point is to follow the above dicta as closely as possible and *consider each decision very*

---

* In our ongoing example this might involve requiring control subjects to attend meetings.

carefully with respect to its ultimate impact on the study's outcomes. Sometimes, actually writing the proposed methodology down or presenting it to an educated audience can enable the researcher to identify potential trouble spots in advance. When it is available, always seek experienced advice. When it is not, assume the worst, act conservatively, and hope to be pleasantly surprised.

SUMMARY

The use of random assignment of subjects to groups is recommended as the most effective means of avoiding the many alternative explanations inherent in the primitive single-group research models discussed in Chapter 6. When all subjects have an equal chance of either receiving an intervention (called the *experimental* group) or not receiving same (called the *control* group), the study's *internal validity* (defined here as the extent to which the study's conclusions are likely to be correct for the sample actually employed) is greatly enhanced. Enhancing internal validity, along with the representativeness of the chosen sample, in turn facilitates the extent to which the study's conclusions are likely to be correct for the population as a whole (which is called *external validity*).

Four relatively common two-group research models employing random assignment are:

1. *The randomized-experimental/control-group–posttest-only model.*
2. *The randomized-experimental/control-group–pretest/posttest model.*
3. *The randomized-experimental/control-group-with-covariates model.*
4. *The randomized-matched-block model.*

Although all are powerful research strategies, the second and third are superior to the first due to the increased statistical precision and power permitted by the use of their premeasures in the analysis of covariance and repeated measures analysis of variance procedures discussed in Part Four. When circumstances permit, *the randomized-matched-block model* adds procedural as well as statistical control by physically facilitating the randomization process.

As powerful as the random assignment of subjects to groups is in the facilitation of a controlled research environment, other steps are also required. Some of these include:

1. *Defining both the experimental intervention and its comparison group carefully and thoughtfully.*
2. *Monitoring them both carefully to ensure their integrity throughout the study.*
3. *Designing the study as unobtrusively as possible.*
4. *Keeping the overt differences between groups as unobtrusive as possible.*
5. *Choosing the research sample as representatively as possible.*
6. *Using common sense.*

REFERENCES

Campbell, D. T., and Stanley, J. C. *Experimental and Quasi-Experimental Designs for Research.* Chicago: Rand McNally, 1963.

Lana, R. E. A further investigation of the pretest-treatment interaction effect. *Journal of Applied Psychology,* 1959, *43,* 411–422.

Webb, E. J., Campbell, D. T., Schwartz, R. D., and Sechrest, L. *Unobtrusive Measures: Nonreactive Research in the Social Sciences.* Chicago: Rand McNally, 1972.

chapter 8

More Sophisticated Models Employing Randomly Assigned Groups

The previous chapter discussed four excellent models for conducting empirical research. All are perfectly acceptable, chiefly because they all share one powerful (and elegant) innovation in common: a comparison group to which subjects are randomly assigned. The chief difference among the four, in fact, resides almost exclusively in the degree of precision and statistical power that the use of the second independent variable (be it pretest, covariate, or blocking variable) is able to bring to the research setting. This is important because:

1. Given the same number of available subjects, statistical significance is more likely via the final three models that employ a pretreatment measure than the first (which does not).
2. In the unlikely event that simple random assignment fails to result in equivalent groups, the use of a pretest or covariate allows the researcher to compensate statistically for this failing; the use of the randomized-matched-block model procedurally prevents nonequivalence.

Although the use of the randomized-experimental/control-group– posttest-only model was not recommended in circumstances in which a pre-measure is available (and is related to the study's dependent variable), the truth of the matter is that we could manage quite well in every discipline in which experimental research is conducted on human subjects if we had nothing more sophisticated than this model at our disposal. It is thus helpful to remember that sophistication and complexity are not ends in themselves. Research is an extremely goal-oriented activity, and often the simplest, most direct path to achieving these goals turns out to be the most productive.

Still, time and resources are limited for researchers as for everyone else. Thus, more efficient research models have been developed that not only enhance precision (and statistical power) but also answer *multiple* research questions. (All the research models discussed so far, for example, answer, or attempt to answer, a single question: Did the intervention work?) This chapter will discuss some of the more widely used (and useful) of these more advanced models. Since they all employ random assignment of subjects to multiple groups, they all correct the serious limitations inherent in the single-group models discussed in Chapter 6 in the same way as their more simple counterparts in Chapter 7. Thus, only strengths and weaknesses *unique* to each model will be discussed here.

MULTIPLE GROUPS REPRESENTING A SINGLE INDEPENDENT VARIABLE

One way to increase the amount that can be learned from a study (and hence its efficiency) is to increase the number of interventions involved. Each of the models discussed in Chapter 7 is amenable to this simple extension.

Adding additional treatment groups to a study is most often done for explanatory purposes. Suppose, for example, that our hypothetical weight-loss study had resulted in a significant difference between the dietary education/exercise regimen treatment and the routine clinical care control in the expected direction. Our hypothetical researcher would justifiably be quite pleased, but there would remain at least one unanswered question: *Why* was the treatment effective? Was it because of the exercise, the dietary education, or were both necessary?

These questions might, or might not, be crucial. Many clinicians would be quite satisfied to find anything that facilitated weight loss among postoperative, cardiovascular patients. Others might feel a need to know *why* the treatment worked, perhaps for theoretical reasons, perhaps for practical ones (the administration of dietary education alone, for example, might save considerable staff time).

Let us, therefore, assume that it is important for our researcher to know exactly which component of the treatment accounted for the effect. There are three possibilities:

1. The dietary education alone (which will now be designated as E_1).
2. The exercise regimen alone (E_2).
3. Both education and exercise (E_3).

One method of determining which of the above possibilities constituted the active element in the effect would appear to be to conduct three separate studies using one of the designs presented in Chapter 7. In other words, E_1

would be contrasted to routine clinical care (C), followed by E_2 versus C and E_3 versus C experiments.

There are two problems with such a strategy. The first is the obvious inefficiency of conducting so many separate studies. The second problem lies in the fact that the researcher would not be able to compare the three treatments with one another directly unless all groups were randomly selected from the same pool of subjects at the same time. Otherwise, sampling errors would simply be too great to permit the statistical comparison of discrete groups from independent studies, even when run by the same researcher employing similar procedures.

What, then, are the alternatives? The researcher could not be expected to conduct three more separate two-group studies, this time comparing each treatment with each of the other treatments (that is, E_1 versus E_2, E_1 versus E_3, and E_2 versus E_3). The solution is probably obvious. The researcher could:

1. Randomly assign subjects to four separate groups (that is, E_1, E_2, E_3, and C).
2. Administer all four conditions simultaneously.
3. Statistically conduct all the pairwise comparisons between the four groups that are of interest.

Compared to the alternatives, this is a very elegant and efficient solution, since the researcher need only employ one control group. Diagrammatically, this model and its resultant comparisons might be represented as shown in Figure 8-1.

All four experimental models discussed in the previous chapter can be easily and logically extended in this fashion. For example, by weighing each subject in each group prior to the administration of the treatments we have a direct extension of the randomized-experimental/control-group–pretest/ posttest model. Substituting a different premeasure, we would have a multiple-group extension of the randomized-experimental/control-group-with-covar-

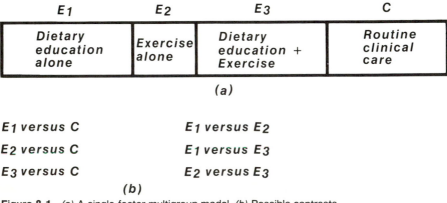

Figure 8-1 *(a)* A single-factor multigroup model. *(b)* Possible contrasts.

iates model. Alternatively, either pretreatment weights or any other continuous variable could be used to rank order subjects into blocks of four (since there are four groups), producing a variant of the randomized-matched-block model. In each case we still have one independent variable (that could be called treatments or conditions) with four levels or groups (instead of two) and one dependent variable.

Adding groups in this manner does nothing to change either the logic behind a model or its inherent strengths and weaknesses with one exception. Nothing is without some cost, and what is lost here is a marked degree of statistical power for the individual contrasts presented in Figure 8-1. If the availability of subjects is not a problem, then this potential liability can be completely compensated for by simply increasing the sample size. Unfortunately, the increased need for subjects is greater than it would appear to be at first glance, since even maintaining the same number of subjects per group (which would necessitate employing a great many more overall) will result in an overall *decrease* in statistical power for each individual pairwise comparison. As will be explained in greater detail later, this is due to the fact that the alpha level must be reduced when multiple comparisons are made within the same study. Thus if a study possessed six individual comparisons as detailed in Figure 8-1, an originally set alpha level of .05 would have to be adjusted downward by a factor of 6, or $.05/6 = .0083$. As discussed in Chapter 4, this would mean that in order to maintain the same statistical power, more subjects would have to be contained in each group. Thus, a two-group study (say E_3 versus C) containing 40 subjects may actually possess more statistical power than a four-group study containing 80 subjects would *for any single pairwise comparison* (say E_3 versus C).

As desirable as the increased explanatory power of multiple-group designs is, sufficient statistical power is far more important. Nothing is achieved, much less explained, if a study is conducted that has no real chance of achieving statistical significance. *For this reason I counsel against multiple-group experiments unless sufficient subjects are available to give such studies a reasonable chance of rejecting the null hypothesis if indeed the null hypothesis is false.*

In our hypothetical weight-loss example, given the normal shortage of subjects in a clinical setting, the researcher would probably be better advised to contrast the potentially most powerful treatment (that is, dietary education plus an exercise regimen) singularly with a control using the most precise two-group model feasible (the randomized-matched-block model, for example). Any study that finds *one* treatment that works would be labeled an unqualified success by any experienced investigator, hence the following advice:

When the number of subjects is limited, use as few groups as possible.

FACTORIAL MODELS

Fortunately, there exists a more efficient strategy to increase the explanatory power of a study than the horizontal (see Figure 8-1) addition of groups. This

E   *C*

Figure 8-2   A simple two-group model.

entails the addition of new groups via the addition of one or more new independent variables.* The purpose of such a strategy is usually to study the effect of a given treatment on different types of people, although occasionally it is used to document that effect under varying conditions.

Let us examine what such a model might look like in our weight-loss study. In the first place, the new variable will have a limitation placed on it that is not present in the simple, single-factor (that is, one-independent variable) model: it must be capable of being crossed with the groups comprising the original independent variable (or factor). Instead of attempting to define what this term *crossing* means, consider the following example.

First, let us return to the hypothetical two-group weight-loss study in which the single treatment consisted of a combination of dietary education plus exercise and the single control group consisted of routine clinical care (Figure 8-2). Now suppose the researcher wished to try out a variant of *E* that would logically require a corresponding adjustment to *C*. For example, suppose that there was some question as to how long the dietary/exercise treatment should last in order to be optimally effective. Let us further suppose that subjects were not available for repeated testing, which would probably be the case in most studies where the measures would be more reactive (that is, where the first administration might affect performance on the second) or where subjects were not routinely available and had to be called in or sought out for data collection purposes.

The most common strategy in such circumstances would be the constitution of *two* control groups: one consisting of routine care for six weeks, the other of routine care for twelve weeks. We now have *two* independent variables instead of one. The treatment variable (that is, dietary education + exercise versus routine clinical care) remains, but now we also have another comparison that, for want of a better title, we could call *length of treatment* (that is, 6 weeks versus 12 weeks). This new, two-factor model is best depicted in two dimensions (horizontally and vertically) rather than one, because the two independent variables are *crossed:* the two treatment lengths each have a treatment and a control component while the two treatment levels (that is, *E* versus *C*) each have two time components (Figure 8-3).

---

* It will be remembered that the four groups (treatments and control) depicted in Figure 8-1 are all visualized as different levels of the same independent variable, a variable that, for want of a better name, was called treatments or conditions.

Treatment length

		T_1	T_2
		Six weeks	**Twelve weeks**
E	Dietary education + Exercise		
C	Routine clinical care		

Figure 8-3   A two-dimensional factorial model.

There are four discrete groups in this model. They are:

E-T_1 = the 6-week treatment
E-T_2 = the 12-week treatment
C-T_1 = the 6-week control
C-T_2 = the 12-week control

There are two independent variables: *treatments* (E versus C) and *length* of treatment (6 versus 12 weeks). We will assume that the single dependent variable remains the number of pounds each subject is overweight at the end of the study.

The chief advantage of this strategy over the horizontal addition of groups depicted in Figure 8-1 is an increase in statistical power. This will be explained in greater detail later, but basically it occurs because the factorial model allows the researcher to combine groups, hence resulting in greater numbers of subjects (and hence greater statistical power) for these combined comparisons. In the factorial model depicted in Figure 8-3 for example, the overall E versus C comparison really involves E-T_1 + E-T_2 versus C-T_1 + C-T_2. Thus, if there were 20 subjects available per group, this comparison would involve a binary comparison of 40 subjects versus 40 subjects, instead of 20 subjects versus 20 as depicted in the pairwise comparisons depicted in Figure 8-1.

Before proceeding further, it should be noted that it is far more common for researchers to employ a second independent variable contrasting different types of subjects rather than different types of conditions. Thus, our hypothetical researcher might hypothesize that the experimental treatment would be more effective for males than females, extroverts than introverts, highly educated than poorly educated subjects, patients whose surgical procedures were less extensive versus those with more extensive surgeries, or younger patients as opposed to older ones.

The logic behind the addition of a subject-related independent variable is identical to that behind the addition of a second *manipulated* variable, although the assignment of subjects is quite different. In the above example, time was manipulated by the researcher because each and every subject had an equal chance of being assigned to a condition (whether E or C) lasting either 6 or 12 weeks. If the second variable chosen had been something like extroversion versus introversion, however, the same situation does not exist. John Smith can still be randomly assigned to either E or C, for example, but he either has an extroverted personality or he does not. He can't be made an extrovert for research purposes.

What the researcher must do in this case is identify two separate groups of subjects: one classified as extroverts and one as introverts. Subjects within each of these two groups are then randomly assigned to E and C groups (Figure 8-4). This yields a model that is structurally identical to the two-dimensional factorial model depicted in Figure 8-3 (Figure 8-5). The chief difference between studies involving the addition of a manipulatable versus a nonmanipulatable variable is *interpretive*. When subjects are randomly assigned to receive a manipulation or not, the quality of the resulting evidence is much greater than when intact groups are employed. This will be discussed in greater detail in Chapter 9, but the distinction is basically that between experimental and correlational research.

When subjects are randomly assigned to treatments and we later observe a difference between those treatments following an experimental intervention, we know that this difference is a function of the intervention *because* that is the only way the treatments differed.* When intact groups of subjects such as extroverts and introverts are studied, we cannot assume that these groups do *not* differ in other ways as well.

The quality of the evidence accruing for the effect of the treatment on weight loss is thus much higher than that for the relationship between personal-

* Assuming that the experiment was carried out properly and that a Type I error (see Chapter 4) did not occur.

Figure 8-4   Personality types are randomly assigned to conditions.

Personality

		P₁	P₂
		Extroverts	*Introverts*
E	Dietary education alone		
C	Routine clinical care		

Figure 8-5 Treatment × personality.

ity (that is, extroversion and introversion) and weight loss. With this distinction in mind, let us assume that the following pattern of means were observed for the four groups depicted in Figure 8-5:

E-P_1, $\overline{X} = 14.2$ pounds lost
E-P_2, $\overline{X} = 10.4$ pounds lost
C-P_1, $\overline{X} = 4.2$ pounds lost
C-P_2, $\overline{X} = 4.1$ pounds lost

Figure 8-6 shows the results of placing these values into the diagram of the aforementioned 2×2 table. There are three distinct and independent questions to be answered in a model such as this:

1. Is there any difference between the levels (or groups) belonging to the first independent variable?

or, in more specific language:

Does a program of dietary education plus an exercise regimen result in postoperative cardiovascular patients losing more weight on the average than similar patients receiving routine clinical care?

Note here that no mention is made of the personality factor. Whether subjects are extroverts or introverts is temporarily ignored, thus this question is said to address the treatment's *main effect*. The numbers addressing the above question are therefore collapsed or averaged across P_1 and P_2. In other words, the mean number of pounds lost for E becomes

$$\frac{\overline{E\text{-}P_1} + \overline{E\text{-}P_2}}{2} = \frac{14.20 + 10.40}{2}$$

$$= 12.30$$

	P₁ (Extroverts)	P₂ (Introverts)
E	14.2	10.4
C	4.2	4.1

Figure 8-6   Hypothetical results for the 2 (*E* versus *C*) × 2 (extrovert versus introvert) example.

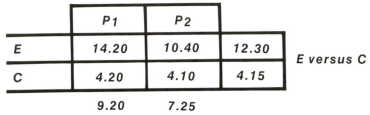

	P₁	P₂	
E	14.20	10.40	12.30
C	4.20	4.10	4.15

E versus C

9.20   7.25

Figure 8-7   Extroverts (*P₁*) versus introverts (*P₂*).

The mean number of pounds lost for *C* is similarly

$$\frac{\overline{C\text{-}P_1} + \overline{C\text{-}P_2}}{2} = \frac{4.20 + 4.10}{2} = 4.15$$

> *2. Is there any difference between the levels (or groups) belonging to the second independent variable?*

or

> *Is there a difference between extroverted and introverted postoperative cardiovascular patients with respect to the mean amount of weight they lose 6 weeks after their surgery?*

Here, of course, all *E* versus *C* differences are ignored in order to assess the main effect due to personality type. The value for *P₁* is found by collapsing across both *E-P₁* and *C-P₁* [(14.20 + 4.20)/2 = 9.20] with a similar procedure effected for *P₂* [(10.40 + 4.10)/2 = 7.25]. Figure 8-7 illustrates the summary data used to answer both this and the previous question. Since each independent variable has now been examined separately, it stands to reason that they must now be considered together. Said another way, their *interaction* with one another with respect to the dependent variable must be now examined. In words, this question becomes:

  3. Is there an interaction between the two independent variables?

or

  Is the treatment differential with respect to patient personality?

or

  Is the dietary/exercise program more effective in inducing average weight loss for one type of patient personality than another?

  This question is answered by contrasting any difference between E and C (that is, with respect to weight loss) for extroverts with any E versus C difference for introverts. In other words, given that the average E-P_1 subject lost considerably more weight than his/her average C-P_1 counterpart (that is, 14.20 versus 4.20 or a mean difference of 10 pounds), did the average experimental introverted patient lose approximately 10 pounds more than the average introverted patient in the control group?

  Note the word approximately (which could be replaced with proportional) here. Mean differences in research are almost never exactly zero. What interactions really address are *patterns* and the best way to visualize them are to construct graphs where the vertical axis reflects the scale on which the dependent variable is measured (average pounds in the present case) and the levels of one of the independent variables constitutes the horizontal axis.

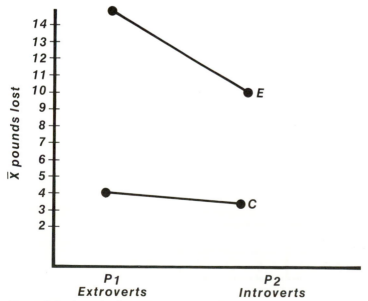

Figure 8-8　A graph of the data in Figure 8-7.

In this way, the hypothetical means in Figure 8-7 would be represented as shown in Figure 8-8. The most direct way to interpret a graphed interaction is to judge whether or not the lines are approximately *parallel*. If they are perfectly parallel, then there is definitely no statistically significant interaction between the independent variables. If the lines are obviously not parallel, then there may be an interaction. The determination of the statistical significance of the interaction depicted in Figure 8-8 must await statistical analysis (see Chapter 15), although this figure certainly appears to represent one since the difference between E and C is greater at P_1 than P_2 (10 pounds versus 6.3 pounds). Thus while the dietary/exercise program seemed to work for both personality types, the effect was even more pronounced for extroverted than introverted subjects. Again, whether or not this interaction, as well as the overall E versus C (question 1) and P_1 versus P_2 (question 2) differences are statistically significant must await statistical evaluation.

Another Example

Although there are a great many different possibilities for a 2×2 interaction, let us examine the most extreme and obvious example of a nonparallel graph. Suppose that the results shown in Figure 8-9 were obtained from our hypothetical study.

If nothing more than the main effects were tested, we would conclude that the experimental intervention was completely ineffectual: E subjects lost exactly the same amount of weight as C subjects by the study's completion (15 pounds). Similarly we would conclude that there was absolutely no difference between personality types. The interaction between the two independent variables reveals an astonishing (and potentially extremely important) phenomenon: a program for dietary education coupled with an exercise regimen is quite effective for introverted subjects but is actually as harmful for extroverted subjects as it was beneficial to introverted subjects. Graphed this effect becomes even more apparent, as shown in Figure 8-10a. Obviously these lines are about as far from parallel as two lines can be and the interaction they represent would almost certainly be statistically significant.

Although a 2×2 model is the most simple factorial design possible, the possible combinations of answers it can provide are truly impressive, since the two independent variables and their interaction are all independent of one

	Extrovert	Introvert	
E	10	20	15
C	20	10	15
	15	15	

Figure 8-9   One possible interaction for a 2×2 model.

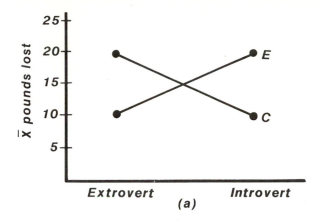

$$
\begin{array}{c}
\text{Possibilities} \\
(1)\quad (2)\quad (3)\quad (4)\quad (5)\quad (6)\quad (7)\quad (8)
\end{array}
$$

	(1)	(2)	(3)	(4)	(5)	(6)	(7)	(8)
Question 1 (first main effect)	yes	yes	yes	yes	no	no	no	no
Question 2 (second main effect)	yes	yes	no	no	no	no	yes	yes
Question 3 (the interaction)	yes	no	yes	no	no	yes	no	yes

(b)

Figure 8-10 *(a)* A graph of the data in Figure 8-9. *(b)* Eight possible outcomes for a 2 × 2 model.

another. In other words, the answers to questions one through three on pages 117–119 can be any combination of yes and no responses. This yields eight possibilities (Figure 8-10b).

For each yes answer to a main effect question, however, there are two possibilities: the first group (for example, E) can be significantly greater than the second group (C) or vice versa. This in itself increases the number of unique possibilities from 8 to 18. To make things even more complicated, however, there are 10 different ways a statistically significant interaction can manifest itself in a 2 × 2 model:

1. E less effective than C for extroverts, more effective than C for introverts.
2. E more effective than C for extroverts, less effective than C for introverts.
3. E more effective for both extroverts and introverts, but proportionally more so for introverts.
4. C more effective for both extroverts and introverts, but proportionally more so for introverts.

5. *E* more effective than *C* for both extroverts and introverts, but proportionally less so for introverts.*
6. *C* less effective than *E* for both extroverts and introverts, but proportionally less so for introverts.
7. No difference between *E* and *C* for extroverts, *E* less effective than *C* for introverts.
8. No difference between *E* and *C* for extroverts, *E* more effective than *C* for introverts.
9. No difference between *E* and *C* for introverts, *E* less effective than *C* for extroverts.
10. No difference between *E* and *C* for introverts, *E* more effective than *C* for extroverts.

Three or More Levels per Factor

All its possible permutations aside, the interpretation of the results accruing from a 2×2 factorial model is actually quite straightforward. All of the above-mentioned combinations are very easy to interpret via a simple examination of the means involved, especially when they are graphed.

Factorial models can be expanded to three or more levels, of course, just as can the two-group models discussed in Chapter 7. Once this extension is made, their interpretation becomes somewhat more complicated. We could, for example, employ the same four levels of the treatment variable depicted in Figure 8-1 in our two-factor personality study. This would be done by randomly assigning each personality group to the four conditions separately to produce the two-dimensional model shown in Figure 8-11. Now, not only are there many possible individual pairwise differences within the overall four-group treatment main effect, the occurrence of a statistically significant interaction can be quite complicated to interpret with this many groups. Such an interaction can still be graphed, but now it is necessary to evaluate whether or not *four* lines are parallel with one another rather than two.

To illustrate, consider the possibilities shown in Figure 8-12. Figure 8-12a represents a situation in which the treatments appear to differ from one another

* Represented by Figure 8-8.

	Extrovert	Introvert
E_1 Dietary education alone		
E_2 Exercise alone		
E_3 Dietary education + Exercise		
E_4 Routine clinical care		

Figure 8-11 A 4×2 factorial model.

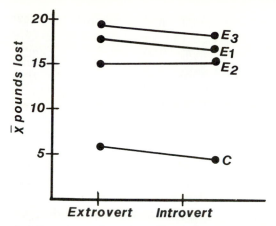

(a) Treatment main effect but no interaction.

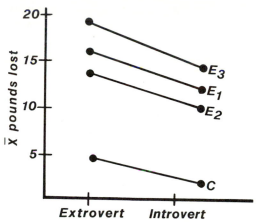

(b) Treatment and personality main effects but no interaction.

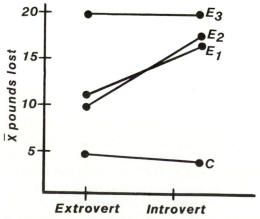

(c) Treatment main effect and interaction.

Figure 8-12 Some possible outcomes from a 4 × 2 model.

(with C registering less favorable outcomes than the three treatments), but none appears to be differentially effective with respect to personality since *the four lines appear to be roughly parallel with one another.* We would therefore expect the interaction not to be statistically significant.

Figure 8-12b depicts a situation in which there is both a difference between treatments and personality types, but no interaction. Again the four lines are roughly parallel with one another or, said another way, the order (that is, E_3, E_1, E_2, then C) among the four levels of the treatment main effect is approximately the same (as is the relative difference among them) for each personality type.

The third scenario reflects both treatment differences and a probable interaction. Although statistical significance must be determined by an analysis of variance procedure (see Chapter 15), Figure 8-12c appears to indicate a situation in which all three treatments are superior to the control, but one in which those treatments involving exercise are less effective for extroverts.

These are only three of a literal plethora of possible outcomes from a 2 (introvert versus extrovert) $\times$ 4 (treatments) factorial model such as this. There is no question that such models dramatically increase the amount we can learn from a study. To repeat a recurrent theme, however, nothing in research is free. Thus, just as with the multiple-group model from which this latter example was extended (Figure 8-1), there is a problem with statistical power with respect to individual comparisons between treatments and with respect to interpreting interactions. I strongly suggest, therefore, that *when the number of subjects is limited, groups should be kept to a minimum: two per factor being optimal* unless there is a strong reason to assume that an additional group will produce *dramatically* different results.

To see why interpretability of the results must at least be considered, let us examine a study where four levels of personality are used instead of two. In addition, let us suppose that a new factor containing three levels of education has also been included. There is, after all, no theoretical limit on either the number of factors that can be included in a study or on the number of levels (groups) per factor. In actual practice more than four of either are rare because of (1) the difficulty of obtaining enough subjects per cell, (2) the increased complexity of interpreting the results, and (3) the difficulty of identifying additional independent variables that can reasonably be expected to interact with the treatment.

To illustrate this first point, let us diagram the 4 (personality) $\times$ 3 (education) $\times$ 4 (treatment) model alluded to above. For ease of exposition the four treatment groups will be redesignated as A_1 through A_4, the four types of personality as B_1 through B_4, and the three levels of education as C_1 through C_3 (Figure 8-13). Since this model has 48 cells, a great many more subjects will obviously be needed to fill it than the 2×2 or the 4×2 factorial models presented earlier. Interestingly enough, the number of subjects do not have to be increased by factors of 12 and 6 respectively (that is, there are 6 times as many cells in a $4 \times 3 \times 4$ as in a 4×2 model) to maintain high statistical power for the original contrasts.

		C_1				C_2				C_3			
		B_1	B_2	B_3	B_4	B_1	B_2	B_3	B_4	B_1	B_2	B_3	B_4
A_1	Dietary education alone												
A_2	Exercise alone												
A_3	Dietary education + Exercise												
A_4	Routine clinical care												

Figure 8-13   A $4 \times 3 \times 4$ model.

The addition of the new education variable does not change the number of subjects available for either of the two other main effects (treatment and personality type) or for the treatment $\times$ personality interaction over and above the requirements imposed by the addition of the two additional personality types. The reason for this is that all three of these effects are tested by summing across levels of education. The main treatment effect, for example, collapses across all nonpersonality boundaries, the treatment $\times$ personality interaction collapses across education levels, and so forth. The chief additional requirement for subjects (and hence statistical power) is for the contrasts between individual cells, which will be discussed below as a three-way interaction between treatment, personality, and education.

Sample size problems do take another form in higher-level factorial designs such as this and that is the difficulty of finding enough subjects meeting cell requirements to fill them. This is seldom a problem with groups to which subjects can be randomly assigned, since by definition any subject can be placed in any cell. Thus, the original pool need only be great enough to numerically fill the cells to the desired size (thus, if it were determined that the above design needed five subjects per cell to ensure adequate power, the necessary sample size would be $48 \times 5 = 240$). With the two nonassignable variables in the present example, however, the researcher must not only find substantial (and preferably equal) numbers of subjects fitting each personality definition and each education level, he or she must also find sufficient numbers of, say, personality type B_1 who are educated at levels C_1, C_2, and C_3. This requirement can be extremely problematic when subjects are limited and when the indepen-

Education

	C_1	C_2	C_3
B_1			
B_2			
B_3			
B_4			

Personality

Figure 8-14   Education × personality.

dent variables are related (such as when it is more common to find poorly educated people possessing personality type B_1), thus making it extremely difficult to fill *all* the $B \times C$ cells equally.

To illustrate how such problems might arise, let us consider the tactics of assigning subjects to a model such as this. First, personality and educational data would need to be collected on an available sample. We will assume that the researcher possesses some sound, nonarbitrary basis for dividing subjects into the four chosen personality and three educational levels. Subjects' names (or identification numbers) are then placed into a 4 × 3 table corresponding to the appropriate levels of the personality and education variables (Figure 8-14). Finally, subjects within each cell are randomly assigned to one of the four treatment groups. This is done separately, with subjects in cell B_1C_1 randomly assigned to groups A_1 through A_4, followed by the subjects in cell B_1C_2, and so forth.

The chief problem with this strategy is having sufficient subjects to fill each of the above 12 cells. Some researchers, failing in this regard, resort to first defining one variable's level, say personality type, and then cutting each of the resulting groups into thirds with respect to education. What happens here is that the cutting points will most likely differ for each personality type, hence highly educated subjects in B_1 may be equivalent to moderately educated subjects in B_2. I would therefore suggest that *cell membership be defined via a defensible, a priori* (that is, before examining the data) *method. If sufficient subjects are then not available to fill all the cells in the desired factorial model with roughly even numbers, the problematic variable(s)/factor(s) should be dropped.* Two additional pieces of advice might be:

1. Employ as few factors as possible. Do not add variables/factors unless absolutely necessary. Hunches and/or intuition are not a good enough reason to add variables to a factorial model.
2. *Employ as few levels or groups per factor as possible. Two is optimal. More is inviting unnecessary complexity. If one of the factors is defined by a continuous variable* (such as education), *always dichotomize: a medium group seldom adds anything to the interpretation of an inter-*

action unless a nonlinear relationship of some sort exists among the variables.

Let us now examine the various questions which a higher-level factorial model such as illustrated in Figure 8-13 addresses. It will be remembered that a two-dimensional model tested two main effects and the interaction between them. The addition of the third variable in the present example naturally introduces additional questions, for not only do the three questions discussed on pages 117–119 remain relevant (that is, the overall effects of the treatments, of personality types, and the interaction between them), four additional questions are generated: one due to the additional main effect for education, the other three due to interactions between the three independent variables. In words, these questions are:

4. Is there a difference between the subjects in the three educational levels with respect to how much weight they will lose 6 weeks after their surgery?

This question is addressed by collapsing across all treatment and personality cells to assess the relationship between education and the dependent variable (number of pounds lost).

5. Are the treatments differentially effective with respect to the patients' educational levels?

This is the treatment-by-education interaction and is obtained by collapsing across personality level. It basically compares the way education is related to the dependent variable within each of the four treatment groups. Thus, if higher education patients tend to lose more weight than moderately and less-educated patients in treatment A_1 (dietary information alone), does this same pattern hold for treatment groups A_2, A_3, and A_4? If it does, the treatment × education interaction will not be statistically significant and the answer to question 5 above will be no. (Note that this interaction can be turned around to compare the way in which A_1 through A_4 relate to the dependent variable within each educational level.)

6. Is there an interaction between personality and education with respect to subjects' weight loss?

The personality-by-education interaction is interpreted similarly to question 5 except, of course, the treatment variable is ignored.

7. Considering all three independent variables simultaneously, are certain treatments differentially effective for certain combinations of educational levels and personality types?

This is called a three-way interaction because there are three independent variables or factors involved. It is a relatively difficult concept for many beginning researchers to grasp, thus it deserves some additional explanation.

Three-Way Interactions

It will be recalled that the easiest way to interpret a statistically significant two-way interaction is to graph the manner in which the different levels of the two independent variables relate to the dependent variable. The same strategy works quite well for higher-level interactions except for the fact that a single graph no longer suffices.

For illustrative purposes, let us suppose that a statistical analysis revealed a significant three-way interaction. For ease of exposition let us further assume that only two levels existed for each independent variable producing the results shown in Figure 8-15.

This collection of cell means can be graphed in one of three ways: AB on C, AC on B, and BC on A, depending on how the researcher wishes to conceptualize the situation. (All will result in identical interpretations.)

Let us arbitrarily choose AB on C (Figure 8-16). The key to interpreting these graphs is to compare the C_1 and C_2 graphs to one another simultaneously. Whether or not the lines are parallel to one another in any one graph is immaterial. The idea is to attempt to superimpose the two graphs on *one another*. If this is done, a difference between the two becomes apparent. The dietary/exercise (A_1) treatment is superior to routine clinical care for both introverts and extroverts without a great deal of education (C_1) but appears to be only effective for extroverts among subjects with more education (C_2).

Although three-way interactions are not always this straightforward, they are usually fairly easily interpreted via graphs of the sort represented by Figure 8-16. The situation does become geometrically more complex with the use of more than three factors. If we were to add a fourth factor (which we'll simply designate as D), for example, not only would four main effects be produced, there would now be ten interactions to consider: six 2-way (AB, AC, AD, BC, BD, and CD), three 3-way (ABC, ACD, and BCD), and one 4-way $(ABCD)$. This simply becomes too complicated for most beginning- (or even intermediate-)

	C_1		C_2	
	B_1	B_2	B_1	B_2
A_1	12.8	14.4	4.2	14.2
A_2	4.1	5.2	4.1	5.1

Figure 8-15   Hypothetical data for a statistically significant three-way interaction.

AB on C₁ (low education)

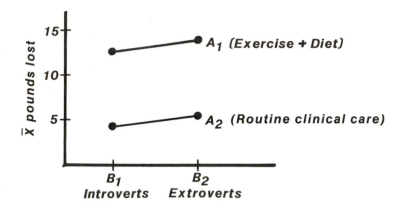

AB on C₂ (high education)

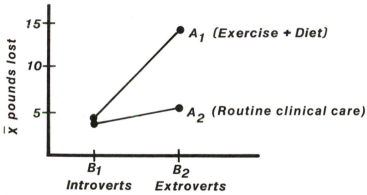

Figure 8-16   A graph of the three-way interaction represented by Figure 8-15.

level researchers to handle. In addition, sample size constraints and the difficulty of assigning subjects usually make such models impractical in actual practice.

MIXED FACTORIAL MODELS

So far factorial studies have been treated as though they are all direct extensions of the randomized-experimental/control-group–posttest-only model. There is no logical reason that the factorial logic cannot be extended to all of the design options discussed in the previous two chapters. Each of the models just discussed could have just as easily employed a pretest or a covariate, for example. They could also have employed groups to which subjects were either assigned

Time

		(*B1*) Posttest	(*B2*) Retest after 6 months
Treatments	*A1* Exercise + Diet		
	A2 Routine clinical care		

Figure 8-17   A repeated measures model.

via a randomized matching procedure or that simply constituted repeated measures on the same subjects. Let us illustrate this latter concept.

Suppose our hypothetical researcher had some concern with respect to how long the overall treatment effect was likely to last. For example, even though it was hypothesized that the education/exercise treatment would be effective over the short run, it was suspected that it would begin to dissipate with time.

One way to test this suspicion would be to administer the dependent variable (that is, weigh the patients) twice, once immediately after cessation of the 6-week program, once again perhaps 6 months later. Such a strategy would result in a model that could be conceptualized as a 2 (treatments: *E* versus *C*) $\times$ 2 (testing intervals: immediate versus 6 months later) model where the new independent variable (which could be conceptualized as time for want of a better label) differs from the original treatment factor in one very important way: subjects were randomly assigned to the two levels of the latter while the *same* subjects are contained in the two levels of the former. When a factor contains randomly assigned subjects in its various groups, it is called *a between-subjects factor* because any comparison made between said groups is between different subjects. When a factor contains the same (or matched) subjects in its different groups, it is called a *within-subjects factor* simply because any comparison between groups entails comparing scores that are correlated with one another (either due to matching strategy or the fact that the same subjects are contained within the groups). When the same measure is administered more than once across time as in the present case, the repeated administration factor is sometimes called a *repeated measures* (Figure 8-17).

Conceptually, this factorial study involving one within-subjects factor is identical to one involving randomly assigned subjects to all groups. There are still two main effects and a single interaction, although the time main effect would not be particularly interesting, since it involves collapsing across all the treatment cells. Also, as in all factorial studies, interpretation of either main effect must be tempered by examination of the interaction. For example, if a treatment effect does occur, is it more (or less) pronounced at 6 months than immediately after the cessation of the experimental protocol?

The process of assigning subjects to a model such as this is identical to that of randomly assigning subjects to a simple, two-group experimental model. Each subject is randomly assigned to either the experimental or the control group and then tested twice. Models employing repeated measures thus require no more subjects than single-factor studies while providing answers to additional questions. Their disadvantage (since nothing is free) resides in the sometimes considerable procedural difficulty of repeatedly administering a measure over time. In the present study, for example, subjects would have probably left the clinical setting long before the 6-months retesting interval was up, hence necessitating reconvening them or going to their homes for the second weighing. This would undoubtedly result in experimental mortality, since some subjects may have moved, some might be unwilling to participate further, and some may have died or been rehospitalized. Subject loss in models that employ within-subjects factors can be especially problematic, since the statistical analysis requires that a subject missing from one observation be dropped from the entire study. (Thus, data from subjects present only in the B_1 cells of Figure 8-17 cannot even be used in evaluating the relative effectiveness of the two treatments at time B_1.) This disadvantage is usually outweighed, however, by the increased statistical power inherent in within subjects designs.

Many more variations exist on this theme than can be mentioned here. All of the models discussed in this and the previous chapter can be mixed and matched, depending on the researcher's unique needs. There is no question that this capacity greatly magnifies the potential amount of knowledge that can be generated from a single research study. At the risk of sounding repetitious, I counsel against complexity for its own sake. The more complex a study is, the more easily things can go wrong with it and the more difficult it is to conduct. Furthermore, a simple two-group study documenting the efficacy of a single treatment may possess the potential of making a greater contribution to science than do dozens of studies employing sophisticated research models that address basically trivial issues. Admittedly it is a fine line to walk, but the best advice that can be offered here is to design a research study in such a way that it can best answer the primary question of interest. If this necessitates multiple-groups factors, then by all means employ them. If it does not, then I recommend opting for simplicity.

SUMMARY

Although complexity is never recommended for its own sake, the addition of either multiple groups or multiple factors to a research model is capable of greatly increasing a study's explanatory power. A *single-factor multigroup model* can be visualized as a simple extension of the two-group research models presented in Chapter 7. Here, additional groups are employed but they are conceptualized as all belonging to a single dimension (or constituting a single independent variable). A *factorial model,* on the other hand, involves at least one additional independent variable or factor and is capable of addressing more than one research question within a single study. A two-dimensional factorial model, for example, addresses the independent effects of both independent variables employed as well as their interactive effects on one another. More complex models address even more questions, although I counsel beginning researchers to strive for simplicity whenever possible.

REFERENCE

Winer, B. J. *Statistical Principles in Experimental Design,* 2nd edition. New York: McGraw-Hill, 1971.

chapter *9*

Nonrandomly Assigned Research Models

The random assignment of subjects to groups occasionally entails such difficulties that researchers opt for alternative research models. Fortunately, there are stronger alternatives that the primitive single-group models outlined in Chapter 6.

THE NONEQUIVALENT-CONTROL-GROUP MODEL

One of the characteristics that made the single-group models so unacceptable was the absence of a reasonable comparison group. One possible solution to this problem is to administer an experimental intervention to an intact group of subjects and then to select an equivalent group to which the intervention will not be administered to serve as a comparison (or control). Certainly such a procedure possesses a certain intuitive appeal over the randomly assigned control when subjects are in limited supply or when objections exist to the randomization process.

A chief disadvantage of such a procedure is that the very reason one group is selected as target of the intervention (for example, convenience, a friendly administrator, subject cooperativeness) may *ensure* its nonequivalence to the group selected not to receive a treatment. Even when the researcher has the option of flipping a coin to determine which of two intact groups will receive the treatment, there is still no guarantee that the two groups will be equivalent to begin with.

This strategy, which is sometimes called the nonequivalent-control-group–posttest-only model, has very few advantages over the very weakest of

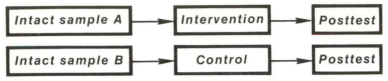

Figure 9-1   The nonequivalent-control-group–posttest-only model.

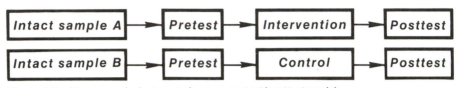

Figure 9-2   The nonequivalent-control-group–pretest/posttest model.

the one-group models discussed in Chapter 6 (Figure 9-1). Given the fact that there is no way to guarantee the initial equivalence of sample A versus sample B (the two of which could be classrooms, clinics, or hospital wings), the three possible outcomes from such a study (that is, $E > C$, $C > E$, and $E = C$) could all be explained in terms of initial nonequivalence. Thus, if sample A proved superior to sample B on the posttest, said difference might be due entirely to A's initial superiority on either the attribute being tested or on some related attribute. The converse could be true if sample B wound up superior to A, while no final difference between the two groups would lead to exactly three possible explanations:

1. There really was no effect for the intervention (introduced to A).
2. The intervention really worked, but sample A began with a disadvantage with respect to B (thus, the intervention was able to bring A subjects up to B subjects' initial level).
3. The intervention was actually detrimental, but since A subjects were initially superior, it only served to bring them down to B's starting point.

Although the nonequivalent-control-group–posttest-only model has other weaknesses as well, this initial nonequivalent possibility is such an overriding concern that it alone pretty much serves to make the strategy useless. For this reason the model is seldom seen any longer in the more prestigious research journals. Instead, either a pretest (Figure 9-2) or a covariate (Figure 9-3)—or both—is employed producing one of the following models:

Returning to the hypothetical weight-loss study used throughout the previous few chapters, either model might be employed if the researcher believed it was not feasible to assign subjects randomly within a single clinic. The search would then be for a similar sample that was not targeted to receive the dietary/exercise intervention. Possibilities might include: (1) postoperative, overweight

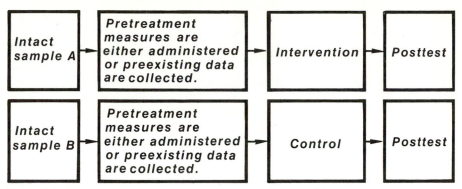

Figure 9-3   The nonequivalent-control-group-with-covariates model.

cardiovascular patients who elected not to enroll in the weight-loss clinic, (2) subjects who did enroll but subsequently dropped out, and (3) similar patients enrolled in a clinic operated by another hospital that offered neither dietary education nor an exercise regimen.

The first two comparisons would be so obviously flawed that it is surprising that any researcher would employ them. Their chief problem is that they *begin* with subjects who select themselves into the two groups *because* they are different. For example, overweight patients who elect not to receive postoperative help (either by not seeking it in the first place or by dropping out of an organized program) may do so because:

1. They are less conscientious.
2. They do not have sufficient time because of high-pressure jobs.
3. They believe they can't lose weight because of past failures.
4. They believe they *can* lose weight on their own because of past successes.
5. They don't believe that diet and exercise have anything to do with their health.
6. They are in such terrible physical condition that they are afraid to exercise.
7. They are so fond of high-fat and high-cholesterol foods that they don't want to give them up.
8. They are not recovering as well from their surgery as their peers and are thus unable to attend the clinic.
9. They are systematically different in any number of ways.

Any of these factors could serve to invalidate such a makeshift comparison as a true control. There is, in fact, no reason why the two groups could not differ on *combinations* of these or other alternative explanations that can only be guessed at. The point here is that *the researcher can never know all the ways the two types of subjects do or do not differ from one another.* Weighing subjects prior to the study can have no influence on the possible presence of these inherent differences. It is quite possible for two groups to be perfectly matched with respect to their need to lose weight (that is, their scores on the pretest or other covariates), for example, but severely mismatched with respect to their *propensity* (or their ability) to lose weight.

Even when the self-selection of subjects into groups is not as obvious as when overt refusals or dropouts are used as the control, the use of a pretest or other covariate can do very little to invalidate the possibility that two intact groups differ with respect to their *propensity to change on the dependent variable*. Suppose in the present example that a comparable clinic from a neighboring hospital was selected to serve as the comparison group instead. It would still be possible that this neighboring clinic might:

1. Make attendance easier (or more difficult) than the one receiving the experimental intervention.
2. Be associated with a more- (or less-) successful surgical department.
3. Serve a hospital that attracted a slightly different clientele (for example, from a different socioeconomic strata or differing religious backgrounds).
4. Be less successful in maintaining contact with their clients (which would result in a differential subject loss).
5. Differ (or serve clients who differed) in any number of additional ways.

Certainly, many of these hypothesized differences between the clinics and their clients could be tested and thereby possibly discounted if enough extra data* were collected that resulted in a stronger hypothesis test than the use of subjects from the same site who elected not to participate. To be useful, this additional data must be correlated (or capable of being correlated) both with subjects' weight loss and their reactions to the experimental intervention. Still, the overriding problem remains that no one can be sure that the two groups did not differ in some systematic way capable to invalidating the basic comparison no matter how much data are collected. The only way of truly ensuring equivalence is to assign subjects randomly.

Remedial Steps

When the stronger research models discussed in the last two chapters are not feasible and when the researcher is determined to conduct the study, there are certain steps that can be taken to ensure as strong a hypothesis test as possible. Some of these are:

1. *Select intact groups that are as comparable as possible.* Avoid any comparison between obviously different groups or settings. Be honest and approach the task from a critic's perspective (that is, set out to

---

* Examples might be severity of illness, previous history of weight loss and exercise, type of life-style engaged in, and perhaps even such affective information as amount of perceived control over one's health.

discover differences between the groups, not document similarities). This may involve a certain amount of legwork, such as actually interviewing people familiar with each setting, but in the long run is worth the extra effort.

2. *Collect as much background data as possible on potential differences between groups (or settings).* Although only one or two controlling variables (see Chapter 14) are likely to be employed for any given analysis, the more information that is systematically collected, the better. If nothing else, the two groups can be statistically compared on these variables in order to make a case for or against initial equivalence. Although this case will always be circumstantial in comparison to groups composed of randomly assigned subjects, the more such evidence, the better.

3. *Be creative in the search for potential intergroup differences.* All too often the previous step is accomplished with preexisting demographic information (for example, age, sex, marital status) that was collected for other purposes. It must be remembered that the real variable of interest is either a preexisting propensity to change on the dependent variable or a propensity to profit from the specific intervention being introduced. Our weight-loss researcher therefore might be wise to collect some life-style and affective information on the two groups of subjects in order to rule out as many of the alternative explanations (as discussed on the last few pages) as possible. For example, subjects could be queried about past weight-loss successes and failures, their opinions regarding the importance of diet and exercise, the demands of their jobs, and so forth. Such questions could be incorporated into a short questionnaire administered to both groups of subjects prior to the study. Should the two groups differ systematically along some of these dimensions, the researcher would probably be wise to search for a more initially comparable control group, since it is doubtful that differences of this sort can be statistically controlled via procedures such as analysis of covariance (see Chapter 14) or multiple regression (as discussed in Chapter 16).

4. *Monitor the progress of both groups carefully.* Although this is always a good practice, it is especially important when employing intact groups that are physically separated or are likely to be subjected to different administrative regimens. It is all too easy in such cases for the two groups to have different histories over the course of the study. A prior clinical or administrative commitment to avoid any unnecessary changes in the comparison group's daily routine over the course of the study would be helpful. So, too, would careful monitoring of both groups, which will enable the researcher to attempt to persuade the interested parties to postpone any major procedural changes until the study is completed. (In the dietary/exercise study, an example of such an invalidating procedural change might occur when clinical staff in charge of the comparison group read of, and decide to implement, an innovative new program for encouraging subjects to lose weight. If allowed to occur, this would obviously invalidate the group as a treatment-as-usual control.)

Recommendation

Although this is probably a minority opinion, I recommend against the use of nonequivalent control groups, especially for beginning researchers. In many ways, quasi-experimental research (as these models are sometimes called) is more difficult to perform well than research involving the random assignment of subjects. Such research is also seldom conclusive, since it is subject to so many alternative explanations.

Furthermore, I find arguments for the value of such procedures as preliminary efforts (or pilot studies) for later experimental research not particularly persuasive. The results (whether positive or negative) of research employing nonequivalent controls are almost always subject to so many alternative explanations that final conclusions await more definitive study. Why not therefore begin with definitive research models in the first place?

USING SUBJECTS AS THEIR OWN CONTROL

One alternative to employing nonequivalent control groups is to use the same subjects in *both* the experimental *and* the control groups, thus obviating all nonequivalence-related alternative explanations *if* (and this is a big if) the very act of serving in both roles does not itself make the same subjects nonequivalent over time. In a sense, the one-group–pretest/posttest model is a primitive example of subjects serving as their own controls, but the limitations of this procedure are so severe that it has already been pretty much dismissed from serious scientific consideration.

A slightly superior version might entail using a temporal baseline, equivalent in duration to the experimental interval as the control. Thus, assuming a 6-week intervention, the ongoing weight-loss study might be designed as shown in Figure 9-4. The basis of comparison here between E and C, of course, is the change from O_2 to O_3 versus the change from O_1 to O_2.

This strategy does possess some redeeming qualities, but unfortunately suffers from many of the same alternative explanations as its one-group–pretest/posttest relative. It also possesses some very real tactical disadvantages that include:

1. Doubling the length of the study.
2. Withholding the intervention from all subjects over the initial interval.
3. Measuring subjects three times instead of two (which can be problematic with certain measures, especially paper-and-pencil instruments).

Practical concerns aside (any one of which can make the model completely infeasible), it may be helpful to reexamine the original objections (that is, threats to internal validity) to the one-group–pretest/posttest model in light of the above procedural innovation.

External events, other than the intervention, occurring during the course of a study capable of influencing its outcome While still a potential problem,

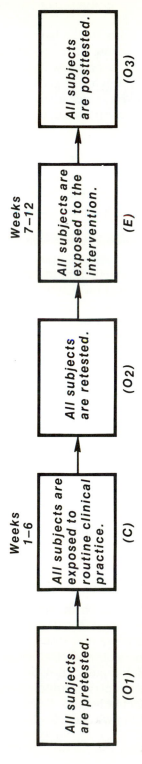

Figure 9-4 The single-group – baseline/intervention model.

(O₁) All subjects are pretested.

Weeks 1–6

(C) All subjects are exposed to routine clinical practice.

(O₂) All subjects are retested.

Weeks 7–12

(E) All subjects are exposed to the intervention.

(O₃) All subjects are posttested.

these confounding historical events at least have as good a chance of occurring during the baseline period as during the experimental interval. This is little compensation, however, in the case of the fictitious television program dealing with the importance of losing weight for cardiovascular patients posited in Chapter 6. Such an event could produce a false-negative result if it occurred during the first 6 weeks, a false-positive result if it occurred during the second 6 weeks.

An inborn propensity of the sample itself to change with regard to the dependent variable irrespective of the intervention This potential problem is addressed to a certain extent by the addition of the baseline. Thus, while the patients who volunteered to participate may have been more motivated to lose weight than those who did not (or the clinic from which the subjects were selected happened to serve an especially motivated clientele), there is no apparent reason why this propensity to lose weight should wait until the beginning of the seventh week to manifest itself. Unfortunately, what could occur is a selection × treatment interaction, in which the type of subjects selected would be especially amenable to reacting to the experimental intervention. As an example of how such an effect might manifest itself, suppose that the type of patients selected for the study were more eager to please their clinicians than the population as a whole. Since no indication that losing weight was a desirable behavior would be given in the first 6 weeks, such subjects would have no motivation to do so. When they were encouraged to lose weight during the second 6 weeks, such patients might happily comply, irrespective of the weight-loss program.

A preexisting characteristic possessed by the study's subjects (or by their environment) that predisposes them to change on the dependent variable The present model does control for maturation effects to a certain extent. There is no reason to believe that such an effect would wait until the seventh week to manifest itself. If such a propensity did exist, a researcher thoroughly familiar with the clinical situation (and the natural history of the types of patients therein) would probably be aware of it. It is possible, of course, that such a propensity could increase over time, thus while occurring to a slight degree during the first 6 weeks it might pick up enough in intensity during the final phase of the study to produce a false-positive result. (The opposite situation, which is probably more likely, in which an initially strong tendency tapered off over time, could just as easily mask a true treatment effect and produce a false-negative result.) The best preventive strategy is to know as much about the types of patients involved as possible and plan the study's time line around this knowledge. Short of that, a small pilot study prior to the full-blown effort in which the progress of similar patients is monitored with respect to their changes on the dependent variable might be helpful. Examining records (if they exist) or discussing the problem with knowledgeable clinicians would also be a good idea.

A statistically demonstrable tendency for subjects chosen because they possessed extreme scores on a pretest to exhibit less-extreme scores on a posttest as a function of chance alone As discussed earlier, statistical regression need be considered only if subjects are selected *because* of their extreme scores on the dependent variable. The single-group–baseline/intervention model pretty much controls for this possibility from a false-positive perspective because the bulk of any regression effect will be dissipated between O_1 and O_2. (Since the intervention is not introduced until after O_2, this artifactual shift in scores due to regression cannot be attributed to the intervention.) It is conceivable, however, that this phenomenon could serve to mask a relatively weak intervention effect, thereby producing a false-negative result.

Subjects were lost from the study who would have scored differently on the posttest from those who were actually measured Unfortunately, the present model does very little to address the problem of experimental mortality when it does occur. Prevention remains the best solution.

Changes occurring in the measuring process over the course of a study If anything, the chances of instrumentation are even greater in the single-group–baseline/intervention model than designs employing only two administrations of the dependent variable. The more times a measure is administered, and the greater the interval between those administrations, the greater the chances that some type of systematic error will creep into the measuring process. Careful monitoring and remediation should prevent this problem, which of course is of greater concern for more subjectively scored measures.

A tendency of subjects to score higher on their second exposure to a measure purely as a function of their first exposure Measures for which testing is a possibility (most notably cognitive and affective ones) are probably not appropriate for any model employing more than two test administrations. In my opinion, taking the same paper-and-pencil test three times in a relatively short time period simply makes the study itself too transparent, regardless of whether the testing artifact is likely to be present. An exception might be an educational study in which the students know that their task is to learn a certain body of knowledge, thus repeated testings might be expected whether research was being carried out or not. In general, I would counsel that:

> *To be employed in any model utilizing more than one testing administration, the testing procedure itself should be unobtrusive and not subject to a substantive practice effect of any kind.*

With this dictum in mind, two variations on the single-group–baseline-intervention theme will now be discussed. Although neither can substitute for random assignment, each does possess certain advantages over the primitive single-group model.

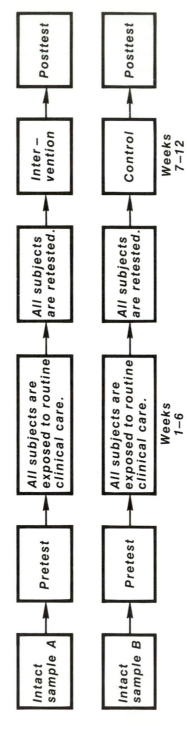

Figure 9-5 The nonequivalent-control-group–baseline/intervention model.

The first involves the simple addition of a nonequivalent control group, represented in Figure 9-5. The main contribution of this model lies not so much in the control of history, selection, maturation, and so forth, as in the intuitive argument it permits: namely, that there is no reason why their effects should be observed between weeks 7 and 12 for the experimental group and not for the control. The two groups still cannot be assumed equivalent with respect to their propensity to change on the dependent variable (and everything said previously about addressing this problem applies here), it is just that the addition of the baseline interval permits greater credence in a positive effect. In other words, why should the experimental group choose the 7-to-12-week time interval to change when the control group did not? (One possibility, of course, is some variant of a selection $\times$ treatment interaction mentioned previously that, if present, might well be completely immune to the addition of a nonequivalent control group. Other threats to internal validity can also interact specifically with an experimental treatment, although all such secondary threats are usually not considered especially virulent in most research settings.) The nonequivalent-control-group–baseline/intervention strategy thus remains an exceedingly weak research model, yet it may be worth employing (as opposed to the single-group models discussed so far) when the random assignment of subjects is truly not feasible.

Interrupted Time-Series Studies

Another variation on this same theme is a category of research models called *interrupted time-series designs.* Just as there are many more varieties of research models employing both randomly assigned or intact control groups than have been presented in the last few chapters,* so are there many more variations on the time-series theme than can be covered here.

Basically, however, interrupted time-series models attempt to impose an element of procedural control via *multiple* measurements, both before and after the introduction of an intervention. In some ways, then, these models are extensions of the baseline/intervention strategies just discussed.

As an example, consider Figure 9-6, which shows a single-group interrupted time-series model (where O is used to designate a test administration or a recorded observation of some sort). Here, the multiple observations or tests on the same group of subjects serves as a sort of control group, since selection, maturation, history, testing, and most of the other threats to internal validity have an equally good chance to occur between O_1 and O_2, O_2 and O_3, and O_3 and O_4 as they do between O_4 and O_5, where the intervention is actually introduced.

Thus, if there is a natural tendency for subjects to improve on the dependent variable over time, this trend can be noted and partialed out of any observed improvements after O_4. This is not to say that this particular time-

---

* For one of the better treatments of the former available, see Campbell and Stanley (1966). For the latter, see Cook and Campbell (1979).

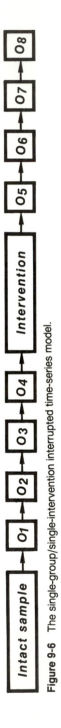

Figure 9-6   The single-group/single-intervention interrupted time-series model.

series model is immune from all possible threats to the internal validity of a study. The fact of the matter is that it is a relatively weak research model for several reasons. In the first place, it is subject to the possible interactive effects of selection and the introduction of the experimental treatment. Second, even though an extraneous event of some sort could have just as easily occurred between say O_3 and O_4 as between O_4 and O_5, there is no way of knowing whether or not such an event did occur except via careful monitoring. Similarly, unless a good deal of data are available for a relatively long period of time, natural cyclical or seasonal variations may be misinterpreted as intervention effects. About the best that can be said for this particular single-group model is that it does increase the probability that an O_4-to-O_5 change, in the absence of any other changes, is in fact due to the experimental intervention.

The chief advantages of multiple measurements prior to the treatment, then, are their ability to detect natural, systematic trends as well as random fluctuations in the data. This helps prevent such changes from erroneously being interpreted as intervention effects. (The multiple post-intervention observations are used to continue this documentation *as well as* to detect noninstanteous intervention effects.)

So far, in fact, it has been assumed that all interventions either produce an immediate effect or none at all. An intervention can just as easily take time to manifest itself. It may also produce a short-lived effect, or it may produce no immediately obvious effect at all but simply subtly change a preexisting trend. By way of illustration, consider the outcomes from a single-group/single-intervention interrupted time-series model as applied to our hypothetical weight-loss study shown in Figure 9-7.

Although constituting only a small number of possible outcomes from such a study, these three examples do illustrate some of the strengths of the interrupted time-series strategy. Figure 9-7a, for example, depicts an outcome that might have been misinterpreted as an intervention effect if O_1 had constituted the sole pretest and O_5 the sole posttest, since there is obviously an O_1-to-O_5 change (which would probably have been statistically significant). The introduction of additional observations makes it quite clear, however, that subjects had a natural tendency to lose weight over time. (Interrupted time-series models can detect intervention effects even when such a trend exists if the O_4 and O_5 change is *greater* than all of the individual O_1-to-O_4 changes.)

Figure 9-7b reflects one of the most obvious possible intervention effects that could occur in this type of study. There is no apparent trend at all between O_1 and O_4 for subjects to lose weight. A marked decrease occurs right after the intervention, however, followed by a continued stable line. Certainly, this occurrence would be interpreted as an intervention effect unless some confounding event also happened to occur between O_4 and O_5. Other possibilities here would be for the weight-loss trend to continue after O_5 or for subjects to begin to gain weight starting at O_6. Both occurrences would still be interpreted as an intervention effect.

The final example (Figure 9-7c) is somewhat less decisive. The effect does not occur concomitantly with the introduction of the treatment but shortly

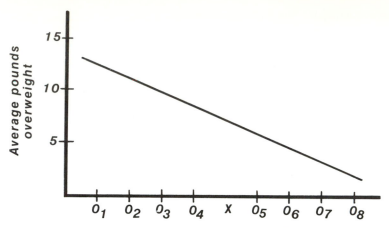

(a) A maturation, but no intervention, effect.

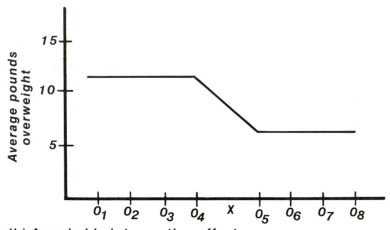

(b) A probable intervention effect.

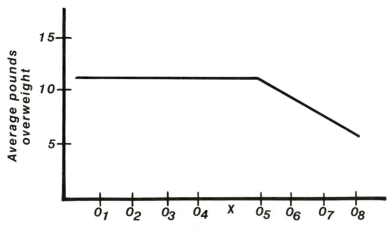

(c) A delayed intervention effect.

Figure 9-7 Three outcomes from a single-group/single-intervention interrupted time-series model (where X = the intervention). *(a)* A maturation, but no intervention, effect. *(b)* A probable intervention effect. *(c)* A delayed intervention effect.

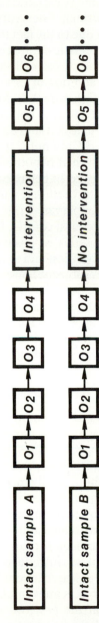

Figure 9-8 The two-group/single-intervention interrupted time-series model.

147

thereafter. Probably the researcher would interpret such a finding as indicative of the fact that the intervention took some time to work, but certainly history or some other alternative explanation has increased plausibility here.

All in all, the single-group/single-intervention interrupted time-series model is a relatively weak strategy due to the fact that regardless of the number of observations employed, only one basic comparison exists: observations collected before the intervention versus those collected afterward. One obvious improvement on this model is the addition of a second group, even if it consists of an intact, nonequivalent control (Figure 9-8). More credence can be placed in an O_4-to-O_5 change if the same effect is not observed for the comparison sample. There is still no guarantee that said shift could not be a function of, say, some extraneous event that affected E but not C subjects, but the existence of a comparison group does make such rival hypotheses considerably less likely.

Another strategy often employed in behavioral research with single subjects is the reintroduction of the intervention (Figure 9-9). Although obviously appropriate only for short-lived, nonpervasive interventions, this strategy does add a considerable amount of procedural control. It is difficult to offer a plausible alternative explanation for a series of positive shifts that always occur exactly after an experimental intervention and at no other time. Such a model requires a great deal of control over subjects, however (which is why it is usually used in a clinical setting), since the intervention is repeatedly introduced and then capriciously (at least from the subject's point of view) whisked away. (Many variations exist of this and all the models discussed so far. For example, the addition of a comparison group to the single-group repeated-intervention time-series model depicted in Figure 9-9 strengthens the procedure.)

Disadvantages of Interrupted Time-Series Models

Although capable of adding a certain amount of procedural control to an otherwise weak quasi-experimental research model, time-series methodologies are seldom practical. There are several reasons for this. In the first place, few dependent variables can be administered repeatedly without fear of the development of a testing artifact or without fatally increasing the study's obtrusiveness. Such studies also typically require more time to complete and more effort on the part of the researcher both to run them and to collect the additional data. Finally, empirical results are seldom as neat and clear-cut as we would like. In a repeated-intervention time-series model, for example, the intervention might perversely work the first two times it was introduced and have no effect at all the third time. What, then, would the researcher conclude? That the intervention worked most of the time? That subjects grew insensitive to the repeated introduction of the intervention? That the first two effects were simply chance occurrences? That subjects grew disgruntled over the repeated denial of a successful (hence popular) intervention?

For these reasons, the most appropriate applications of interrupted time-series designs may well be for (1) very powerful effects (such as the effects of reinforcement on performance), which can be relied on to manifest themselves

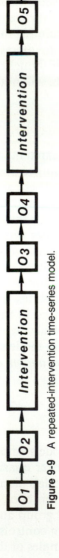

Figure 9-9 A repeated-intervention time-series model.

repeatedly on demand, or (2) large-scale, post hoc evaluations of interventions introduced for other than research purposes (for which no real alternative models exist), such as a state's introduction of spot checks for drunk drivers.

The analysis of interrupted time-series data can also be problematic, requiring specialized statistical procedures with which not many professionals are really that conversant at this point. Still, there are situations in which these models are the only viable alternative to no research at all. It is only for such circumstances, and for those researchers who engage in single-subject investigations, that I recommend interrupted time-series models. (Interestingly, many of the latter type of researchers avoid the use of the above-mentioned inferential statistical procedures altogether, claiming that if the experimental effect is not large enough to be obvious, it is of no interest to them anyway. Since this book represents an alternative school of thought, this philosophy, which is sometimes found in behavioral research, will not be discussed here further.)

OTHER RESEARCH MODELS

The reader should not view the research models presented in this and previous chapters as rigid frameworks within which a study must somehow be forced, whether it fits comfortably or not. There are many, many more models than have been discussed on these pages, and there is absolutely no reason why different models cannot be adapted (or mixed and matched) to fit a particular research purpose rather than the other way around. The chances are, in fact, that almost any conceivable combination or adaptation so fabricated has already been employed (and possibly even named) by someone.

Counterbalanced models (Figure 9-10), for example, which combine aspects of both interrupted time-series and nonequivalent control-group models have not even been discussed in this book. In many instances, such hybrid strategies can be quite powerful when creatively applied, approximating the control present in experimental models. Since approximation is the best that can be hoped for, however, *the random assignment of subjects to groups is always preferable when feasible.*

SUMMARY

Although lacking the power of models employing the random assignment of subjects to groups, there are stronger quasi-experimental alternatives to the primitive single-group research models discussed in Chapter 6. The two basic types of such models discussed in this book include those involving a second, potentially nonequivalent control group and those single-group models that allow subjects to serve as their own controls.

The two most common examples of the first category are:

1. The *nonequivalent-control-group – pretest/posttest-only model.*
2. The *nonequivalent-control-group-with-covariates model.*

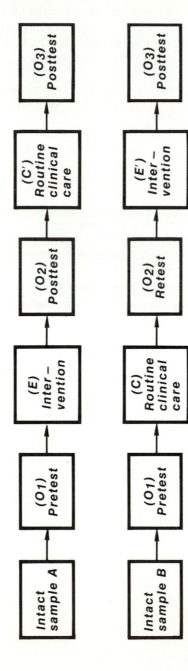

Figure 9-10 A typical counterbalanced model.

151

The primary problem with both of these alternatives involves the very real possibility that original differences (perhaps undetectable with existing measuring instruments) may account for the results rather than the experimental intervention itself. Common sense procedures exist to work against this and other alternative explanations. Among these are:

1. Selecting intact groups as comparable to one another as possible.
2. Collecting as much background data as possible on potential differences between groups.
3. Monitoring the progress of both the experimental and the comparison groups carefully during the course of the study.

Examples of research models employing subjects as their own controls include:

1. The *single-group–baseline/intervention model.*
2. The *nonequivalent-control-group–baseline/intervention model.*
3. The various types of *interrupted time-series models.*

Although each represents some improvement over the one-group–pretest/posttest model, I counsel against the use of all quasi-experimental strategies when the random assignment of subjects to groups is feasible.

REFERENCES

Campbell, D. T., and Stanley, J. C. *Experimental and Quasi-Experimental Designs for Research.* Chicago: Rand McNally, 1966.
Cook, T. C., and Campbell, D. T. *Quasi-Experimentation: Design and Analysis Issues for Field Settings.* Chicago: Rand McNally, 1979.

three

MEASUREMENT

chapter 10

Measuring Human Subjects

The previous three chapters discussed strategies for structuring the research environment to facilitate the collection of meaningful data. In research involving human subjects, these data almost invariably entail the measurement of human attributes or reactions, thus the three chapters that comprise this section are concerned with ensuring the appropriateness and utility of this type of measurement.

From a research perspective, the most crucial consideration in the measurement process is the selection of an *important and appropriate* criterion on which subjects or groups will be compared. This selection has a major impact on the potential importance of a study. It occurs, of course, during the original formulation of the research question, since the attribute or reaction that will be used in its answer is explicitly specified in the question (or hypothesis) itself. As in the previous section, we will therefore assume that the research question has already been formulated.

Since we can now also assume that an appropriate research model has been selected, the only decisions remaining with respect to this variable is how it will be *measured*. At first glance the measurement of most human attributes may seem qualitatively very different from the type of measurement carried out in the physical sciences. Physical attributes appear to be so much more concrete, observable, and objective. No one can see or touch the thing psychologists call intelligence, for example. No one can even prove that it *exists*. Measurement specialists have responded to this challenge by developing an impressive array of creative and (in some cases) complex procedures basically designed to address two issues:

1. *Is the measurement procedure* (the method by which numbers are assigned to attributes) *stable, consistent, and/or precise?* That is, regardless of what is being measured or even of whether the procedures involved are appropriate, are numbers assigned to said attribute in a stable, consistent, and precise way?
2. *Do the numbers so assigned truly measure the desired attribute?* That is, assuming a positive answer to the first question, is the procedure being employed measuring what the researcher thinks it is measuring?

Both of these questions really address a specific genre of issues. Separate techniques were thus developed for each.

The first question, dealing with stability, consistency, and precision has been given the general name of *reliability*. Among the more specific issues that it deals with are questions such as:

1. Can different people use the same procedure to arrive at similar results?
2. Can the same person use the procedure consistently at different times?
3. Regardless of who is using it, does the procedure itself assign numbers consistently?
4. How much error is involved in the numbers assigned by this procedure?*

The second question regarding what is truly being measured has been given the general name of *validity*. This term covers an even wider range of issues, a sample of which includes:

1. Are the numbers assigned by a given procedure similar to the ones that would be assigned by other procedures designed to measure the same attribute?
2. Can the numbers assigned by this procedure predict future behaviors or performance appropriate to the attribute being measured?
3. Do the different components of the measurement procedure (which are usually items) match the different constituents of the attribute being measured?
4. Do subjects differentiated by this procedure as possessing relatively more (or less) of the attribute in question behave as they should (or possess the right mix of related characteristics)?†

Separate chapters will be devoted to both reliability and validity due to their relative prominence in the literature dealing with the conduct of empirical research. In truth, the former is a much more useful concept. Issues related to

* The procedures used to address these questions are each given their own special names. Respectively they are: (1) interrater reliability, (2) intrarater reliability, (3) internal consistency or test-retest reliability (depending on the circumstances), and (4) precision (which is assessed via a statistic called the standard error of measurement).

† These in turn are called (1) concurrent validity, (2) predictive validity, (3) content validity, and (4) construct validity.

the reliability in the measurement of human subjects are also more tangible, since they are not really that different from that of physical measurement. The concept of validity, on the other hand, is relatively foreign to physical measurement and a case will be made later that questions its utility in the types of research dealt with in this book as well.

PHYSICAL VERSUS NONPHYSICAL MEASUREMENT

At first glance, even the questions related to reliability may seem to have very little relevance to physical measurement. Taking the measurement of length as perhaps the most simple example from the physical domain, no one really questions the consistency with which, say, a yardstick can be used to assign numbers. It is also assumed that two reasonably intelligent people can use the instrument to obtain similar results and that there is little if any error associated with its use.

To a certain extent all this is true, due in large part to refinements made in the procedure over the years. Today, a standard exists under lock and key to which all yardsticks can be calibrated. This standard is rigidly prescribed, from the material with which it is made to the temperature at which it is kept (since length changes slightly with temperature).

A few centuries ago, this process was not nearly so precisely standardized. Then, the measurement of length was in terms of hands (spans) or other body parts (such as feet, which we still use) that (1) could alter decidedly from measurer to measurer, (2) probably were difficult even for the same measurer to apply in a consistent manner from situation to situation, and (3) were difficult to break down into fractional parts. Even with a precisely standardized yardstick, however, situational problems arise that affect the accuracy of its use. Measuring the height (or length) of a ten-year-old child, for example, is much easier to effect with a yardstick than measuring the length of an infant. The former can at least be told to stand up straight, the latter must be positioned by the measurer. The former may still stand straighter at one measuring session that another, just as the infant may be positioned in a slightly different manner by two different measurers, causing slight discrepancies. Precision too is relative. A yardstick marked off in eighths of an inch is, for most people, probably precise only to the nearest sixteenth of an inch. For many purposes, this is not nearly precise enough, hence a different measurement instrument and a different, more detailed procedure for using it is indicated.

The same situation holds for all other physical measures. The stability and precision with which they can be used to assign numbers is a function not only of the instrument itself, but also of the situations and the conditions in which it is employed. In this regard, the only real difference between physical and nonphysical measuring instruments is that the former are generally more precise and the conditions under which they can be employed are more precisely specified.

Questions that ask "How do we know the instrument is measuring what we think it is measuring?" are quite a different matter however. A researcher developing a scale designed to measure, say, attitudes toward totalitarianism is expected to address this question. After all, no one can see, touch, hear, smell, or feel an attitude, thus such nonphysical measures are considered somehow to be less objective or real. The truth of the matter is that physical attributes such as length or weight have no objective reality either. They are constructs or hypothetical attributes that have been found to be *useful* over the years *for certain purposes.* True, we have come to view most objects from their perspectives, but this is more a function of habit than it is of any scientific or epistemological imperative.

In physical measurement, then, scientists know what the measurement of length means. They do not ask if it is a valid measure, they only ask if it is relevant (for example, it is not when applied to a liquid) or a useful measure (for example, it is not when intelligence is being addressed). Since we are not as comfortable with relatively new measures such as attitudes toward totalitarianism, additional steps have traditionally been required to justify or validate their use. I believe that nonphysical measurers should take the cue supplied by their colleagues in the more established sciences and assume, in Popeye's terms, that a measure "am what it am" and concentrate more on whether or not it is useful for a specific purpose. Because this is still very definitely a minority view, however, the concept of validity as it is presently employed in the human sciences will be treated in greater detail in Chapter 12.

THE MEASUREMENT OF HUMAN SUBJECTS

There are literally tens of thousands of instruments that can be used to assign numbers to human subjects. Obviously, a book of this size cannot discuss even a fraction of them in any detail. What will be attempted is:

1. An enumeration of the major categories.
2. A presentation of a brief guide to sources of published instruments.
3. A description of different types of instrumentation.
4. An overview of different methods for collecting data.

Categories of Measures

It is difficult even to enumerate all the major categories of measures that can be applied to human subjects. Without burdening the reader with academic definitions, some of these categories are:

1. *Demographic or factual measures,* including measures of social status (for example, socioeconomic status), occupational status, personal characteristics (for example, sex, age, income), and so forth.
2. *Affective measures,* including attitudes, interests, values, self-concept, and satisfaction.
3. *Cognitive measures,* including achievement tests (which can be wide-ranging standardized versions administered to large groups of students

or teacher-made instruments specific to a given instructional unit) and measures of intelligence, creativity, curiosity, and development.
4. *Personality measures,* including projective and self-report varieties.
5. *Physiological measures,* including height, weight, blood pressure, levels or densities of various substances in the body, and many varieties of medical tests.
6. *Psychomotor or behavioral measures,* including tests of skills and performance (for example, typing speed or professional competence).

Sources of Measurement Instruments

The above categories are very general, perhaps too general to be of much real help. For each category and subcategory, there are hundreds, sometimes *thousands,* of instruments designed for specialized circumstances, purposes, and groups of people. *The Eighth Mental Measurements Yearbook,* for example, lists over 200 personality measures alone.

It is probably safe to say that, outside of achievement tests designed to assess learning of specialized instructional units or *very* specialized affective measures, published instruments exist that can be used for most research purposes. Given that the development of a satisfactory measuring instrument can be as difficult and time consuming a task as the research designed to employ it, it is definitely cost effective to devote the time necessary to locate an existing measure. It is almost an *impediment* to scientific progress to use a wide variety of instruments to measure the same constructs, since replicability and generalizability become very difficult under such circumstances.

The most direct (and probably the best) source of such instruments is found in the related literature review discussed in Chapter 2. Obviously, research employing the same variables as the study being designed had to employ some sort of measuring device to assign numbers to their subjects. If not, they are likely to cite studies that do. If one of the measures employed is not published, a call or letter to its developer will most likely result in a copy plus permission to use it. (When calling, one should not ask the researcher to return a call at his or her own expense. A self-addressed, stamped envelope may also facilitate receiving a copy of the instrument.)

When a suitable instrument is not found via the literature, a number of compilations exist. Below is a partial list compiled in part by Dr. Shirley Damrosch and Lynada Johnson. Any research librarian can probably supplement it.

Compendia and Sources of Measuring Instruments

Andrulis, R. S. *Adult Assessment: A Source Book of Tests And Measures of Human Behavior.* Springfield, IL: Charles C Thomas, 1977.
Bauer, J. D., Ackerman, P. G., and Toro, G. *Clinical Laboratory Methods,* 8th Edition. St. Louis: Mosby, 1974.
Beere, C. A. *Women and Women's Issues: A Handbook of Tests and Measurements.* San Francisco: Jossey-Bass, 1979.

Bonjean, C. M., Hill, R. J., and McElmove, S. D. *Sociological Measurement: An Inventory of Scales and Indices.* San Francisco: Chandler, 1967.

Brook, R. H. et al. *Conceptualization and Measurement of Health for Adults in the Health Insurance Study,* vol. 8. Santa Monica, Calif.: Rand, 1979.

Buros, O. K., ed. *Intelligence Tests and Reviews.* Highland Park, N.J.: Gryphon Press, 1975.

Buros, O. K., ed. *Eighth Mental Measurements Yearbook,* 8th edition. 2 vols. Highland Park, N.J.: Gryphon Press, 1978.

Buros, O. K., ed. *Personality Tests and Reviews I, II.* Highland Park, N.J.: Gryphon Press, vol. I, 1970 and vol. II, 1975.

Buros, O. K., ed., *Reading Tests and Reviews.* Highland Park, N.J.: Gryphon Press, vol. I, 1968 and vol. II, 1975.

Buros, O. K., ed. *Vocational Tests and Reviews.* Highland Park, N.J.: Gryphon Press, 1975.

Cattell, R. B., and Warburton, F. *Objective Personality and Motivation Tests: A Theoretical Introduction and Practical Compendium.* Urbana: University of Illinois Press, 1967.

Chun, K. T., Cobb, S., and French, J. R. P., Jr. *Measures for Psychological Assessment: A Guide to 3,000 Original Sources and their Applications.* Ann Arbor, Mich.: Survey Research Center Institute for Social Research, 1975.

Ciminaro, A. R., Calhoun, K. S., and Adams, H. E., eds. *Handbook of Behavioral Assessment.* New York: Wiley, 1977.

Comrey, A. L., Backer, T. E., and Glaser, E. M. *A Sourcebook for Mental Health Measures.* Los Angeles: Human Interaction Research Institute, 1973.

Cromwell, L., Weibell, F. J., and Pfeiffer, E. A. *Biomedical Instrumentation and Measurements,* 2nd edition. Englewood Cliffs, N.J.: Prentice-Hall, 1980.

Farrell, H. K., Woog, P., and Hyman, R. B. *Current Non-projective Instruments for the Mental Health Field.* New York: Atcom, 1978.

Ferris, C. *Guide to Medical Laboratory Instruments.* Boston: Little Brown, 1980.

Fomar, S. L. *Nutritional Disorders of Children: Prevention, Screening, and Follow-Up.* Washington, D.C.: DHEW, 1976, HSA 76-5612.

Geddes, L. A., and Baker, L. E. *Principles of Applied Biomedical Instrumentation.* New York: Wiley, 1975.

George, L., and Landerman, L. R. *The Meaning and Measurement of Attitudes toward Aging.* Durham: Duke University Medical Center, 1978.

Goldman, B. A., and Busch, J. C. *Directory of Unpublished Experimental Mental Measures,* 2 vols. New York: Human Sciences Press, 1974 and 1978.

Johnson, O. G., and Commarito, J. W. *Tests and Measurements in Child Development: Handbook I.* San Francisco: Jossey-Bass, 1971.

Johnson, O. G. *Tests and Measurements in Child Development: Handbook II,* 2 vols. San Francisco: Jossey-Bass, 1976.

Kane, R., and Kane, R. *Assessing the Elderly.* Toronto: Lexington Books, 1981.

Kegan, D. L. *Scales/RIQS: An Inventory of Research Instruments.* Evanston, Ill.:Technological Institute, Northwestern University, 1970. (Organizational measures.)

Lake, D. G., Miles, M. B., and Earle, R. B., Jr. *Measuring Human Behavior.* New York: Teachers College Press, 1973.

Lyerly, S. *Handbook of Psychiatric Rating Scales,* 2nd edition. Rockville, Md.: National Institute of Mental Health, 1973.

McCubbin, H. I., and Patterson, J. M. *Systematic Assessment of Family Stress, Resources, and Coping: Tools for Research, Education, and Clinical Intervention.* Family Stress and Coping Project, University of Minnesota: St. Paul, 1981.

Miller, D. C. *Handbook of Research Design and Social Measurement,* 4th edition. New York: David McKay, 1983.

Mitchell, J. V. *Tests in Print III.* Lincoln: University of Nebraska Press, 1983.

Pfeiffer, W. J., and Jones, J. E. *Instrumentation in Human Relations Training,* 2nd edition. La Jolla, Calif.: University Associates, 1976.

Price, J. L. *Handbook of Organizational Measurement.* Lexington, Mass.: Heath, 1972.

Robinson, J. P., Athanasiou, R., and Head, K. B. *Measures of Occupational Attitudes and Occupational Characteristics.* Ann Arbor: Institute for Social Research, University of Michigan, 1969.

Robinson, J. P., Rush, J. G., and Head, K. B. *Measures of Political Attitude.* Ann Arbor: Institute of Social Research, University of Michigan, 1966.

Robinson, J. P., and Shaver, P. R. *Measures of Social Psychological Attitudes.* Ann Arbor, Mich.: Survey Research Center Institute for Social Research, 1973.

Shaw, M. E., and Wright, J. M. *Scales for the Measurement of Attitudes.* New York: McGraw-Hill, 1967.

Strauss, M. A., and Brown, B. W. *Family Measurement Techniques—Abstracts of Published Instruments, 1935–1974,* Revised Edition. Minneapolis: University of Minnesota Press, 1978.

U.S. Department of Health, Education, and Welfare. *Instruments for Measuring Nursing Practice and Other Health Care Variables,* 2 vols. Hyattsville, Md, 1977.

Walker, D. K. *Socioemotional Measures for Pre-school and Kindergarten Children.* San Francisco: Jossey-Bass, 1973.

Ward, M. J., and Lindeman, C. A., eds. *Instruments for Measuring Nursing Practice and Other Health Care Variables,* 2 vols. Washington, D.C.: Government Printing Office, 1979.

Weiss, M. *Biomedical Instrumentation.* Philadelphia: Chilton, 1973.

Wylie, R. *The Self Concept: A Critical Search of Pertinent Research Literature.* Lincoln: University of Nebraska Press, 1961.

Wylie, R. *The Self Concept: A Review of Methodological Considerations and Measuring Instruments.* Lincoln: University of Nebraska Press, 1974.

Types of Instrumentation

Within each category and subcategory of measurement instruments there exists several methods of instrumentation or general devices for assigning scores to individuals. In cognitive measures, for example, where responses can be judged as correct or incorrect, the major options include the following.

1. Multiple Choice

> *Example* The first English settlement in America was located in:
> (a) Plymouth
> (b) Boston
> (c) Jamestown
> (d) Cambridge
> (e) St. Augustine

Generally, multiple-choice items constitute good discriminators among subjects. The technique also permits precise scoring, since an item (if properly written) is either answered correctly or incorrectly. Its chief disadvantage resides in the difficulty of constructing good distractor options (that is, options that people who do not know the correct answer are likely to choose). In the above example, if no one selected Boston or St. Augustine, the discriminatory power of the item as a whole would be greatly decreased to the extent that the overall proportion of subjects selecting the correct response was increased.

Recommendation   This is the procedure of choice for most cognitive tests.

2. True/False

    Example   The first English settlement in America was located in James-town.   T   F

True/False items are generally easier to write than their multiple-choice cousins and, if skillfully constructed, may function quite well. They usually do not discriminate as well among people, since they are normally *easier* than multiple-choice items and often contain cues that tip off test-wise individuals to the correct answer. Like multiple-choice items, however, there is little likelihood of scoring error.

Recommendation   Use cautiously. Use more items than would be normal for a multiple-choice test to compensate for the decreased level of difficulty and discriminatory power.

3. Fill in the blank

    Example   The first English settlement in America was located in _____.

These are especially easy items to write and generally discriminate well between people. Such tests cannot be machine scored and do permit a certain amount of scoring subjectivity (for example, a correct answer to the above question could be Virginia, 1609, an unhealthy area, and so forth).

Recommendation   Use only when multiple choice is not feasible. For certain subject matters, however (such as mathematics), it may be the preferred procedure since supplying the response via a multiple-choice format may cue the respondent to the correct answer.

4. Matching

    Example   Match the following English settlements with the religious affiliations of their settlers:

Rhode Island	Catholic
Maryland	Baptist
Jamestown	Church of England
Plymouth	Calvinism

Among this format's advantages are the ability to include a large number of items in a limited space and relative ease of construction. Disadvantages include (a) the necessity for all the items to be very close in content, (b) the fact that responses are not independent (missing one match usually necessitates missing another), and (c) the necessity for subjects to process simultaneously several bits of information.

Recommendation   Try to avoid for research purposes.

5. Recall

Example   Name the religious affiliations of the original English settlements in America.

The chief advantage of this type of item is the ease with which items are constructed. Ceiling effects (whereby the majority of the subjects get extremely high scores on the measure) are also avoided, but scoring subjectivity can be a problem.

Recommendation   Use only when the subject matter demands and then only after carefully training scorers. The difficulties involved in scoring this and the next type of test usually cost more time than is saved by the relative ease with which they are constructed.

6. Essay

Example   Describe the religious affiliations of the early English settlements.

The chief advantage of this type of item is its ease of construction.* Two different scorers seldom agree that well when assigning scores to the same essay (Coffman, 1971); thus the quality of the scores accruing from their use is usually poor.

Recommendation   Do not use for research purposes.

All of these options have different variations and all can be used satisfactorily for research purposes. All share the characteristic that the final number that

---

* Other commonly advanced advantages, such as the capacity to tap a different level of knowledge, remain largely unsubstantiated (Coffman, 1971).

they assign to an individual is a composite of several different parts or items, namely, the total number of questions answered correctly. (Even an essay exam, to be graded consistently, must contain a scoring key comprised of points or items that should be covered.) To a large extent, this characteristic differentiates cognitive, affective, psychomotor, and personality instruments from most physiological and demographic/informational measures. Body temperature, for example, consists of a single, indivisible number. Similarly, only one item is needed for someone to report his or her sex.

Even more instrumentation options exist for measures comprised of responses that cannot be judged as either correct or incorrect. Like their dichotomous (that is, correct or incorrect) counterparts, they too normally presuppose at least one composite score comprised of the summation of responses to individual items. A sample of the types of options availble for such items includes the following.

1. Bipolar Scales These are comprised of a number of statements or characteristics that the respondent rates. *Likert-type* scales are a special subset here, consisting of statements with which the respondent either agrees or disagrees, such as:

Overall I felt this instructor was an excellent teacher.

1	2	3	4	5
Strongly agree	Agree	Undecided	Disagree	Strongly disagree

Alternately, the responses can be given other anchors, such as:

Overall, how do you rate this instructor's teaching ability?

1	2	3	4	5
Excellent	Good	Satisfactory	Poor	Completely unsatisfactory

Both strategies basically result in the same type of information when summed. Other options, such as 7-point and 9-point scales, produce very similar results, as does simply requiring the respondent to mark yes or no, or true or false to a series of questions/statements. [There is some empirical evidence that 5-point scales or higher tend to give more stable results than dichotomous ones (Nunnally, 1978).]

Recommendation For most research purposes, this is the technique of choice.

2. Forced-Choice Scales Here, respondents are presented with a series of paired statements that may differ from one another only slightly along some predetermined dimension. For each pair of statements, the respondent must select the one with which he or she agrees with more, the theory being that the subtlety of the difference between the two choices will:

a. Reduce any tendency to try to please the researcher by giving desirable answers.
b. Force the respondent to put more thought and effort into the task, hence reducing any tendency to mark all 5s, say, on a 5-point scale.

A respondent's total score is normally a function of the total number of favorable (as determined a priori by judges) choices between pairs.

There is some evidence that the forced-choice technique may indeed work in these regards (Zavala, 1965). It has the disadvantages of:

a. Being very difficult to construct, given both the difficulty of coming up with good statement pairs and the fact that these pairs must be weighted by judges prior to the instrument's use to determine where each lies along the predetermined dimension being rated.
b. Being tedious to fill out.

An example of a forced-choice instrument assessing racial prejudices might include instructions for the respondent to select one statement within each of the following preweighted sets of pairs:

a. People should be allowed to refuse to sell their houses to blacks if they choose.
b. People should be allowed to send their children to private, noninte-grated schools if they choose.

a. Blacks are presently assured the right to vote in all states.
b. Blacks should be assured proportional representation through redistricting if necessary.

Recommendation When there is reason to suspect that bipolar rating scales may not yield sufficiently high-quality data, this is a recommended strategy. If the scale must be constructed, the beginning researcher should definitely seek expert help.

3. Rank Ordering Another technique often used (too often in my opinion) to elicit responses to noncognitive items is to ask subjects to rank a series of questions, items, or statements from lowest to highest along some specified dimension. Thus, given a series of 20 items, for example, each will be assigned a unique number from 1 to 20 based on their perceived ordering.

Disadvantages of this procedure are:

a. A total score cannot be derived, since all responses will add up to the same number.
b. It is difficult for respondents to consider all the items simultaneously, especially if there is a large number of them.
c. The range or variation among items is artificially inflated, thus a few

divergent responses can influence the overall results to a greater extent than any other technique discussed here.*

The single advantage of rank-ordered items lies in the intuitive appeal of being able to report that item *C*, say, was considered the single most important (or whatever other dimension the items were ranked upon), item *D* the second, and so forth. Actually, the same effect can be obtained by rating the items on a 5-point bipolar scale, computing mean ratings for each item based on the research sample, and then rank ordering the means.

Recommendation   Do not use. Rank order mean ratings instead, thus combining the intuitive advantages of ranks with the statistical advantages of ratings.

4. The Q-Sort   This is a relatively unique method of ordering a large set of items (perhaps between 50 and 100) in such a way that respondents are forced to discriminate between them. Respondents are given the items written out on individual cards and asked to sort them into individual piles with predetermined numbers of cards in each pile. Sixty items might be distributed as follows:

PILES:	Least important	*1*	*2*	*3*	*4*	*5*	*6*	*7*	*8*	*9*	Most important
NUMBER OF ITEMS PER PILE:		1	3	7	11	16	11	7	3	1	

Disadvantages of the technique are that:

a. It is time consuming.
b. The procedure must be explained carefully to respondents who may have never used it before.
c. It cannot be used to derive a total score, since the sum of each person's item weights will yield the same figure (subscores are still possible of course).
d. It requires more items than are normally available (or necessary) for any single topic.

On the positive side, Q-sort methodology probably does result in superior discrimination among items, since subjects do not have the option of responding the same way to large numbers of items. When time is not a consideration, subjects sometimes enjoy the novelty of this methodology as well.

Recommendation   Use only when time permits and when the added discriminatory potential of the technique is needed.

* If 40 entities are rank ordered, for example, the difference between the most and least favored will be 39 units. If these same entities were rated on a 5-point scale, the most and least favored could differ only by four points.

Although there are other instrumentation options for self-report, paper-and-pencil measures, these are the most commonly employed. It is probably safe to say that the most important and interesting research questions cannot be addressed solely by analyzing the marks respondents make on a piece of paper. The reason that such measures are used so extensively in human subjects research is probably due to the relative ease with which the data can be collected. Thus, while a medical continuing education program may be designed to change a specific practice or behavior, program evaluators are most likely to assess the effectiveness of the program by using cognitive or affective paper-and-pencil measures administered at the end of the course due to the relative ease with which such data can be collected. An administrative intervention designed to improve the quality of psychotherapy received by patients might be best assessed via its effect on actual improvement in patients' conditions, but would most likely be assessed via patients' *satisfaction* with the treatment they received, since such a measure can be administered en masse within a 20-minute time period.

In some cases there is no substitute for such practices simply because researchers have no viable options. In many instances, however, more veridical *outcome* measures can be devised with a little creativity. Therefore, I counsel beginning researchers to at least consider the possibility of using alternative types of measures. Examples of such techniques include the following.

1. Checklist Direct observation of behavior is quite possibly the most difficult type of data to collect. Certainly, its collection is the most labor intensive, often requiring the observer's presence at a clinical site for an extended period of time. It also requires a great deal of preparation, since interobserver consensus on the assignment of numbers to constantly moving objects is not easily obtained. Extensive pilot work is also required, beginning with the preparation of a checklist by which the presence, absence, duration, intensity, or quality of a behavior (or set of behaviors) can be recorded in a systematic fashion.

Once constructed, observers are typically trained in the checklist's use and given practice observations. This is done both to refine the checklist and to document agreements and disagreements among different observers recording the same behaviors (see the *interrater reliability* discussion in Chapter 11). Obviously, this is a much more involved procedure than the self-report, paper-and-pencil measures discussed above. Despite the difficulties involved, there are occasions when no acceptable substitute for direct observation of behavior or performance exists. Though considerable, these difficulties can be overcome through extensive preparation and constant monitoring of the observational process.

Recommendation When appropriate, use them. Special attention should be paid to interrater reliability issues (see the next chapter) prior to its final use in the study. Where possible, previously employed, published observational instruments should be used. The beginning researcher would definitely benefit from access to an individual who is experienced in direct observational research.

2. Physiological Measures Since, with the exception of some of the vital signs (for example, blood pressure, heart rate, temperature), dimensional assessments (such as height and weight), and sensory or perceptual measures (such as visual acuity or tonal discriminations), special expertise (and sometimes even licensure) is needed for the administration and interpretation of many physiological measures, this type of dependent variable will not be discussed in this book, although everything said about reliability and validity in the next two chapters are just as applicable to the numbers assigned by, say, a laboratory test as they are to a 5-point Likert scale.

Recommendation When appropriate, and when the requisite expertise exists, use them. Do not consider such measures necessarily more objective or valid, however, since physiological indicators are subject to the same constraints as other types of measures.

There are many, many additional methods of assigning numbers to human attributes and reactions than have been mentioned in this brief overview, such as logs (whereby people record their own behaviors over a period of time), scenarios (which consist of brief stories to which the reader is asked to respond in certain ways), and unobtrusive measures (such as systematically observing the way discharged psychiatric patients dress at follow-up interviews as one indicator of their posttreatment adjustment [see Webb, Campbell, Schwatz, & Sachrest (1972) for a more thorough discussion of unobtrusive measures]. The actual form that an instrument takes is not as important as the consistency with which it assigns numbers to individuals or the usefulness of those numbers for the empirical purposes for which they are employed. After a brief overview of some of the more common data-collection procedures, these two crucial issues will be examined for all types of instrumentation.

DATA-COLLECTION PROCEDURES

The most common way to collect the data required for an empirical study is either:

1. To convene subjects in a convenient location and administer the measuring instruments (usually paper and pencil) en masse.
2. To administer the instruments as subjects become available (which is usually the way in which physiological or direct observational techniques must be employed).

There are occasions, however, when subjects are either not physically available for testing or when the data are collected routinely by nonresearch personnel for nonresearch purposes. In the first case, the researcher must go to the subject, whether in person or via the telephone or mail. In the second instance, the subjects' records must be culled for the necessary information.

1. The Personal Interview Although quite costly, actually going to the subject's home and conducting an in-depth interview probably results in the highest-quality data obtainable in survey research. It affords a high response rate (that is, fewer people refusing to be interviewed), allows more data to be collected (since it is easier to hold the respondent's attention once the interviewer's foot is in the door), and permits probing/follow-up questions for more in-depth information. Its disadvantages are primarily economic and tactical (for example, often a single interviewer can reach no more than two respondents per day and occasionally these respondents live in unsafe areas).

Recommendation Employ only when necessary. If other means for collecting the same data exist, consider using them (especially if resources are limited). Use experienced interviewers when possible. When not, ensure sufficient practice and training prior to the final data collection.

2. The Telephone Interview This is the method most commonly employed by professional pollsters because of its speed, convenience, and relative economy. A skilled interviewer can also elicit a reasonable response rate, perhaps because people have reasonably polite telephone etiquette and have difficulty saying no to a persistent caller. The number of questions that can be asked is more restricted than the personal interview and since rapport is more difficult to establish, highly sensitive information is difficult to obtain. When answers are not clear, probing is still possible. (The population to which results can be generalized is, of course, limited to those people who have a telephone.)

Recommendation Probably acceptable for most survey purposes. Again, experienced interviewers are helpful and practice/training is necessary.

3. Mailed Questionnaires Practically anything that can be asked in person or over the telephone can also be asked in written form via a questionnaire, although the investigator must be satisfied with the written responses obtained, since follow-up questions (or probing) are usually not possible. The chief disadvantage of mailed questionnaires resides in the low response rates normally obtained. Even when self-addressed, stamped envelopes and follow-up letters are employed, return rates typically fall in the 40 to 60 percent range (Miller, 1983). For respondents who receive a great deal of mail or who are very busy (such as doctors or business executives), the return rate can be drastically lower (Fottler, 1981; Miller, 1975). To the extent that it is important to generalize to the entire population from which the sample was drawn, low response rates can be extremely problematic given the fact that nonrespondents may be quite different from respondents. The chief advantages of the mailed questionnaire lie in its relatively low cost (at least with respect to interviewer time) and the number of respondents that can be surveyed.

Recommendation This is not a particularly good procedure for purely descriptive studies, due to the response rate problem. If the main purpose of the study is correlational in nature, then moderate response rates may be less serious. When other methods are available, they should be used. When not, all available means should be taken to increase the response rate (such as keeping the questionnaire as brief as possible and giving it as professional an appearance as possible).

4. Record Reviews The final data-collection procedure that will be discussed here involves the abstracting of data that were not necessarily generated for research purposes. Such data can be used either prospectively (for example, when the researcher institutes an intervention but uses data routinely collected by other people to assess its effect) or retrospectively (when past records are employed to assess relationships).

Hospitals, schools, clinics, governmental agencies, indeed almost all societal institutions, maintain records on their clients. These records thus constitute a fertile source of research data. Their major problems are incompleteness and inaccuracy, since it is very rare for entries to be checked systematically. Busy clinicians thus often fail to complete entire sections of a record (or do so in such a sketchy, offhanded manner as to make them almost useless) that have little relevance to them but which may be crucial to a discrete research study.

If a study is prospective in nature, administrative support may result in better quality data being made available for the duration of a particular study. Generally speaking, however, relying on others to collect one's data is a hazardous enterprise and should be monitored as closely as possible. On the positive side, though, clinical records often contain some of the most important outcome data available to researchers.

Recommendation Use when comparable data are not available from other sources. Monitor the abstracting of these data carefully, since inaccuracies and incompleteness here can be as serious as in the original recording of the data.

DESIGNING/SELECTING A DATA-COLLECTION INSTRUMENT

Regardless of the actual procedure employed, a written, data-collection instrument must either be selected or designed prior to the conduct of any study not employing exclusively physiological measures. Even when records are reviewed or when respondents are interviewed personally, the specific answers to be gleaned (or questions to be asked) are written out in questionnaire form. The fact that the research subjects may never actually see this form (although in most cases they do) does not negate the paramount importance of its careful design.

There is such a staggering variety of nonphysiologically oriented data-collection instruments employed in research involving human subjects that specific suggestions regarding the design of each cannot be given in a book of this size. There are some general rules that apply to all types of data collection, however, whether the instruments employed are developed specifically for the study at hand or are selected from preexisting options (which is normally recommended). Some of these include the following.

Do Not Collect More Information Than Is Needed

Adding items to a questionnaire is a pervasive temptation in research. After all, the argument goes, "who knows what will turn up in the data?" The problem with this procedure is that the more that is required of subjects, the lower will be the response/participation rate. It is also a truism that very little of importance ever turns up in an empirical fishing expedition. The researcher is therefore well advised to cut out as many irrelevant questions as possible.

This dictum applies even to the standard demographic information (for example, marital status, religion) routinely collected in most studies. My impression is that such variables are seldom related to anything, and even when they are, the relationships seldom are of much practical or theoretical import. The favorite argument that they are useful in describing the sample has little validity either if norms do not exist on the population from which the sample is drawn or if said information is not related to the variables of interest.

A good procedure for reducing the amount of information collected in a questionnaire or other device is to go through the form item by item, asking oneself exactly what purpose each item will serve. Simply being interesting is not reason enough for inclusion. An attempt should also be made to visualize how the numbers that will result from responses to a particular item will be handled statistically. If they are to be used descriptively, will other researchers be interested in this description? If they are to be correlated to other variables, is a statistically significant relationship likely? If so, will it have any practical or theoretical import? (Defending every piece of data to be collected to a skeptical colleague playing the role of devil's advocate is an excellent item reduction technique.)

A final piece of advice in the same vein: no single study can resolve all the unanswered questions in an area. If a study answers even one question adequately, it is a truly exemplary piece of research. It is always better to address one issue soundly than several superficially.

Strive for Clarity and Simplicity

If the data-collection instrument contains questions to be asked of people, *make sure the wording is clear and unambiguous.* This is perhaps the single most important rule in measurement. If a written questionnaire is to be employed, care should be taken that the vocabulary used is consonant with the targeted respondents' reading levels. Unless the instrument in question has been successfully used before with similar subjects, there is really no substitute for pilot testing the procedure on a number of typical respondents with specific instructions for them to identify items that they find confusing. Though they are no substitute, knowledgeable colleagues can be helpful in this regard as well.

If subjects do not fully understand what the researcher is asking of them, a measuring instrument is not likely to be either reliable or valid.

Use Clear, Explicit Instructions

No assumptions should be made regarding respondents' previous experience with data-collection instruments. Include instructions that explicitly (and briefly) tell them exactly how to fill out (or otherwise answer) each section of the instrument, including what to do if they do not know the answer to an item or if it is not applicable to them.

Design the Response Options as Carefully as the Item Stems Themselves

It is important to remember that numbers will be assigned to most questions contained in a measuring instrument designed for empirical research use. It is the responses themselves (for example, disagree/agree, yes/no) that are used in this process, so an excellently conceived question can be useless if the answer is not in a usable form or is itself allowed to be ambiguous.

Whenever possible, open-ended questions whose answers must later be classified or ordered should be avoided. An exception to this rule is when open-ended responses can be sufficiently cued. For example, the desired response for the following question is not at all ambiguous:

How many hours of sleep do you get in a typical night? _____ hours

Further, it is more sensitive statistically than the typical practice of arbitrarily supplying the respondent with categories (for example: __ less than 4 hours, __ 4–6 hours, __ 6–8 hours, __ 8–10 hours, __ over 10 hours).

Finally, all the possible responses and their meanings for a given item should be considered in advance. At first glance, for example, the following item would appear quite straightforward.

Were the instructor's explanations clear and his/her presentations interesting? yes no

A yes response is indeed quite unambiguous. Consider the possible meanings of no on the other hand. It could indicate that the instructor's explanations were unclear and her/his presentation was uninteresting. What about the possibility, however, of clear explanations couched in a most boring lecture? This question would best be reformulated as two separate items.

Make Responding to the Measuring Instrument as Attractive as Possible

When soliciting participation, explain the importance of the study. (If a persuasive case cannot be made here, then perhaps the study's importance is questionable.) Prospective respondents should be given a realistic appraisal of the amount of time that will be required of them. Arriving at such an estimate in advance via a pilot study may also serve as an impetus to streamline the measurement process.

Finally, when possible, make responses anonymous and underline this fact for prospective respondents. When this is not feasible, steps should be taken to assure them that their responses will at least be confidential.

Make Sure the Final Product Looks Professional

Any materials received by respondents should be attractively printed and pack-aged. Questionnaires should have an uncluttered look. (It is better to reduce the size of the print, as long as small children or the elderly are not involved, than to have practically no margins or spaces between items.) When possible, use a typewriter or printer that employs metal impressions and nonrenewable carbon ribbons. Finally, do not go to all of this trouble and then duplicate the finished product on a substandard photocopier. The extra expense of offset printing would be worthwhile in such circumstances.

LEVELS OF MEASUREMENT

To this point a very general overview of the measurement process has been presented, along with some very general suggestions for facilitating that process. The next two chapters will provide more specific information on the technical evaluation of the quality of the numbers assigned to human subjects via these procedures.

Prior to this discussion some additional consideration of the statistical uses to which said numbers can be put is probably in order. The most widely used taxonomy is undoubtedly S. S. Stevens's (1946) formulation of the con-cept of scales or *levels of measurement.*

According to Stevens, all numbers generated by measuring instruments can be placed into one of four hierarchical categories:

1. *Nominal.* Here the numbers serve only as category *names.* If a survey asked respondents what type of car they owned, each different model could be arbitrarily assigned a unique number for convenience. For example, Rolls Royce could be listed as 1, Chevrolet as 2, and Oldsmobile as 3. The fact that Chevrolets were coded as 2 and Oldsmobile as 3 did not mean that one was less than, greater than, before, or after the other. The numbers serve as nothing more than labels and could be completely reshuffled (for example, Oldsmobile = 1, Chevrolet = 2, and Rolls Royce = 3) with no data analysis implications at all.

2. *Ordinal.* As the term implies, such numbers can be used to designate an ordering along some dimension (such as from less to more, from small to large, from sooner to later, and so forth). If a group of people were asked to rank order a list of three cars that they would most like to own, the results might indicate that their first choice was a Rolls Royce, their second choice was an Oldsmobile, and their third choice a Chevrolet. For analysis purposes, Rolls Royce could be assigned the number 1 to indicate that it was indeed the first choice, Oldsmobile a 2, and Chevrolet a 3. These particular numbers are not interchangeable.* A 2 means something in relation to a 3: it means that people would prefer to own an Oldsmobile over a Chevrolet.

3. *Interval.* Now the distinctions become a bit more subtle. Returning to the ordinal example, it cannot be assumed from the way in which our three numbers were assigned that people prefer a Rolls Royce to an Oldsmobile to the same degree that they prefer an Oldsmobile over a Chevrolet. This is true even though the numerical difference between the two choices is identical (that is, $2 - 1 = 1$ and $3 - 2 = 1$). It may be, in fact it is almost a certainty, that people would *greatly* prefer a Rolls Royce to an Oldsmobile while the relative intensity of their preference for an Oldsmobile over a Chevrolet would be much less. In other words, the *intervals* on this little scale are not the same; the relative distance from 1 to 2 is probably much greater than from 2 to 3.

Suppose, on the other hand, that respondents had been asked to rate the cars on a scale from 1 to 100 where 1 was defined as the object that they would least want to own and 100 as the object they would most want to own. Suppose further that the average (or mean) rating for each car was then computed and those mean ratings were substituted for the above-mentioned ranks. If the Rolls Royce were rated 72.3, the Oldsmobile 32.5, and the Chevrolet 24.1, the relative intensity of people's preferences would be far better represented than the numbers 1 through 3. It still would not be safe to say that a Rolls Royce was three times as desirable as a Chevrolet (that is, $24.1 \times 3 = 72.3$) because we don't know enough about this 100-point scale for that. However, we can safely say that the difference between people's preference for a Rolls Royce and a Oldsmobile is considerably greater than the difference between an Oldsmobile and a Chevrolet. We can also make the assumption that the intervals between the points on this scale are *approximately* the same.

The majority of the measurements used for human subjects fall in this category. That is, their scales *aspire* to equal-sized intervals. The difference between a score on a 100-item mathematics achievement test of 90 and one of 95 could be considered *approximately* the same as the difference between scores of 50 and 55. There is no good reason to believe that these intervals are *exactly* the same, since some items may be much more difficult than others (and thus indicative of much more sophisticated mathematical achievement), but there is also little reason to care if they are *slightly* off.

4. *Ratio.* Ratio scales have two unique characteristics. The intervals between points can be demonstrated to be precisely the same *and* the scale has a conceptually meaningful zero point. If the average retail cost of our three cars were of interest, the resulting dollar values would constitute a ratio scale. If the average price for a Rolls Royce was $104,000, an Oldsmobile cost $12,400, and a Chevrolet $10,400, very precise comparisons between the three values could

---

* Although it doesn't really matter whether their order runs from high to low or low to high.

be made. Here the Rolls Royce could be said to cost exactly ten times as much as a Chevrolet. A few physiological measures probably qualify as ratio scales. A person who weighs 200 pounds, for example, weighs exactly twice as much as someone who weighs 100 pounds. Furthermore, a difference of 1 pound is the same regardless of where it occurs on the scale. (Whether an absolute zero makes sense is questionable, since no one could weigh absolutely nothing, but it at least has some kind of abstract meaning.)

The distinctions among these four scales would have no real significance if it were not for the position taken by some methodologists that the more powerful and useful statistical procedures (for example, the Pearson r, analysis of variance, multiple regression) can only be appropriately used for measures that assign numbers that demonstratably meet the criteria of interval or ratio scales. All other numbers, this position maintains, must be analyzed via a category of procedures classified as nonparametric statistics (for example, chi-square, rank-order correlation coefficients, median tests).

From a strictly logical point of view, this would preclude just about all nonphysical measures from being subjected to the more powerful statistical techniques, since it is very difficult to demonstrate absolute equality of intervals for such scales. This untenable state of affairs has been avoided by traditionally assuming that certain scales (for example, cognitive tests, personality inventories, affective scales) are interval enough, while others (for example, single-item Likert scales) have been designated as more ordinal than interval.

As discussed in Chapter 5, I believe that parametric statistics may be used with a clear conscience for any numbers for which an arithmetic mean makes sense and that this dictum really only excludes nondichotomous nominal measures.* Certainly this is not a unanimous opinion in empirical research, however, hence the best course of action for the beginning researcher is probably to adopt the most commonly employed practice in his or her own discipline.

SUMMARY

The most crucial consideration in the measurement process is the selection of an important and appropriate criterion or dependent variable. Once selected, the measurement procedure used to assign numbers to that attribute or reaction is normally evaluated with respect to its reliability (that is, are the numbers assigned in a stable, consistent, and/or precise manner) and validity (that is, do the assigned numbers actually measure the desired attribute or reaction).

These issues are basically common to all types of measurement, physical and nonphysical. There are a great many categories of measures appropriate to human subjects and even more sources of measurement instruments. Within

---

* Actually, there is an exception even to this nonrestrictive rule. A nondichotomous nominal variable can be recoded as a series of dichotomous values and used in procedures such as multiple regression. (This is called dummy coding, and in the example of our three cars, the overall variable of type of car could be recoded to three separate dichotomous variables: Rolls Royce—yes/no; Oldsmobile—yes/no; Chevrolet—yes/no.)

each category, several instrumentation options also exist, making the design or selection of a data-collection instrument relatively complex.

General guidelines for facilitating this test include:

1. Collecting only necessary information from subjects.
2. Striving for clarity, simplicity and explicitness in the measurement process.
3. Making responding as attractive to subjects as possible.

REFERENCES

Coffman, W. E. "Essay Examinations," in R. L. Thorndike, ed. *Educational Measurement.* Washington, D.C.: American Council on Education, 1971.
Fottler, M. D. Manpower utilization and task delegation: present patterns and future potential of physicians' practices. *Evaluation and the Health Professions,* 1981, *4,* 365–384.
Martuza, V. R. *Applying Norm-Referenced and Criterion-Referenced Measurement in Education.* Boston: Allyn and Bacon, 1977.
Miller, D. C. *Handbook of Research Design and Social Measurement.* New York: Longman, 1983 (pp. 102–106).
Miller, D. C. *Leadership and Power in the Bos-Wash Megalopolis.* New York: Wiley, 1975 (p. 380).
Nunnally, J. M. *Psychometric Theory.* New York: McGraw-Hill, 1978.
Osgood, C. E., Suci, G. J., and Tannenbaum, P. H. *The Measurement of Meaning.* Urbana: University of Illinois Press, 1957.
Stevens, S. S. On the theory of scales and measurement. *Science,* 1946, *103,* 677–680.
Webb, E. E. et al. *Unobtrusive Measures: Nonreaction Research in the Social Sciences.* Chicago: Rand McNally, 1966.
Zavala, A. Development of the forced-choice rating scale technique. *Psychological Bulletin,* 1965, *63,* 117–124.

chapter 11

Reliability

It is now time to consider the most fundamental concept in measurement: *error.* No matter how carefully a measuring instrument is constructed, be it yardstick, thermometer, or rating scale, it will have built-in limitations. A ruler marked off in centimeters, for example, can hardly be expected to be accurate to the nearest millimeter. A scale calibrated in pounds would not be accurate for the determination of ounces. Similarly, no measurer is perfect either. Given enough opportunities, everyone occasionally makes mistakes. Given enough different people performing a measurement, individual differences will contribute to error.

The problem with the cognitive, affective, psychomotor, perceptual, and psychosocial measures used in empirical research involving human subjects is that the error involved is both greater and harder to conceptualize than it is in physical measurement. Fortunately, however, measurement theory is so far advanced that this error can be estimated quite accurately. The first step in understanding how this feat is accomplished involves understanding the concept of *reliability.*

Perhaps the easiest way to achieve such an understanding remains the classical compartmentalization of every score or number assigned to a human attribute into two elements: a *true score,* which represents the true measurement of an object (or the true amount of a given attribute possessed by a person *sans* any error at all) and an *error* score, which is comprised of nothing but random noise emanating from human or instrumental deficiencies.

No one ever knows either of these two elements. Fortunately, reliability theory has given us the means of estimating both. If the actual score assigned by a measuring instrument is comprised of both an error and an errorless component, it should also follow that *the observed variation* (or variance) *in a set of scores is also comprised of true variation* (that is, differences between scores due to real individual differences on the attribute being assessed) *and variation due to error. Reliability,* as a matter of fact, *is defined as the proportion of true variation that exists in the actually observed variation in a set of scores:*

$$\text{Reliability} = \frac{\text{true variance*}}{\text{total variance}}$$

The problem with this definition, of course, resides in the fact that no one knows how much of the observed variance in a set of scores is due to true variations between people and how much is due to deficiences in the measurement process. However, it is often extremely important for a researcher to be able to estimate the amount of error residing in the measurement of a dependent variable. *If a measure is sufficiently unreliable,* for example, *there is no possible way* (other than by chance alone) *that any sort of statistically significant relationship or difference with that measure can be documented.* What this means, in effect, is that *the results of a study employing an unreliable measure are themselves unreliable.*† From a less extreme (and more likely) perspective, this means that studies employing dependent variables possessing substantial error components suffer loss of statistical power (which basically can only be compensated for by using larger sample sizes).

It therefore follows that it is extremely important to be able to estimate the error component involved in the measurement of a study's variables. Fortunately, this can be done in a number of ways, as illustrated by the following questions that *can* be answered and that, taken together, illustrate the multifaceted concept called reliability:

1. *Alternate forms reliability.* Would the same group of respondents score similarly on two equivalent forms of the same measure?
2. *Internal consistency.* Would the same group of respondents score similarly on two *parts* of the same measure?
3. *Test-retest reliability.* Would the same group of respondents score similarly on the same measure at two different points in time?
4. *Interrater reliability.* Would two different scorers assign the same group of respondents similar scores on the same instrument?
5. *Intrarater reliability.* Does the same scorer assign scores in a consistent fashion?

These five questions are important and deserve some thought. The first thing that should be clear is that reliability is not a unitary concept and, thus,

---

* Note that this book deals only with the reliability of measures for which the mean and the standard deviation (or variance) are appropriate descriptions. For criterion referenced measures involving mastery/nonmastery decisions, see Martuza (1977).

† Strictly speaking, reliability (and validity) relate to the scores assigned by measuring instruments rather than to the instruments themselves. For ease of exposition, ignore this definitional distinction.

short and simple definitions are not especially helpful. The first two questions, for example, address *equivalency* of instruments and/or items designed to measure the same constructs. Test-retest reliability addresses the *stability* (Cronbach, 1951) of a measure rather than equivalency between instruments or parts of instruments. Questions four and five address the consistency of scoring itself, which in some ways is a completely separate issue from those raised by the first three questions.

MEASURES INVOLVING SINGLE VERSUS MULTIPLE COMPONENTS (OR ITEMS)

Although there are many ways to categorize measures, the only two of any real relevance to our consideration of reliability and validity are whether or not:

1. The mean and standard deviation are appropriate descriptions of the numbers a measure assigns.
2. The numbers so assigned are indivisible or are composites of some sort.

The first point has already been discussed; basically, this book is only concerned with measures that assign numbers for which the mean and standard deviation are appropriate.* The second point deserves some additional explanation.

Measures of attitudes, personality, knowledge, intelligence, achievement, and aptitude are usually (but not always) composed of multiple parts or items. Most paper-and-pencil measures, in fact, employ composite scores of some sort. Measures addressing physiological, perceptual, performance, or behavioral attributes are more likely to be based on a single, indivisible score (e.g., body temperature or typing speed).

From a measurement perspective, the only practical difference between measures based on composites and those based on a single, indivisible number is the type of reliability and validity coefficients that are relevant to each. All five reliability questions, for example, could theoretically be applied to a composite measure. For a measure that cannot be broken into smaller units, however, alternate forms reliability or a coefficient of internal consistency do not apply. Test-retest, interrater, or intrarater reliabilities, on the other hand, may be quite appropriate. [Similar distinctions also apply for validity as well, since content validity (see Chapter 12) has no meaning for anything but composite measures.]

The reader is therefore requested to keep this basic distinction between composite and indivisible scores in mind as this and the next chapter are studied. It should also be mentioned that terms such as tests, scores, and items used in these chapters must be interpreted generically, rather than literally

---

* This in effect excludes criterion referenced measures (see Martuza, 1977 for a description of appropriate reliability and validity indices).

(taking a person's body temperature, for example, is a form of *testing* while the resulting temperature is visualized as a score from a purely measurement perspective).

THE UNIT OF ANALYSIS

One further preliminary issue must be reemphasized prior to discussing the five reliability-related questions. Both reliability and validity coefficients are computed on the scores (generically defined) that are actually subjected to statistical analysis (see Chapters 13 to 16).

Thus, if measure X possesses five subscores and if these subscores are analyzed separately, then reliability and validity must be considered for each separately. If the subscales are summed and analyzed only as a total score, however, then reliability and validity need to be considered only for the total score. If both subscores and a total score are considered at some point, then everything discussed concerning reliability and validity is relevant for both subscores and the total score. The reader should keep this fact in mind, since for ease of exposition the discussion that follows in this and the next chapter will generally be presented in terms of a single score.

ALTERNATE FORMS RELIABILITY

This type of reliability is seldom used in research because of the difficulty of constructing two versions of the same test with different, but identically functioning, items. Although difficult, the mechanics behind this construction are quite straightforward:

1. All the possible items that measure a given construct, attribute, or domain are identified.
2. These items are then administered to a sample of subjects representative of the ones that will actually be used in the study.
3. Items are weeded out that are too difficult, too easy, or that do not correlate with the total score (see Increasing the Instrument's Homogeneity below).
4. Those items that remain are rank ordered with respect to difficulty* and randomly assigned in pairs to two alternate forms (using the same procedure as when subjects are randomly assigned to groups in the randomized-matched-block model).

This procedure results in two almost identical forms of the same test *if* the above steps are carried out carefully with a reasonably large sample of both subjects and items. The two forms will have almost identical means and standard deviations. They should also correlate very highly with one another *if* the items measure anything consistently, since there is no way the two forms could measure different things given the way in which they were constructed. It is this

---

* And often stratified according to content.

correlation, in fact, that constitutes the alternate forms reliability of the measure in question. It is obtained by administering both forms of the test to a second sample of subjects and correlating the two sets of scores via the classic correlation model as illustrated by the following hypothetical data set.

	Form A	Form B
S_1	42	40
S_2	58	57
S_3	49	49
.	.	.
.	.	.
.	.	.
S_{30}	24	24

If the measure in question does indeed assign scores consistently to subjects, then one would certainly expect subjects who scored high on form A also to score high on form B and subjects who scored low on form A to score low on form B. This it will be remembered is exactly what the Pearson r assesses, thus in this special instance the Pearson r *is* the reliability coefficient.

The theory here is quite straightforward. There are two types of variation in the two sets of scores above, true variance and error variance. Since error variance is random, error will cause nonsystematic* fluctuation between any given subject's score on form A and form B, which will in turn lower the correlation (hence the reliability) coefficient. The only way, therefore, in which a high correlation coefficient can be obtained between the two sets of scores is for there to be very little error (nonsystematic variation) involved. The less the error, the higher the reliability. The more error, the lower the reliability.

However, reliability coefficients are interpreted somewhat differently from simple Pearson correlation coefficients. In the first place, reliability coefficients are visualized as ranging only from 0 to 1.00. Negative reliabilities are thus not defined. If a negative r were obtained (and this is *extremely* unlikely), the reliability would simply be reported as zero. Second, statistical significance has no real meaning for a reliability coefficient. The only thing of significance is its absolute size: the closer to 1.00 the better. Finally, reliability coefficients are never squared. They are interpreted directly. A reliability coefficient of .88, for example, is interpreted as indicating that 88 percent of the variance of the measure is systematic and 12 percent is due to error (or unreliability).

Advantages and Disadvantages of Alternate Forms Reliability

Most measurement theorists believe that alternate forms reliability gives a less inflated estimate of the true reliability of a measure than the other techniques

---

* Note the word nonsystematic. If the mean for form A were slightly higher than for form B, for example, this would not in itself affect the correlation coefficient (and hence the reliability), because such an artifact would be *systematic*. A constant added to one set of scores will not affect a correlation coefficient.

that will be discussed in this chapter. The construction of two truly equivalent forms of the same test is an extremely time-consuming process, however, and since the assessment of reliability is usually tangential to the primary objectives of most studies, the technique is seldom employed in research. Instead, alternate forms reliability is more likely to be reported for widely used standardized tests where two (or more) versions can be helpful in preventing:

1. Respondents from improving their scores on a second testing.
2. Items from being remembered and shared with other test takers.
3. The specific contents of a test from being taught.

A researcher is therefore most likely to encounter alternate forms reliability as a characteristic of a published measure. In this sense, it is a perfectly acceptable index if the sample on which the reliability coefficient was computed is *roughly* comparable to the population from which the research sample will be drawn.

Recommendation Impractical for most research purposes.

INTERNAL CONSISTENCY

The truth of the matter is that alternate forms reliability is far too unwieldy to be of much practical use to a researcher attempting to do anything other than construct a measuring instrument. Even when it has already been computed, as with preconstructed, standardized tests, it is often a good idea for researchers to report how reliably their measures functioned for the actual research samples employed under the specific research conditions.

What is obviously needed, then, is a more practical form of reliability. Fortunately one exists, based on a variation of the alternate forms logic. Here, instead of constructing two parallel forms of the same test, a single test is administered to a single group of subjects. What in effect happens, then, is that the single test is treated as though it is really two separate forms with a correlation coefficient being computed between the two.

The logic still holds. If we define all the odd items, say, as form A and the even items as form B, would not a correlation coefficient computed between the two forms be an estimate of the measure's reliability? Would not random error variance still cause the correlation coefficient to be lower?

The answer to both questions is yes with one qualification, and that is since the test has been split in half (hence the term *split-half reliability*), the resulting estimate is for a shorter version of the real measure (which is forms A and B combined). Since the systematic variance in a test tends to accumulate faster than error (or random) variance as items are added, longer tests tend to be more reliable than shorter ones. The correlation computed between two halves of the same test must therefore be corrected in some way before it can be used as an estimate for the combined total.

A very handy little formula, called the Spearman-Brown formula for correcting a split-half correlation coefficient (after its originators), exists for doing this:

$$\text{Rel}' = \frac{2r_{ab}}{1 + r_{ab}} \qquad (11\text{-}1)$$

where Rel' = the estimated reliability coefficient of the combined measure
          r_{ab} = the correlation between the two halves of the measure

To illustrate how a split-half reliability coefficient might be computed, let us suppose that a 30-item test of some sort has been administered to a sample of 30 subjects. Let us further suppose that the responses to these 30 items are normally added up to achieve a total score. The researcher might then divide the test into two halves, one consisting of the even-numbered items and one the odd items. Two subscores would be computed for each half for each subject, producing the following correlational model:

	Form A (items 1 + 3 + 5 + $\cdots$ + 29)	Form B (items 2 + 4 + 6 + $\cdots$ + 30)
S_1	12	14
S_2	8	8
S_3	15	14
.	.	.
.	.	.
.	.	.
S_{30}	4	4

If the correlation coefficient between the two halves was found to be .70, this value would be substituted into Equation 11-1 as follows:

$$\text{Rel}' = \frac{2 \times .70}{1 + .70}$$

$$= \frac{1.40}{1.70}$$

$$= .82$$

Thus, the split-half reliability of the total measure would be estimated to be 0.82 instead of .70.

There was a time when this type of reliability was probably the most common form reported in the literature. It does have one logical flaw, however, and that is the arbitrariness of splitting a test into only two parts when there are so many other possible ways of doing so. After recognizing this problem, Lee J. Cronbach (1951) developed an index called *coefficient alpha,* which today is the most commonly used reliability coefficient for multiple-item measures that can only be administered once. It is conceptually appealing because it can be viewed as an average of all the possible split-half reliabilities that can be computed for a given measure. It is also computationally quite simple, although most researchers use the computer to derive it. Basically, all that is needed is the variance of the total measure plus the variances of each individual item. These values can then be plugged into the coefficient alpha* formula:

$$\text{Alpha} = \frac{\text{no. of items in the test}}{\text{no. of items in the test} - 1} \times \left(1 - \frac{\Sigma \text{ individual item variances}}{\text{total variance}}\right)$$

$$(11\text{-}2)$$

To illustrate how this formula is used, suppose a researcher administered a five-item Likert scale to five subjects (naturally both more items and certainly more subjects would be employed in actual practice). Suppose further that the responses shown in Table 11-1 were obtained for each item:

$$\text{Variance of total} = \frac{\Sigma X^2 - \frac{(\Sigma X)^2}{N}}{N - 1}$$

$$= \frac{1{,}386 - \frac{(80)^2}{5}}{5 - 1}$$

$$= 26.5$$

$$\text{Variance of item 1} = \frac{\Sigma X^2 - \frac{(\Sigma X)^2}{N}}{N - 1}$$

$$= \frac{79 - \frac{(19)^2}{5}}{5 - 1}$$

$$= 1.7$$

$$\text{Variance of item 2} = \frac{44 - \frac{(14)^2}{5}}{4}$$

$$= 1.2$$

$$\text{Variance of item 3} = \frac{79 - \frac{(19)^2}{5}}{4}$$

$$= 1.7$$

* Note that the Kuder-Richardson formula 20, which is often used to address the internal consistency of cognitive tests whose items are scored dichotomously (that is, scored as either correct or incorrect), is identical to coefficient alpha for this special case. Coefficient alpha is the more generic index, however, being applicable to a wide range of responses, hence it is the only measure of internal consistency discussed here.

$$\text{Variance of item 4} = \frac{58 - \frac{(16)^2}{5}}{4}$$

$$= 1.7$$

$$\text{Variance of item 5} = \frac{34 - \frac{(12)^2}{5}}{4}$$

$$= 1.3$$

Placing these values into Equation 11-1 we have:

$$\text{Coefficient alpha} = \frac{5}{4}\left[1 - \frac{1.7 + 1.2 + 1.7 + 1.7 + 1.3}{26.5}\right]$$

$$= 1.25\,(1 - .29)$$

$$= .89$$

As computationally simple as this formula is, it is not particularly helpful in conceptualizing exactly what coefficient alpha *is*. Perhaps the best way of doing this is to visualize coefficient alpha as an *average correlation of each item with each other item:* in other words, the correlation of item 1 with item 2, item 1 with item 3, and so on to item 4 with item 5. This, then, is equivalent to splitting the test into its smallest possible components and taking the average of all of them, thereby answering the primary objection to the old split-half procedure.

We must, however, take one final step. In the original odd/even split-half example, it was necessary to correct the resulting correlation to take into account the fact that the test length had been split in half. Here it is even more crucial to correct for test length, since in effect the test was split into *fifths.* (If a 40-item test had been used, it would have been split into fortieths.) To do this it is only necessary to apply the generic version of the Spearman-Brown formula to the average correlation between the individual items, yielding another version of the coefficient alpha formula.

Table 11-1 HYPOTHETICAL RESPONSES FOR A FIVE-ITEM LIKERT SCALE

	Subjects					Item total
	1	2	3	4	5	
A	5	4	5	5	4	23
B	3	3	3	3	2	14
C	4	3	4	4	3	18
D	5	3	5	2	1	16
E	2	1	2	2	2	9
ΣX	19	14	19	16	12	80
ΣX^2	79	44	79	58	34	1,386
$\overline{X}$	3.8	2.8	3.8	3.2	2.4	16.0

$$\text{Coefficient alpha} = \frac{k\bar{r}_{items}}{1 + (k-1)\bar{r}_{items}} \qquad (11\text{-}3)$$

where $\quad k =$ the number of times the real test is longer than the shortened versions (five in the present example)

$\bar{r}_{items} =$ the average inter-item correlation coefficient

As was mentioned above, the almost universal availability of computers obviate the need for actually employing either Equation 11-2 or 11-3. An examination of the latter, however, should help to highlight three important characteristics of coefficient alpha as a reliability index:

1. Alpha is only appropriate for multi-item measures whose total scores are the sums of individual item responses.
2. The more items involved, the higher the alpha.*
3. The higher the average correlation between items (which translates to the more they measure the same construct/attribute), the higher the alpha.

Advantages and Disadvantages of Coefficient Alpha

The chief advantage of coefficient alpha resides in its convenience. It can be computed on a single administration of a measure. It is, in fact, often performed following the completion of a study (although this precludes the researcher's taking corrective action should the measure prove to be unreliable). The coefficient's chief disadvantage lies in its tendency to give a slight overestimate of a measure's true reliability. When this tendency is recognized, coefficient alpha probably deserves its preeminent place in empirical research.

Recommendation When a composite score is used and consistency across time is *not* the preeminent issue, coefficient alpha is the procedure of choice for most research purposes.

TEST-RETEST RELIABILITY

The question that test-retest reliability addresses (that is: *would the same group of respondents score similarly on the same measure at two different points in time?*) has a great deal of intuitive appeal. If an instrument measures nothing with any real consistency (that is, if the scores it assigns are comprised totally of random error), then the reliability of that instrument would be expected to be zero and the correlation between two administrations would be expected to be zero as well. If, on the other hand, the instrument measured something with perfect consistency, an individual's score should be relatively the same at time 2 that it was at time 1 (assuming that nothing of import intervened in the interval), yielding a correlation and a reliability of 1.00.

---

* That is, assuming that the additional items are of adequate quality.

However, there are a number of practical problems with this approach. What, for example, if the number of items and the time between their administration were very limited. Taking an extreme example, what if the measure consisted of a single item and that item was administered twice within a 5-minute time interval? Obviously, even if the respondents to whom the item was administered had no idea what the item even meant, most would probably respond the same way at the second administration as the first, thus producing a spuriously high correlation for the sample as a whole. If the interval between the two administrations were increased to a week or more, however, this remembering would not be as important a factor.

Taking the other extreme, what if a measure of, say, attitudes toward alcoholics were administered to a classroom of students before and after the airing of a network television program that had the effect of dispelling negative attitudes toward alcoholism? Since some of the respondents would have seen the show and others would not, the correlation between the total class' first and second administration scores might well be low, thus resulting in a lower correlation coefficient and an artifactually low reliability estimate.

The moral here is that test-retest reliability can be a tricky proposition. For it to be used the researcher must make two very tenuous assumptions, namely that:

1. Enough time has elapsed for the respondent not to remember previous responses to items.
2. Nothing has intervened in that time interval that is capable of affecting responses to those items.

If the first assumption is not met, a spuriously high reliability coefficient is likely. If the second is violated, an artifactually low one will result. Unfortunately, the researcher can seldom be sure which has or has not occurred.

Test-retest reliability should therefore be used primarily when *stability across time* is desired. This occurs when the researcher wishes to address such questions as:

1. Do subjects respond to the measure similarly at time 1 versus time 2?
2. Is the attribute being measured *stable* across time?

When the researcher is not so much interested in these questions as in the consistency with which the measuring instrument assigns scores to people, then the test-retest technique is not recommended.

Advantages and Disadvantages of Test-Retest Reliability

The chief disadvantage of test-retest reliability resides in the practical difficulty of requiring that the same measure be administered to the same group of people twice. This requires more time on the part of both the researcher and the subjects. Also, unless captive, intact groups are used, it is often impractical to convene the same group of subjects twice. It also requires some creativity on the part of the researcher to explain why an identical measure is being administered twice in a relatively brief time period.*

A second disadvantage is that the test-retest procedure, like coefficient alpha, tends to give a slight overestimate of a measure's true reliability, possibly due to subjects' remembering their responses from the previous administration. Since a reliability estimate does not need to be extremely precise for most research purposes, however, this is not a serious problem. It can also be ameliorated by increasing the number of items (which makes it slightly more difficult to remember individual responses) and the length of time between administrations. This latter strategy must be weighed carefully, since the longer the intervening time period, the greater the chance that some intervening event (including maturation) may occur to change subject's scores on the measure and hence artifactually lower the reliability coefficient. Cureton (1958) has proposed as reasonable a rule of thumb here as any: test the subjects at the beginning of the week in the morning and at the end of the following week in the afternoon. (Testing at different times of the day will help balance out such cyclic variation as general fatigue, motivation, and so forth.)

On the other side of the coin, there are circumstances in which the test-retest procedure is the only viable alternative. The first is the situation in which the researcher is specifically interested in assessing stability across time, as for an attitudinal attribute that should be temporally stable by definition.

The second situation in which test-retest reliability is the procedure of choice is far more common and pragmatic. As discussed in the beginning of this chapter, there are many measures that are not comprised of a collection of individual items, but consist of a single irreducible number. Examples might be a single, self-reported item, such as an estimate of how many hours on the average a person reports watching television per week or a physiological measure such as a person's standing pulse rate.† Certainly, alternate forms reliability doesn't make any sense for such measures, since there is basically only one way to measure the attributes in question. (A differently worded item tapping self-reported television-watching behavior, for example, would result in a spuriously high agreement if administered at the same time as the original item simply because respondents would *try* to answer the two questions consistently.) Similarly, coefficient alpha would not even be possible, simply because inter-item correlations (see Equation 11-3) are not possible for a single item.

---

* Some researchers compute test-retest reliability based on a dual administration of a measure to a control group (as in the randomized-experimental/control-group – pretest-posttest model) since the data are being collected anyway. I see nothing wrong with this convenience as long as (1) the time intervals between the administrations is reasonable and (2) a true control group is used (which means that nothing is done to the subjects that is capable of changing their scores on the measure in question).

† The latter is a good example of a measure on which an index of temporal stability might be useful. A machine-scored pulse rate might be extremely accurate at the time it was recorded, but a subject's pulse rate might itself be quite unstable from one time period to another. A test-retest reliability coefficient computed for such a measure is thus an indicator of both the stability of the measurement procedure *and* of the attribute (pulse rate) itself.

Table 11-2 HYPOTHETICAL TEST-RETEST
RELIABILITY MODEL

	Self-reported hours watching TV — time 1	Self-reported hours watching TV — time 2
S_1	20	20
S_2	10	12
S_3	0	0
.	.	.
.	.	.
.	.	.
S_{30}	14	18

The only real alternative for both examples, then, would be to administer the identical measure twice to the same group of subjects under as near identical conditions as possible with a reasonable time interval in between (perhaps using a variant of Cureton's advice for the self-report item, while perhaps a few hours or a day would suffice for pulse rate).

The actual computation of a test-retest reliability coefficient involves the classical correlational model with time of administration substituted for the two variables normally present (Table 11-2). The resulting Pearson r would thus be the test-retest reliability coefficient. (Note that this model precludes respondent anonymity, since subjects' first scores must be individually matched with their second scores. When this is a problem, codes instead of names may be employed, such as the final four digits of subjects' social security numbers or their mothers' maiden names and first initials.)

Recommendation For those occasions in which an irreducible score is used or in which the researcher is specifically interested in stability over time, test-retest reliability is the only viable alternative. For most other research purposes, coefficient alpha remains the procedure of choice.

THE RELIABILITY OF OBSERVATIONS AND JUDGMENTS

So far, we have implicitly assumed the use of measures on which there is little probability of substantive disagreement between different measurers. This is a reasonably safe assumption for paper-and-pencil cognitive, affective, and personality measures where the scoring protocols are rigidly (and clearly) specified. There is really no reason that two conscientious people should not assign the same test sheet the same score as long as they use the same scoring key. Certainly some errors are possible, but for a *set* of scores the overall effect of these efforts should be trivial. (This is even more true of machine-scored tests of course.)

There are many instances in empirical research involving human subjects in which scoring is not, and cannot be, so precisely operationalized. The most common examples of this occur in observational research, where one or more individuals record behaviors. Here, the dependent variable becomes what subjects *do* rather than what they know, think, feel, or say they do. No matter how clearly specified the rules for recording these behaviors and how conscientious the observers are at their task, a new source of error creeps into the resulting scores. It is error associated with the observers themselves.

There are many sources of this error. Some of them are:

1. *Individual differences between the observers.* Some people are simply more skillful or conscientious than others. Different individuals also *interpret* what they see differently.
2. *Two individuals observing the same scene may be attending to different things in that scene, thus one observer may actually see something the other does not.* Alternatively, one observer may be recording one behavior while another behavior is occurring. (Sometimes things happen so quickly that the blink of any eye can obscure them.)
3. *Since most observations must be recorded according to some sort of classification scheme, judgmental errors or even legitimate differences of opinion can surface.*

For whatever the reason, errors associated with individual differences between observers or judges are always present. One need only watch the scoring of a figure skating contest or boxing match to see how widely experienced observers viewing the same events can differ from one another. Obviously the quality of the resulting scores is greatly affected by the consistency with which different observers assign scores to the same individuals or events. This consistency is documented in the guise of an *interrater reliability* coefficient.

Interrater Reliability

As in health, prevention is the best cure for unreliable measures. This is especially true where interrater differences are a potential problem. The first preventive step is to draw up carefully the rules for assigning numbers to the phenomenon in question. This is best done by either personal, or personally supervised, pilot work in which observers (also called *raters*) receive adequate training prior to actual data collection by:

1. Carefully and explicitly going over rules and procedures (which should always be written out) with all observers.
2. Giving observers practice in recording the types of behavior that will be required of them in the actual study.

When possible, *all raters should observe the same cases, after which scores should be compared and discussed.* Discrepancies in scoring should be ironed out with each divergent rater, discussing why a particular score was assigned followed by, when necessary, new rules being drawn up to cover such cases. This process should be continued until as high a degree of consistency as possible is obtained between observers, regardless of how many trials are necessary. (Video or audio recordings are especially helpful in such training sessions.)

Even when an apparently high degree of consensus is achieved, other common sense safeguards should be taken to minimize the recurrence of later interrater differences. Some of these are:

1. *Use as few observers as possible.* The more individuals assigning scores to subjects, the more chances there are of discrepancies. (An exception to this is when each subject or phenomenon is observed by more than one person, with an average score thus being assigned. In this relatively unusual situation, the more observers the better, since the more scores going into a composite or mean score, the more stable it will be.)
2. *Select observers with similar levels of experience and training.* An experienced research assistant, for example, paired with an undergraduate new to research will probably result in greater interrater discrepancies than the use of two experienced observers. When possible, replace observers who consistently deviate from their colleagues.
3. *Randomly assign subjects (or phenomena) to observers.* Under no circumstances should one observer be responsible for, say, all experimental subjects and the other for all controls. Such a situation would undoubtedly confound a degree of systematic bias with the experimental treatment.
4. *If feasible, schedule one or more meetings during the course of the study to allow the observers to discuss unusual cases not covered in training as well as to review the original set of rules.* If the study is of relatively long duration, observers should be compared again occasionally to see if their degree of consensus has slipped.

To actually assess the degree of interrater reliability it is, of course, necessary for the same observers to rate the same phenomena at the same time. This is best done before the advent of the final study and involves a reasonable number of observations (probably no fewer than fifteen). When only two observers are used, a simple correlation coefficient between the two sets of ratings yields as good an estimate of interrater reliability as any, if a mean rating is not used and if absolute differences between observers is of no interest.*

The model for this correlation coefficient is set up as follows:

	Observer *A*	Observer *B*
S_1	15	12
S_2	16	14
S_3	17	17
.	.	.
.	.	.
.	.	.
S_{15}	10	10

---

* It will be remembered that a constant added to all the scores in one set of ratings (or to one variable) will not affect a correlation coefficient. Thus, observer *A* could assign *consistently* higher scores than *B* and not affect the correlation between the two.

It should be noted that the unit of analysis for the computation of inter-rater reliability must be the same as for the final study. Thus, if a single composite score is to be used as the dependent variable, a single *r* between the two observers across observations is sufficient. If 10 individual categories are to be used, however, then 10 individual interrater reliability coefficients must be computed.

If more than two observers are involved, the situation is slightly different. Some experts have argued that an average correlation coefficient between all possible pairs of observers is a reasonable measure of interrater reliability (Peters and Van Voorhis, 1940), while others, such as Ebel (1951), suggest an analysis of variance as the procedure of choice. Everything else being equal, the two procedures usually yield comparable results, although analysis of variance is a more flexible approach. For a more detailed discussion of this technique, the reader is referred to the within-subjects analysis of variance example presented in Chapter 14.

Intrarater Reliability

The final question regarding the consistency with which scores are assigned to individuals relates to the stability of a single observer:

Does the same rater assign scores in a consistent fashion?

This question, of course, is relevant when a single observer is used for all subjects. Here, individual differences between observers is not a concern, although the danger is present that this single observer can either systematically change over time or simply never assign scores with any real consistency.

Perhaps this can be visualized more easily if the reasons for low interrater reliability are considered. In the simplest case involving two raters, a low coefficient can be due to one of three sources:

1. The raters simply use different rules or perceptions for assigning numbers to individuals.
2. They do not consistently use the same rules for different subjects (or cannot perceive whatever is being observed well enough to make consistent judgments).
3. One rater does assign numbers consistently, but the other does not.

With intrarater reliability, the third possibility is no longer relevant. The single rater either does or does not assign numbers in a consistent manner. The easiest way to ascertain this is to have this single rater observe the same phenomenon twice and rate it twice, a task that is normally easier said than done unless a video or audio recording is available. If it is, then the observer can rate several *S*'s (preferably at least 15) and then rate them again several weeks later when enough time has elapsed for each individual case to have been forgotten (along with the way in which it was rated). What results, therefore, are two observations on each S that, of course, conforms to the correlation model discussed in Chapter 5. Consequently, the Pearson r between the two observations is an estimate of intrarater reliability for the rater in question.

Since it is possible for even the same rater to change over time (such as becoming more expert, more disinterested, fatigued, or whatever), it is often a good idea to recompute the intrarater reliability later on in the study if the study is of very long duration or if a great many S's are involved. This can be done in exactly the same way by either using the same taped observations (if enough time has elapsed for them to have been completely forgotten by the rater) or with new ones.

The procedures for ensuring high intrarater reliability are really quite similar to those used with more than one rater. Normally, of course, within- (intra-) rater differences will be considerably fewer than between- (inter-) rater differences, both because people are more similar to themselves than they are to other people and because intrarater reliability coefficients are artifactually increased by observers remembering how they rated something the first time around. This can and should be compensated for by requiring a slightly higher *intra-* than interrater reliability coefficient. To ensure a reasonable degree of stability, it is always a good idea to practice assigning numbers to subjects via a pilot study during which detailed rules for the assignment of numbers to unusual circumstances may be drawn up. (The researcher should never rely on memory when rating complex behavioral phenomena. Each new situation should be written down along with whatever decision was made concerning it at the time it was made. Then, whenever the situation recurs, the observer can refer back to this ever-expanding, written document.)

Substituting Interrater for Intrarater Reliability

The taping of human behavior solely for the purpose of establishing intrarater reliability is seldom a luxury that can be afforded. It is always important, however, to establish the consistency with which observers assign scores. When the documentation of intrarater reliability is not practical, I recommend that two raters observe a number of subjects in common (preferably during a pilot study), even when a single rater is to be used in the actual study. An interrater reliability coefficient is then computed between the two sets of observations as described above.

The obtained coefficient can then be interpreted as an *under*estimate of the intrarater reliability, since a moderate-to-high interrater reliability coefficient means that *both* raters must be consistently assigning scores to individuals or phenomena. (It is simply not possible for two individuals' ratings to agree if they are not first consistent with themselves.) In other words, acceptable interrater reliability assumes acceptable intrarater reliability, although the reverse is not true.

To take this line of reasoning one step further, it could be argued that intrarater reliability is not an essential procedure, since:

1. Interrater reliability can always be substituted for it.
2. In many ways, an interrater reliability coefficient is of more scientific interest because it is an indication that at least the observational elements of the study in question can be replicated.

Recommendation Use interrater reliability instead of intrarater reliability when the services of a competent second observer are available.

Nonobservational Applications of Intra/Interrater Reliability

Although studies in which scores on the dependent variable are assigned via direct observations are the most common applications of intra/interrater reliability procedures, they are by no means the only ones. Any scoring procedure that requires even a modicum of judgment on the part of the scorer is an equally good candidate. Examples are open-ended, nonstructured questions whose responses must be categorized, free recall items, and essay tests.

All such situations require considerable preparation and pilot work to achieve high interrater consensus. This preparatory work is basically the same described for observational variables. Detailed protocols, for example, must be worked out for acceptable and unacceptable responses for scoring either free or cued recall (an example of which might be: "List five characteristics of a schizoid temperament"), since synonyms and approximations of the desired responses are usually the rule rather than the exception. Practice sessions using the same test forms are also recommended, as well as periodic checks to ensure that an originally acceptable degree of interrater reliability has not slipped over time.

Answers to open-ended items (for example: "What aspect of this course did you find the most interesting?") must often be forced into closed categories before they can be of any use in empirical research. Here, too, it is important to establish as detailed rules as possible to ensure that two or more raters can independently place the resulting responses into the same categories with a reasonably high degree of consensus. When the categories involve a natural progression of some sort, then this consensus is documented via the same procedures discussed above (for example, a Pearson r for two raters, or, when the categories are completely nominal, a percentage of agreements between scorers, along with a statistic called kappa, is as good an index of interrater consistency as any).

INCREASING THE RELIABILITY OF A MEASURE

So far, reliability has been treated as though it were a fact of life, as though a measure is either sufficiently reliable or it is not. The true utility of the concept, however, lies in its potential for ensuring that a new instrument being developed (or an existing one being adapted) for a specific research purpose will indeed assign scores with sufficient consistency to fulfill that purpose. There are a number of strategies that can be undertaken to ensure this. Some involve nothing more than common sense, such as:

1. Making the directions for completing the instrument as explicit and clear as possible.
2. Deciding on the optimal conditions under which the instrument should be administered and striving to obtain them. (A very noisy examining room, for example, can easily cut down on the reliability of resulting scores.)
3. Choosing a format that delimits scoring subjectivity to the maximum degree possible.
4. Most important (at least for paper-and-pencil measures), writing items as clearly and as nonambiguously as possible, making sure that the reading level (and vocabulary) is consonant with the targeted sample's abilities.

There are other strategies that are a little less obvious. We will discuss these now.

1. Increasing the Instrument's Length

Everything else being equal, the more data points going into a score, the more stable that score becomes. Thus, a total score comprised of 20 individual items will be more reliable than a total score comprised of only 10 items. The reason for this derives from the fact that all scores (total and individual item) are comprised of two sources of variation: systematic and random error. When added, as we do when arriving at a total score, systematic variation tends to accumulate faster than error, simply because the former is all in the same direction while the latter is not (since it is assumed to be random).

This phenomenon is easiest to visualize in terms of the second coefficient alpha formula presented earlier in this chapter:

$$\text{Coefficient alpha} = \frac{(\text{number of items}) \, \bar{r}_{\text{items}}}{1 + (\text{number of items} - 1) \, \bar{r}_{\text{items}}}$$

Thus, if the average inter-item correlation for a set of items is .20 ($\bar{r}_{\text{items}}$), the difference between the estimated reliability of a 10-item measure based on this set versus a 20-item combination can be calculated as follows:

$$\text{Rel' of 10 items} = \frac{10 \times .20}{1 + (10 - 1) \, .20}$$

$$= .71$$

$$\text{Rel' of 20 items} = \frac{20 \times .20}{1 + (20 - 1) \, .20}$$

$$= .83$$

Increasing the number of items thus increases a measure's internal consistency. In this case, doubling the number of items adds 12 percent (.83 − .71) of true (systematic) variance to the final score.

This phenomenon can be extremely useful to researchers trying to develop sufficiently reliable instruments, since the more systematic variance in a measure the greater the study's statistical power. All this assumes, of course,

Table 11-3 THE RELATIONSHIP BETWEEN TEST
LENGTH AND RELIABILITY

Number of items	Reliability			
10	.20	.40	.60	.80
15	.27	.50	.69	.86
20	.33	.57	.75	.89
25	.38	.63	.79	.91
30	.43	.67	.82	.92
35	.47	.70	.84	.93
40	.50	.73	.86	.94
45	.53	.75	.87	.95
50	.56	.77	.88	.95

that the additional items are of equal quality (and measure the same attributes) as the original ones (which is another way of saying the $\bar{r}_{items}$ is assumed not to change).

Table 11-3 indicates the extent to which the reliability of a measure can be actually improved by adding items. These estimates are based on one of the most useful formulas yet developed in the field of measurement (and from which coefficient alpha was derived), the general Spearman-Brown formula:

$$\text{Rel}' = \frac{k\,(\text{Rel}_{xx})}{1 + (k-1)\,\text{Rel}_{xx}} \tag{11-4}$$

where   Rel′ = estimated reliability
k = the number of times the test is increased in length
Rel_{xx} = reliability before test length is increased

Thus, a 10-item test with an original, completely unacceptable reliability of .20 can be expected to possess a marginally acceptable reliability of .56 by adding 40 items (or of increasing the test length fivefold), while the same increment to length will increase an original reliability from .40 to .77. [This table can be used in a variety of ways. One is to choose the reliability column most consonant with the original reliability possessed by one's test and observe the effect of adding items. Thus, an original reliability of .60 (the third reliability column) will be increased to .75 by doubling the test length, whatever the original number of items happens to be.]

Although increasing a test's length is perhaps the single most useful strategy available to a researcher wishing to increase a measure's reliability, adding items is not the panacea that it might appear to be at first glance simply because of the sheer numbers of items that must be added to have any substantive effect. It is usually quite difficult to double a measure's length (especially since the additional items must be of equal quality to the original ones and since test developers usually include their best items to begin with); it also requires considerably more time to administer such an instrument. Still, as evidenced by Table 11-3, increasing a measure's length can be a relatively effective strategy, especially when coupled with some of the strategies that follow.

2. Increasing the Instrument's Homogeneity

At the risk of repetitiveness, adding items to a measure increases its reliability only to the extent that the new items are both well constructed and assess the same construct as their original counterparts. Adding ambiguous, poorly worded items to a scale can actually decrease that scale's reliability; adding excellent items that measure a new, unrelated construct can also decrease reliability.

To understand why this is true, it is only necessary to remember that coefficient alpha is really nothing more than an indicator of the average correlation between all possible pairs of items in a scale. Items that contain nothing but random error variance will not correlate with other items, hence their inclusion will decrease the average intercorrelation between items and hence decrease alpha. Items that measure unrelated constructs will also not correlate highly with one another, hence their inclusion will have the same effect.

Paradoxically, then, while the addition of items to an existing scale normally increases its reliability, there are occasions when deleting bad items will have the same effect. The best strategy for discovering the existence of deleterious items is via a pilot test followed by an item analysis that assesses both the intercorrelations between all the items plus the correlation between each separate item and the measure's total score.

To illustrate, suppose that a five-item Likert-type scale were administered to a sample of 20 subjects prior to the conduct of the actual study. Table 11-4 illustrates some of the output that a typical computer program might yield. Computer programs differ widely with respect to the amount of psychometric information they supply. Any of the elements in Table 11-4 can be very helpful in evaluating the results of a pilot test. If only a correlation matrix were presented, the researcher would need to examine the general trends therein to see if

Table 11-4   HYPOTHETICAL ITEM ANALYSIS INFORMATION

	Correlation matrix				
	Item 1	Item 2	Item 3	Item 4	Item 5
Item 1	1.00	.45	.50	.02	.44
Item 2		1.00	.48	.00	.50
Item 3			1.00	−.04	.52
Item 4				1.00	.08
Item 5					1.00

Coefficient alpha = .68

Items	Item-to-total correlation	Corrected item-to-total	Coefficient alpha if item is deleted
1	.64	.58	.58
2	.68	.62	.57
3	.65	.59	.57
4	.10	.02	.79
5	.69	.62	.55

one or more items tended to correlate relatively poorly with the rest. In the present example, it is quite clear that item 4 does not go with the other four, since its intercorrelations are .02, .00, − .04, and .08 while the remaining intercorrelations average .48. By substituting this latter figure into Equation 11-3 the researcher could approximate how much the dropping of this unrelated item would facilitate the measure's internal consistency.

The second part of Table 11-4 provides much more directly useful information. The item-to-total correlations provide a measure of how well each of the five items are functioning with respect to the total score. Column 2 is an even better index, since the uncorrected correlations in column 1 are to a certain extent tautological: the uncorrected correlation of item 1 with the total (.64) is the Pearson r between each subject's response on item 1 and his or her response on the sum of items $1 + 2 + 3 + 4 + 5$, thus it is in part a correlation between something and itself. The corrected item-to-total correlation between item 1 and the rest of the test is the Pearson r between each item 1 score and the total *minus* item 1.

Obviously, based upon these results, item 4 would be dropped from future administrations of the measure because of its near zero correlation with the rest of the test. The final column confirms the wisdom of this decision, indicating that the overall alpha of .68 would actually be increased to .79 with this deletion, while the deletion of any other item would decrease the reliability of the resulting shortened test.

Item analyses of pilot test results are thus potentially of great benefit to the researcher. Their most obvious benefit, the computation of a reliability coefficient (.68 in the present example), gives an indication as to whether or not the measure in question can function adequately with the type of sample being employed. The item-to-total correlations, or the alpha estimates when each item is deleted, provide good hints as to which items are not functioning adequately. (When such items are identified, they may either be rewritten or deleted. In either case, their true effect on the internal consistency of the new measure cannot be ascertained until a separate administration to a separate sample of subjects is performed, although the computer can be used to give an estimate of what those results may be by recomputing alpha using various combinations of items within the existing data set.)

3. Increasing the Target Sample's Heterogeneity

Although usually neither feasible nor desirable, one method of increasing the effective reliability of a measure is to administer that measure to a very heterogeneous sample. (By heterogeneity is meant a sample in which there are large individual differences between subjects with respect to the attribute being tested.) This phenomenon also stems from the fact that reliability (at least from the internal consistency perspective) is reducible to correlation coefficients between items and, as discussed in Chapter 5, the more variance in a set of scores, the higher will be any correlations involving those scores.

This phenomenon possesses the potential for abuse, such as a standardized test whose reliability is computed on a sample of children from a wide distribution of grade levels, or a researcher who combines untaught control group subjects with instructed experimental subjects to *ensure* heterogeneity for the documentation of a measure's reliability. The truth of the matter is that the phenomenon has very limited research utility, but it is helpful in explaining two generalities that are quite useful in empirical research involving either the development of a new measure or the adaptation of an existing one:

1. *The more variability contained in each individual item of a measure, the more reliable the whole.* In effect, when the heterogeneity of the subjects to which a measure is administered is increased, what is really happening is that the variance of individual items is being increased. A legitimate research application of this phenomenon, then, becomes the construction of items with as much variance as possible. Said another way, *the best way to increase the reliability of a measure is to include items that differentiate between people* (with respect to the attribute being tested) *to the maximum degree possible.*

For cognitive tests, this translates to writing items that approximately half of the subjects will answer correctly and half will not (Nunnally, 1978). (The closer to a 50-50 break the better.) For items that are not scored as correct or incorrect, such as affective, personality, or other psychosocial measures, the greater the spread of responses on each item, the better. (Thus, for Likert-type items, one would hope that everyone would not select 4's and 5's on a 5-point scale, but instead would distribute responses throughout the scale.)

2. *The reliability of a test is not a constant entity. It depends on the sample to which it is administered.* This generalization follows directly from the previous discussion. To understand why, let us suppose that the same cognitive test is administered to two different samples. In the first, approximately half of the subjects answer each item correctly. The second sample, however, is comprised of higher-ability subjects who answer almost every item correctly. Coefficient alpha will be considerably higher for the first sample than the second, even though the test itself did not change, simply because the more closely the items approximate a 50 percent-correct/50 percent-incorrect split, the more reliable the measure will be. What this means in practical terms is that a researcher cannot rely on the published reliability of any measure unless that reliability coefficient was computed on a sample very similar to the one being employed for the study at hand. For this reason, *I recommend that the reliability of all research measures be reestablished each time they are administered.* I do *not* necessarily recommend that a pilot study be designed specifically to reestablish the reliability of a measure for which a reliability coefficient has already been published, unless the targeted sample is *extremely* divergent from the original. In most cases, a coefficient alpha computed after the study

has been completed will indicate a very similar value to any preestablished value.*

4. Increasing the Number of Observations per Data Point

So far, the individual has been assumed to be the unit of analysis. There are
occasions, however, when the unit of analysis is based on a mean value, such as
in:

1. Observational research, where two or more raters can assign scores to
   the same subjects or phenomena.
2. Studies of clinical performance (for example, clinical outcomes of a
   group of patients receiving care from the same person) or teacher
   competence (as defined by satisfaction ratings made by an entire
   classroom of students).
3. Studies involving entire organizations (such as comparing a number of
   divisions within a large corporation with respect to their employees'
   work satisfaction).

In all of these instances, a simple, unadjusted reliability coefficient is no
longer appropriate. Means are far more stable than individual scores. The effect
of adding data points to the unit of analysis (such as in using two observers to
record behavior rather than one), in fact, is exactly comparable to adding items
to increase a test's length, which means that the Spearman-Brown formula (see
Equation 11-4) can be used to estimate the increment to reliability resulting
from these additional data points. This increment can be truly dramatic, depending on the number of observations going into the mean being used in lieu
of a single score.

To illustrate with an extreme example, let us suppose that a cognitive test
was found to have an internal consistency of only .35 when the unit of analysis
was individual elementary school children. If this same test were used as a
measure of teacher performance, however, and if the average classroom for a
sample of teachers contained 25 students, the reliability of the resulting mean
would be comparable to increasing the test length 25 times. Using the Spearman-Brown formula to estimate what the actual reliability would be, we have:

$$\text{Rel}' = \frac{k \cdot \text{Rel}}{1 + (k-1)\,\text{Rel}}$$

$$= \frac{25 \times .35}{1 + (24 \times .35)}$$

$$= \frac{8.75}{9.40}$$

$$= .93$$

* Note that this recommendation applies only to existing measures with sufficiently high,
preestablished reliability coefficients. For new instruments, or for radically new applications of
existing ones, a pilot test is still recommended.

Obviously, it is seldom practical to increase the number of observations going into a study's data points in such a dramatic way unless means are naturally indicated. There are occasions, however, where more than one observation per data point (or per subject) is possible, especially when measures collected close together are available on an otherwise relatively unstable score. Examples might be continuously monitored heart rates or a performance indicator of some sort.

TYPES OF VARIABLES TO AVOID

These then are the primary mechanisms by which the consistency with which a measure assigns scores can be protected. Some types of measures start out with built-in limitations that even the most stringent steps cannot completely ameliorate. These are best avoided by researchers, especially for use as dependent variables. Some of the more common include the following.

1. Difference Scores

Although intuitively attractive, the practice of subtracting one score from another (say a pretest from a posttest) results in a hybrid score that is less reliable than *either* of its parents. The problem with this approach is that when one score is subtracted from another, the resulting number really represents a *third* measure that is based in part on that part of its parents' scores that are not shared. This means that if the two original measures are correlated with one another (which they normally are), a large part of this unshared variance is due to error.

Cronbach and Furby (1970) have provided a formula for estimating what this reliability decrement will be that basically demonstrates that the higher the correlation between the two measures, the greater the problem.* Difference scores are thus best avoided in empirical research. Fortunately, their use is practically never necessary. If gains between two groups, say experimental versus control, are to be computed, the pretest can be used as a covariate in an analysis of covariance procedure (see Chapter 14). If a third variable is to be correlated with the difference between two administrations of a measure, then the partial correlation between the second administration and the new variable (with the first administration being partialled out) can be employed (see Chapter 5).

For those rare instances in which a difference score between two variables is actually hypothesized to be the measure of choice for a new construct, the researcher might well heed Cronbach and Furby's (1970, p. 79) admonition:

> The claim that an index has validity as a measure of some construct carries a considerable burden of proof. There is little reason to believe, and much empirical reason to disbelieve the contention that some arbitrary weighting function of two

* For example, if two measures, each with a reliability of .80, were correlated .70 with one another, the reliability of any difference score computed by subtracting one from the other would be only .33.

variables will properly define a construct. More often, the profitable strategy is to use the two variables separately in the analysis so as to allow for complex relationships.

2. Individual Items

Although not always possible, the use of individual items as separate variables is a practice that should be avoided. There are occasions when the individual items making up a test are interesting enough in their own right to merit separate analysis. Since reliability is computed on the actual data points used in a statistical analysis, the reliability of the individual item (or behavior), not that of the total test, would become the relevant consideration.

To illustrate why individual items are seldom that reliable, consider a 30-item measure with an internal consistency of .85. Turning the Spearman-Brown formula around, we could estimate the reliability of any single item as follows:

$$\text{Rel}'_{\text{item}} = \frac{\frac{1}{k}(\text{Rel}_{xx})}{1 + \left(\frac{1}{k} - 1\right)\text{Rel}_{xx}}$$

$$= \frac{\frac{1}{30}(.85)}{1 + (-.966).85}$$

$$= \frac{.028}{.179}$$

$$= .156$$

where $\text{Rel}'_{\text{item}}$ = the estimated reliability of the average item in the test

Obviously, this is not a very impressive index. Certainly, individual items can be more reliable than this, but in general they do not assign scores to subjects nearly as consistently as do composite scores.

3. Essay Exams, Unstructured Interviews, and Open-Ended Responses

These strategies and their disadvantages have already been discussed. Generally speaking, *I recommend their use only in pilot work designed to construct structured items or closed categories, not as variables in and of themselves.* All too often, their appearance in empirical research is dictated by the lack of time or motivation to complete the proper pilot work.

ADDITIONAL CONSIDERATIONS

The final two issues that will be discussed relate to (1) the precision of individual scores and (2) the practical question of minimum reliability standards for empirical research.

The Precision of Individual Scores

All the different types of reliability coefficients discussed so far speak to the consistency with which scores are assigned to a sample. Since most empirical research does indeed involve groups of people, this is as it should be. There are rare occasions, however, when the precision of an individual score is desired or, said another way, when it is necessary to know how close the score assigned to an individual subject is to his or her *true score* on the attribute in question.

The *standard error measurement* speaks to this issue. It is a function of both the test's reliability and its standard deviation:

$$\text{S.E.}_{\text{meas}} = \text{S.D.}_x \sqrt{1 - \text{Rel}_{xx}} \tag{11-5}$$

where $\text{S.E.}_{\text{meas}}$ = the standard error of measurement
   S.D._x = the standard deviation of test x
   Rel_{xx} = the reliability of test x

and it is interpreted in much the same way as a standard deviation in the sense that it can be used to set up confidence intervals around an individual's true score.

Suppose, for example, the standard deviation of an instrument is 5 and its reliability equals .75. Feeding those values into the formula above yields a standard error of measurement for the instrument of 2.5 ($5\sqrt{1 - .75} = 5\sqrt{.25} = 2.5$). What this means is that on the average any single score achieved on the instrument in question will be within ± 2.5 units of the person's true score 67 percent of the time (and within ± 5 units 95 percent of the time).

Some characteristics of the standard error of measurement should probably be examined at this time, prior to any further discussion concerning its use. In the first place, it should be obvious that the standard error of measurement is an inverse function of the reliability coefficient. (It will, furthermore, always be less than the standard deviation except in the unlikely case of a measure with zero consistency.) To examine this relationship more closely, note the way in which the size of the standard error of a measure decreases as its reliability increases (but its standard deviation remains constant at 5.0) (Table 11-5). As the reliability continues to increase, the relative size of the standard error of measurement decreases at an accelerated pace; thus, the gain in the precision of a single score when the reliability is increased from .80 to .90 is over twice that achieved when raising the reliability from .30 to .40.

The second characteristic of the standard error of measurement that should be kept in mind is that it is an *average* quantity. It is the average amount of deviation of observed from true scores present in a normally distributed sample. Scores at either the positive or negative extremes are skewed in the opposite direction (Nunnally, 1978), although over the long run, these differences average out.

A third characteristic is not quite as obvious, but has important implications in measurement theory. *The standard error of an instrument tends to be a relatively constant entity that does not change drastically due to the characteristics of an individual sample.* At first glance, this statement may appear to be contradictory, since the formula is also a function of the standard deviation,

Table 11-5 STANDARD ERROR OF MEASUREMENT
FOR VARIOUS RELIABILITY LEVELS
WHEN THE STANDARD DEVIATION REMAINS
CONSTANT AT 5.0

Reliability	S.E.$_{meas}$
1.00	.00
.90	1.58
.80	2.24
.70	2.74
.60	3.16
.50	3.54
.40	3.87
.30	4.18
.20	4.47
.10	4.74
.00	5.00

which can fluctuate widely due to changes in the characteristics of the sample. With a little thought, however, the reader will recall that reliability also increases as a function of the standard deviation (or variance, since the S.D. = $\sqrt{var.}$); hence what is lost by increasing the size of the standard deviation is gained by an increase in the size of the reliability, which causes the two to have the effect of canceling one another out.

Finally, as is indicated above, the standard error really sets confidence intervals around the true score, not around the observed score. For practical purposes, this distinction is often ignored, which is not unreasonable as long as the researcher is cognizant of the slight distortions that are likely to ensue.

The standard error of measurement is of primary use when individual scores are used for decision-making purposes. In this regard, it is most crucial in cognitive or clinical measurement where important decisions often ride on individual test results (such as entry into an educational program or a dangerous treatment procedure). If, for example, an individual scores within two points of the cutoff point for such a decision, and the standard error of measurement is five points, the chances are quite good that the decision itself is in error. For that reason, the standard error of measurement should always be taken into consideration when decisions are made concerning individual scores. Its applicability to most research situations is quite limited, however, since differences or relationships between groups of subjects are usually of more interest than differences between individuals. It has been presented here primarily as a means of tying together the concepts of consistency and *precision*.

Reliability Standards

The question of how reliable an instrument must be before it is useful depends on the use to which the resulting scores are to be put. As demonstrated in the previous section, the precision of individual scores is heavily dependent on the

Table 11-6 EXAMPLES OF THE RELATIONSHIP BETWEEN RELIABILITY AND VALIDITY

1	2	3	4
Reliability of existing measure(s)	Maximum possible correlation when one measure is assumed to be perfectly reliable (true correlation = 1.00)	Maximum possible correlation when both measures' reliability is given in column 1 (true correlation = 1.00)	Maximum possible correlation when both measures' reliability is given in column 1 (true correlation = 0.70)
1.00	1.00	1.00	.70
.90	.95	.90	.63
.80	.89	.80	.56
.70	.84	.70	.49
.60	.77	.60	.42
.50	.71	.50	.35
.40	.63	.40	.28
.30	.55	.30	.21
.20	.45	.20	.14
.10	.32	.10	.07
.00	.00	.00	.00

reliability of the measure that assigned them. Thus, for scores on which important individual clinical or educational decisions are to be based, one would hope that a reliability coefficient of over .90 would be obtained. (In my opinion, there is really no reason why any commercial test designed for such purposes should not be able to obtain such a figure.)

Since researchers are seldom interested in the stability of a single score, their chief concern with respect to the reliability lies in its relationship to the concept of statistical power. Unreliable variables can make it very difficult to achieve statistical significance.

The extent to which this is a problem can perhaps best be demonstrated via the following formula:

$$r_{xy} \text{(maximum)} = \sqrt{\text{Rel}_{xx}} \qquad (11\text{-}6)$$

where r_{xy} (maximum) = the largest possible nonchance correlation between measure x and any other measure (y)

Thus, if we assume that measure y is *perfectly* reliable (which is never the case), column 2 of Table 11-6 gives an indication of the highest possible nonchance correlations* that could accrue between it and measure x as the reliability varies from .00 to 1.00. If x possesses a reliability of .60, for example, r_{xy} cannot exceed .77 (row 5, column 2). Column 3 gives an indication of the corresponding value when the reliability of both measures varies from .00 to 1.00 as determined by Equation 11-7:

* Although the Pearson r is used as an example, the same principle holds for other statistical procedures, such as t-test between E and C groups (in which case group membership or the independent variable becomes measure y).

$$r_{xy} \text{ (maximum)} = \sqrt{\text{Rel}_{xx} \cdot \text{Rel}_{yy}} \qquad (11\text{-}7)$$

Thus, if y also possesses a reliability of .60, r_{xy} is not likely to exceed .60 (row 5, column 3).

The fourth column represents the hypothetical scenario in which the constructs measured by x and y actually correlate .70 instead of 1.00 (which is *highly* unlikely, since a perfect correlation would indicate that measures x and y really addressed the *same* construct). Here, the maximum possible r_{xy} would be only .42 (row 5, column 4).

For other reliability and true correlational values, Equation 11-8 may be used to determine the highest possible nonchance correlation coefficient that the researcher can expect to obtain.

$$r_{xy} \text{ (maximum)} = r_{xy} \text{ (true)} \cdot \sqrt{\text{Rel}_{xx} \cdot \text{Rel}_{yy}} \qquad (11\text{-}8)$$

where r_{xy} (true) = the true correlation between the attributes being measured (this value is never really known).

What makes the decrements in the correlation coefficients caused by unreliability important is the fact that the smaller maximum possible r obtainable from a study, the more subjects will be necessary to achieve statistical significance. Thus, in the hypothetical situation in which the true correlation between constructs x and y is .70, only nine subjects would be necessary to achieve statistical significance with perfectly reliable measures of those constructs. If the imperfections in the measures (Rel_{xx} and Rel_{yy}) dictate that only a correlation of .60 (r_{xy}) can actually be obtained, then 12 subjects are necessary to document statistical significance. If the maximum possible correlation that could be expected is only .20 (when the reliabilities of both measures x and y are .30), almost 100 subjects are required simply to achieve statistical significance.

The point here is that although it is quite possible to achieve statistical significance employing relatively unreliable measures, the loss in statistical power and concomitant need for larger numbers of subjects makes their use extremely inefficient. *I recommend that unless extremely large samples are being employed, researchers should not employ measures whose reliabilities are much below .60.* If the true correlation is much below .70, then even this figure is suspect.

SUMMARY

The reliability of a measure is defined primarily in terms of five questions:

1. Would the same group of respondents score similarly on two equivalent forms of the same measure?
2. Would the same group of respondents score similarly on two *parts* of the same measure?
3. Would the same group of respondents score similarly on the same measure at two different points in time?

4. Would two different scorers assign the same group of respondents similar scores on the same instrument?
5. Does the same scorer assign scores in a consistent fashion?

Questions 1 and 2 are theoretically relevant only to measures employing composite scores. Questions 3, 4, and 5 are potentially relevant to all types of measures, including those consisting of single, indivisible numbers (such as many physiological or perceptual measures).

For composite measures, coefficient alpha is usually the most practical reliability coefficient. For indivisible scores, test-retest reliability is often the only viable option (unless the subjectivity of raters is also perceived as a problem).

Strategies for increasing the reliability of a measure include:

1. Increasing the instrument's length (relevant only to composite scores).
2. Increasing its homogeneity (also relevant only to composite scores).
3. Increasing the target sample's heterogeneity.
4. Increasing the number of observations per data point.

The reliability of a measure is directly related to the confidence that can be placed upon any individual score (quantified via the standard error of measurement) and to the maximum possible nonchance correlation that can be obtained between it and any other variable. This latter characteristic of reliability is an especially essential consideration, since most empirical research involves establishing the existence of such a relationship (or of a difference among groups with respect to a measure).

REFERENCES

Cronbach, L. J. Coefficient alpha and the internal consistency of tests. *Psychometrika,* 1951, *16,* 297–334.
Cronbach, L. J. and Furby, L. How we should measure change — or should we? *Psychological Bulletin,* 1970, *74,* 68–80.
Cureton, E. E. The definition and estimation of test reliability. *Educational and Psychological Measurement,* 1958, *18,* 715–738.
Ebel, R. L. Estimation of the reliability of ratings. *Psychometrika,* 1951, *16,* 407–424.
Martuza, V. R. *Applying Norm-Referenced and Criterion-Referenced Measurement in Education.* Boston: Allyn and Bacon, 1977.
Nunnally, J. C. *Psychometric Theory.* New York: McGraw-Hill, 1978.
Peters, C. C. and Van Voorhis, W. R. *Statistical Procedures and Their Mathematical Bases.* New York: McGraw-Hill, 1940.

chapter 12

Validity

The two chief catchwords in measurement theory are reliability and validity. Standard texts tell their readers that the first step in studying a measure is to assess its reliability, then, assuming adequate results, its validity. This progression answers the two essential questions in measurement:

1. Are scores being assigned to S's consistently?
2. Do these scores measure what the researcher intends them to measure?

Such a neat compartmentalization ignores some serious problems, however. As the last chapter should indicate, there are many ways of conceptualizing and assessing the reliability of a measure. Furthermore, regardless of the method used, the resulting assessment is situation *and* sample specific. Nevertheless, there is usually *one* generally acceptable way of measuring reliability, and it is conveniently communicated via a coefficient with a value between zero and one. The same is, unfortunately, not true of validity.

Robert Ebel (1961) seriously questioned prevailing notions of validity over 20 years ago when he listed four indications that something was seriously wrong with the concept:

1. All the giants of the field of measurement (e.g., Gulliksen, Cureton, Lindquist, Edgerton, and Cronbach) seemed to have different definitions of the word.
2. There is a vast array of types of validity, each of which is substantively different from one another (for example, content, predictive, concurrent, construct, face, factorial, intrinsic).

3. Two surveys conducted 30 years apart on samples of published, standardized tests indicated that validity was either not addressed at all or was inadequately addressed. Ebel suggests that this state of affairs may not simply indicate incompetence on the part of test developers; it may indicate that the concept itself is faulty.

4. The concept of validity is all but nonexistent in physical measurement. Even when two different measures of, say, the hardness of a solid, give disparate results, the physical scientist does not tend to ask which method was more valid.

Ebel concludes this excellent discussion by a very apt quotation: "Have we, in Berkeley's words, first raised a dust and then complained that we cannot see?"

In my opinion, it usually is more useful to visualize the various aspects of both the reliability and validity concepts as lying on the same continuum, which for want of a better word could be called a continuum of *utility*. Certainly a measure is not useful if it does not measure something reliably and certainly this something may or may not be the construct or attribute that the researcher has in mind. The trouble is that what is really being measured can rarely be precisely ascertained. Much of the time, researchers in the human (or softer) sciences cannot even be sure that what they want to measure even exists. (Who, for example, has ever seen an attitude? How do we know that anxiety or stress actually exist over and above the observable symptoms we attribute to them? Are we really sure that clinical behaviors x and y signal competence while z does not?) In the final analysis, all that can be done is to attempt to ascertain whether or not an instrument is appropriate (or useful) for a specific research purpose.

In effect, this is the purpose of all the procedures discussed in the previous chapter, which were equally relevant for the selection of an existing instrument or the creation of a new one. In effect, this is also what the myriad types of validity are all about as well. Thus, while the overall concept called validity may be too diffuse to have much utility in and of itself, some of the specific techniques used to assess and ensure its many facets can be quite helpful in ensuring that a given instrument can indeed be useful in answering a specific research question.*

The first order of business, therefore, will be to discuss what is commonly meant by the various types of validity and the circumstances under which the techniques recommended for their assurance can be useful. The reader should be warned at the onset, however, that this discussion will not result in any truly satisfying degree of resolution, since it is seldom (if ever) possible to state categorically that a measure is absolutely *valid* for any given purpose.

CONTENT VALIDITY

Some time ago, the American Psychological Association recognized four distinctly different types of validity: content, predictive, concurrent, and construct

---

* As with reliability, the techniques discussed will be primarily relevant to measures in which the arithmetic mean and variance are appropriate descriptors (as opposed to criterion-referenced measures that are seldom used in empirical research).

(APA, 1974). The first of these, content validity, when applied to a multiple-item measure, is really nothing more than a sampling issue. The items (or constituents) contained in any given measure can be visualized as a sample drawn from a larger population or domain. This population, however, is not comprised of subjects; it is comprised of all the possible items, tasks, or behaviors that could be used to define what the researcher wishes to measure. The problem with the concept is that there is usually no way to observe or catalogue this population. This means that there is no way to ensure that any given test is, indeed, a representative sample from it.

The utility of content validity as a concept is directly proportionate to the amount that is known about the entity to be measured. In some cognitive measures, for example, content validity can be addressed quite directly. If a researcher is interested in ascertaining how well a sample of third-grade students have mastered their multiplication facts, it is extremely important that the test used for this purpose does, indeed, contain a representative sample of these multiplication facts. Representativeness can, furthermore, be assured because there are exactly 100 multiplication facts between 0×0 and 9×9, these facts can be listed, and an actual random sample drawn from that population.

The assurance of content validity becomes more and more difficult as the measurement process becomes more abstract. How could anyone ever define the population of all possible items for an anxiety scale, for example? How could, in fact, anyone even be sure that such a thing as anxiety exists?

What usually passes for content validity in more abstract measurement problems, therefore, is some statement to the effect that "a group of experts in the field examined the test and judged it to possess content validity." Without further specification such a statement is of very little use, since it could mean only that the test was examined by two or more friends of the developer who said it looked all right after making a few suggestions.

This is not to say that the potential existence of a domain of test items measuring a particular construct should be ignored. If anything, the difficulties involved make such a consideration even more crucial. The test developer should thus be *very* conversant with all the relevant research and theory surrounding the targeted construct, for this is where ideas for items will ultimately come. In fact, I would argue that the assurance of content validity precedes reliability on the utility continuum (see Figure 12-3). It is true that no measure can be valid if it is not reliable, but even if scores are consistently assigned to individuals no measure can be useful if its contents do not match (or reflect) its purpose.

The assurance of content validity in all but the most straightforward situations (such as the aforementioned example involving a clearly specifiable item domain) is basically a two-phased process. Reduced to questions, they become:

1. Do the items selected to measure a given construct reflect all known facets of that construct?
2. Do all the items so selected truly measure the construct?

Both questions are exceedingly difficult to answer authoritatively. The completeness of the instrument (question 1) will primarily be a function of how much is known about the construct. The safest approach is undoubtedly to list all the different aspects or constituents of a construct that are known or have been suggested. If the construct in question is cognitive, this reduces to listing instructional or behavioral objectives. If something more complex is involved, such as a personality inventory, previous theory and research will be the chief sources of these constituents.*

Once this blueprint has been developed, it should be subjected to expert review to assure that all the objectives or categories of constituents have indeed been listed and are indeed relevant. (This step can either be formal — see the technique suggested below — or informal.) Once the test blueprint has been decided upon, items should be written or selected for each category. These items should then be subjected to knowledgeable critique by as many experts in the field as possible. Since one purpose of this critique is to weed out questionable items, it is always a good idea to begin with as large a pool of items as possible.

Various measurement specialists have suggested means by which content validity can be expressed in terms of a single coefficient. Rovinelli and Hambleton (1976) and Hambleton, Swaminathan, Algina, and Coulson (1975) propose quantifying judges' ratings of content validity that, although developed for cognitive tests, have a great deal of potential for improving the content validity of any multiple-item measure.

Martuza (1977) proposes an excellent adaptation for assessing the agreement between such expert judgments. He suggests that a number of experts rate all the items available to measure a given attribute according to some sort of scale, such as:

1	2	3	4
Not relevant	Somewhat relevant	Quite relevant	Very relevant

(Alternatively a dichotomous relevant/not relevant judgment could be used.)

If two raters are available, each item can then be judged independently by each rater and placed into Figure 12-1.

Thus, if item 1 is perceived as quite relevant by rater 1 and not relevant by rater 2, it would be placed in cell B as illustrated in Figure 12-2. If item 2 were considered quite relevant by both raters, it would be placed in cell D.

Suppose, then, that a 15-item test were rated by two judges (Figure 12-2). An interrater agreement can now be calculated by dividing the number of items contained in the congruent cells ($A + D$) by the total number of items (cells $A + B + C + D$):

---

* Generally, I would counsel beginning researchers to select, with expert help, existing instruments designed to measure such phenomena rather than to attempt to develop them on their own.

Rater #1

	Not relevant or somewhat relevant	Quite or very relevant
Rater #2 Not relevant or somewhat relevant	A	B
Quite or very relevant	C	D

Figure 12-1 Interrater reliability model for content validity.

Rater #1

	Not relevant or somewhat relevant	Quite or very relevant
Rater #2 Not relevant or somewhat relevant	A Items #5 (n = 1)	B Items #1 (n = 1)
Quite or very relevant	C Items #6 #7 (n = 2)	D Items #2 #10 #15 #3 #11 #4 #12 #8 #13 #9 #14 (n = 11)

Figure 12-2 A computational example.

$$\text{Interrater agreement} = \frac{A + D}{A + B + C + D}$$

$$= \frac{1 + 11}{1 + 1 + 2 + 11}$$

$$= \frac{12}{15}$$

$$= .80$$

Alternatively (and here I deviate from Martuza's discussion), the researcher could opt for a more direct content validity coefficient by using only cell D (which contains only those items considered valid by both judges) as the numerator:

$$\text{Content validity coefficient} = \frac{D}{A + B + C + D}$$

$$= \frac{11}{15}$$

$$= .73$$

Since none of these procedures is well established, common sense alterations and adaptations are quite permissible. Should more than two judges be used, for example, all combinations of interrater matchups could be computed (with an average coefficient reported) or items could be placed in a single table where cells A and D would represent consensus between all judges involved and with cells B and C being combined and simply allowed to represent disagreements of any sort.

Regardless of the specific technique used, this general strategy is only as good as the judges employed. Its use makes the occasionally tenuous assumption that said judges do indeed know what a construct looks like. If this assumption is reasonable, then the formal use of interrater consensus in the documentation of content validity can be an extremely useful strategy, either in the construction of a measure or in the choice of an existing one. Certainly in the development of a new measure it would be expected that items falling in cell A (and possibly in B and C) would either be deleted or rewritten. (This may even be reasonable when using an existing instrument, if the researcher has more confidence in his or her judges than in the test developer.)

Face Validity

Although vaguely similar to content validity, the once-fashionable concept of face validity has today fallen into deserved disuse. Originally, it was used to designate whether or not a measure looked like it was measuring what it was purported to be measuring. Charles Mosier's (1947) classic article, "A Critical Examination of the Concepts of Face Validity," probably did a great deal to undermine the concept's credibility. Basically, Mosier broke the term down into some of its more common meanings, such as what he called validity by assumption, validity by definition, and the appearance of validity.

Simply *assuming* that a test is valid pretty much speaks for itself; all tests would pass this criterion, since the simple existence of a measure would attest to this form of validity. Validity by definition is really synonymous with content validity and has already been discussed. Validity by appearance harks back to the assumption that, at least from a consumer's point of view, the test ought to look like it measures what it purports to measure. Since no one knows what many measures should look like, however, the concept is of little utility, although it is basically this aspect of face validity that is being attested to when experts *informally* examine a test in a *cursory* fashion. Suffice it to say that content validity is really nothing more than a term used to describe the item writing/selection process, while face validity is often nothing more than a means of informally justifying (or rationalizing) the completed process.

CRITERION-RELATED VALIDITY

The next two conceptualizations of validity are related in the sense that both assume the existence of a separate, established measure or indicator of the construct under consideration.

Predictive Validity

Every measure ever constructed was at least implicitly designed to predict something. The rare exceptions may be the types of items that pollsters occasionally ask that have some intrinsic meaning in and of themselves (such as, "Do you favor administration X's handling of foreign policy?"), and even here responses are often used for larger inferences, such as satisfaction or dissatisfaction with the president's leadership or as an indication of whether or not said president is likely to be reelected.

In the assessment of such things as attitudes, learning, personality, and so forth, the researcher usually predicts a relationship between the construct(s) being studied and some other criterion (for example, behaviors or prognoses). When a measure is explicitly developed to serve such a purpose, then the extent to which it does or does not function in this regard is defined as the measure's predictive validity.

In this regard, predictive validity is very different from content validity. If an attitudinal scale is developed to predict which patients will and will not comply with a certain treatment regimen, for example, and if said scale is not found to predict compliance, this result does not say that the instrument in question did not adequately measure attitudes. It may have measured the attitudinal domain that the researcher had in mind perfectly (although no one is ever likely to know for sure); it was simply not useful in predicting (and, therefore, measuring) compliance.

In classical measurement theory, predictive validity is assessed in terms of a correlation coefficient computed between the instrument in need of validation and the criterion (compliance in this case). In actual practice, this line of reasoning has become obsolete, thanks in large part to the popularity of multiple regression as an analytic technique.

Research experience and familiarity with its literature will preclude even the most optimistic researcher's expectation of a very high correlation between two disparate measures, especially when they are separated by a substantial amount of time. Thus, a university admissions officer, charged with the task of assessing the predictive utility of the SAT's with respect to later college success (for example, grade-point averages), might be quite satisfied with a correlation of .30 between the two measures. In classical measurement terms, the predictive validity of the measure (that is, of the SAT scores) would be said to be .30

with respect to later college success. Said another way, only 9 percent (r^2) of the criterion (later college success) variance could be explained by the SAT scores, hardly an auspicious figure.

The reason that the classical concept of predictive validity is pretty much obsolete is that no one any longer expects much from a single correlation coefficient. Our admissions office would undoubtedly use the SAT's as only one of a set of predictors (which might include high school GPA, other available standardized tests, sex, race, and so forth), hence, the real utility of the measure would be assessed in terms of the unique variation in students' later college success that the SAT's were able to explain (that is, their unique increment to R^2: see Chapter 16).

Predictive validity really involves those specialized, and relatively rare, instances when a measure is designed primarily for use as a predictor of future behavior. When this is the case, it is often established on existing data (for example, students upon whom SAT scores and later academic success indicators are already available). This, of course, is retrospective rather than true prediction. To establish the latter, the relationships should be recomputed prospectively with a new sample of students, although this is seldom done due to the patience required in waiting the necessary time for the data to become available.

Concurrent Validity

The concept of concurrent validity is similar to its predictive counterpart in the sense that it is *criterion related*. The chief distinctions between the two are that in the former:

1. The administrations of the two measures involved (that is, the instrument being developed or selected and the criterion) are not temporarally separated.
2. Both the instrument being validated and the criterion are assumed to measure the same construct.

In other words, all that one need do to establish the concurrent validity of a measure is to administer both it and a criterion to the same sample at approximately the same time (so that it is reasonable to assume that the respondents could not have changed substantively with respect to their possession of the attribute in question). *The resulting correlation coefficient is then defined as the concurrent validity of the measure in question.*

At first glance, concurrent validity would appear to be a very straightforward method of determining whether an instrument does indeed measure what the researcher thinks it measures. It does not take much thought, however, to find a flaw in this appealing logic:

> If a criterion exists that is *known* to measure a construct validly, then what need is there for another instrument that will correlate imperfectly at best with this valid criterion?

If, on the other hand, no criterion exists, then the assessment of concurrent validity is not *possible.*

Finally, if a criterion exists but its efficacy is questionable, then the assessment of concurrent validity is not reasonable because concurrent validity requires one ironclad, uncompromising assumption: the criterion is valid. (The empirical testing of this assumption is not possible, because it leads only to an infinite regress, for whence comes the criterion to test the criterion?)

It is the existence of a reasonable criterion, therefore, that limits the utility of concurrent validity. This problem was not as severe in predictive validity, since there is no lack of important variables that we would like to be able to predict. There, too, the only assumptions regarding a criterion are that it is itself psychometrically sound and that it is important enough to merit the effort needed to predict it.

The concept of concurrent validity is very different in the sense that it is only appropriate if the construct of interest can be measured twice by two different means at approximately the same time. About the only excuse for its consideration is when the existing measure (criterion) is deemed too long or too expensive to administer. When this is the case, a new, shorter, or more easily administered measure can be developed and then correlated with the original. If the obtained coefficient is extremely high, then it may be assumed that the two measures function equivalently. When the coefficient is more moderate (e.g., .50 to .70), as is more usually the case, then additional study is required to see if the two measures are equally *useful* (for example, do they predict the same criterion equally well?).

At the risk of belaboring the point, concurrent validity is a method of assessing the utility of an instrument for one particular purpose. Researchers who routinely collect demographic information on their subjects at the same time that they collect responses on their instrument, and subsequently correlate the former with the latter, are not engaged in concurrent validation. Concurrent validation assumes an established criterion that measures the same construct as the instrument under development. Even those instances where the researcher wishes to adapt an existing instrument to make it relevant to a special sample (such as rewriting an anxiety scale so that children can respond to it) do not fit the concurrent model, unless the same sample can be measured by both instruments (and even here the resulting correlation coefficient is likely to be inconclusive).

The Use of a Pilot Test in Criterion-Related Validity

Just as item analyses can be quite useful in facilitating the reliability and content validity of a measure being developed, so too can item data from a pilot test be used to increase either the predictive or concurrent validity of a new measure. To accomplish this, all that is really necessary is for criterion information to be available on a sample to which the measure in question is being administered.

Then, in addition to the item-to-total correlations (and other information presented in Table 11-4 relevant to determining how each item contributes to the measure's reliability), each item can be correlated with the criterion. Those that correlate very poorly can be assumed not to be contributing to the measure's criterion-related validity and thus be deleted or replaced. Naturally, it is wise to recompute this correlation coefficient using the new set of items to ensure that the measure's validity is indeed being increased by the deletions.* It is also essential that said correlation be recomputed with a separate sample of subjects (called cross-validation), since the original coefficient is almost certainly inflated due to the method by which items were dropped.

CONSTRUCT VALIDITY

The final type of validity that will be discussed here is undoubtedly the most complex and evasive of the four. It is also potentially the most useful. It is called construct validity and is not reportable in terms of a single correlation coefficient. It is never even possible to determine whether or not a measure does or does not possess it. Rather, its evaluation is the evaluation of a gestalt of evidence, of a body of research.

The first step in its consideration involves the definition of exactly what constitutes a construct, no mean task in and of itself. Nunnally (1978) discusses the term as follows:

> To the extent that a variable is abstract rather than concrete, we speak of it as being a construct. Such a variable is literally a construct in that it is something that scientists put together from their own imaginations, something that does not exist as an isolated, observable dimension of behavior. A construct represents a hypothesis (usually half-formed) that a variety of behaviors will correlate with one another in studies of individual differences and/or will be similarly affected by experimental treatments.

Cronbach and Meehl (1955) give a similar, more succinct definition:

> A construct is some postulated attribute of people presumed to be reflected in test performance.

Certainly, it will be agreed that just about every attribute that we can conceive of measuring is a construct. Even objective attributes such as height and weight can be visualized as constructs, for they have no objective reality. They are really nothing more than ideas or *words,* and as Nunnally puts it, it is really not possible to validate a name of something:

> It is more defensible to make no claims for the objective reality of a construct name, e.g., anxiety, and instead to think of the construct name as being a useful

---

* It is also wise to recompute the reliability coefficient, since the shortened instrument may be slightly less stable.

way to label a particular set of observable variables. Then the name is "valid" only to the extent that it accurately communicates to other scientists the kinds of observables being studied.

Construct validation, then, involves the assessment of relationships between generalized names for sets of behaviors or attributes that are perceived to share something in common. In other words, construct validity is a means of assessing whether a measure is related to the world in the same way that the construct it represents is *hypothesized* to relate to the world.

In the final analysis, this assessment involves the computation of correlation coefficients (or comparable statistics) between two or more variables that are assumed either to measure the constructs in question or be related thereto. Borrowing again from Nunnally, the concept of construct validity involves four hypotheses:

1. Construct A and construct B correlate positively.
2. X is a measure of construct A.
3. Y is a measure of construct B.
4. X and Y correlate positively.

Obviously, only the correlation between X and Y can actually be empirically tested, which means that the first three hypotheses must rest on assumptions. If the chief purpose of testing hypothesis 4 is to lend credence to X being a measure of A, then the researcher is assessing the construct validity of an instrument. If the outcome of the correlation between X and Y is as expected, then hypothesis 1 will be true if both 2 and 3 are true (assuming the absence of a false-positive finding and that the correlation is not due to some third construct to which X and Y are related). If X and Y do not correlate, then this lack of correlation will be due to a faulty theory (hypothesis 1), faulty measurements of the constructs in question (hypotheses 2 and 3), or faulty research design.*

If all this is confusing, then the reader may be in the process of grasping the basic rationale behind construct validity. *The process of construct validation is nothing more or less than the scientific process.* Obviously, then, a statement such as "the construct validity of measure X has been established" will never be made by a serious researcher, although certainly evidence to support such a statement can and should be presented.

A natural question thus becomes: *What constitutes evidence of construct validity?* Said another way: *How does a researcher convince other scientists that measure* X *does indeed measure construct* A*?* The answer is by (1) developing the best measure possible and (2) assessing how this measure fits into the overall scheme of what is known, suspected, or believed about the way that construct relates to the world (which is called current knowledge, theory, or in the philosophy of science, the nomological net).

---

* Unfortunately, it is seldom possible to sort out which of these hypotheses is correct.

THE UTILITY CONTINUUM

Construct validity, as I conceive it, can be visualized as the final stop on the aforementioned continuum representing a measure's* utility for a given purpose. Diagrammatically, this continuum might be depicted as shown in Figure 12-3. The first step in developing the best possible instrument thus lies in the item-writing process and the attempt to assure content validity (where applicable). Content validity, in fact, is really synonymous with an a priori consideration of construct validity, since, as stated earlier, the actual domain from which items are theoretically drawn is seldom known, thus forcing the test developer to draw on everything known or hypothesized about the attribute (construct) in question.

The second step involves assuring the instrument's reliability. A totally unreliable measure will have absolutely no construct validity (and possess absolutely no utility for *any* purpose), simply because it is incapable of measuring anything, including the targeted construct. Related to this process is the assessment of the instrument's internal structure as discussed in the previous chapter. So far, we have assumed that the instrument measures a single entity. At some point this assumption probably needs to be tested, which is usually done via a statistical procedure called factor analysis, a device that describes the internal structure of a measure. If the construct in question is believed to be a single entity and a factor analysis indicates the presence of five independent dimensions, then something is either wrong with the theory or with the instrument itself (although it is quite conceivable that *one* of the factors may measure the targeted construct†). This second step may involve a number of alternative approaches to reliability as well, such as inter/intrarater reliability if the subjectivity of scoring is problematic, or test-retest reliability if the stability of the instrument (or construct) over time is a consideration.

If a recognized measure already exists for the attribute in question (that is, a measure whose construct validity/utility has already been adequately documented), then the establishment of concurrent validity could be the final step on this continuum. Otherwise, the distinctions between criterion-related validity and construct validity begin to blur into a final step consisting of seeing how the measure in question fits with whatever theory (or network of empirical relationships) has been developed concerning the construct. This fit is described in terms of either correlation coefficients or experimental outcomes and is

---

* It will be remembered that reliability and validity actually address the scores assigned by a measure rather than the measure itself.

† A factor analysis will *usually* result in more than one independent dimension. Since one of these dimensions is usually much larger than the others and since all the items usually contribute at least a little variance to this large factor, the overall instrument is usually capable of assigning scores consistently (and probably validly) despite its multidimensionality. For this reason, I would argue that if an indicator such as coefficient alpha is sufficiently high, the measure in question is capable of being *useful* (and by implication, valid) even if its internal structure is not thoroughly documented (as via factor analysis). It is primarily for this reason and the fact that so many subjects are required that factor analysis (or other scaling techniques) is not routinely required for all measurement situations. However, such a procedure is always recommended where practical.

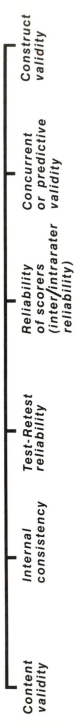

Figure 12-3   The utility continuum.

Content
validity

Internal
consistency

Test-Retest
reliability

Reliability
of scorers
(inter/intrarater
reliability)

Concurrent
or predictive
validity

Construct
validity

usually very difficult to evaluate, since such results can often be viewed from several different perspectives.

AN EXAMPLE

To illustrate this multiple step process, let us consider the well-established practice of evaluating college courses via student ratings. Suppose that a researcher wished to make a case that ratings were really measures of teacher proficiency (that is, that student ratings measured the construct called teaching proficiency). How would such a case be made?

To begin with we would hope that the course evaluation questionnaire would consist of items that thoroughly tapped those behaviors currently thought to reflect teaching proficiency (for example, clarity of explanation, knowledge of subject matter, enthusiasm for the topic). To ensure this, the scale developer would take all the relevant steps necessary to ensure content validity (including reviewing the literature, examining existing course evaluation questionnaires, and subjecting the resulting item pool to formal scrutiny).

It would also be hoped that the resulting instrument would be pilot tested on a reasonably large sample, followed by item-analysis techniques to identify items that detracted from the scale's overall reliability (that is, items that did not correlate reasonably well with the total score). Such items would be subsequently deleted, replaced, or altered.

Assuming that a reasonably reliable course evaluation instrument were then developed, how would its construct validity be tested? If some other acceptable criterion existed by which good and bad instructors could be identified (for example, peer ratings or observational techniques of some sort), the task would be relatively simple. Student ratings of the good and bad instructors would be compared. If a statistically significant difference existed between the two (in the proper direction), then evidence of construct validity would be obtained. (Note the similarity here with concurrent validity, which again is really able to be subsumed under the concept of construct validity as I visualize it.)

Unfortunately, as previously stated, the existence of a completely acceptable criterion seldom exists. Thus, while the above comparison using, say, peer ratings could be performed, we wouldn't be sure that they would be any more valid than student ratings. (This, along with the procedural diversity between the two measures, would preclude the comparison's acceptability as evidence of concurrent validity.) Campbell and Fiske (1959) have addressed this dilemma by suggesting that researchers administer a number of measures to the same sample of subjects, some of which, using the present example, would address teacher proficiency via two or more different *methods* and some of which would address related constructs but would employ the same general methods. (In other words, multiple methods of assessing the same construct versus multiple constructs assessed by the same methods.)

In theory, this is a quite elegant procedure, allowing the researcher to (1) check hypotheses regarding relationships that should (convergent) and should not (discriminant) occur as well as (2) separating out the effects of using common measuring techniques. In reality, the multitrait-multimethod procedure is not very practical, given the difficulty of obtaining several measures of each of several constructs and administering them all to the same sample. Furthermore, it has been my experience that the common variance associated with the same procedures is not great enough to cause that much concern, thus questioning the necessity for so elaborate a procedure.

What, then, are the alternatives? The researcher could simply collect data on a number of variables (some of which should be related to the construct at hand, some of which should not) and assess their relationship with the measure under consideration. The problem here is in determining exactly which relationships constitute positive evidence of construct validity and which constitute negative evidence.

Suppose, for example, that our researcher administered the course evaluation questionnaires in the classrooms of a heterogeneous sample of instructors with respect to instructor sex and faculty rank. Since no theoretical or empirical rationale exists to predict that females should be better or poorer instructors than males, a nonsignificant relationship between ratings and sex would be hypothesized. Statistically nonsignificant relationships are more common than statistically significant ones, however, thus such a discriminant finding would be very weak evidence for the construct validity of student ratings.

Hypothesizing a direction for the relationship between student ratings and faculty rank illustrates an even more serious limitation in the usual practice of construct validation. Reasonable arguments could be made both for and against the existence of such a relationship and, given its existence, for it being in either direction (higher-ranked faculty, for example, presumably have more expertise in their fields as well as more teaching experience; junior faculty may be fresher, more enthusiastic, and better able to relate to students). Thus, regardless of the way the correlation came out, the researcher would not be much better off than before. (Perhaps an exception to this would be the unlikely scenario in which a very high correlation coefficient were obtained. Here, the researcher might conclude that the instrument addressed prestige or some related variable, since there is no reason to expect a near perfect correlation between rank and teaching proficiency.)

Another potentially more useful technique involves the generation of a critical, experimental test of a measure's construct validity. In our student rating example, Holmes (1972) provides an excellent illustration. One of the arguments against student ratings constituting a valid measure of teaching proficiency is the oft-observed relationship between the grades students *expect* from instructors and the ratings they assign them. (Students expecting A's rate their instructors higher than students expecting D's, for example.)

The problem with this relationship, as with that between faculty rank and ratings, is that it is subject to several alternative explanations. It may be that instructors who assign high grades do so because their students have profited more from their instruction, or it may be that they simply bought higher ratings with their leniency. From a within-class perspective, an opposite argument could be made. Is it not equally reasonable that the instructor may have been more effective for those students receiving A's than those receiving D's? Alternatively, of course, students may assign ratings based on their expected grade irrespective of anything the instructor did or did not do.

Holmes's study was interesting in this regard because he decided to manipulate grades *experimentally* to see if the relationship held. It would seem to follow,* then, that any relationship between ratings and experimentally manipulated grades would constitute evidence of construct *in*validity, since the instructor's teaching proficiency was obviously not affected by the manipulation. To accomplish this manipulation, Holmes randomly assigned students who were expecting a given grade based on actual classroom performance to one of two conditions: they were either told that they were to receive the grade they had earned or they were informed that they were to receive a lower grade than they were legitimately expecting. As hypothesized, those informed that they were receiving lower grades than justified rated the instructor lower. Although at first glance this would appear to be clearly indicative of rating invalidity, the omnipresent problem of alternative interpretations of the same result, even though experimentally determined, surface. Would not, for example, an equally legitimate interpretation be that the cheated students should have rated this instructor lower? Is not grading fairness (or appropriateness) one facet of instructional competence? Viewed from this perspective, could not the same result constitute evidence of construct validity?

The bottom line, here, is not that it is impossible to formulate a critical hypothesis that can bear on the construct validity of a measure. It is not even that correlational evidence cannot be brought to bear on the subject. However, I contend that:

1. *Construct validity really encompasses all the other types of validity* (for example, content, predictive, concurrent).
2. *Since each of these has severe practical problems* (for example, the difficulty of identifying a suitable criterion measure), *so has construct validity.*
3. *Construct validity can almost never be established by a single study, rather it is best assessed by an entire gestalt of evidence.*†
4. *This gestalt is itself difficult to assess, given:*
   (a) *The multiple interpretations usually possible for any single relationship.*
   (b) *The difficulty of marshaling all this evidence* (there are hundreds of studies involving student ratings, for example).

My conclusion, therefore, although undoubtedly antithetical to the majority of the research community, is that we have indeed raised a dust through

---

* From this point on, I deviate at will from Holmes's arguments, thus any logical discrepancies should not be laid on his doorstep.

† Naturally, the better developed the empirical and theoretical evidence around a given construct, the better the chances of coming to some reasonable conclusion regarding one of its measures' validity.

which it is impossible to see, that the multifaceted concept of validity is empirical research's version of the emperor's new clothes parable, and that researchers employing paper-and-pencil or observational measures follow the lead of their hard science colleagues and disregard validity unless the purpose of the study at hand is primarily measurement oriented. In other words:

> *If a measure is reliable, appears to possess adequate content validity, and appears to be relevant for the research purposes at hand, use it until a better measure is developed.*

Useful measures will survive, worthless ones will not. No one has ever consciously set out to assess the validity of blood pressure as a physiological measure, yet its utility has been well established over the years for certain purposes through empirically demonstrated relationships with other variables (for example, the incidence of strokes). No one uses head circumference as a measure of intelligence anymore, but rest assured that its demise was brought about by decades of negative results, not by a single study. The best that individual researchers can realistically expect to accomplish is to choose or develop their measures with enough care to ensure that their studies have a reasonable chance of achieving their purposes. If done properly, their results may very well ultimately be included in the literature that decides the fate of a construct or the means of measuring it.

SUMMARY

Although a case can be made for evaluating a measure's utility rather than its validity, the four most common types of validity are content, concurrent, predictive, and construct. Content validity addresses the adequacy and appropriateness of a measure's items as a sample of all the possible items that could be employed to assess an attribute. As such, it is relevant only for composite scores. Concurrent and predictive validity assess the relationship between a measure and a criterion of some sort, while construct validity is seen as the final point on a utility continuum. As such, it is visualized as a process consisting of (1) developing the best measure possible and (2) assessing how this measure fits into the overall scheme of what is known, suspected, or believed about the fit between the measured construct and current knowledge or theory. Given the difficulty inherent in the validation process, I counsel beginning researchers to search primarily for reliable measures that appear to possess adequate content validity and to be relevant for their research objectives.

REFERENCES

American Psychological Association. *Standards for Educational and Psychological Tests and Manuals.* Washington, D.C: American Psychological Association, 1974.

Campbell, D. T., and Fiske, D. W. Convergent and discriminant validation by the multitrait-multimethod matrix. *Psychological Bulletin,* 1959, *56,* 81–105.

Cronbach, L. J., and Meehl, P. E. Construct validity in psychological tests. *Psychological Bulletin,* 1955, *52,* 281–302.

Ebel, R. L. Must all tests be valid? *American Psychologist,* 1961, *16,* 640–647.

Hambleton, R. K., Swaminathan, H., Algina, J., and Coulson, D. Criterion-referenced testing and measurement: review of technical issues and developments. Paper presented at the Annual Meeting of the American Educational Research Association, 1975.

Holmes, D. S. Effects of grades and disconfirmed grade expectancies on students' evaluations of their instructors. *Journal of Educational Psychology,* 1972, *63,* 130–133.

Martuza, V. R. *Applying Norm-Referenced and Criterion-Referenced Measurement in Education.* Boston: Allyn and Bacon, 1977.

Mosier, C. I. A critical examination of the concepts of face validity. *Educational and Psychological Measurement,* 1947, *7,* 191–205.

Nunnally, J. C. *Psychometric Theory.* New York: McGraw-Hill, 1978.

Rovinelli, R., and Hambleton, R. K. On the use of content specialists in the assessment of criterion referenced test item validity. *Laboratory of Psychometrics and Evaluation Research Report No. 24.* Amherst, Mass: The University of Massachusetts, 1976.

four

STATISTICAL ANALYSIS

chapter 13

Data Analysis: An Overview

There was a time in the not too distant past when the statistical analysis of data was one of the most time consuming and tedious aspects of the research process. I can personally recall spending an entire weekend performing a particularly complex analysis of covariance on a four-function calculator. Today, given the almost universal availability of computers and (equally important) easy-to-use statistical programs, data analysis is undoubtedly the most straightforward (and probably the easiest) component of the research process. Both computers and the statistical routines written for them come in a great many shapes and forms. Some machines are no larger than a pocket calculator and either have their statistical programs built into their circuits or are programmable via small magnetic tapes. Data are normally entered manually by simply touching keys and are usually erased from the machine's memory as soon as the electric current is turned off, hence necessitating reentry for additional analyses. These are undoubtedly the quickest and most convenient computers for use with relatively small data sets and for relatively simple analyses.

In general, the popularity of these very small machines is declining rapidly because of the growing availability of personal computers. These machines are about the size of a typewriter and come equipped with a video screen, a printer, or both. They possess far greater storage capability and many have the very important advantage of storing data on magnetic disks for reanalysis. Most also have sophisticated preprogrammed statistical packages (an absolute necessity) as accessories. Personal computers are convenient, relatively inexpensive, and will probably someday be the primary data analysis choice of most practicing researchers.

The third type of machine used for data analysis is the mainframe computer owned by large institutions. These machines have such enormous capacities that they can be used by many people at the same time. They are normally more flexible than their smaller counterparts, having more programs (called software) and often being able to accept data via a number of methods (such as cards, tape, or direct entry). They are especially useful for extremely large-scale analyses that may exceed the capacity of personal computers. They are also often accessible to researchers who do not have the funds to purchase their own machines.

Statistical programs come in as many shapes and forms as the machines for which they are written. Each computing system has a variety of programs written especially for them, but by far the most commonly used routines are those contained in large, statistical packages encompassing dozens of procedures. The most popular (and, in my opinion, the best) of these are:

1. SPSS^x [Statistical Package for the Social Sciences: SPSS, Inc. (1983), McGraw-Hill.]
2. BMDP [Biomedical Computer Programs: Dixon et al. (1981), University of California Press.]
3. SAS [Statistical Analysis Systems: (1982), SAS Institute.]

Systems such as these are so powerful and applicable to such a wide range of research endeavors that I strongly suggest that anyone interested enough in empirical research to contemplate conducting a study take the time to become familiar with one of them. It is a skill that will be used over and over again. It is also a skill that can be acquired fairly quickly via the use of a good tutor.

Thus, while it is always possible simply to hire someone to perform one's data analyses, in the long run this is neither a cost effective nor a wise strategy. Statistical analysis is such an integral part of the research process that a researcher must at least know *how* to analyze his or her own data (even if a decision is ultimately made to hire someone else to do it) for at least three reasons:

1. A simple error in data analysis can invalidate an otherwise perfectly executed study. The researcher who does not understand the concepts involved is unlikely to catch such an error.
2. Very profitable future research studies are often suggested by creatively sifting through data. This is very difficult to do by remote control.
3. It is just plain fun to be the first to see a new piece of knowledge. I have found nothing, in fact, to be more intellectually stimulating.

To illustrate the use of a computer for testing a typical hypothesis, let us actually illustrate the steps involved via a hypothetical set of data.

AN EXAMPLE OF A COMPUTER ANALYSIS

Suppose that our ongoing weight-loss study had been performed using the randomized-experimental/control-group–posttest-only model with the data

Table 13-1   HYPOTHETICAL STUDY DATA

E (Dietary education/ exercise regimen) number of pounds lost		C (Routine clinical care only) number of pounds lost	
S_1	14	S_{11}	6
S_2	12	S_{12}	4
S_3	24	S_{13}	18
S_4	20	S_{14}	9
S_5	19	S_{15}	2
S_6	0	S_{16}	0
S_7	10	S_{17}	0
S_8	14	S_{18}	6
S_9	9	S_{19}	2
S_{10}	19	S_{20}	8

shown in Table 13-1 resulting. Normally a full-scale study would employ more subjects than this. In addition, more data would be obtained on the subjects (for example, prestudy weight, clinical indicators of prognosis, demographic information), but for the time being let us assume that the investigator's only interest was to answer the following question:

Does a program of dietary education and supervised exercise result in greater weight loss than routine clinical care employing neither of these strategies?

Since subjects were randomly assigned to the two groups, the assumption can be made that everyone began with an equal propensity to lose weight, hence what the investigator really wants to know is:

Is there a statistically significant difference between the two groups with respect to the means of the dependent variable?

To answer this question the researcher needs to know three things:

1. What the independent variable is.
2. What the dependent variable is.
3. That the *t*-test for independent samples is the statistical procedure of choice.

As will be discussed in more detail later:

1. If differences between means are desired.
2. If there are only two means involved.
3. If scores from different, unmatched subjects make up those means.
4. If there are no controlling variables.
5. Then the procedure of choice is the *t*-test for independent samples.

If the t-test were to be performed manually, the 20 numbers presented in Table 13-1 would be plugged into the t-test formula as follows:

$$t = \frac{\overline{X}_E - \overline{X}_C}{\sqrt{\dfrac{\text{Var}_E}{n_E} + \dfrac{\text{Var}_C}{n_C}}}$$

$$= \frac{14.10 - 5.50}{\sqrt{\dfrac{47.43}{10} + \dfrac{29.17}{10}}}$$

$$= \frac{8.60}{2.77}$$

$$= 3.11$$

The t-value of 3.11 would then be compared to its appropriate critical value in a table representing the t-distribution. Since the obtained t is larger than this value, the researcher would infer that the program of dietary education plus exercise did indeed result in greater average weight loss than the absence thereof.

If the t-test were to be done on a personal computer, all that would be necessary would be for the researcher to insert the appropriate program and key in the 20 numbers according to that program's instructions. At the press of a button the t-statistic, the two means and standard deviations, and possibly the exact probability of said statistic occurring by chance alone would either be printed out or displayed on a screen.

If the researcher chose to use one of the statistical packages available on a large computer, the process would be a little more involved but still quite straightforward. The first step in the use of one of these programs (as well as in the use of a personal computer for that matter) in the analysis of data, such as that depicted in Table 13-1, would be to code that data via a variable-by-subject matrix format with the variables being listed horizontally and the subjects vertically. Coding forms are available for such purposes, normally being 80 columns wide and 24 rows deep.

The rules for setting up such a matrix are very simple. Variables are assigned to columns, subjects to rows. The same variables are always coded in the same columns, with the right-most column representing the lowest-valued digit ("ones" if no decimals are involved), the next column to the left the next-highest digit ("tens" if no decimals are involved), and so forth. The present data might use the following format:

Weight loss codebook		
Columns	**Variable**	**Code**
1–2	Subject I.D.	The researcher could simply begin with 01 and proceed to 20.
4	Group membership	1 = Experimental 2 = Control
6–7	Weight loss	Number of pounds lost

Columns

Rows	1	2	3	4	5	6	7	8	9	10	11	12	. . . . .
1	0	1		1		1	4						
2	0	2		1		1	2						
3	0	3		1		2	4						
4	0	4		1		2	0						
•	•	•		•		•	•						
•	•	•		•		•	•						
•	•	•		•		•	•						
17	1	7		2			0						
18	1	8		2			6						
19	1	9		2			2						
20	2	0		2			8						

Figure 13-1 The data from Table 13-1 coded for computer entry.

Coded, the information would look as shown in Figure 13-1. Once checked, the data could now be entered into the computer, either directly via a terminal keyboard or via cards (tapes are normally reserved for larger data sets). Although the type of coding form depicted in Figure 13-1 was originally developed for cards, I recommend its use for all types of data entry due to the increased accuracy it affords.

Regardless of how the data are entered, they should always be checked for accuracy. The first step in this process involves checking the coding forms against the raw data, then asking the computer to print out descriptive statistics for each variable, including the mean and the highest and lowest values each take. [The mean for group membership here should thus be 1.50, with the lowest value being 1 and the highest value 2. If the highest value were 4, the researcher would thus know that either a coding or a data entry error had been made. He or she could then ask the computer to print out the raw data (which would look like Figure 13-1) to find the error.]

Once the researcher is satisfied that the data are accurate, a number of basic things must be communicated to the computer. These can be visualized in terms of 10 steps, the number and order of which may vary from computing system to computing system and from program to program:

1. The researcher's account number and identification number (since mainframe computing time is assigned only to authorized personnel).

2. The name of the program (for example, SPSS, BMDP, SAS) to be used.
3. The number of variables being employed (two in the present case).
4. The way the data are to be entered (for example, card, tape).
5. Where the variables are located in the variable x subject matrix (columns 4, 6, and 7 in the present case).
6. The number of subjects involved (20 in the present case).
7. The statistical procedure to be used (independent sample *t*-test).
8. What the independent and dependent variables are.
9. An indication of the point at which the commands are over and the data are beginning.
10. An indication that the data have all been read.

Once entered the following output would be expected:

1. *Means and standard deviations of the two groups.* These descriptive statistics are interesting in their own rights and would appear in the final research report. Furthermore, I suggest that the means themselves be checked via a pocket calculator (using the coding forms) as a quality control device. This is not particularly time consuming, except for very large data sets, and it does protect against format or procedural command errors that are quite common with computer use.
2. *The number of subjects in each group.* This too is reported in the final write-up. It can serve as a flag to detect errors, since the researcher already knows how many pieces of data should be available for the analysis.
3. *A test for the homogeneity of the two groups' variances.* Theoretically, the variance of the control group should not differ significantly from that of the experimental group. In reality, if the number of subjects is the same in each group, this doesn't make much difference, although the program provides a more conservative *t*-statistic for those situations in which the variances of the two groups do differ significantly.
4. *The* t-*statistic and its probability level.* Both are necessary for the final research report. The presence of the significance level avoids the necessity of consulting a table of the *t*-distribution.

Advantages and Disadvantages of Computer Analysis

Computers are a great boon to researchers. Many of the more complex statistical analyses are practically impossible without them. For others, countless hours of toil are saved. More importantly, computers are *far* more accurate than human beings, which ironically points to their chief disadvantage: *computers do exactly as they are instructed.* They do not second-guess their masters, hence if an incorrect command is given, this command will be carried out regardless of the consequences.

As an example, suppose that the location of the subjects' weights (command 5) had been inadvertently written as though it were in columns 7 and 8 instead of columns 6 and 7. This very small mistake would cause column 6 in

Figure 13-1 (the "tens" digits) to be ignored altogether. Instead, the old "ones" digit would now be read as the "tens" digit while column 8 (in which nothing at all is coded) would be incorrectly read as the new "ones" digit. Thus, the computer would treat the first experimental subject (01) as though he or she had lost 40 instead of 14 pounds, the second as though 20 pounds had been lost instead of 12, and so on down to the final control subject (20), who would be treated as though he or she had lost 80 pounds when in reality only 8 had been lost.

If this error were to go undetected, the *t*-statistic would have turned out to be .25 (which is not statistically significant) with the control group actually registering numerically greater weight loss (45 versus 41 pounds) than the experimental group. An error of this sort is all too possible, although it would have been easily detected if reasonable precautionary measures had been taken. To repeat, therefore, I wholeheartedly recommend the use of a computer for data analysis of research studies with the following stipulations:

1. That the raw data be coded as they will be entered into the computer (either on an 80-column coding sheet or other form especially set up for computer entry).
2. That this coded data be checked against the raw data for accuracy.
3. That the data entered into the computer be checked against the coding sheets (this is normally done by a process called verification).
4. That the means and ranges (or other relevant statistics, such as a frequency distribution) be examined for each variable for appropriateness and, when possible, one or more of these be checked for accuracy via a pocket calculator (assuming the sample size is not prohibitively large). When this latter strategy is impractical, the highest and lowest value for each variable identified by the computer should at least be checked for appropriateness. [In the above error, the researcher would immediately know that no one could have lost 90 pounds as subjects 05, 09, 10, and 14 (see Table 13-1) would have via this format error.]

REDUNDANCY AMONG STATISTICAL PROCEDURES

What the computer will *not* do for researchers, of course, is either tell them what statistics are appropriate for what situations or interpret the results accruing from their use. Given the fact that the computer *will* calculate whatever statistic is chosen, and even tell the researcher how likely that statistic would have occurred by chance alone, selection and interpretation of the proper statistic becomes by default the most important (and difficult) aspects of data analysis.

One contributor to this difficulty for beginning researchers lies in the fact that there is seldom one and only one way to analyze the data accruing from any given study. This is partly due to an almost ridiculous redundancy between seemingly diverse statistical procedures. It has been said, in fact, that practically all the parametric statistical procedures (that is, statistics appropriate for data for which means and standard deviations are appropriate) can be viewed as extensions of the Pearson *r*. The data presented in Table 13-1, for example, would certainly almost always be analyzed via a t-test. As will be discussed in the next chapter, however, it could just as easily be analyzed via a one-way analysis of variance procedure, in which case an F-ratio would replace the t-statistic. Thus, F would be 9.67 which, not coincidentally, is exactly equal to 3.11^2 (the original t computed for these data).

These data could also be visualized as reflective of a situation in which the *relationship* between group membership (that is, E versus C) and the number of pounds lost was desired. Viewed from this perspective, a Pearson r could be used to analyze the data, now set up in the classical correlational model as shown in Table 13-2. The r computed on these numbers would result in a coefficient of $-.59$, which again not coincidentally, would be statistically significant at exactly the same level as a t of 3.11 and an F of 9.66. Furthermore, two numbers generated from the calculation of the F-ratio (see Chapter 15) can be combined as follows to produce r^2:

$$r^2 = \frac{SS_{\text{between groups}}}{SS_{\text{total}}}$$
$$= .35$$
$$= (-.59)^2$$

Table 13-2 THE DATA FROM TABLE 13-1 REFORMULATED INTO A CORRELATIONAL MODEL

	X Group membership: $1 = E; 2 = C$	Y Number of pounds lost
S_1	1	14
S_2	1	12
S_3	1	24
S_4	1	20
S_5	1	19
S_6	1	0
S_7	1	10
S_8	1	14
S_9	1	9
S_{10}	1	19
S_{11}	2	6
S_{12}	2	4
S_{13}	2	18
S_{14}	2	9
S_{15}	2	2
S_{16}	2	0
S_{17}	2	0
S_{18}	2	6
S_{19}	2	2
S_{20}	2	8

The same data could also have been analyzed via a procedure called *eta* or the point biserial correlation coefficient, all of which would produce the same basic results.

Although other examples abound, the point here is that there is truly a great deal of redundancy in seemingly disparate statistical procedures. Therefore, there are always several correct ways to analyze the same data, thus any scheme designed to help beginning researchers to choose *the* one correct method to test a hypothesis must by necessity have a degree of arbitrariness about it. Still, there is usually one most common way to analyze any particular situation. The data presented in Table 13-1, for example, would be analyzed via an independent samples *t*-test by the vast majority of practicing researchers. If the subjects in the experimental and control groups were matched, then these same researchers would just as surely use a dependent samples *t*-test, even though a repeated-measures ANOVA or a partial correlation would produce the same results.

In my opinion, the beginning investigator would be wise to employ those procedures most commonly used for any given situation, if for no other reason than the comfort it will bring the people who read his or her final research report. The following three chapters are therefore dedicated to enabling beginning researchers to select and interpret those statistics that most appropriately address their hypotheses.

SELECTING AN APPROPRIATE STATISTICAL PROCEDURE

The first step in selecting a statistical procedure involved differentiating between the study's independent and dependent variables. Let us therefore review this important distinction.

Independent versus Dependent Variables

A variable is considered independent when it is conceived of as being capable of influencing another variable under study, either by itself or in combination with other variables. In experimental and quasi-experimental research, this includes the experimental manipulation or group membership (for example, experimental versus control, which are considered two levels of the *same* independent variable) *and* any other variables that might act in conjunction with that manipulation or that are essentially nonmanipulatable (such as sex). The dependent variable in such a model is the attribute that the experimental manipulation is designed to manipulate. Thus, in the evaluation of our clinical program designed to help subjects lose weight, the experimental intervention and its control constitute two levels of the independent variable, with weight loss being the dependent variable. If we wished to see if a variable such as personality acted in conjunction with the experimental intervention to affect weight loss (or, viewed in another way, if the experimental intervention were differentially effective for different personality types), then personality type would be a second independent variable.

In correlational research, independent variables are normally conceived of as *potentially* influencing (since nothing is manipulated in such studies) or at least predating the dependent variable. Similarly, variables employed primarily for statistical control (whether in experimental or nonexperimental research) are visualized as independent variables* as well.

Assumptions Regarding Selection of Statistics

The statistical procedures discussed in this book assume the presence of only one dependent variable per study. It is further assumed that the arithmetic mean can be used to appropriately describe the sample's scores on this dependent variable.

If a study's dependent variable is categorical in nature, then chances are that a nonparametric statistical procedure is called for and the reader is referred to either Siegel (1956) or Hollander and Wolfe (1973). If a study possesses more than one dependent variable, the researcher has two basic options. These are:

1. Using a multivariate statistical procedure.
2. Analyzing each dependent variable separately using one of the statistical procedures disucssed in this book.

The first option is unquestionably preferred by most present-day methodologists. However, I believe that some degree of advance training is required for the proper use and interpretation of most multivariate statistical procedures. In lieu of this, I recommend that a beginning researcher collaborate with a colleague who has had such training if this option is employed.

Although there are definitely differences of opinion on this matter, I believe that the second option will not result in major distortions as long as the number of dependent variables is not excessive and especially if a more stringent alpha level is employed. Thus, an alpha level of .01 might be selected instead of .05 or, more properly, the alpha level could be set at .05 divided by the number of dependent variables employed.†

Let us assume that a study does possess only one dependent variable for which the arithmetic mean is an appropriate descriptor. How then does one go about selecting an appropriate statistical procedure? In the first place, the following question must be addressed:

Is the hypothesis stated in terms of differences between groups or relationships between variables?

Differences Between Groups   If differences between groups are of interest, there are two additional questions that must be answered.

---

* They are also called matching variables, control variables, and covariates.
   † As an example, if four *t*-tests were to be performed between the same two groups, the a priori significance level could be set at .0125 (.05 divided by 4).

1. *Are any of the independent variables included primarily for statistical control?*
2. *How many groups are involved?*

If the answer to the first question is yes, then the statistical procedure of choice will probably be some sort of *analysis of covariance*. These procedures are discussed in the next two chapters. If there are no controlling variables and only two groups involved (question 2), then a *t*-test will be employed.* If more than two groups are involved, then some sort of *analysis of variance* procedure will be employed. (These are also discussed in Chapters 14 and 15.)

Relationships Between Variables   The first question that must be addressed here is:

How many variables are involved?

If two, then the Pearson *r* is the statistic of choice as long as the arithmetic mean is appropriate for both. If three or more variables are to be employed in assessing the same relationship, then the procedure of choice is probably either:

1. A *multiple correlation* (the procedure itself is most often referred to as *multiple regression*) when the combined impact of two or more independent variables upon a single dependent variable is desired.
2. A *partial correlation* when all but two of the variables are partialled out (or used for statistical control).

SUMMARY

Statistical analysis today is almost universally performed via computer. Although recommended, computer analysis requires care both in respect to data entry and the selection of an appropriate statistical procedure.

Although considerable redundancy exists among the statistical procedures available, there is usually one most commonly employed procedure for any given situation. If only one dependent variable is employed and if this variable can be appropriately described by the arithmetic mean, then the statistical procedure of choice is usually one of the following:

1. *Hypotheses dealing with differences between groups.*
   a. t-*test* (two groups, no controlling variables).
   b. *Analysis of variance* (three or more groups, no controlling variables).
   c. *Analysis of covariance* (one or more controlling variables).
2. *Hypotheses dealing with relationships between variables.*
   a. *Pearson* r (two variables appropriately described by the mean).

---

* If the two groups contained different, unmatched subjects, then the *t*-test used is called an independent samples *t*-test. If matched or identical subjects are present in the groups, then a correlated or dependent samples *t*-test is indicated.

b. *Partial correlation* (three or more variables as described in Chapter 5).
c. *Multiple correlation* or *multiple regression* (three or more variables as described in Chapter 5 and discussed in Chapter 17).

REFERENCES

Dixon et al. *Biomedical Computer Programs.* Los Angeles: University of California Press, 1981.
Hollander, M., and Wolfe, D. A. *Nonparametric Statistical Methods.* New York: Wiley, 1973.
SAS User's Guide: Basics. Cary, N.C.: Statistical Analysis System Institute, 1982.
Siegel, S. *Nonparametric Statistics for the Behavioral Sciences.* New York: McGraw-Hill, 1956.
SPSS, Inc. *SPSS^x: User's Guide.* New York: McGraw-Hill, 1983.

chapter *14*

Single-Factor (One-Way) Analysis of Variance and Covariance

As discussed in Chapter 8, it is not unusual for more than two groups to be employed in a single study. Let us therefore assume that the data shown in Table 14-1 resulted from the three-group example presented therein. With these results the researcher will be interested in three mean differences: 14.10 (E_1) versus 5.50 (C); 12.90 (E_2) versus 5.50 (C); and 14.10 (E_1) versus 12.90 (E_2). One option would be to employ three separate, independent-sample t-tests for the purpose, one for each mean difference. It will be recalled, however, that the distribution for the t-statistic is applicable to one test of one mean difference per experiment. To compute more for nonindependent* data increases the probability of obtaining statistically significant differences by chance alone. In other words, it changes the study's original alpha level and thereby violates one of the most important logical assumptions in hypothesis testing (see Chapter 4).

The researcher therefore has three alternatives:

1. The t-distribution itself (and thus the alpha level) can be adjusted for the number of contrasts contemplated (three in the present example).
2. A limited number of independent, a priori contrasts can be hypothesized.
3. A procedure (analysis of variance) whose statistic's distribution is already adjusted for the number of mean differences involved can be employed.

---

* The concept of independence or orthogonality of contrasts is discussed later in this chapter.

Table   14-1   HYPOTHETICAL DATA FOR A THREE-GROUP SINGLE-FACTOR DESIGN

E_1 (Dietary education and exercise regimen) number of pounds lost		E_2 (Dietary education only) number of pounds lost		C (Routine clinical care only) number of pounds lost	
S_1	24	S_{11}	22	S_{21}	9
S_2	20	S_{12}	20	S_{22}	2
S_3	14	S_{13}	14	S_{23}	6
S_4	12	S_{14}	10	S_{24}	0
S_5	19	S_{15}	18	S_{25}	18
S_6	0	S_{16}	5	S_{26}	4
S_7	10	S_{17}	8	S_{27}	0
S_8	14	S_{18}	12	S_{28}	8
S_9	9	S_{19}	3	S_{29}	2
S_{10}	19	S_{20}	17	S_{30}	6
$\Sigma X = 141$		$\Sigma X = 129$		$\Sigma X = 55$	
$\overline{X} = 14.10$		$\overline{X} = 12.90$		$\overline{X} = 5.50$	
S.D. = 6.89		S.D. = 6.42		S.D. = 5.40	
Var. = 47.43		Var. = 41.21		Var. = 29.17	

Although each of these options can be appropriate (the first two are discussed in more detail later in the chapter), the third is the most commonly chosen. There are several reasons for this:

1. The number of t-tests necessary to test all the contrasts contained in some studies can become somewhat unwieldy as the number of groups proliferates (five groups imply ten mean differences, for example).
2. A priori contrasts contain stipulations that are sometimes too restrictive for certain situations (as explained later in this chapter).
3. The analysis of variance procedure allows the researcher to ascertain the discriminatory power of all involved groups in combination. (As will be explained below, this is reported in terms of the amount of variance in the dependent variable that is accounted for by group membership.)

THE BETWEEN-SUBJECTS MODEL

The analysis of variance (ANOVA) counterpart of the independent samples t-test is referred to as either a *between-subjects* (because different, unmatched subjects are contained in each group), *one-way analysis of variance* (because only one independent variable is involved) or a *between-subjects, single-factor analysis of variance* (again because of the single independent variable or factor).

Relationship to the *t*-Test for Independent Samples

One-way ANOVA is a direct extension of the *t*-test. In fact, the two statistics yield identical results when applied to two-group designs. (On page 232, for example, we found the *t* between E_1 and C means to be 3.10. An ANOVA computed on these same data would result in a statistic, called an *F*, of 9.61. It is not coincidental that $\sqrt{9.61} = 3.10$ and $3.10^2 = 9.61$. For the two-group model, the *t*-test gives identical results to ANOVA: $t^2 = F$; $\sqrt{F} = t$.)

Given the similarity between the two statistics, the same assumptions governing the use of the *t*-test would also be expected to apply to ANOVA. This indeed is the case, with ANOVA being basically appropriate for:

1. Any dependent variable for which the arithmetic mean is appropriate.
2. Any independent variable lending itself to defining two or more discrete groups.
3. Any distribution of scores that does not violate the homogeneity of variance assumption (that is, that the variance within any single group is not statistically different from that within any other group).*

Conceptual Basis

As with the *t*-test, the almost universal availability of digital computers makes it no longer necessary to know *how* to compute an analysis of variance. Blind faith in anything, however, including a computer routine, is not a characteristic normally found in serious researchers. Therefore, a true *understanding* of the conceptual basis of the fundamental statistical procedures used in empirical research has very real affective and practical advantages.

All ANOVA procedures operate under the assumption that distinct sources of variation exist among subjects. These sources possess the following characteristics:

1. They are logically identifiable *prior* to analysis.
2. They are from two basic sources (explainable versus unexplainable).
3. The ratio between the two is indicative of the relative confidence that can be placed in the judgment that any observed differences are *real* and not a function of chance.

The key to understanding all ANOVA type procedures lies in the ability to identify all the possible sources of variation within any given design. Once identified and computed, the size of the explained or systematic variance is directly contrasted to that of its unexplained, nonsystematic counterpart to yield an *F*-ratio:

---

* As with the *t*-test, ANOVA is relatively robust to this assumption unless the numbers of subjects within groups also differ. Corrections do exist, however, which are basically extensions of the separate variance *t*-test to three or more groups. The most accessible of these procedures are the Welch and Brown-Forsythe statistics that are available via the Biomedical computer programs (Dixon, 1981) and that provide more conservative tests.

$$F = \frac{\text{explained variation}}{\text{unexplained variation}} \qquad (14\text{-}1)$$

This F-ratio is then compared to a distribution of like statistics (just as was done for the t) to determine its probability level.

Review of Statistical Variation

Prior to discussing how these different sources of variation are identified, let us first review the computational basis of variance from Chapter 3. It will be remembered that the variance of a set of scores may be computed in one of two ways:

$$\text{Variance} = \frac{\Sigma(X - \bar{X})^2}{n - 1} \qquad (14\text{-}2)$$

$$\text{Variance} = \frac{\Sigma X^2 - \dfrac{(\Sigma X)^2}{n}}{n - 1} \qquad (14\text{-}3)$$

The first formula is conceptually clearer, showing variance as a sort of average squared deviation score (hence the use of the term sum of squares in the numerator). The second formula is mathematically equivalent to the first, that is

$$\Sigma(X - \bar{X})^2 = \Sigma X^2 - \frac{(\Sigma X)^2}{n}$$

and although not as appealing conceptually, it will be employed in this chapter because of its computational advantages.

Once the conceptual and computational basis of variance is grasped, a visual image of a study's design, such as the one presented in Table 14-1, should be examined to differentiate explained from unexplained sources. When this is done, all that remains is to substitute the appropriate data points in Equation 14-3 and compute the F-ratio.

Source I. Systematic (Between-Group) Variation

The most obvious source of variation among the scores in Table 14-1 lies in the group membership of the 30 subjects involved. Subjects in different groups *should* systematically differ from one another; the creation of such differences constitutes the chief purpose of the study.

It is possible to use either group means or group sums to compute the between-group variance. In either case, it is necessary to correct the chosen data point (that is, group sums or group means) for the number of subjects involved. For present purposes, let us use the *total* number of pounds lost by each group (which will have to be corrected by dividing by 10, since each total is made up of 10 individual scores):

$$\text{Variance}_{\text{between groups}} = \frac{\Sigma X^2 - \dfrac{(\Sigma X)^2}{n}}{n_{\text{groups}} - 1}$$

$$= \frac{\overbrace{\dfrac{(\Sigma X_{E_1})^2}{n_{E_1}} + \dfrac{(\Sigma X_{E_2})^2}{n_{E_2}} + \dfrac{(\Sigma X_C)^2}{n_C}}^{(\Sigma X^2)} - \overbrace{\dfrac{(\Sigma X_{\text{total}})^2}{n_{\text{total}}}}^{(\Sigma X)^2}}{n_{\text{groups}} - 1}$$

$$= \frac{\dfrac{(141)^2}{10} + \dfrac{(129)^2}{10} + \dfrac{(55)^2}{10} - \dfrac{(325)^2}{30}}{3 - 1}$$

$$= \frac{3{,}954.7 - 3{,}520.83}{2}$$

$$= \frac{433.87}{2}$$

$$= 216.94$$

This figure, 216.94, represents the systematic, between-group variation in our three-group, single-factor design. All that remains is to locate and calculate its nonsystematic counterpart and divide the two to obtain the F-ratio.

Source II. Nonsystematic (Within-Group) Variation

If we return to our data model in Table 14-1, it should be apparent that there are two remaining sources of variations. One is the total variance of all 30 subjects considered as a whole, irrespective of group membership. It is computed as though subjects were not assigned to groups at all and as such is of little interest, since it represents a combination of systematic and nonsystematic components. The remaining source therefore must be the object of our search. It is the variation within groups and it represents nonsystematic or error variance. It is the source to which the systematic variation resulting from the experiment will be compared.

The logic behind this concept is quite straightforward. We can explain why subjects differ from one another between, say, groups E_1 and C; it is because subjects in E_1 were treated differently from those in C. How can we explain why S_8 *within* E_1 lost more weight following the intervention than S_9 but lost less than S_1?

Without additional information we cannot. Without additional information we must assume that this within group variation is nonsystematic and represents error. It is this source then that constitutes the denominator of the F-ratio and is calculated by (1) computing separate sums of squares (that is, the numerator of the variance formula:

$$\Sigma X^2 - \frac{(\Sigma X)^2}{n})$$

for each group), (2) adding these three values together, and (3) dividing this sum by the total number of subjects minus the number of groups included $[30 - 3 = 27$, which can also be visualized as $(N_{E_1} - 1) + (N_{E_2} - 1) + (N_C - 1)$ or $9 + 9 + 9 = 27]$:

$$\text{Variance}_{\text{within groups}}$$

$$= \frac{\text{sum of squares}_{\text{within } E_1} + \text{sum of squares}_{\text{within } E_2} + \text{sum of squares}_{\text{within } C}}{(n_{E_1} - 1) + (n_{E_2} - 1) + (n_C - 1)}$$

$$= \frac{\left[\Sigma X^2_{E_1} - \dfrac{(\Sigma X_{E_1})^2}{n_{E_1}} \right] + \left[\Sigma X^2_{E_2} - \dfrac{(\Sigma X_{E_2})^2}{n_{E_2}} \right] + \left[\Sigma X^2_C - \dfrac{(\Sigma X_C)^2}{n_C} \right]}{(n_{E_1} - 1) + (n_{E_2} - 1) + (n_C - 1)}$$

$$= \frac{\left[2{,}415^* - \dfrac{(141)^2}{10} \right] + \left[2{,}035 - \dfrac{(129)^2}{10} \right] + \left[565 - \dfrac{(55)^2}{10} \right]}{9 + 9 + 9}$$

$$= \frac{426.90 + 370.90 + 262.50}{27}$$

$$= \frac{1{,}060.30}{27}$$

$$= 39.27$$

Calculating and Evaluating the F-Ratio

The final ANOVA calculation is simplicity itself:

$$F = \frac{\text{Variance}_{\text{between groups}}}{\text{Variance}_{\text{within groups}}} = \frac{216.94}{39.27} = 5.52$$

The evaluation of this statistic is also quite simple. One only need look up its critical value in a table (found in practically all statistical texts) such as the one depicted in Table 14-2. If the tabled value at the designated alpha is larger than the computed F (5.52), then the systematic variance is not statistically greater than the nonsystematic variance and the group means do not differ significantly from one another. If the tabled F is equal to or less than 5.52, then the opposite is true.

To illustrate, let us actually find the tabled F value for our data. The first thing that will be noted when examining Table 14-2 is that the F-distribution is two dimensional. This is necessary because the F-statistic represents a *ratio* of two numbers (that is, systematic variance to nonsystematic variance), each of which is based on a different number of observations.

Each of these tabled F-ratios thus represents a unique data model. Each column represents a study involving a different number of *groups,* each row one

---

* $\Sigma X_{E_1}^2$ is found by squaring and summing each number contained in group E_1 ($24^2 + 20^2 + 14^2 + \ldots + 19^2$).

Table 14-2   A PORTION OF AN *F*-TABLE (.05 LEVEL OF SIGNIFICANCE)

	df for numerator				
	1	**2**	**3**	**4**	**5**
1	161.4	199.5	215.7	224.6	230.2
2	18.51	19.00	19.16	19.25	19.30
3	10.13	9.55	9.28	9.12	9.01
4	7.71	6.94	6.59	6.39	6.26
5	6.61	5.79	5.41	5.19	5.05
6	5.99	5.14	4.76	4.53	4.39
7	5.59	4.74	4.35	4.12	3.97
8	5.32	4.46	4.07	3.84	3.69
9	5.12	4.26	3.86	3.63	3.48
10	4.96	4.10	3.71	3.48	3.33
11	4.84	3.98	3.59	3.36	3.20
12	4.75	3.89	3.49	3.26	3.11
13	4.67	3.81	3.41	3.18	3.03
14	4.60	3.74	3.34	3.11	2.96
15	4.54	3.68	3.29	3.06	2.90
16	4.49	3.63	3.24	3.01	2.85
17	4.45	3.59	3.20	2.96	2.81
18	4.41	3.55	3.16	2.93	2.77
19	4.38	3.52	3.13	2.90	2.74
20	4.35	3.49	3.10	2.87	2.71
21	4.32	3.47	3.07	2.84	2.68
22	4.30	3.44	3.05	2.82	2.66
23	4.28	3.42	3.03	2.80	2.64
24	4.26	3.40	3.01	2.78	2.62
25	4.24	3.39	2.99	2.76	2.60
26	4.23	3.37	2.98	2.74	2.59
27		3.35	2.96	2.73	2.57
28	4.20	3.34	2.95	2.71	2.56
29	4.18	3.33	2.93	2.70	2.55

df for denominator

involving a different number of *subjects*. For convenience the *F*'s are tabled with respect to the denominator of both the systematic and nonsystematic variances (also called *degrees of freedom*) or the number of observations minus one.

As illustrated in Table 14-2, the first step involves locating the appropriate column and row in which the *F*-value representing our particular study is located. Since the columns represent the denominator of the systematic variance (or the number of *groups* minus one) and the rows represent the denominator of the unsystematic variance (or the number of subjects minus the number of groups), our critical *F*-value will be located in column 2, row 27. Since the obtained *F* of 5.52 is larger than this figure (3.35), we may conclude that the three groups did indeed differ significantly from one another.* If we wished to ascertain if the obtained *F* was statistically significant at or beyond the .01 level, it would be compared to the .01 level tabled value in the same way.

---

* We still do not know which groups differ statistically from one another. To ascertain this, we must perform one of the a posteriori tests described in the next section.

Assessing the Magnitude of the Effect

The size, or significance level, of an F-ratio tells very little about the overall strength of the relationship between the independent and dependent variables. The reason for this failing is that both the absolute size and the significance level of the F-statistic are directly related to the size of the sample. What is needed, therefore, is an index similar to R^2 that reflects the total amount of the dependent variable's (weight loss) variance that is shared with the independent variable (group membership). The simplest way to obtain such a value is to compare the study's systematic variation to its total variation. Since the variances themselves are not additive (because they have different denominators), it is easier to work with sums of squares (or the numerator of the variance formula), which does not have this limitation.

Our study's systematic sum of squares is, of course, the same as the previously computed between-groups sum of squares. The total sum of squares is the combination of both between- (systematic) and within- (nonsystematic) group sources. The ratio of the two is called, among other things, eta^2 (or simply R^2) and ranges from 0 to 1.0.

For the above example, it would be calculated as follows:

$$\text{Shared variance} = \frac{\text{sum of squares}_{\text{between groups}}}{\text{sum of squares}_{\text{total (between + within groups)}}} \quad (14\text{-}4)$$

$$= \frac{433.87}{1,494.17\dagger}$$

$$= .29$$

In other words, 29 percent of the variation in subjects' scores (that is, their weight loss) can be explained by the experimental interventions.*

In many ways, a numerical value of shared or explained variance such as this possesses considerably more conceptual clarity than the F-ratio itself, which is primarily an indicator of a study's level of statistical significance. Therefore, I recommend that a statistic such as R^2 be reported along with the significance level of the F-ratio.

REPORTING THE RESULTS

All the information normally needed for the final research report is present in Tables 14-3 and 14-4. Depending on the amount of the space available, it would normally be communicated in two tables: one presenting summary statistics, the other the ANOVA table itself.

---

* Some authors (e.g., Kirk, 1982) maintain that a more conservative estimate, such as omega^2 be used for this purpose. This will result in a comparable, but slightly lower estimate of shared variance:

$$\text{Omega}^2 = \frac{\text{mean square}_{\text{between groups}} - (\text{number of groups} - 1) \text{ mean square}_{\text{within}}}{\text{sum of squares}_{\text{total}} + \text{mean square}_{\text{within}}}$$

$\dagger$ $1,494.17 = 433.87 + 1060.30$.

Table 14-3 SUMMARY STATISTICS

	E_1 (N = 10)	E_2 (N = 10)	C (N = 10)
$\overline{X}$	14.10	12.90	5.50
S.D.	6.89	6.42	5.40

Table 14-4 ANOVA SUMMARY TABLE

Source	SS[a]	df[b]	MS[c]	F	p
Treatments	433.87	2	216.94	5.52	<.01
Error	1,060.30	27	39.27		
Total	1,494.17	29			

[a] SS stands for sum of square or the numerator of the appropriate variance formula.

[b] df stands for degrees of freedom or the denominator of the appropriate variance formula.

[c] MS stands for mean square, which is a synonym for variance.

When space is at a greater premium, the ANOVA summary table may be completely replaced with a statement such as:

The results of the one-way analysis of variance clearly indicated that the three groups did differ with respect to the average amount of weight loss [F (2, 27) = 5.52 p < .01]* following the experimental interventions.†

THE WITHIN-SUBJECTS MODEL

The between-subjects, one-way analysis of variance just discussed assumes the existence of two or more groups, each of which contains its own discrete subjects. There are occasions when these groups either share the same or contain matched subjects (as with the randomized-matched-block model discussed in Chapter 8). When either of these scenarios occurs, a different type of analysis of variance is performed, called either a *within-subjects* or a *repeated-measures analysis of variance.*

To illustrate the differences between these two types of analyses, let us return to the data set presented in Table 14-1. For these numbers to represent a within-subjects model, we must visualize S_1, S_{11}, and S_{21} as either having been matched on a blocking variable of some sort or actually being multiple measurements on the same person. Since the particular example being used isn't amenable to having the same subjects in the three treatments, let us assume that we have administered or collected a premeasure of some sort known to be related to weight loss, rank-ordered people with respect to this variable, and

---

* The first number within the parentheses refers to the degrees of freedom for the numerator of the *F*-ratio, the second to the denominator.

† Some journals prefer not to print ANOVA summary tables in order to conserve space.

randomly assigned them in blocks of three. What would result, therefore, is a situation in which everything else being equal, S_1 would be more similar to S_{21} with respect to propensity to lose weight than he or she would be to, say, S_5, S_{10}, or any other subject except S_{11}. The challenge inherent in a within-subjects analysis of variance, then, becomes the necessity of computationally taking these similarities within blocks of subjects into account.

Relationship to the Dependent Samples *t*-Test

To illustrate the difference between studies employing independent subjects in their groups (between-subjects models) versus matched subjects, let us actually compute a dependent samples *t*-test on the E_1 versus C data and compare the results to the result obtained in Chapter 4 [$t = 3.1$ (df = 27), p < .01]. Using the formula presented therein we have:

$$t = \frac{X_E - X_C}{\sqrt{\dfrac{\text{Var}_E}{N_E} + \dfrac{\text{Var}_C}{N_C} - \dfrac{2r\,(\text{SD}_E)}{\sqrt{N_E}}\dfrac{(\text{SD}_C)}{\sqrt{N_C}}}}$$

where r is the correlation between matched subjects' weight loss in the two groups as illustrated in the following correlational model:

Weight loss for E subjects		Weight loss for C subjects	
S	Pounds	S	Pounds
S_1	24	S_{21}	9
S_2	20	S_{22}	2
.	.	.	.
.	.	.	.
.	.	.	.
S_{10}	19	S_{30}	6

This figure happens to be .45, thus plugging this and the other values contained in Table 14-1 into the above formula we have:

$$t = \frac{14.10 - 5.50}{\sqrt{\dfrac{47.43}{10} + \dfrac{29.17}{10} - 2 \times .45 \times \dfrac{6.89}{\sqrt{10}} \times \dfrac{5.40}{\sqrt{10}}}}$$

$$= \frac{8.60}{\sqrt{7.66 - 3.35}}$$

$$= 4.13$$

This value is obviously larger than the independent samples *t*-test calculated on the same data. The reason for this lies in the nonzero correlation between the matched subjects in the two groups. The larger this correlation, the greater the discrepancy between the t's.

As was the case with the between-subjects model, a one-way analysis of variance could have been computed in lieu of the t-test. If a one-way, within-subjects ANOVA has been so computed, the resulting F-ratio would have been 17.06, which, again not coincidentally, happens to be equal to 4.13^2 ($\sqrt{F} = t$; $t^2 = F$).

The same general assumptions apply to the within-subjects as the between-subjects ANOVA, with the additional constraint that a correlation is expected to exist across groups, whether matched subjects or the same subjects are represented. Said another way, we assume that subjects within blocks (that is, S_1, S_{11}, and S_{21}) are more similar to one another with respect to the dependent variable than they are to anyone else. If this assumption is violated for one reason or another, the only real penalty is a loss in statistical power over the between-subjects model. (If a correlation does exist, then a sizable increment to statistical power is realized.)

Conceptual Basis

The conceptual basis for a within-subjects ANOVA is identical to that of its between-subjects counterpart; we still assume the existence of explained versus unexplained sources of variation and the ratio between the two is still translatable to an F-ratio to which a probability can be assigned. The within-subjects ANOVA does have one major advantage over its less-powerful counterpart. Much of the variation that we were forced to label as unexplained in the between-subjects model can now be explained via the dependence (that is, the correlation) in scores between groups brought about by the way in which subjects were assigned to these groups.

Let us illustrate using the data in Table 14-1. Formerly, it was necessary to assume that all variation between the amount of weight loss between subjects within the same treatment group was unsystematic. In other words, since we couldn't *explain* why S_8 within E_1 lost more weight following the intervention than S_6, but lost less weight than S_3, we had to label all these within-group discrepancies as error.

Now, however, we have a different situation. Now we may be able to explain some of this variation due to variations between *blocks* of subjects. Since each block of subjects (that is, S_1, S_{11}, and S_{21} or S_2, S_{12}, and S_{22}) is *expected* to be different from every other block, these differences between blocks can be subtracted from the error variance.

To illustrate, let us repeat the Table 14-1 data, this time summing scores within blocks (Table 14-5). Any differences in the total column can now be explained by the fact that matched subjects were assigned to blocks. In other words, the total for block 8 is less than the total for block 1 *because* three subjects were assigned thereto who were judged to have a greater propensity to lose weight over time. The fact that the total weight loss is different across blocks attests to the general success of the blocking variable in predicting weight loss.

**Table 14-5   A NUMERICAL EXAMPLE FOR A
WITHIN-SUBJECTS ANOVA**

Blocks	E_1	E_2	C	Total $(E_1 + E_2 + C)$
1	24	22	9	55
2	20	20	2	42
3	14	14	6	34
4	12	10	0	22
5	19	18	18	55
6	0	5	4	9
7	10	8	0	18
8	14	12	8	34
9	9	3	2	14
10	19	17	6	42

These differences, or the variation due to blocks (that is, the variance of the total column), will thus be used to reduce the final error term.

This does not mean, of course, that there is *no* unexplained variation within the three groups. For that highly unlikely (if not impossible) scenario to occur, the *pattern* of scores within each block would have to be identical.* A cursory examination of the scores in Table 14-4 indicates that this obviously is not the case. The control subject who lost the most weight, for example, was located in block 5 while the E_1 and E_2 subjects in block 5 were ranked only third within their respective groups. Similar discrepancies exist for other blocks as well, and the sum total of these discrepancies can be visualized as constituting the unexplained variation in a within-subjects analysis of variance. (To the extent that the overall pattern of scores is similar from block to block, however, the experimental error will be decreased. The larger the discrepancies, the greater the error.)

A Computational Example

Let us now examine the computational basis of the within-groups analysis of variance procedure using the same data on which the between-subjects ANOVA was performed. The computation of the total sum of squares, the between-groups sum of squares, and the within-group sum of squares remains identical. Since the numbers themselves have not changed, the values will be the same as those presented in Table 14-3 (that is, $SS_{total} = 1494.17$, $SS_{between groups}$ or $SS_{treatment} = 433.87$, and $SS_{within groups} = 1,060.30$).

The primary change in the two analyses, then, resides in the fact that the variation between blocks must be subtracted out of the within-groups variation to produce the new error sum of squares:

$$SS_{error} = SS_{within groups} - SS_{blocks}$$

* Said another way, the correlation between the E_1, E_2, and C scores in Table 14-5 would all have to equal 1.00.

The sum of squares for blocks is computed as follows:

$$SS_{blocks} = \frac{\Sigma \text{ each block total}^2}{N \text{ of scores per block}} - \frac{(\Sigma X_{total})^2}{N}$$

$$= \frac{(55)^2 + (42)^2 + \cdots + (42)^2}{3} - \frac{(325)^2}{30}$$

$$= 4{,}325 - 3{,}520.83$$

$$= 804.17$$

Thus, $SS_{error} = 1{,}060.30 \, (SS_{within\,groups}) - 804.17 = (SS_{blocks}) = 256.13$.

This example should illustrate that within-subjects designs can dramatically reduce the variance that we cannot explain in an experiment. The above figure is not yet the error term, however, since it must be divided by the appropriate number of degrees of freedom. Since the sum of squares within groups no longer represents unexplained variation, it is no longer appropriate to use its degrees of freedom for this purpose. Actually, the degrees of freedom for error is determined in exactly the same way as was the sum of squares for error, by subtracting the degrees of freedom associated with blocks from the sum of squares within groups:

$$df_{error} = df_{within\,groups} - df_{blocks}$$

$$= [(N_{E_1} - 1) + (N_{E_2} - 1) + (N_C - 1) - [N \text{ of blocks} - 1]$$

$$= 27 - (10 - 1) = 18$$

Thus, the variation (or MS) due to within-subjects error (which translates to all of the unexplained variance in this model) is computed as follows:

$$MS_{error} = \frac{SS_{error}}{df_{error}}$$

$$= \frac{256.13}{18}$$

$$= 14.23$$

This figure can be used to calculate the F-ratio representing differences between the three groups means by dividing it into the variation due to those groups:

$$F = \frac{MS_{treatments}}{MS_{error}}$$

$$= \frac{216.93}{14.23}$$

$$= 15.25$$

This value is then compared to the critical value found within the F-distribution for 2 and 18 degrees of freedom. Obviously, it greatly exceeds this value at both the .05 and .01 levels of significance, indicating that statistically significant differences do exist between at least two of the three group means.

Table 14-6 WITHIN-SUBJECTS ANOVA SUMMARY TABLE

Source	SS	df	MS	F	p
Between blocks	804.17	9			
Treatment	433.87	2	216.93	15.25	<.001
Error	256.13	18	14.23		
Total	1,494.17	29			

Table 14-7 AN ALTERNATIVE WITHIN-SUBJECTS ANOVA SUMMARY TABLE

Source	SS	df	MS	F
Between people[a]	804.17	9		
Within people	690.00	20		
Treatments	433.87	2	216.93	15.25[c]
Residual[b]	256.13	18	14.23	
Total	1,494.17	29		

[a] A more common label than between blocks.

[b] Another name for error.

[c] $p < .001$

Reporting the Results

The results of the above analysis would be reported via the same basic format as described for the between-subjects ANOVA. Means and standard deviations would be presented as in Table 14-3, while the ANOVA summary table (if reported at all) would need to be altered to depict the new source (between blocks) of variation (Table 14-6).

This is only one of several legitimate ways to present a within-subjects ANOVA summary table. Other authors suggest alternative labels for the sources of variation. Winer (1971) uses the layout shown in Table 14-7.

As with the between-subjects ANOVA, many journals do not encourage the presentation of a summary table. Those that do are not normally too concerned regarding the exact form of the table as long as the basic constituents are clearly laid out. Regardless of whether or not the summary table is presented, authors should indicate clearly in the text that a *within-subjects* ANOVA was computed, since in the absence of this information readers would typically assume the use of a between-subjects analysis.

A Measurement Application

As discussed in Chapter 11, a repeated-measures ANOVA is usually the analytic procedure of choice to determine interrater reliability. To illustrate, let us assume that the following results accrued from a situation in which three observers rated ten subjects on some parameter (Table 14-8).*

* Note that the independent variable (or the groups) for this analysis consists of the observers. The analysis is conceptualized as a repeated-measures (or within-subjects) model because each group (or observer) contains measures on the same subjects.

Table 14-8 **REPEATED-MEASURES ANOVA SUMMARY TABLE**

Source	SS	df	MS	F	p
Between people	804.17	9	89.35		
Within subjects	690.00	20			
Observers	433.87	2	216.93	15.25	
Error	256.13	18	14.23		
Total	1,494.17	29			

Although many computer routines would print the interrater reliability coefficient directly, the values listed in the MS column can be used to generate it if this option is not available (Ebel, 1951) via the interrater reliability equation:

$$\text{Interrater reliability} = \frac{MS_{between\,people} - MS_{error}}{MS_{between\,people} + (\text{number of observers} - 1)MS_{error}}$$

or   (14-5)

$$\text{Interrater reliability} = \frac{89.35 - 14.23}{89.35 + (3 - 1)14.23}$$

$$= .64$$

If different observers are used to rate different subjects within the final study, a better estimate of interrater reliability may accrue from adding the variation due to differences between observers to the MS_{error}. In the present example, this would be done by adding the two relevant figures in the SS column and dividing by the df_{error} + the $df_{observers}$:

$$\frac{SS_{observers} + SS_{error}}{df_{error} + df_{observers}} = \frac{433.87 + 256.13}{18 + 2}$$

$$= 34.50$$

which becomes the new MS_{error} for Equation 14-5.

$$\text{Interrater reliability} = \frac{89.35 - 34.50}{89.35 + (3 - 1)34.50}$$

$$= .35$$

This reliability figure is less than the previous one because there is a systematic observer bias, as attested by the statistically significant F-ratio for observers (due to the relatively low scores assigned by observer 3) and it is now appropriate to consider this bias as error since observer 3's scores will be mixed with those of the other observers in the final data analysis.

ANALYSIS OF COVARIANCE

As discussed in Chapter 8, and actually illustrated in the preceding section, within-subjects models (such as the randomized-matched-block) possess a major advantage over their between-subjects counterparts. Not only are they more efficient and precise, they also considerably increase the probability of achieving statistical significance. Within-subjects models are unfortunately not always feasible. Using the same subjects in different treatments has numerous pitfalls and randomly assigning matched subjects to groups in blocks presupposes that the researcher has access to the entire sample prior to the beginning of the study.

Subjects often trickle into a setting, for example, and have to be randomly assigned and administered the treatment as they become available. This could very easily be the case if our current weight loss example were conducted at a clinic of some sort to which people came as they either felt the need or were discharged from an acute care hospital. Here, premeasures could certainly be obtained on subjects, but there is no way that such measures could be used as a matching variable since the treatment would be running either continuously or in waves. Fortunately, there is a statistical technique that mimics the effects of a within-subjects design by using one or more of these premeasures as a form of statistical (as opposed to procedural) control. It is called analysis of covariance and, when properly used, can be almost as effective as a randomized-matched-block model.

An Example

Let us suppose that we were forced to conduct our three-group weight loss experiment at a clinic in which only about five new subjects were enrolled per week. Let us further suppose that we have made the decision to administer each

Table 14-9 DATA FOR A HYPOTHETICAL THREE-GROUP ANALYSIS OF COVARIANCE MODEL

	E_1			E_2			C_3	
	Motivation to lose weight	Number of pounds lost		Motivation to lose weight	Number of pounds lost		Motivation to lose weight	Number of pounds lost
S_1	9	24	S_{11}	6	22	S_{21}	7	9
S_2	6	20	S_{12}	9	20	S_{22}	7	2
S_3	7	14	S_{13}	7	14	S_{23}	7	6
S_4	7	12	S_{14}	7	10	S_{24}	6	0
S_5	8	19	S_{15}	8	18	S_{25}	9	18
S_6	7	0	S_{16}	7	5	S_{26}	7	4
S_7	7	10	S_{17}	7	8	S_{27}	7	0
S_8	7	14	S_{18}	7	12	S_{28}	8	8
S_9	7	9	S_{19}	7	3	S_{29}	7	2
S_{10}	8	19	S_{20}	8	17	S_{30}	8	6
$\overline{X}$ =	7.30	14.1	$\overline{X}$ =	7.30	12.9	$\overline{X}$ =	7.30	5.5
S.D. =	0.82	6.89	S.D. =	0.82	6.42	S.D. =	0.82	5.4

of the three conditions (E_1, E_2, and C) individually as subjects became available.

What we would do, then, is to assign subjects randomly as they enrolled in the clinic (assuming of course that they agreed to participate in the study). To mimic the error-reducing capability of a within-subjects model, we could administer one or more premeasures to all subjects (E and C) to serve as a statistical control. There are few rules regarding the form such measures must take as long as they *are linearly correlated with the dependent variable.* They can, for example, be values gleaned from clinical records (such as prognosis or severity of illness) or they can be actual instruments administered directly to the subjects. Let us assume the latter, that a special 10-point scale designed to assess motivation to lose weight existed and was known to be predictive of how much weight patients actually do lose. The final data set thus might look like Table 14-9.

Conceptual Basis

A one-way analysis of covariance (ANCOVA) is conceptually very similar to a one-way, within-subjects ANOVA, since both procedures employ a second variable to reduce a study's error variance. ANCOVA involves an additional use of this second variable (called a covariate*), however, which is to adjust statistically posttreatment means for any pretreatment differences in the covariate. This second step is not necessary in a within-subjects ANOVA, because the groups are procedurally forced (either via matching or by employing the same subjects in the various groups) to be very nearly identical with respect to the premeasure prior to the beginning of the study.

Of course, when subjects are randomly assigned to groups we would expect the pretreatment means to be almost identical with respect to practically any identifiable measure, simply because high- (or low-) scoring subjects would tend to be evenly distributed among groups. Random assignment does not always result in a *perfect* distribution, however, thus this additional feature of statistically adjusting posttreatment means (in the presence of pretreatment differences) can be valuable insurance when randomized matched blocking is not an option.

Basically, what analysis of covariance does is subtract or partial out the relationship between the covariate and the dependent variable from the two primary sources of variation that are of interest in all analysis of variance procedures: systematic (or between-subjects) and nonsystematic (within-subjects) variation. The size of the Pearson r between the covariate and the dependent variable directly influences the procedure's ability to do this. If there were no relationship between motivation to lose weight and actual weight loss in our present example, there would be absolutely no statistical adjustment to either

---

* For ease of exposition, *one* covariate will be assumed. There is no theoretical limit on the number of covariates that can be employed (assuming enough subjects), although the use of more than two is rare.

source of variation. Since this is usually not the case, and is not the case in the data presented in Table 14-8 where the r is .43 between the two variables, let us examine how ANCOVA tends to affect these two sources of variation.

Error Variance   In a between-subjects ANOVA, it will be remembered that individual differences within groups must be considered error variance simply because we cannot explain them. Between-group variation we can explain (for example, we know that one reason S_1 may have lost more weight than S_{21} is because S_1 received a treatment designed to help him or her lose weight while S_{21} did not). What the addition of a covariate does is bring some more information to bear on why S_1 may have lost more weight than S_2. If S_1 had a greater initial propensity to change on the dependent variable based on a higher score on some pretreatment measure, then his or her actual greater change is now explainable. To the extent that a covariate is able to explain within-group differences a study's error variance can be reduced.

In the present data, the Pearson r of .43 would reduce the MS_{error} from 39.27 (see Table 14-4) to 33.08, while leaving the $MS_{treatments}$ alone since the three groups did not differ with respect to the covariate (and hence the dependent variable means would not be adjusted). This results in an increase in the F-ratio from 5.52 to 6.56, which in other circumstances could mean the difference between statistical significance and lack of statistical significance.

Between-Group or Treatment Variance   In the present example, the variation between groups remains the same following an ANCOVA simply because the means of the three groups are identical with respect to motivation to lose weight. Although in actual practice the means would not be identical, ANCOVA does not normally result in much of a change in between-group variance in true experiments simply because the groups would not be expected to differ substantively on the covariate. In nonrandomly assigned studies, the situation can be quite different, however, since conceivably the groups may differ widely on the covariate. If we had used intact groups in our hypothetical study, for example, and if the control group had proved a most unmotivated lot with respect to losing weight, it is possible that ANCOVA could have completely wiped out the significant effect for treatments. It would have done this by adjusting the two treatment groups downward and the control group upward with respect to the amount of weight loss *due to* the original discrepancy in motivation. Since the F-ratio in an analysis of covariance tests significant differences between *adjusted* dependent-variable means, the ANCOVA F-ratio might very well not have been statistically significant.* However, this is a very unusual occurrence in empirical research. Normally analysis of covariance results in a higher probability of achieving statistical significance and as such is a valuable addition to the researcher's arsenal.

---

* Of course, the opposite is also true. If the experimental groups had started off with a motivational deficit as compared to the control group, the resulting adjusted means would reflect this discrepancy by increasing the treatment effect.

Assumptions

All of the assumptions governing the use of analysis of variance also apply to the use of analysis of covariance. As would be expected, there are some additional ones specifically associated with the use of the covariate. Some of these are quite similar to those governing the use of a blocking variable. Others are related to the unique capability of a covariate to actually adjust posttreatment dependent variable means.

1. *The covariate should be correlated* (preferably .30 or better) *with the dependent variable.* This also assumes, of course, that the covariate is a measure for which the arithmetic mean makes sense. If the covariate is not correlated with the dependent variable, the penalty (though present) is not as severe as that associated with using an ineffectual blocking variable.*

2. *The covariate should be a measure that is in existence prior to the advent of the treatment* (and thus cannot possibly be affected by the treatment). ANCOVA is a very sophisticated, powerful procedure and must be used with caution. If for convenience sake our particular covariate had been administered at the end of the first week of the study, the resulting adjustment of the posttreatment means could completely invalidate the study. To illustrate how this could happen, suppose that the first few treatment sessions were quite motivational in nature, being designed to make patients want to lose weight (or to scare them into losing it). What would result, then, is that although the experimental group subjects might not have lost much weight by the end of the first week, their scores on the motivation scale would have increased dramatically with respect to the controls. At the data-analysis stage, the ANCOVA procedure would then adjust the legitimate weight loss differences favoring the experimental treatments downward based on this initial nonequivalence with respect to experimentally induced motivation. If the effect were large enough, a statistically significant difference favoring E_1 and E_2 might be inappropriately wiped out or reduced.

   In nonexperimental studies, the researcher must further guard against selecting covariates that run counter to the purposes of the study. An example might be a study designed to assess the effect of clinical experience. One way to do this study would be to employ intact groups of clinicians, one with a great deal of experience and one with very little. Suppose, however, that the researcher decided to use age as a covariate. What would happen is that the ANCOVA procedure would statistically adjust the two groups of subjects so that they in effect had the same age, at least as far as the dependent variable is concerned. Since clinical experience is highly correlated with age, the very differ-

---

* ANCOVA reduces the degrees of freedom for the error term at the rate of one per covariate. A randomized-block ANOVA reduces the df error at the rate of number of blocks minus 1. Everything else being equal, the *more* degrees of freedom possessed by MS_{error}, the greater the statistical power.

ence between the groups that interested the researcher in the first place would be washed out.

3. *The correlation between the covariate and the dependent variable is approximately the same in each group.* This is a loose translation of an assumption discussed in slightly more advanced statistical treatises such as Winer (1971, pp. 764–771) or various computer manuals such as SPSS (Nie et al., 1975). For experimental studies involving the random assignment of subjects to groups, the assumption is very seldom violated. For nonexperimental research using intact groups, the assumption should probably be checked. For those situations, the researcher is directed to one of the above references.*

Reporting the Results of an ANCOVA

An analysis of covariance looks exactly the same as an ANOVA. The summary tables are identical, the F-ratio too is interpreted identically except that it tests for differences between *adjusted* means. It is these means that are reported, then, not the raw unadjusted dependent-variable means. When describing the data analysis in the final report, the researcher should very clearly differentiate between the dependent variable and the covariate, for example:

> *A one-way analysis of covariance was performed for the three groups using the number of pounds lost as the dependent variable and motivation to lose weight as the covariate.*

INDIVIDUAL COMPARISONS BETWEEN TREATMENT MEANS

ANOVA and ANCOVA procedures do possess one limitation when applied to three or more groups and this is related to the fact that they produce only one statistic with only one attendant probability level. This is not a problem for two-group designs, since a significant result can only refer to the one existing mean difference. In our three-group example, all that the statistically significant F-ratio tells us is that at least two of the group means are reliably different from one another. Since there are three possible mean differences, it is necessary to take an extra step to determine if E_1 differs from E_2, E_1 from C, or E_2 from C. Any or all possibilities exist when the F-ratio is statistically significant.

Strategy 1

One way to ferret out this difference (or differences) is to compute multiple t-tests: one between each possible pair of group comparisons. The problem with this strategy is that we would be capitalizing on chance, using statistical distri-

---

* The assumption is tested by computing within-regression weights between the covariate and the dependent variable and testing them via the t-test for differences between correlation coefficients (see, for example, Bruning & Kintz, 1977). If the weights do not differ significantly, the assumption is not violated.

butions set up for single, independent comparisons on multiple, dependent data sets. We could partially compensate for this defect by lowering the study's alpha level by dividing the alpha of choice (normally .05) by the number of mean differences we want to test. In the three-group example, this would be done by using the corrected alpha level equation:

$$\text{Corrected alpha} = \frac{\text{desired alpha}}{\text{number of tests}} \qquad (14\text{-}6)$$

$$= \frac{.05}{3}$$

$$= .0167$$

Thus, to be judged statistically significant, any individual t-statistic would need to be larger than the critical value for .0167 rather than for .05.

After three groups, the number of possible contrasts begins to increase dramatically, causing the alpha level to decrease just as dramatically. In a four-group study, for example, there are six possible comparisons ($E_1 - E_2$, $E_1 - E_3, E_2 - E_3, E_1 - C, E_2 - C, E_3 - C$), which yields a corrected alpha of .0083; for five groups the corrected alpha is .005, and so forth.

Strategy 2

The problem with the above strategy is that although it does correct for the number of tests, it does nothing about the dependency problem.* To compensate both for this and the number of contrasts planned, techniques called a posteriori or post hoc tests have been developed that, in effect, lower the alpha both as the number of comparisons and as the mean difference between them increases. There are quite a few of these techniques, ranging from the very liberal (that is, more likely to result in statistical significance) to the very stringent. For those readers desiring the most liberal test most good journals will accept, I suggest either the Newman-Keuls procedure or one developed by Dunnett [for the special case in which the only comparisons of interest involve direct contrasts with the control (for example, E_1 versus C and E_2 versus C)]. For a more conservative test, Scheffé is recommended. Most ANOVA computer programs compute these tests automatically for the researcher. Those who must compute them without the aid of a computer are referred to Winer (1971, pp. 170–176).

---

* To understand this meaning of independence, consider the situation in which the subjects in one treatment somehow managed to be superior to the subjects in all the others by chance alone (such as by sampling error). In such a case, all comparisons involving this group would be influenced by this sampling error. If, however, separate, *independent* studies had been conducted for each contrast involving the treatment in question, the chances of the same sampling error occurring repeatedly for the same treatment group by chance alone would have been practically nonexistent. Obviously, it is not practical to conduct separate independent studies, but insurance against an artifactually inflated group mean resulting in statistical significance can be had by effectively decreasing the required alpha level for all extreme comparisons.

Strategy 3

There are occasions when the researcher is not particularly interested in all possible comparisons between groups. When this is the case and when those comparisons that are of interest can be hypothesized in advance, more powerful statistical procedures exist than the above mentioned a posteriori tests. The most common of these are simply called a priori orthogonal contrasts and are applicable when the following two constraints are acceptable:

1. The number of comparisons can be limited to the number of groups minus one.
2. Only independent comparisons are needed.

Let us illustrate via our weight-loss data. The first constraint means that we would be limited to no more than two comparisons (number of groups − 1). The second is somewhat more involved, since these two comparisons must be independent of one another. This means that if we decide to compare E_1 with E_2, then we cannot compare either E_1 or E_2 with C separately. In fact, there is only one single-group comparison that can be made in an a priori contrast involving a three-group model, since the same group cannot be used singularly more than once. This obviously forces the other contrast to be a combination of some sort.

The most likely choice for our particular study would be as follows: $E_1 + E_2$ versus C to see if, taken as a whole, the treatments are effective, and E_1 versus E_2 to see if there is any difference between the treatments themselves. This particular combination involves two independent (or orthogonal) contrasts, because each contrast was completely unrelated with the other. If we had chosen to couple an E_1 versus C contrast with the E_1 and E_2 versus C choice, then we could hardly make an argument for independence, since E_1 was used singularly in both. Of course, we could have chosen E_1 versus C and E_2 versus $E_1 + C$ or E_2 versus C and E_1 versus $E_2 + C$ instead, but neither seem like contrasts that would have been selected prior to examining the data (which is a necessity when doing a priori contrasts).

To avoid confusion regarding which contrasts are and are not orthogonal, statisticians have worked out a very simple algorithm. Taking the three-group example again, we can represent the comparisons we wish to make with positive and negative numbers that add up to zero for any given comparison. For example, the combination of E_1 and E_2 with C could be designated as follows;

E_1	E_2	C
+1	+1	−2

This type of nomenclature is interpreted as follows:

1. Positive numbers are always contrasted to negative numbers. (Thus, the two positive numbers under E_1 and E_2 mean that, in combination, these two groups will be contrasted to the group containing a negative number—which is C.)

2. The relative size of the numbers indicate the weight that will be placed on the corresponding group means. (In the present case, we are really contrasting an average of E_1 and E_2 with C, thus each treatment is counted half as much as the control. This fact is reflected in the absolute size of the numbers corresponding to these groups: 2 for the control and 1 for each of the treatments.)
3. The numbers used to represent any given contrast must add up to zero. [Thus $(+1) + (+1) + (-2) = 0$.]

Our other chosen contrast, E_1 versus E_2, would be represented as follows:

$$\frac{E_1 \qquad E_2 \qquad C}{+1 \qquad -1 \qquad 0}$$

Again, the positively numbered group (E_1) is contrasted to the negatively numbered one (E_2). (A zero indicates that the group so designated does not enter into a comparison at all, which is another way of saying that it is weighted zero.)

Let us now examine all the possible contrasts inherent in our two-group example:

	E_1	E_2	C
(A)	+1	+1	-2
(B)	+1	-1	0
(C)	+1	0	-1
(D)	+1	-2	+1
(E)	0	+1	-1
(F)	-2	+1	+1

Note that each row adds up to zero. To determine which pairs of rows or contrasts are orthogonal, it is necessary to multiply the two numbers under each group together and then add up the products. If the sum of these products is equal to zero, then the comparisons are orthogonal. If the sum is anything else, then the two contrasts in question are dependent.

Thus contrasts (A) and (B) are orthogonal because:

	E_1	E_2	C
(A)	+1	+1	-2
(B)	+1	-1	0
	$(+1) \times (+1) = +1$	$(+1) \times (-1) = -1$	$(-2) \times (0) = 0$
	$(+1) \qquad +$	$(-1) \qquad +$	$(0) \qquad = 0$

While (A) and (D) are not because:

	E_1	E_2	C
(A)	$+1$	$+1$	-2
(D)	$+1$	-2	$+1$
	$(+1) \times (+1) = +1$	$(+1) \times (-2) = -2$	$(-2) \times (+1) = -2$
	$(+1) \qquad +$	$(-2) \qquad +$	$(-2) \qquad = -3$

Although the actual computations are a bit more complicated (and the number of contrasts permutate drastically), the same algorithm works for studies involving more than three groups.

Recommendation The decision regarding which procedure to use to determine exactly which groups differ significantly from one another is largely a matter of personal choice. When the differences between groups are relatively large, all the methods just discussed would probably result in the same outcome. In the specific example used, the hypothetical data presented in Table 14-1 would yield the same conclusion regardless of the technique employed; both E_1 and E_2 were superior to C, but there is no statistically significant difference between E_1 and E_2.

In most cases, however, researchers are much too curious to pass up the opportunity to make all the possible contrasts inherent in a set of data, hence a procedure such as Newman-Keuls or Scheffé* should probably be routinely computed following a statistically significant F-ratio unless statistical power is very weak (that is, the number of subjects is limited). It is probably only when statistical power is at a premium that a priori contrasts should be used, since it is possible for a single contrast to be statistically significant even when the overall F-ratio resulting from the analysis of variance is not. (Thus, it is not even necessary to compute or report an overall F-ratio when a priori contrasts are used.)

Reporting the Results

With the Newman-Keuls, Scheffé, and Dunnett tests, many journals require only the reporting of the ANOVA (or ANCOVA) results, as described earlier, followed by a description of the type of post hoc test employed and the results so obtained. For example,

Following the significant F-ratio, a Newman-Keuls procedure was performed to evaluate mean differences between the three groups. Both E_1 and E_2 were found to be significantly different (p < .01) from C, although no statistically significant differences existed between the two treatments.

---

* These procedures are available automatically via all of the statistical packages mentioned in the previous chapter. For a more thorough explanation, see Winer (1971, pp. 185–204).

For both the alpha-corrected *t*-test (which is not a common procedure) and the a priori orthogonal contrasts, it is not always necessary to report the initial ANOVA/ANCOVA results since it is the individual contrasts that are of interest. In each case the procedure may simply be described and the appropriate statistics (*t*'s or *F*'s) reported parenthetically as described earlier. (As always, group means and standard deviations should be reported.)

SUMMARY

Between-subjects, one-way analysis of variance is the statistical procedure of choice to evaluate differences among means of three or more groups to which subjects have been randomly assigned. The resulting statistic is called an *F* and is defined as the ratio between systematic (between-group) and unsystematic (within-group) variation. A within-subjects analysis of variance is used either when matched subjects are assigned to groups or when identical subjects are present within each group. This procedure normally results in a substantial increment to statistical power since the unsystematic variation in such a study is reduced. A one-way analysis of covariance is not only capable of increasing a study's statistical power, this procedure is also capable of statistically adjusting posttreatment means to reflect any pretreatment differences on the covariate(s). Assumptions regarding the use of a covariate include the following:

1. The covariate should be correlated with the dependent variable.
2. The covariate should be a measure that is in existence prior to the advent of the treatment.
3. The correlation between the covariate and the dependent variable is approximately the same in each group.

Since one-way ANOVA and ANCOVA procedures yield only one probability level to represent three or more individual mean differences, a second step is usually required when the results are statistically significant. This normally takes the form of an a posteriori (for example, Newman-Keuls or Scheffé) or a priori contrasts between individual group means.

REFERENCES

Bruning, J. L., and Kintz, B. L. *Computational Handbook of Statistics.* Glenview, Ill.: Scott, Foresman, 1977.

Dixon, et al. *Biomedical Computer Programs.* Los Angeles: University of California Press, 1981.

Ebel, R. L. Estimation of the reliability of ratings. *Psychometrika,* 1951, *16,* 407–424.

Kirk, R. E. *Experimental Design: Procedures for the Behavioral Sciences,* 2nd edition. Belmont, Calif.: Brooks/Cole, 1982.

Nie, H. N. et al. *Statistical Package for the Social Sciences,* 2nd edition. New York: McGraw-Hill, 1975.

Winer, B. J. *Statistical Principles in Experimental Design,* 2nd edition. New York: McGraw-Hill, 1971.

chapter *15*

Factorial ANOVA

In the single-factor analyses discussed in Chapter 14, the presence of an additional independent variable was used solely to ensure either statistical (with ANCOVA) or procedural (with the randomized-matched-block model) control. As discussed in Chapter 8, however, there are occasions when such a variable is also hypothesized to moderate the effects of (or interact with) the treatments being tested. Suppose, for example, that our weight-loss researcher hypothesized that the dietary education plus exercise treatment (E_1) would be relatively more effective than dietary education alone (E_2) for one specific type of patient. Let us again assume that this dimension on which E_1 and E_2 were hypothesized to be differentially effective was extroversion versus introversion.

To test this hypothesis, both extroverted and introverted subjects would naturally have to be subjected to all treatments. As discussed in Chapter 8, this would first entail classifying or grouping subjects prior to the study with respect to their personality type and then randomly assigning subjects within each of these two groups to one of the three experimental treatments. As far as the conduct of the study is concerned, this is the only difference between this particular factorial model and a single-factor study; the treatments would be administered and the data would be collected in the same way.

The statistical analysis of the resulting data would be handled quite differently, of course, although the basic logic common to all ANOVA and ANCOVA procedures remains that of contrasting systematic or explained variation to nonsystematic or unexplained variation. The primary difference between a factorial ANOVA/ANCOVA and the one-way within-subjects

ANOVA procedures discussed so far lies in the use to which this second independent variable is put.

We have already demonstrated how these other procedures employ their second independent variables to reduce unexplained (or error) variation. To facilitate this demonstration, the same scores used throughout the previous chapter will be used. The only difference between the data presented in Table 15-1 and that contained in Table 14-1, therefore, is that subjects are now placed into six compartments instead of three to reflect the way in which they were assigned to treatments.

UNEXPLAINED VARIATION IN A FACTORIAL MODEL

In a one-way, between-subjects model, it will be remembered that we could *not* explain any individual differences in the amount of weight loss within treatment groups, hence all such differences were treated as error variance for analytic purposes. We could not explain why S_1 lost more weight than S_7, for example, since both people received exactly the same treatment. In both the randomized-matched-block data (represented by Table 14-5) and the ANCOVA data (represented by Table 14-8), this problem was solved to a certain extent by bringing new information to bear via the addition of a blocking variable or a covariate, respectively.

The addition of a second independent variable in a factorial model entails a variation on this logic. Now we at least have a hypothesis for why S_1 may have lost more weight than S_7; even though they received the same treatment (dietary education plus an exercise regimen), they possessed a *different* type of personality (S_1 was extroverted, S_7 was introverted), which itself was hypothesized to be related to weight loss. In other words, differences between extroverted and introverted subjects are no longer considered error because they can

Table 15-1 HYPOTHETICAL DATA FOR A TWO-DIMENSIONAL FACTORIAL MODEL

Personality		B_1 Dietary education + exercise regimen S	X		B_2 Dietary education alone S	X		B_3 Routine clinical care S	X
Extrovert (A_1)	A_1B_1	S_1	24	A_1B_2	S_{11}	22	A_1B_3	S_{21}	9
		S_2	20		S_{12}	20		S_{22}	2
		S_3	14		S_{13}	14		S_{23}	6
		S_4	12		S_{14}	10		S_{24}	0
		S_5	19		S_{15}	18		S_{25}	18
Introvert (A_2)	A_2B_1	S_6	0	A_2B_2	S_{16}	5	A_2B_3	S_{26}	4
		S_7	10		S_{17}	8		S_{27}	0
		S_8	14		S_{18}	12		S_{28}	8
		S_9	9		S_{19}	3		S_{29}	2
		S_{10}	19		S_{20}	17		S_{30}	6

be *explained.* Only differences *within* one of the six cells will now be completely unexplainable. Thus, the experimental error will be reduced and the statistical power of the analysis will increase to the extent that the researcher is correct in assuming that extroverts will differ from introverts with respect to the amount of weight they lose over the course of the study. In this sense, then, factorial ANOVA is very similar to the within-subjects ANOVA and the ANCOVA models already discussed. Its success depends entirely on the relationship between the new independent variable (personality) and the original dependent variable (number of pounds lost) or, said another way, the mean weight loss in the six cells represented in Table 15-1 (that is, cells A_1B_1 through A_2B_3) will differ from one another in *some* systematic way.

ADDITIONAL SOURCES OF SYSTEMATIC VARIATION

To illustrate how the addition of the new independent variable (personality type in the present case) affects the error term, let us reanalyze the data presented in Table 15-1 by taking into account the two new sources of variation (that is, the personality's main effect and its interaction with the three treatments).

To begin this process, it is helpful to add the scores within each cell and place the sum in a table as follows:

	$B_1(E_1)$ Diet and exercise		$B_2(E_2)$ Diet alone		$B_3(C)$ Routine care		Total	
A_1 (Extrovert)	89	($n = 5$)	84	($n = 5$)	35	($n = 5$)	208	($n = 15$)
A_2 (Introvert)	52	($n = 5$)	45	($n = 5$)	20	($n = 5$)	117	($n = 15$)
Total	141	($n = 10$)	129	($n = 10$)	55	($n = 10$)	325	($n = 30$)

The treatment sum of squares is computed the same and will remain the same (that is, 433.87) as for the one-way, between-subjects ANOVA analyzed in the previous chapter simply because neither the numbers of subjects nor their scores have been changed for illustrative purposes. (Naturally, nothing this clean and neat would accrue from a real study.) The sum of squares for personality is computed in basically the same manner by completely ignoring the treatment variable:

$$SS_{personality} = \left[\frac{(\Sigma X_{ext})^2}{N_{ext}} + \frac{(\Sigma X_{int})^2}{N_{int}} \right] - \frac{(\Sigma X_{total})^2}{N_{total}}$$

$$= \frac{208^2}{15} + \frac{117^2}{15} - \frac{325^2}{30}$$

$$= 2{,}884.27 + 912.60 - 3{,}520.83$$

$$= 276.04$$

The within-groups sum of squares is also calculated in the same basic way as in Chapter 14, except there are now six groups instead of three, hence this number will change somewhat:

$$\mathrm{SS}_{\mathrm{within\,groups}} = \left[\Sigma X_{A_1B_1}^2 - \frac{(\Sigma X_{A_1B_1})^2}{N_{A_1B_1}} \right]^* + \left[\Sigma X_{A_1B_2}^2 - \frac{(\Sigma X_{A_1B_2})^2}{N_{A_1B_2}} \right]$$

$$+ \cdots + \left[\Sigma X_{A_2B_3}^2 - \frac{(\Sigma X_{A_2B_3})^2}{N_{A_2B_3}} \right]$$

$$= \left[24^2 + 20^2 + 14^2 + 12^2 + 19^2 - \frac{(89^2)}{5} \right] + \left[22^2 + 20^2 \right.$$

$$+ \cdots + 18^2 - \frac{(84^2)}{5} \right] + \cdots + \left[4^2 + 0^2 + 6^2 - \frac{(20^2)}{5} \right]$$

$$= \overbrace{\underset{92.8}{A_1B_1}} + \overbrace{\underset{93.8}{A_1B_2}} + \cdots + \overbrace{\underset{40.0}{A_2B_3}}$$

$$= 748.80$$

The final source of variation to be computed for this model is unique to factorial studies. It is called the interaction term, and it is basically composed of variation between subjects, scores on the dependent variable that can be explained only by the differential reaction of extroverted and introverted subjects to the three experimental treatments. In other words, it is completely independent of any overall effects due to treatments or to differences between people's personalities, thus it is computed by simply *subtracting* the sum of squares due to these main effects from the overall differences among the study's six cells (that is, A_1B_1 to A_2B_3):

$$\mathrm{SS}_{\mathrm{interaction}} = \frac{(\Sigma A_1B_1)^2}{N_{A_1B_1}} + \frac{(\Sigma A_2B_1)^2}{N_{A_2B_1}} + \cdots + \frac{(\Sigma A_2B_3)^2}{N_{A_2B_3}} - \frac{(\Sigma X_{\mathrm{total}})^2}{N_{\mathrm{total}}}$$

$$- \mathrm{SS}_{\mathrm{treatment}} - \mathrm{SS}_{\mathrm{personality}}$$

$$= \frac{89^2}{5} + \frac{52^2}{5} + \cdots + \frac{20^2}{5} - \frac{325^2}{30} - 433.87 - 276.04$$

$$= 4{,}266.20 - 3{,}520.83 - 433.87 - 276.04$$

$$= 35.46$$

CALCULATING AND EVALUATING THE RESULTING *F*-RATIOS

We have now calculated three sources of systematic variation (actually the numerators or sums of squares of these sources have been calculated) and one nonsystematic source. These are variation due to:

1. Treatments.
2. Personality.
3. The interaction between treatments and personality.
4. Error.

*

$$\left[\Sigma X_{A_1B}^2 - \frac{(\Sigma X_{A_1B_1})^2}{N_{A_1B_1}} \right]$$

for example, is calculated by using the five scores found in cell A_1B_1 in Table 15-1:

$$(24^2 + 20^2 + 14^2 + 12^2 + 19^2) - \frac{(24 + 20 + 14 + 12 + 19)^2}{5} = 92.8$$

As always, the calculation of the F-ratios involves nothing more than dividing each source of systematic variation by its nonsystematic counterpart. The present case involves three such computations that in effect test the following three null hypotheses:

1. There is no difference in the average amount of weight loss between postoperative cardiovascular patients receiving a program of dietary information coupled with an exercise regimen, a program of dietary information alone, or a program consisting of routine clinical care alone.
2. There is no difference in the average amount of weight loss between introverted and extroverted postoperative cardiovascular patients.
3. There is no interaction between the three treatments and types of personality with respect to average weight loss among postoperative cardiovascular patients.

The actual computation of these F-ratios requires the conversion of each of the previously calculated sums of squares to a variance (or mean square). This is done, it will be remembered, by dividing each sum of squares by one less than the number of observations (or degrees of freedom) that went into the calculation of each figure. In the present case, these degrees of freedom would be calculated as follows:

1. $\quad df_{total} = $ number of subjects $- 1 = 30 - 1 = 29$
2. $\quad df_{treatments} = $ number of treatments $- 1 = 3 - 1 = 2$
3. $\quad df_{personality} = $ number of levels of personality $- 1 = 2 - 1 = 1$
4. $\quad df_{interaction} = df_{treatments} \times df_{personality} = 2 \times 1 = 2*$
5. $df_{within groups} = \Sigma$ (number of subjects per cell $- 1$)
$\qquad = (5 - 1) + (5 - 1) + (5 - 1) + (5 - 1) + (5 - 1) +$
$\qquad (5 - 1) = 24$

Note that the degrees of freedom associated with sources (2) through (5) always equal the df_{total}: $2 + 1 + 2 + 24 = 29$

To convert the three systematic sums of squares and the error sum of squares to variances (or mean squares), all that remains is to divide each of these degrees of freedom into their respective sums of squares. Thus, the personality mean square is computed as follows:

$$MS_{personality} = \frac{SS_{personality}}{df_{personality}}$$

$$= \frac{276.04}{1} = 276.04$$

This information is all conveniently represented in a factorial summary table (Table 15-2).

Each F-ratio is then compared to the critical value associated with its

---

* Since six data points went into the calculation of $SS_{interaction}$, it might appear at first glance that $df_{interaction}$ would be $6 - 1 = 5$. It will be remembered, however, that $SS_{treatments}$ and $SS_{personality}$ were *subtracted* from this term. This means that we must also subtract their degrees of freedom, which leaves us with 2 $[(6 - 1 = 5); 5 - 2 \, (df_{treatment}) - 1 \, (df_{personality}) = 2]$.

Table 15-2 FACTORIAL ANOVA SUMMARY TABLE

Source	SS	df	MS	F
A(treatments)	433.87	2	216.94	6.95[a]
B(personality)	276.04	1	276.04	8.85[a]
AB	35.46	2	17.73	0.57
Error	748.80	24	31.20	
Total	1,494.17	29		

[a] $p < .01$

degrees of freedom. Thus, the F-ratio for treatments is associated with 2 and 24 degrees of freedom, the F for personality with 1 and 24, and the interaction F with 2 and 24. Normally, this ANOVA would be performed by a computer that would output the exact probability levels associated with each of the three F's. If the values above were obtained from an F table, it would be found that the ratios associated with the two main effects were statistically significant beyond the .01 level. Note that the F for treatments is greater for this analysis than the one-way ANOVA computed in the previous chapter. This is due to the fact that the MS_{error} was reduced from 39.27 to 31.20 by the addition of an independent variable that was indeed related to weight loss. Thus:

$$F_{treatment} = \frac{MS_{treatment}}{MS_{error}}$$
$$= \frac{216.94}{31.20}$$
$$= 6.95$$

A POSTERIORI COMPARISONS OF MEANS

Just as in the one-way examples discussed in the last chapter, a significant F-ratio does not indicate exactly which means differ significantly from which other means. In the above example, there is no problem with personality type since only two means are involved (and hence there is only one possible mean difference, that between introverts and extroverts). A comparison of the overall means for these two groups (ignoring treatments) indicates that extroverts, on the average, lost more weight (13.87 pounds as opposed to 7.8 pounds for introverts). The three treatment mean differences are evaluated in exactly the same manner as discussed for the one-way model, using either an a posteriori method such as Newman-Keuls or Scheffé or, more rarely, an orthogonal a priori contrast. Basically, the only difference between the techniques for the one-way and factorial model is that the latter brings more power to the comparisons due to the reduced MS_{error}.

Evaluating Statistically Significant Interactions

The interaction between the independent variables is a completely different situation, however. In the present example, since the treatment × personality

Table 15-3 NEW FACTORIAL ANOVA DATA
REFLECTING A STATISTICALLY
SIGNIFICANT INTERACTION

| | E_1 | E_2 | C | |
	B_1	B_2	B_3	Total
Extroverts (A_1)	89	45	35	169
Introverts (A_2)	52	84	20	156
Total	141	129	55	325

Table 15-4 NEW FACTORIAL ANOVA SUMMARY TABLE
BASED ON TABLE 15-3 DATA

Source of Variation	SS	df	MS	F
A(treatment)	433.87	2	216.94	6.95[b]
B(personality)	5.64	1	5.64	.18
AB	305.86	2	152.93	4.90[a]
Error	748.80	24	31.20	
Total	1,494.17	29		

[a] $p < .05$

[b] $p < .01$

interaction was not statistically significant, no individual comparisons are called for. Suppose, however, that the scores in cells A_1B_2 and A_2B_2 had been completely reversed (Table 15-3). On cursory examination of these reformulated scores, it would appear that E_1 and E_2 were differentially effective for extroverts versus introverts.

The factorial ANOVA resulting from these data would be quite different, although the overall, within-groups, and treatments sums of squares would remain the same (Table 15-4). Obviously, the personality sum of squares and the interaction sum of squares will be drastically altered by this switch since, if for no other reason, the overall mean difference between externals and internals has been reduced from 6.07 to .87 ($\frac{169}{15} - \frac{156}{15}$).

Now it will be noted that the treatment $\times$ personality interaction is indeed statistically significant. There are basically two ways of interpreting this effect. The simplest and in especially clear cases such as the present example probably as good a way as any is to graph the cell means as illustrated in Chapter 8. As illustrated in Figure 15-1, a discrepancy becomes immediately apparent in the basic extrovert/introvert pattern; while extroverts register a substantial greater weight loss than introverts for both E_1 and C, dietary information alone (E_2) seems to result in introverts losing more weight than extroverts.

A second, more precise method of interpreting a statistically significant two-way interaction involves the calculation of two or more one-way analyses of variance* while holding one of the factors constant.† In our present example,

* See Winer (1971) for the more complicated use of this procedure, called simple effects tests, for higher-level interactions.

† Actually, only the between-groups variation is recalculated, since the factorial error term remains in force.

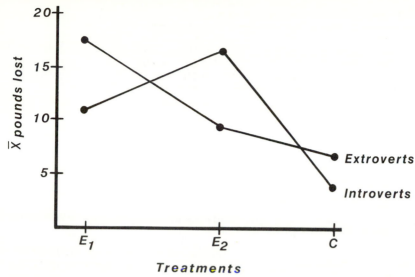

Figure 15-1 Treatments.

this would entail calculating one treatments sum of squares for extroverts and one for introverts or, turning the problem upside down, three sums of squares for personality (one for each treatment). Since the treatment variable is of more interest here, the former option would most likely be selected, although either procedure produces the same basic results. Each individual mean square is then contrasted to the overall error mean square presented in Table 15-4 to arrive at separate F-ratios.

This procedure, called a simple effects test, though not without its drawbacks,* does at least tell the researcher whether or not there is a statistically significant difference between the three treatments with respect to each type of personality. To illustrate how the treatment sum of squares are recomputed for extroverts and introverts separately, consider the following numerical example taken from the values found in Table 15-3.

$$\text{SS (treatments for extroverts)} = \frac{89^2}{5} + \frac{45^2}{5} + \frac{35^2}{5} - \frac{169^2}{15}$$
$$= 330.13$$

$$\text{SS (treatments for introverts)} = \frac{52^2}{5} + \frac{84^2}{5} + \frac{20^2}{5} - \frac{156^2}{15}$$
$$= 409.60$$

These values may then be placed into a simple effects summary table (Table 15-5), converted to variances (MS), and tested for significance.

What this information now tells us is that the treatment means differ significantly from one another both for subjects with extroverted and intro-

* One of which is that the resulting F-ratios are composites of both main effects and interaction.

Table 15-5   SIMPLE EFFECTS SUMMARY TABLE

Source	SS	df	MS	F
Treatments for extroverts	330.13	2	165.07	5.29[a]
Treatments for introverts	409.60	2	204.80	6.56[a]
Error	748.80	24	31.20	

[a] $p < .05$

verted personalities. Since there are three mean differences making up each of these simple effect F-ratios, we must take one additional step and compute an a posteriori (probably Newman-Keuls or Scheffé) test for differences among E_1, E_2, and C means: first for extroverts only, then for introverts alone. What we would find, among other things, is a statistically significant difference favoring E_1 over E_2 for extroverts and a statistically significant difference favoring E_2 over E_1 for introverts. This is the crux of this particular interaction.

All simple effects, especially those testing more complicated interactions, are not this easily interpreted. It is also helpful to remember that while an interaction between two variables is independent of those variables' main effects, a simple effects test is not.* This fact, coupled with a tendency for more complex interactions that have not been specifically hypothesized a priori not to replicate exactly, leads me to counsel caution in overinterpreting interactions. Certainly, this is true of higher-level interactions (that is, three-way or higher), anyway. There are occasions when simply presenting a graph of a statistically significant interaction may be just as satisfactory as conducting simple effects followed by a posteriori tests. For those occasions in which such an intuitive approach will not suffice, several statistical programs calculate simple effects tests automatically.

Unequal Cell Sizes

The same general assumptions regarding the use of one-way ANOVA apply to factorial models. The more complex a factorial model becomes, however, the more difficult it becomes to complete the study with exactly the same number of subjects per cell due to experimental mortality of one sort or another. This is not usually problematic as far as the main effects are concerned, but unequal cell sizes can artifactually contribute to an interaction F-ratio. Since all of the major computer programs mentioned in Chapter 13 contain reasonably acceptable options for dealing with this problem, unequal cell sizes should not pose any real statistical problems for the beginning researcher. To be safe, however, a more stringent alpha level may be employed or, where feasible, subjects may be randomly deleted from the larger cells to arrive at equal cell sizes.

---

* To illustrate, note that when the simple effects sums of squares in Table 15-5 are added, their sum is equal to $SS_{interaction} + SS_{treatment}$ in the original analysis of variance (Table 15-4): $330.13 + 409.60 = 739.73$ and $305.86 + 433.87 = 739.73$.

REPORTING THE RESULTS

Unlike the one-way analysis of variance, it is customary to report both descriptive statistics and the overall summary table for more complicated factorial models. Thus Table 15-2, coupled with Table 15-6, would be the preferred method of displaying the results.

These results might be succinctly reported as follows:

The 3 (treatments) $\times$ 2 (personality) analysis of variance indicated both statistically significant treatment and personality main effects, although no statistically significant interaction was observed. As illustrated in Table 15-6, the personality main effect was due to a decided tendency for extroverted patients to lose more weight, regardless of treatment, than their introverted counterparts (13.87 pounds to 7.80 pounds). Scheffé tests were performed for the overall treatment means and indicated that both E_1 and E_2 subjects lost significantly more weight than controls, although no statistically significant difference existed between the two treatments.

MORE COMPLEX FACTORIAL MODELS

As discussed in Chapter 8, there is no theoretical limit to the number of permutations that can be incorporated into a factorial model. As stated there, the systematic sources of variation also grow geometrically with the number of factors added. As long as these additional factors all represent between-subjects variables, the single error term remains relatively simple, being nothing more than the total sum of squares minus all the main effect and interaction terms. When within-subjects factors are added, however, the number of error terms begins to proliferate.

Suppose, for example, that we had randomly assigned matched subjects to the treatment factor in the 2 $\times$ 3 study just discussed. This would have produced a model containing one within-subjects and one between-subjects factor and *two* error terms, one for the between-subjects main effect and one for everything touching the within-subjects variable. The source of variation portion of the resulting ANOVA summary table would thus look like Table 15-7.

Table 15-6 MEANS AND STANDARD DEVIATIONS FOR THE 3 $\times$ 2
FACTORIAL EXAMPLE

	E_1 Dietary education + exercise regimen		E_2 Dietary education only		C Routine clinical care	
	$\bar{X}$	S.D.	$\bar{X}$	S.D.	$\bar{X}$	S.D.
Extroverts	17.80	4.82	16.80	4.82	7.00	7.07
Introverts	10.40	7.02	9.00	5.61	4.00	3.16

Table 15-7 SOURCES OF VARIATION FOR A TWO-FACTOR ANOVA
(ONE BETWEEN- AND ONE WITHIN-SUBJECTS FACTOR)

Source of variation
Between subjects
A (personality)
Error
Within subjects
B (treatments)
AB
Error

Table 15-8 SOURCES OF VARIATION FOR A THREE-FACTOR ANOVA
(ONE BETWEEN- AND TWO WITHIN-SUBJECTS FACTORS)

Source of variation
Between subjects
A (personality)
Error
Within subjects
B (treatments)
AB
Error
C (time)
AC
Error
BC
ABC
Error

As indicated in Table 15-8, the sources of variation and error terms continue to proliferate as additional variables are added. Here, the use of a second within-subjects variable (which we will define as weight loss immediately after the intervention versus 6 months later) results in still another error term.

Since practically all researchers perform analyses of variance and covariance via computers, it is no longer necessary to be able to calculate these sources of variation. It remains a good idea, however, to at least be aware of what the completed analysis should look like as well as to guess which effects will be statistically significant and which will not by eyeballing the cell means prior to computer analysis. Computers are only as accurate as the instructions they are given, and it is very easy to make a data entry or format error in setting up these more complicated analyses. Unless checked in some way, embarrassing errors can find their way into the professional literature.

SUMMARY

As a statistical procedure, factorial analysis of variance employs one or more additional independent variables both to reduce the amount of unexplained variance within a study (which increases its statistical power) and to test additional hypotheses generated by the potential interaction of these independent variables with respect to the dependent variable. The calculation and evaluation of the resulting F-ratios is a simple extension of one-way ANOVA procedures. Individual differences between main effect means are also evaluated in the same way (usually via a posteriori tests such as Newman-Keuls or Scheffé), although the specific contributions made to a statistically significant interaction involve the use of two or more simpler ANOVAs called simple effects tests. The complexity of a factorial ANOVA increases geometrically with the number of independent variables employed, thus computers are almost universally used in their computation. It remains a good idea, however, both to identify the sources of variation present in a study and to estimate which are likely to be statistically significant prior to computer analysis.

REFERENCE

Winer, B. J. *Statistical Principles in Experimental Design,* 2nd edition. New York: McGraw-Hill, 1971.

chapter *16*

Multiple Regression

Some of the most important variables in the human sciences are not manipulatable and hence are neither subject to research models involving the random assignment of subjects nor even to the quasi-experimental approximations thereof discussed in Chapter 9. Few methodologists would argue, for example, that the cleanest way (that is, subject to the fewest alternative explanations) to assess the effect of tobacco smoking on the development of lung cancer would be to assign a large group of young subjects randomly to two conditions: one that would smoke two packs of cigarettes per day for the rest of their lives and one that would never smoke cigarettes at all.

Even if society could afford to wait two-thirds of a lifetime for such results, and even if human behavior could be controlled so thoroughly, there are some rather obvious ethical problems in either manipulating potentially harmful variables or with depriving subjects of those potentially beneficial treatments to which they would normally have access. Some experiments such as this can be performed on animals (although their indiscriminant use is coming under increasing attack), of course, but many variables do not translate easily across species.

Rats and monkeys, for example, could be (and have been) forced to breathe tobacco smoke, but it is doubtful that such research alone would have widespread impact. The only real option open to researchers interested in essentially nonmanipulatable variables, then, is to study the world as it is, rather than as it could be (which is what the introduction of an experimental manipulation permits). Conceptually, what this translates to is comparing individuals who engage in a particular behavior (for example, who smoke, take drugs,

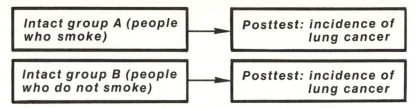

Figure 16-1   Nonequivalent-control-group–posttest-only model.

exercise and watch their diets following cardiovascular surgery) with those who do not. This, of course, bears a distinct similarity to one of the weakest quasi-experimental designs discussed in Chapter 9, namely the nonequivalent-con-trol-group–posttest-only model (Figure 16-1).

However, the reality of this study is somewhat different from the types of questions normally addressed by the quasi-experimental designs discussed so far. When subjects are *completely* free to select themselves into the treatment (that is, smoking) versus nontreatment (nonsmoking) groups, no serious re-searcher (or research consumer for that matter) would consider any conclusion regarding the effects of smoking as credible when so simple a data-collection model was employed. There are simply too many alternative explanations for any results that might accrue, either positive or negative. This is especially true here, since the researcher really did not introduce the treatment to anyone, but simply studied it as it occurred naturally in society.

How then could the study be strengthened? Obviously the addition of a pretest would make no sense, since practically no one would have lung cancer prior to their beginning smoking (and if they did, they probably would not survive until the end of the study). We also could not afford to wait the requisite length of time before collecting our posttest data, thus the most appropriate model yet discussed is probably the nonequivalent-control-group-with-covar-iates model, where the covariates are conceptualized as variables that either existed prior to the advent of smoking or that were not directly influenced by the subjects' smoking behaviors. (It doesn't matter if these variables themselves predispose the subject to smoke.) What normally occurs, then, is an adaptation or extension of this primitive model, whereby statistical control is substituted for the procedural strategies (that is, the introduction of the intervention via one of the experimental or quasi-experimental models discussed in previous chapters).

CHARACTERISTICS OF MULTIPLE REGRESSION STUDIES

For want of a better name, research that must completely substitute statistical control for procedural control will be said to be employing a *multiple-regression model* after the most common (although by no means the only) statistical procedure used to analyze its results. Such studies bear some very striking *dissimilarities* from the types of studies that employ even a modicum of proce-dural control. Some of these include the following.

1. *Studies employing the multiple-regression model normally employ far more variables.* These variables function in much the same way that covariates do in the nonequivalent-control-group-with-covariates model. Here, however, since the primary purpose of the covariates is to increase statistical power and to serve as a facilitator of establishing equivalence between groups, it is very rare for more than two covariates to be employed. The norm, in fact, is one.

In multiple-regression studies, the chief purpose of these additional variables is to serve as substitutes for the procedural control abdicated by studying the variable of interest (still called the independent variable) as it occurs naturally. To understand how statistical control can substitute for procedural control, let us contrast the logic underlying each.

When subjects are assigned either to receive or not to receive an intervention and then subsequently measured on the dependent variable, any postintervention differences between groups thereon are assumed to be a function of the intervention. This assumption is possible because subjects who received the intervention are assumed to have been equivalent to those who did not before the study began. If subjects had an equal chance of either receiving or not receiving the intervention (that is, if they were randomly assigned to groups), then this initial equivalence assumption is usually tenable. Even when subjects are not randomly assigned to groups, the researcher normally makes every effort possible to ensure that experimental subjects are not *obviously* different from control subjects in some important way.

When a variable is not manipulated, but when the subjects themselves (or their environments) are the sole determinants of whether or not they will receive an intervention, then it is far more reasonable to assume that the two types of people involved *are* obviously different from one another. Thus, if smokers are to be contrasted to nonsmokers, it is more reasonable to assume that the two groups of subjects differ on many other dimensions (for example, personality, life-style, exposure to stress) as well. Similarly, if we were to study the relationship between exercise and diet on weight loss among postoperative cardiovascular patients by not manipulating the former, it is almost certain that those patients who engage in exercise and sensible dietary practices on their own differ from those who do not in several ways not specifically related to the parameters of interest (for example, seriousness of the cardiovascular problem, general physical condition, motivation, fear). The purpose behind the use of the multiple-regression model thus becomes the statistical control of all the possible ways in which people who engage in the behavior being studied differ from those who do not with respect to the dependent variable (be it weight loss or the incidence of lung cancer). To do this, all the possible correlates of the dependent variable must be employed as independent variables. (If one of these potentially confounding variables is not related to either the dependent or other independent variables, then it doesn't matter whether or not the groups involved differ thereon or not.) Obviously, all the alternative explanations for an event's occurrence can never be controlled in this manner, but many can and that is both the logic behind the multiple-regression model and the reason why studies employing it use as many independent variables as they do.

2. *Multiple-regression studies normally employ far more subjects.* This characteristic is not unrelated to the fact that multiple-regression studies normally employ so many variables. On an intuitive level, the relationship between the number of subjects and the number of variables can best be visualized in comparing a simple two-group experimental model to a multifactorial model.

In a simple experimental study involving a single experimental and control group, the main consideration in determining the number of subjects needed is the assurance of sufficient statistical power. In most cases, 50 to 60 subjects per group are quite ample. The situation is different when a number of additional independent variables or factors are employed. Suppose that four independent variables were added to this two-group model, each of which possessed three levels (say high, medium, and low). If 100 subjects were present initially, the addition of these four variables would bring the number of subjects available per cell from 50 (that is, 50 in E and 50 in C) to less than one, since the new design would contain $2 \times 3 \times 3 \times 3 \times 3$ or 162 cells.

Obviously, then, what starts out as a reasonable sample size for one or two independent variables becomes patently ridiculous very quickly with the introduction of additional independent variables. Although the factorial model is not strictly applicable to a multiple-regression study, since interactions between independent variables are seldom assessed in any great quantity, it is still helpful to visualize the cells involved along with the numbers that will go into them to make sure that enough subjects exist to test all the alternative explanations in need of testing.

The distribution of subjects with respect to both the independent and the dependent variables must also be considered. As an extreme example, suppose a random sample of a thousand subjects were employed for our smoking study. Since perhaps only two of these subjects would have contracted lung cancer, this particular study would be worthless. One must thus consider both the absolute number of subjects as well as their variability with respect to the variables being studied. (In reality a study such as this would of course not employ a random sample, given the low incidence of lung cancer in the general population. Rather a sample of subjects known to be suffering from lung cancer would probably be contrasted to a group not so afflicted.)

The subject-to-variable ratio   In multiple-regression studies, the issue of how many subjects are needed is usually discussed in terms of how many independent variables are being employed. The reason the two parameters are related stems from the fact that every estimate of shared variation (that is, r^2) between two variables contains two elements: true shared variance and shared variance due to error. The more subjects that are involved in the calculation of any individual correlation coefficient, the greater the true shared variance is likely to be in comparison to the shared variance due to error.

Since a multiple regression entails a progression of Pearson r's performed between each independent variable and a single dependent variable using the *same* sample of subjects, the shared variance due to error is *cumulative* or additive. The smaller the sample size, the greater this cumulative error; the more independent variables involved, the greater this cumulative error. Obviously, then, the worst possible scenario occurs when many independent variables are used with a relatively small sample size (or when the subject-to-variable ratio is relatively small).

As a general rule of thumb, *I recommend that at least 25 subjects be available for each independent variable,* although I am not particularly impressed with any multiple-regression study employing fewer than 200 subjects. This dictum is not carved in stone, but in general it is certainly safe to say that the greater the subject-to-variable ratio, the better. Failing this, I recommend the use of large samples (that is, $n > 200$) for multiple-regression studies.

3. *Multiple-regression studies often restrict their samples in some way.* This has already been touched on with respect to ensuring sufficient variability among all the variables employed. While this could be viewed as a statistical imperative, multiple-regression samples are sometimes restricted for procedural reasons. This often happens when a relationship between the dependent variable and an extraneous independent variable is known to be more powerful than the independent variable of primary interest and when this first relationship is basically irrelevant to the study's specific purpose. To take an extreme example, a researcher interested in investigating the determinants of muscular strength might do well to exclude preadolescent children from the final sample, since the relationship between age and strength is known and probably stronger than anything else the researcher might wish to study. (The researcher in this case might also be wise to restrict the sample to one sex and possibly to an even narrower age range.)

The reason for restricting one's sample in this way may not be obvious at first glance. Certainly it has the disadvantage of limiting the generality of any findings that may accrue from the study. If, however, the extraneous variable is itself strongly related to the dependent variable *and* if the patterns of relationships between the variables of primary interest and the dependent variable are different for the various levels of this extraneous variable, then in effect the researcher basically winds up with two sets of noncomparable data. Suppose, for example, that our researcher was primarily interested in the relationship between certain life-style variables (for example, diet, body weight) and muscular strength. Suppose further that he or she decided to include both males and females in the sample.

In the first place we know that men are stronger than women, thus a major proportion of the individual differences between subjects (that is, the variance) with respect to muscular strength can be predicted by simply knowing what sex they are. More seriously, the chances are excellent that the same variables are not related identically to muscular strength in males and females or that, using the last chapter's terminology, an interaction exists between sex and the other independent variables. What our researcher must do in such a case is to take this possibility into account by either including a test for such interactions within the multiple regression itself or simply conducting two separate multiple regressions, one with each sample, and compare the two. Both strategies require a far larger sample size than would a study restricted to a single sex.

As has been stated before, I counsel all beginning researchers to curb their ambitions to learn everything there is to know about a set of variables in one study. If this translates to restricting the scope of one's research questions, so be it. It is better to answer a small question definitively than a large one ambiguously.

4. *Multiple-regression studies have the potential of addressing more important research questions.* Since multiple-regression studies substitute statistical control for experimenter-introduced interventions, they have the potential of studying variables whose manipulations are prohibited by societal mores (or which are simply impractical to manipulate). Furthermore, experimental and quasi-experimental studies are normally prospective in nature. Multiple-regression studies, on the other hand, are most often retrospective, which allows them the luxury of using variables that may take years (or decades) to manifest themselves.

Thus, returning to the dietary/exercise intervention used throughout this book, any experimental (or quasi-experimental) study introducing this intervention would be pretty much limited to the selection of a dependent variable that could be measured relatively *quickly*.* The selection of weight loss as the criterion to evaluate a program such as this would have been, therefore, primarily guided by expediency. Weight loss in postoperative cardiovascular patients is not particularly interesting in and of itself. It is really a secondary variable *assumed* to be related to real criteria, such as longevity, productivity, or the necessity of undergoing future surgery.

Most experimental researchers do not have the patience or resources to wait the necessary time for such variables to manifest themselves, thus they are relegated to the use of secondary criteria. Large-scale regression studies using retrospective data are under no such constraints, however, since they can use records, self-reports, and even data supplied by someone with intimate knowledge about a possibly deceased or incapacitated subject. (Of course, regression studies do not necessarily rely on retrospective data. They are capable of employing this added dimension and their large samples are even capable of ameliorating some of the weaknesses of this type of data.)

5. *The multiple-regression model permits the study of variables as they occur naturally in society.* Many researchers into the human condition are interested primarily in the study of phenomena as they occur in naturalistic settings. Thus, even though a variable may be manipulatable, such researchers eschew the opportunity for fear of substituting an artificial environment for the real world laboratory in which they are truly interested. There is certainly nothing logically wrong with this perspective, and to the extent that empirical methods are appropriate for such studies,† the multiple-regression model is probably one of the most powerful and useful options available.

---

* Researchers should use both, of course, cashing in on the immediate payoff of an easy criterion while preserving the integrity of the sample for future follow-up studies (even if they must be conducted by other researchers).

† Many researchers (for example, anthropologists, sociologists, and members of other disciplines who employ their methods) interested in this type of research prefer qualitative techniques as opposed to the empirical methods discussed in this book. Although I am undoubtedly biased toward empirical research, I see no reason why the two approaches cannot be profitably combined.

6. *Multiple-regression studies are better suited for continuous variables, hence are capable of greater sensitivity.* Regardless of the dependent variable employed, research introducing experimental interventions is limited to relatively few levels of that intervention. Usually, these gradients are dichotomous in nature; the subjects either receive it (the experimental group) or they do not (the control). Occasionally, other gradients or groups are added (such as our dietary information plus exercise regimen versus dietary information alone), but in the final analysis the values that the independent variable can take are limited.

For most research purposes, this is not that severe a disadvantage. It is usually enough to know that, say, a program of dietary education and supervised exercise results in a statistically significant weight loss. If it were equally important to learn how much exercise and dietary information was optimal, on the other hand, the researcher might do better by conducting a large-scale regression study in which exercise and dietary knowledge were allowed to vary normally. Cutting points could then be developed empirically based on actual practices after other relevant factors (such as age, life-style, weight) had been statistically controlled.

7. *Multiple-regression studies result in weaker causal inferences than research employing experimental designs.* At first glance, this may seem to contradict some of the preceding points, but in reality it does not. Multiple-regression studies do possess some very real advantages over other types of studies, but in the final analysis statistical control is not nearly as powerful as the procedural control afforded by randomly assigned subjects to experimental interventions.

Large-scale correlational studies only approximate experimental control. The more subjects employed and the more creatively alternative explanations are ruled out via the independent variables employed, the better this approximation. Still, when a researcher manipulates intervention X and observes a concomitant change in variable Y for subjects who received X and no change for those who did not receive it, then the inferences that changes in X *caused* changes in Y is about as safe as any that can be drawn.

When values on X are found to be related to values on Y in a single group of subjects, however, there is always the possibility that another unknown variable Z actually *caused* the differences both in X and in Y. In an experimental study, on the other hand, we know what caused the between-group differences on Y; it was the experimental manipulation, since the random assignment of subjects to groups ensured that they did not differ on Z prior to the intervention, regardless of whether we even know what Z is or not.

Viewed from this perspective, the purpose of the additional controlling variables in a multiple-regression study is to ferret out all the Z's, thus ruling out all the alternative explanations. The problem with this approach is that no matter how creatively this is accomplished, the doubts already discussed concerning the validity of quasi-experimental models always manifest themselves. Some researchers react to this problem by arguing that they are not really concerned about causation anyway. It is enough, they argue, to be able to predict the circumstances under which human phenomena occur. Is not prediction as legitimate a scientific concern as control?

Most researchers therefore employ multiple-regression studies in a sort of descriptive manner, with the primary purpose being to identify as many correlates of the chosen dependent variable as possible. Framing this sort of inquiry into the perspective of the types of research and research purposes that have been discussed in this book so far, such studies can be viewed as either:

1. Precursors to experimentation (where promising variables can be identified for later manipulation).
2. Follow-ups of experimental research in which an interesting effect can be studied in the real world laboratory of the multiple-regression model.
3. Simply a convenient way to address a genre of research question (perhaps suggested by experimental study, perhaps not) that can be addressed *only* via the sort of descriptive-correlational manner unique to the multiple-regression model.

As an illustration of this latter situation, an example from my own research will be used to illustrate the conceptual and computational basis of multiple regression. Basically, the study in question was a direct outgrowth of other research — some of it experimental, some of it not — documenting the relationship between cholesterol intake and cardiovascular disease. Given this well-documented, direct relationship, a natural question becomes: Can certain types of people be identified who are less likely to take special steps to regulate their cholesterol intake *without* some kind of special intervention? If so, then we would know what portions of the population are in the greatest need of such an intervention (and by implication, are also at greatest risk for cardiovascular disease). Prior to discussing this study in any detail, however, let us examine some of the procedural and statistical bases of the multiple-regression model.

PROCEDURAL STEPS

Besides the obvious steps of literature review and problem delineation common to all research studies, the following sequence of steps would normally be undertaken for a multiple-regression study.

1. *The independent and dependent variables are selected and operationally defined.* The dependent variable is usually quite straightforward, since its prediction or explanation constitutes the purpose of the study in the first place. Independent variables are generated based on the literature, theory, and clinical knowledge surrounding the network of relationships associated with the dependent variable. Usually, any variable that is known or suspected to be related to the dependent variable is included, whether the relationship is considered potentially direct (causative) or indirect (confounding). The latter corresponds to alternative explanations of the former, thus certain independent vari-

ables are often included as a check or control, with the researcher actually hoping that they will not correlate with the dependent variable. Everything said concerning the insurance of reliability and validity in Chapters 11 and 12 applies here. Measures that are not psychometrically sound will not prove useful, whether used as independent or dependent variables. Thus, pilot work to establish content validity, reliability, and just plain clarity is essential, whether data will be collected via survey, record review, or observation.

2. *The specific sample to be used is identified.* Knowledge of the field, especially clinical knowledge, is often of great importance here when the sample is to be limited in some purposeful manner (such as limiting it to one sex, age group, diagnosis, and so forth).

3. *The data are collected and coded.* Accuracy is extremely important at this stage, since errors will work against achieving the study's primary objectives.

4. *The analytic scheme to be used is selected and the data are analyzed.*

CONCEPTUAL AND STATISTICAL BASIS FOR MULTIPLE REGRESSION

Multiple-regression techniques are direct extensions of the correlational procedures discussed in Chapter 5. Basically, linear multiple regression is a direct extension of the multiple-correlation formula presented therein, although several additional statistics are normally examined relating to:

1. The individual contribution of each independent variable to the total, overall multiple R.

2. The regression equation whereby subjects' scores on the dependent variable can be predicted based on their individual independent variables' scores.

At the risk of oversimplification, there are basically two types of statistical procedures used to analyze the data accruing from a multiple-regression model. The most common, generally referred to as *linear multiple regression,* is used when the dependent variable is measured at something approximating the interval level of measurement (for example, intelligence scores or age, for which the arithmetic mean is an appropriate descriptive statistic). The second, called *discriminant analysis,* is used when the dependent variable is categorical or measured at the nominal level (such as personality type or religious affiliation, for which the arithmetic mean would make no sense).*

Within each of these general procedures, several different analytic options exist that basically produce similar results to one another. The most common are:

---

* Canonical correlation can be used to analyze data accruing from multiple-regression models employing more than one dependent variable. In general, I do not encourage the use of multivariate statistical procedures such as discriminant analysis or canonical correlation without advanced training or expert guidance.

1. *The general model,* in which the total and individual contributions of the independent variable set to the prediction (or explanation) of the dependent variable are determined.

2. *The stepwise model,* in which the independent variables are entered into the equation in order of importance (defined as the amount of variance they individually share with the dependent variable). The advantage of this technique is that it allows the researcher to terminate the analysis at the point at which the remainder of the independent variables no longer constitute a significant contribution to the total correlational scheme. Within this general option, several specific strategies exist, such as:

   (a) *Forward stepwise,* in which the first variable entered constitutes the strongest correlate with the dependent variable, the second variable the second strongest (after the variance accounted for by the first step has been taken into consideration), and so forth.

   (b) *Backward stepwise,* in which the process is begun with all the independent variables already in the equation and variables are systematically dropped beginning with the one making the weakest contribution.

   (c) *Forward and backward,* which is identical to the forward stepwise procedure except variables that enter the equation at one point may be deleted later if their contribution becomes insignificant.*

3. *The hierarchical model,*† in which the researcher specifies the order that some or all of the independent variables enter the regression equation. This technique is most often used for studies where one or more of the independent variables assumes a preeminent role while the others are relegated to serving as statistical controls for ruling out alternative explanations for this (or these) primary relationship(s). In the hypothetical regression study assessing the relationship between smoking and longevity, for example, the amount smoked would be correlated (or entered into the regression equation) with longevity only *after* all the other potentially confounding variables had been entered into the equation to see if smoking was related to longevity *after* all the rival hypotheses that the researcher could come up with had been controlled.

Although all of these options produce the same final multiple R, we will examine the multiple-regression concept from a forward stepwise perspective, since it is probably the most appealing from a conceptual point of view and also

---

* This could occur in the following way. Suppose a variable was entered as the second step because it possessed the highest correlation with the dependent variable when the variable entered on the first step was statistically controlled. This partial correlation would be continually reevaluated in a forward and backward procedure as more and more independent variables were statistically controlled. It is quite possible that an originally statistically significant partial correlation holding one variable constant might *not* be statistically significant once several independent variables were held constant.

† Many statistical programs do not offer this option for discriminant analysis, although there is no good reason for this other than difficulty of programming.

Table 16-1 HYPOTHETICAL CORRELATION MATRIX

	Exercise	Smoking	Dietary habits	Longevity
IV-a (exercise)	—	.02	.70	.44
IV-b (smoking)		—	.04	.24
IV-c (dietary habits)			—	.41
DV-d (longevity)				—

the most commonly employed strategy.* To simplify matters, let us assume a study employing the use of three independent variables (smoking, dietary habits, and frequency of exercise) to predict or explain a single dependent variable (longevity).

The first step in the process would be the computation of a correlational matrix involving all the possible relationships between all the variables involved (Table 16-1). As stated above, the first step taken in a forward stepwise procedure would be to search through the simple correlations between each independent variable (IV) and the single dependent variable (DV) to find the strongest correlate of the latter. In Table 16-1, this translates to the three values in the final column, where the strongest correlation happens to be between exercise and longevity (the dependent variable).

The next step in the process is a bit more complex, since the second-highest independent-dependent variable correlation cannot automatically be chosen. This is because 19.4 percent of the variance associated with the dependent variable has already been explained ($.44^2$); thus, it is the highest correlation with what remains unexplained ($1 - r^2$) that is of interest. This translates to the highest partial correlation between each of the remaining variables when the frequency with which a person exercises is held constant. Because of the relatively high correlation between exercise and dietary habits, the highest partial correlation in which exercise is held constant will involve the subjects' smoking behavior, even though its simple relationship to longevity is smaller than the relationship between diet and longevity (.24 as opposed to .41).

$$r_{bd.a} = \frac{.24 - .02 \times .44}{\sqrt{1 - (.02)^2} \sqrt{1 - (.44)^2}}$$

$$= .26$$

$$r_{cd.a} = \frac{.41 - .70 \times .44}{\sqrt{1 - (.70)^2} \sqrt{1 - (.44)^2}}$$

$$= .16$$

where a = exercise
 b = smoking
 c = diet
 d = longevity

* The forward and backward procedure may be the best choice if it is available, especially if the researcher wishes to know the exact point at which the addition of more independent variables no longer makes a statistically significant contribution to the overall effort.

As discussed in Chapter 5, the *unique* contribution of smoking behavior (*b*) is thus equal to this squared partial correlation coefficient ($.26^2$) times the amount of variation in the dependent variable (longevity) that remains unexplained *after* the variation explained by the first independent variable has been subtracted (in other words, $1 - r_{ad}^2$). Thus, the unique contribution made by the second variable is equal to

$$r_{bd.a}^2 \times (1 - r_{ad}^2) = .26^2 \times (1 - .44^2)$$
$$= .068 \times .866$$
$$= .055$$

The process then continues. The total amount of the dependent variable variance that can now be explained is $.194 + .055 = .249$. The final independent variable (diet or *c*) is then correlated with this unexplained variation in the dependent variable ($1 - R_{d.ab}^2$), which is equivalent to the squared partial correlation between *c* (diet) and *d* (longevity) with *a* (exercise) and *b* (smoking) held constant.

This, then, is the crux of a forward, stepwise, multiple-regression procedure. The only additional statistics (other than R and R^2) accruing that are of much interest for most research purposes are:

1. An *F*-ratio that tests the overall statistical significance of the multiple-correlation coefficient at each step along the way.
2. A series of *F*-ratios that test the statistical significance of the individual contributions made by each independent variable (for the second step in the above numerical example, this would indicate whether or not .055 was a statistically significant increase in the amount of dependent variable variance explained).

ASSUMPTIONS AND GENERALIZATIONS REGARDING THE USE OF LINEAR MULTIPLE-REGRESSION TECHNIQUES

1. Multiple regression is a very general technique. It can basically be used in lieu of any parametric, univariate statistical procedure discussed so far in this book (for example, any kind of ANOVA or ANCOVA). All the assumptions (the most obvious of which is that the dependent variable must be a variable for which the arithmetic mean is an appropriate descriptor) regarding those techniques thus apply to multiple regression used for similar purposes.*
2. The term *linear* multiple regression implies that the relationships between the variables employed are linear. Just as with the Pearson *r*, the primary penalty for violating this assumption will be the underestimation of the relationships involved. Two of the more obvious types of nonlinear relationships are:
   (a) *Relationships involving noncontinuous independent or dependent variables.* Categorical or nominal independent variables would

---

* For a more thorough statistical explanation of this phenomena see Nie et al. (1975, pp. 340–341).

obviously not be expected to bear a linear relationship to a dependent variable measured at the interval level. Such variables (which I suggest avoiding when at all possible) must be recoded in a dichotomous fashion (called dummy coding),* the mechanisms for which are described in most manuals for statistical programs.

(b) *Independent variables that are suspected of interacting with one another* in the classic analysis of variance sense. Such variables should either not be used or the interaction itself should be recoded as a separate variable. (This too is described in most statistical manuals, but it usually entails transforming the two independent variables in some way, such as using their products as the interaction term.)

3. The higher the intercorrelations between the independent variables, the less confidence that can be had in the results of a multiple regression, especially with respect to the independent contribution made by each of the variables involved. When two variables are very highly correlated with one another (say .70 or greater, which indicates that approximately half or more of their variance is shared), the researcher should either employ only one or combine the two into a single composite of some sort. (The SAS regression procedure actually has a routine for assessing the degree to which this phenomenon, called *multicollinearity,* is problematic for any given analysis.)

4. *The more subjects per variable, the better.*

A RESEARCH EXAMPLE

Since the interpretation of a multiple-regression analysis can be relatively complex, the above procedural, conceptual, and statistical points will be illustrated as promised by an actual research example. The four procedural steps outlined above were accomplished as follows:

1. The dependent variable was dictated by the primary purpose of the study itself, which was identifying the types of people who made a conscious effort to reduce their cholesterol intake. The specific item, which was developed to be administered via a telephone interview, was:

* For example, the single-factor multigroup model depicted in Figure 8-1 would normally be analyzed via a one-way ANOVA. The data resulting from this model could just as well be analyzed via a multiple regression employing weight loss as the dependent variable and each of four groups as dichotomously coded independent variables. For our four-group model, then, each subject would be assigned a score on each of three dummy variables as follows:

	Dummy variable 1	Dummy variable 2	Dummy variable 3
Subjects in E_1	1	0	0
Subjects in E_2	0	1	0
Subjects in E_3	0	0	1
Subjects in C	0	0	0

Thinking about your personal diet and nutrition, do you try a lot, try a little, or don't you try at all to avoid eating too many high-cholesterol foods (such as eggs, dairy products, and fatty meats)?

This item was subjected to careful scrutiny by a number of knowledgeable people and tried out in a pilot test to make sure that people could respond to it unambiguously.

The independent variables were primarily chosen by a thorough literature review and clinical knowledge of the area. Each potential item was subjected to the same careful scrutiny and pilot testing procedure as the dependent variable. In brief, the variables chosen were *demographic variables,* such as:

(a) Age.
(b) Sex.
(c) Education.
(d) Income.

compliance with other health-seeking behaviors, such as:

(e) Regulating intake of salt, fat, and sugar (which will be called nutrition composite 1: score range = 0 to 3).
(f) Eating sufficient quantities of fiber, vitamins, and minerals (called nutrition composite 2: score range = 0 to 3).*
(g) A fire safety composite (consisting of owning smoke detectors and a fire extinguisher: score range = 0 to 2).
(h) A driving safety composite (driving at the speed limit and not drinking and driving: score range = 0 to 2).
(i) Wearing seatbelts (score range = 0 to 1).
(j) Exercising strenuously three times per week (score range = 0 to 1).
(k) Not smoking (score range = 0 to 1).
(l) Eating breakfast regularly (score range = 0 to 1).
(m) Having one's blood pressure checked regularly (score range = 0 to 1).
(n) Taking steps to reduce one's stress (score range = 0 to 1).
(o) Getting enough sleep (score range = 0 to 1).
(p) Consuming alcohol in moderation (score range = 0 to 1).
(q) Attempting to avoid home accidents (score range = 0 to 1).
(r) Ensuring sufficient social contacts with friends and relatives (score range = 0 to 1).

attitudes toward preventive behavior, or more specifically,

(s) The importance placed on avoiding cholesterol for ensuring a long and healthy life as measured by a 10-point scale ranging from not at all important (1) to extremely important (10).
2. The target sample to be used was quite straightforward. Since the results were to be generalized to the entire adult population of the United States, a random sample therefrom (actually a random sample of Americans owning a telephone) was used. The sample size was

---

* The two nutritional composite variables employed items very similar to the cholesterol question presented above.

dictated by the resources available and the maximum amount or sampling error that was deemed tolerable. Since this involved over a thousand subjects, the subject-to-variable ratio was quite good for this particular study, even though 18 independent variables were employed.
3. The data were collected, coded, and checked for accuracy using the procedure suggested in Chapter 13.
4. The statistical procedure selected was a forward, stepwise, multiple regression as performed by SAS.

The initial correlation matrix among the 18 independent variables and the extent to which subjects attempted to regulate their cholesterol intake (the dependent variable) are presented in Table 16-2. As a cursory examination will indicate, multicollinearity was not a problem with these data since none of the independent variables tended to correlate that highly with one another. Also, since none of the variables were measured at the nominal level* and interactions among the independent variables were not considered likely or problematic, the major assumptions for the use of multiple linear regression were met.

Table 16-3 presents the results of the first five multiple-regression steps. Step 1, it will be noted, involves nothing more than the selection of the one independent variable that bears the highest simple correlation with cholesterol intake (see column 19 of Table 16-2). This is the first nutritional composite, which correlates .443 with cholesterol intake. This is reflected by value ① (R square) under step 1, which is .197 (.443²). The entire ANOVA summary table underneath this value is a means of testing the statistical significance of this R^2 (which at the first step is equivalent to a simple Pearson r^2). The values of interest are thus the F of 289.74 ② and its probability level of .0001 ③. Basically, then, these three values lead to the following interpretation:

1. The best single predictor of cholesterol intake is self-reported intake of salt, fat, and sugar (nutritional composite 1).
2. This variable explains 19.7 percent of the variability among individuals with respect to their self-reported cholesterol intake.
3. This 19.7 percent figure is statistically significant.

It will be remembered that the next step involves the computation of partial correlations between each of the remaining independent variables and the single dependent variable while holding the first nutrition composite constant. The highest of these turns out to be subjects' perceived importance of limiting cholesterol intake (partial $r^2 = .054$), hence this will be the variable entered at step 2. The R^2 for the second step should be equal to the R^2 for the first step plus the partial r^2 times $(1 - R^2)$ or .197 + .054 $(1 - .197) = .240$. Examination of step 2 will indeed show that this is the case (see ④).

---

* Variables i through q above were assessed dichotomously (that is, subjects either did or did not meet a priori defined standards), but as discussed in Chapter 3, a dichotomously scored variable may be appropriately analyzed using parametric statistical procedures.

Table 16-2 CORRELATION MATRIX

	V1	V2	V3	V4	V5	V6	V7	V8	V9	V10	V11	V12	V13	V14	V15	V16	V17	V18	Cholesterol intake
V1	—	.16	.11	.08	.04	.03	.13	.01	.04	.08	.01	.06	.02	.03	.08	.04	.05	.03	.071
V2		—	.35	.22	.01	.06	.15	.02	.15	.15	.09	.06	.12	.02	.24	.09	.14	.06	.443*
V3			—	.24	.06	.03	.18	.09	.15	.13	.09	.02	.12	.02	.15	.12	.07	.08	.317*
V4				—	.03	.17	.03	.08	.19	.13	.12	.08	.06	.00	.11	.05	.22	.07	.144*
V5					—	.03	.03	.02	.03	.05	−.09	.04	.05	−.05	−.03	−.17	−.16	.09	.014
V6						—	−.03	.01	.17	.08	−.02	.01	−.06	−.06	.01	.03	.03	.11	.051
V7							—	.00	.10	.06	.00	.03	.08	−.01	.07	.01	.01	.11	.116*
V8								—	.02	.05	.00	.04	−.00	.01	.05	−.01	−.02	.10	.017
V9									—	.07	.21	−.01	−.00	.02	.07	.19	.19	.07	.160*
V10										—	−.01	.12	.04	−.03	.02	−.06	−.01	.23	.108*
V11											—	−.06	.06	.02	.10	.22	.21	−.18	.162*
V12												—	.09	.02	.02	−.04	.01	.10	.030
V13													—	−.01	.09	.06	.05	−.09	.060
V14														—	.02	.06	−.12	−.01	.000
V15															—	.15	.12	.07	.352*
V16																—	.05	−.10	.111*
V17																	—	.04	.191*
V18																		—	.020

$V1$ = blood pressure check; $V2$ = nutrition composite 1; $V3$ = nutrition composite 2; $V4$ = eating breakfast; $V5$ = exercise; $V6$ = smoking; $V7$ = stress control; $V8$ = sleep; $V9$ = drinking; $V10$ = seatbelts; $V11$ = driving safely; $V12$ = driving safely; $V13$ = fire safety; $V14$ = avoiding home accidents; $V15$ = social activity; $V16$ = importance of cholesterol; $V16$ = sex; $V17$ = age; $V18$ = education.

Table 16-3 COMPUTER OUTPUT FOR A STEPWISE MULTIPLE REGRESSION

Step 1. Variable entered: nutritional composite 1   R square = .197 ①

	DF	SS	MS	F ②	Probability ③
Regression	1	56.92	56.92	289.74	.0001
Error	1,184	232.60	.20		
Total	1,185	289.52			

	B value	Std error	F	Probability
Intercept	.109			
Nutrition 1	.198	.011	289.74	.0001

Step 2. Variable entered: importance of cholesterol   R square = 0.240 ④

	DF	SS	MS	F ⑦	Probability
Regression	2	69.42	34.71	186.57	.0001
Error	1,183	220.10	.19		
Total	1,185	289.52			

	B value	Std error	F ⑤	Probability ⑥
Intercept	−.193	.012	180.15	.0001
Nutrition 1	.163	.006	67.20	.0001
Importance of cholesterol	.048			

Step 3. Variable entered: nutritional composite 2   R square = .261 ⑧

	DF	SS	MS	F	Probability
Regression	3	75.51	25.17	139.03	.0001
Error	1,182	214.00	.18		
Total	1,185	289.52			

	B value	Std error	F	Probability
Intercept	−.243			
Nutrition 1	.142	.013	128.44	.0001
Importance of cholesterol	.097	.017	33.64	.0001
Nutrition 2	.044	.005	55.08	.0001

Step 4. Variable entered: age   R square = .266 ⑨

	DF	SS	MS	F	Probability
Regression	4	77.00	19.25	106.98	.0001
Error	1,181	212.51	.18		
Total	1,185				

	B value	Std error	F	Probability
Intercept	−.306			
Nutrition 1	.137	.013	118.35	.0001
Importance of cholesterol	.095	.017	32.30	.0001
Nutrition 2	.042	.006	50.15	.0001
Age	.017	.006	8.29	.0041 ⑩

Table 16-3 *(continued)*

Step 5. Variable entered: drinking		R square = .269⑪			
	DF	**SS**	**MS**	**F**⑫	**Probability**⑬
Regression	5 ⑰	77.83	15.57	86.77	.0001
Error	1,180⑱	211.69	.18		
Total	1,185	289.52			
		B value⑮	**Std error**⑯	**F**⑭	**Probability**⑭
Intercept		−.359			
Nutrition 1		.136	.013	115.55	.0001
Importance of cholesterol		.092	.017	30.05	.0001
Nutrition 2		.085	.039	4.61	.0319
Age		.413	.006	48.85	.0001
Drinking		.148	.006	6.04	.0141

Step 2 has two additional statistics that are of interest. They are the F-ratios ⑤ and their probability levels ⑥ in the bottom right-hand corner, which indicate whether or not each of the two variables entered so far does indeed contribute significantly to the overall effort when the other is partialled out (or held constant). The F of 186.57 ⑦ and its probability level of .0001 tests the statistical significance of the overall multiple R at step 2 ($\sqrt{.240}$ or .49).

Perhaps the most interesting information at step 2 is not printed in this particular output, although many multiple-regression programs do provide it. This is the unique contribution to R^2 made by the addition of the second independent variable. We already know that this contribution is statistically significant, but as will soon be seen, statistical significance is not that good a barometer of practical significance when this much statistical power is available (that is, in an analysis containing over a thousand subjects). The unique contribution to R^2 made by the perceived importance of restricting one's intake of cholesterol is found by simply subtracting the multiple R^2 at step 1 from that at step 2, or .240 − .197 = .043. This says that the addition of this particular independent variable explained an additional 4.3 percent of the variation (individual differences) in the dependent variable (which is the degree to which the general population attempts to regulate their cholesterol intake).

Given that a forward stepwise procedure is being employed, the relative contribution made by each independent variable from step 1 on will become progressively smaller. Since a significance level of .05 was specified, each increment to R^2 will be statistically significant, simply because the program will terminate the process when the .05 level of significance is not reached. The contribution to R^2 made by the addition of the second nutritional composite at step 3 is thus equal to ⑧ − ④ or .261 − .240 = .021. (This value of .261 is generated in the same way as .240, except that the partial r^2 now holds both the first nutritional composite and the importance placed on cholesterol intake constant.)

Opinions would be mixed regarding the triviality-nontriviality of adding 2.1 percent to an R^2. Most researchers would probably argue that such a value is of interest, given the number of subjects involved and the fact that it would probably be replicated in another study using a similarly large sample. Opinions would be much less divided concerning the relative importance of age to this prediction scheme, however, since it adds only one-half of a percent to R^2 (.266 − .261 = .005: ⑨ − ⑧). Note under step 4, however, that this increase is statistically significant at the .0041 level of significance ⑩, given the large number of subjects involved. Step 5, though statistically significant at the .0141 level, is even more trivial, adding only .003 to the total R^2. I would therefore suggest that researchers employ an additional criterion to the significance level for judging the unique contribution made to R^2 by independent variables, namely the absolute size of this contribution, which should probably not be below 2 percent. This is admittedly an arbitrary figure with which many experts would disagree. However, few would argue with the fact that an independent variable that adds less than a percentage point to the total R^2 can be considered of little import in most research situations.

The present example was terminated after step 5 because no additional partial r could be found that could add to the total prediction scheme when the first five variables were held constant. This is interesting since 10 of the 18 simple correlation coefficients between each independent variable and the dependent variable were statistically significant (see the final column in Table 16-2). This is normally the case in multiple regression, since one of the functions of the procedure is to identify only the most important relationships when all the intercorrelations between variables have been taken into consideration.

Step 5 in Table 16-3 contains the majority of the information that the researcher would actually need to include in his or her research report. The R^2 of .269 ⑪ of course, is the most important value, indicating that almost 27 percent of the individual difference in cholesterol intake could be predicted by the five variables considered. This may not seem like an especially impressive figure, since 73 percent of the variation remains unexplained, but a multiple R of .52 ($\sqrt{.269}$) is not particularly low for a study employing independent variables consisting of single items (since single items are not particularly reliable and reliability places an upper limit on any relationship involving the variable of interest).

Other statistics of interest at step 5 are the F and attendant probability associated with this final R (⑫ and ⑬), the F-ratios and their probabilities attending the unique contribution made by each independent variable ⑭, and to a lesser extent, the figures under B value and std error (⑮ and ⑯).

These latter values contain the basic elements of the final regression equation, which can be used to predict an individual's dependent variable score based on that individual's scores on each of the independent variables. Although seldom used in empirical research per se, the regression equation would be useful to anyone attempting to apply the results of a study to actual clinical practice.

REPORTING THE RESULTS

As always, there are large individual differences in the way in which a multiple-regression analysis such as this might be reported. Basically, the reader of the

Table 16-4   SAMPLE MULTIPLE-REGRESSION SUMMARY TABLE

Step	Variable entered	B	Contribution to R^2	Cumulative R^2
1	Nutritional composite 1	.136[b]	.197	.197[b]
2	Importance of cholesterol intake	.092[b]	.043	.240[b]
3	Nutritional composite 2	.085[b]	.021	.261[b]
4	Age	.413[a]	.005	.266[b]
5	Alcohol consumption	.148[a]	.003	.269[b]
	Intercept $= -.358$			

[a] $p < .05$

[b] $p < .0001$

research report must be told the exact statistical procedure that was employed, what the independent and dependent variables were, how they were measured, the number of subjects involved, and at least some information on the final R^2, its significance level, and the contributions made by the individual predictors.

The above study thus might be most succinctly described as follows:

A forward, stepwise, multiple regression using the .05 level for inclusion was performed on the 1,186 subjects on whom complete information was available. The dependent variable of interest was the extent to which subjects attempted to restrict their cholesterol intake; the independent variables were a nutrition composite consisting of self-reported behaviors concerning the effort made to restrict fat, salt, and sugar intake, a second nutritional composite. . . . (The list would go on to describe all 18 independent variables. In most cases these variables would be described in some detail in the methods section of the report, perhaps even with the use of a table, thus they would not need to be repeated in the results section.)

Five independent variables were identified that contributed significantly to the overall R^2 of .269 [F = 86.8 (df = 5, 1180),* p < .0001]. These were, in order of importance, (1) nutritional composite 1, (2) the importance placed on restricting one's cholesterol intake, (3) nutritional composite 2, (4) age, and (5) alcohol consumption. As indicated by Table 16-4, however, the contribution made by these final two variables were relatively trivial, amounting to a combined total of less than 1 percent of the overall amount of explained variance.

Since there is so much variation in the way the results of a multiple-regression analysis can be reported, the beginning researcher would probably be best advised to consult the journal to which he or she is planning to submit the research report to see the most often-reported form. Table 16-4 does communicate most of the essential information (especially since the overall R and its attendant F and degrees of freedom are reported in the text), thus most varia-

* See (17) and (18) of Table 16-3.

tions will be organizational in nature. For a much more in-depth treatment of multiple regression, see Kerlinger and Pedhazur (1973) or for a somewhat less-exhaustive but still very helpful discussion, Darlington (1968).

SUMMARY

Many of the most important variables affecting human subjects are either not manipulatable or are better studied in naturalistic settings. In such circumstances, statistical control must be substituted for procedural control, usually via a multiple-regression model employing a number of independent or predictor variables. Although a number of analytic options exist, one of the most commonly employed consists of a forward stepwise regression procedure, in which independent variables are rank-ordered with respect to their unique explanatory power. Regardless of the specific option chosen, a multiple-regression procedure normally yields the following information:

1. An overall multiple correlation coefficient, which when squared (denoted as R^2) indicates the total percentage of dependent variable variation accounted for by all the independent variables in combination.
2. The individual contribution of each separate independent variable to the total R^2 when all the other independent variables are held constant (partialled out).
3. The statistical significance of the overall R^2 (1) and the unique contribution made thereto by each independent variable (2).

Some of the more important assumptions regarding the use of linear regression techniques include:

1. That the independent and dependent variables be measures for which the arithmetic mean is an appropriate descriptor.
2. That the relationships between these variables be linear.
3. That the interrelationships among the independent variables not be excessively high.
4. That a reasonably high subject-to-variable ratio (25:1 is recommended) be employed.

REFERENCES

Darlington, R. B. Multiple regression. *Psychological Bulletin,* 1968, *65,* 161–182.
Kerlinger, F. N., and Pedhazur, E. J. *Multiple Regression in Behavioral Research.* New York: Holt, Rinehart, and Winston, 1973.
Nie, N. H., Hull, C. H., Jenkins, J. G., Steinbrenner, K., and Brent, D. H. *Statistical Package for the Social Sciences.* New York: McGraw-Hill, 1975.

five

EVALUATING AND COMMUNICATING THE RESULTS

chapter *17*

Evaluating and Communicating the Results

Once the data have been analyzed and interpreted, it is important for a re-searcher to step back and evaluate the now-completed study as objectively as possible. This is often difficult, but it is a task that no one is in a better position to accomplish than the person who has actually conducted the study. For some, the evaluation of a study is more easily done following the preparation of the final research report. When the task is accomplished is not so important as how well it is accomplished, although obviously any written report must ultimately reflect its author's honest appraisal of how cleanly and appropriately a study was conducted.

Basically, any empirical research study should be evaluated with respect to the importance of the questions (or hypotheses) it addressed and the confi-dence that can be placed in the answers (or conclusions) it generated. These two parameters pretty much represent the entire research process as outlined in Chapter 1 and discussed in detail throughout the remainder of this book.

Rather than present an exhaustive checklist* for what is basically a sub-jective process, I counsel researchers to use the contents of this book to attempt to answer the following two questions:

1. How important were the questions (or hypotheses) addressed by my study?

If the study was clinical in nature, what effect will the answers obtained have on clinical *practice?* If the study was theoretical, can any of the answers

* Of those checklists that have been published, I recommend Isaac and Michael (1977, pp. 156–158).

either substantively challenge or support the theory being tested? If the study was an empirical extension of other research, can any of the answers explain previously unexplained phenomena? In other words, are there any real uses to which the obtained answers can be put?

2. To what extent can the resulting answers be trusted?

In other words, was the study conducted cleanly using a research model that effectively limited the most plausible and virulent alternative explanations for the obtained results? Were the variables employed measured appropriately? Are the interpretations drawn from these results evenhanded and defensible?

Assuming the absence of a decidedly negative answer to either of these questions, all researchers have the obligation to prepare a written report to communicate their findings to other professionals. There are at least two reasons for this obligation. In the first place, the conduct of all research involves the expenditure of increasingly limited societal resources. Second, and obviously related to this, the whole idea behind empirical research is to accumulate knowledge by testing hypotheses and theories. Obviously, nothing of substance can accumulate if researchers cannot build on one another's work.

Research reports are typically either published in a research journal, presented at a professional conference, or both. Occasionally, it will be readily available only to members of the author's institution as an internal report (although usually such documents are available to outside researchers on request). Very rarely, the study will comprise a separate publication of its own, such as a monograph or a book. For graduate students, of course, the finished product is most often their bound thesis or dissertation, which will be available in their institution's library or on microfilm.

Regardless of the specific medium in which the final research report appears, its basic components are always the same. These have already been discussed in Chapter 1 and are:

1. *An introduction to the problem under investigation.* This will include an explanation of exactly what the problem is, why it is important enough to study, how it relates to previous theory and research, and perhaps a formal statement of the research questions or hypotheses being investigated. (In a thesis or dissertation, the relationship to previous work will comprise a separate chapter. For most other reports, all of the above elements are normally blended together.)
2. *A description of the procedures used to address the problem.* This basically encompasses:
   (a) How subjects were selected for the study.
   (b) How many were used.
   (c) How they were assigned to groups (if they were so assigned).
   (d) *Precisely* what was done to them (including how, when, and for how long).
   (e) How they were measured (including salient reliability and validity data on the measurement instruments themselves).

3. *A description and presentation of the results.* This includes a description of the statistical procedures used to test the hypothesis(es), the outcome(s) thereof, summary statistics where appropriate, and, usually, subsidiary findings of interest.
4. *A discussion of the study findings.* This section explains why the results probably manifested themselves in the way they did and what these results signify with respect to the previous research upon which the study was originally based.

In other words, the research report is really no more (or less) than a written record of the basic components making up the research process discussed in Chapter 1. Its function is to delineate, as economically and in as unadorned manner as possible, the study's purpose, the rationale for that purpose, the way in which it was accomplished, the results obtained, and the interpretation of the final results. The report should be written based on the assumption that its audience may wish not only to understand each step in the process, but also to *evaluate* and possibly *replicate* the study as a whole.

All of this results in an undeniable fact; for many people, the actual writing of a research report is a difficult, time-consuming, and tedious task. In many ways, it is the least enjoyable aspect of the research process. In the final analysis, however, it is also one of the most important, for it is only through the communication of the research process that a researcher's efforts are ultimately rewarded.

REASONS TO WRITE A RESEARCH REPORT

There are basically two motivations for writing research reports: altruistic and egocentric. Both have been touched on, but both are important enough to deserve additional discussion.

Altruism

Building empirical knowledge is an endless journey comprised of enumerable, tiny steps. In most cases, these individual steps are discrete research findings found in published research reports. One step taken may either lead to another or prevent the necessity of someone else taking it. A step taken but not communicated can help no one. Since empirical research is an expensive endeavor, whether it is formally funded or not, and since resources of all kinds are limited, including time and material, researchers have an obligation to make their studies count for something, even if it is to prevent others from making similar mistakes or going down blind alleys.

Ego

For better or worse, personal reinforcement is a far more effective motivator than altruism. In universities, professional appointments, advancement, tenure, and salaries are decisively influenced by the presence of published research reports on one's curriculum vitae. Even when the professional is not operating under the publish-or-perish imperative, the existence of an impressive publication list opens up additional vistas and options. Everything else being equal, the researcher with a vitae containing research publications will be in a more advantageous position than one without such a track record, whether it is in applying for research grants (where an impressive list of published research reports is definitely to one's benefit) or (to a lesser extent) for nonacademic (and nonresearch) positions. In many, many ways, especially in academe, research publications are the coin of the realm. To conduct research and not to publish it is a form of professional masochism.

Such considerations aside, the personal satisfaction that comes from presenting a paper to a large group of interested colleagues or of seeing one's name in print in a prestigious journal may be the best reason of all to write a research report. Personally, I have found nothing in my professional life more rewarding than the discovery of a new, previously unknown relationship. This is followed closely by seeing my first few studies in print.

Another Reason

Although these are the primary reasons for writing a research report, there is one other and it is that the process *is not nearly as difficult as it seems.* Furthermore, it is a behavior possessing a definite practice effect. Research reports are so stylistically prescribed that after the format has been gone through once, subsequent reports become geometrically easier to prepare. For this reason, it is unfortunate that most beginning researchers' first exposure to writing research reports is via the cumbersome, redundant, long-winded, and often oversupervised thesis or dissertation format. The average manuscript prepared for the typical research journal is probably no more than one-tenth as long (and probably about one-tenth as difficult to write).

REASONS NOT TO WRITE A RESEARCH REPORT

The only good reasons that I can think of for not writing a research report are:

1. The research is flawed to such an extent that sufficient confidence cannot be placed in its results or conclusions.
2. The research makes no contribution to the literature (and hence really should not have been carried out in the first place).

Avoidance of these two situations constitutes much of the subject matter of this book. Assuming that they can be overcome, the advantages of writing a research report far outweigh any negative rationalizations.

ESSENTIAL CHARACTERISTICS OF A RESEARCH REPORT

The underlying purpose of a research report is the communication of factual information. Clarity, conciseness, and complete veracity are therefore absolutely essential characteristics of the final document. Professionals read research studies to be enlightened, not entertained. Figures of speech, lyrical prose, and amusing anecdotes usually have no place in a research report. Neither do lengthy digressions or unnecessary detail, since space is almost always at a premium (and even when it is not, the reader's time is).

All of this is not to say that the researcher's writing style is not important. It also is not meant to imply that a research report need be dull; the more interesting it is, the greater will be both its audience and its impact. Everything else being equal, a researcher with a clear, concise, and interesting writing style will find it easier to publish and will find a larger audience than the researcher cursed with obtuse, rambling prose. A passable writing style, however, is not an inborn trait. It is an acquirable skill that can be developed through conscious effort, skin thick enough to accept proofreaders' suggestions, and enough patience to keep revising a paper until it is acceptable. Some very good references exist to facilitate these efforts as well, including Strunk and White's *The Elements of Style* (1978), Zinsser's *On Writing Well* (1985), *A Manual of Style* (1982) published by the University of Chicago Press, and the *Publication Manual of the American Psychological Association* (1983) (which not only is used as the style guide for a number of journals, but also contains a good deal of advice relevant to the writing of research reports in general).

Truthfulness

If there is one salient characteristic of a professional researcher and a professional research report it is absolute, uncompromising honesty. This characteristic should permeate every section of the final research report. Its *introduction,* for example, should not exaggerate the study's importance; literature should not be cited that has not been read (such as pirating sections of other people's literature reviews). Of equal importance, all ideas taken from other sources should be cited. Plagiarism is as serious an offense in research as in all other forms of scholarship. The *methods* section must report things as they occurred, not as they should have occurred. *Anything* that potentially affects a study's validity must be reported. Needless to say, outright untruths (such as pretending that subjects were randomly assigned to groups when in fact intact groups or purposeful assignment were used) have no place in research and can seriously impede progress in a discipline. (Granted, honesty can be difficult at times, but there is really no alternative. If it is any consolation, I have always found that journal reviewers appreciate an author's honest appraisal of a study's flaws. Mentioning them up front can even have the effect of stealing a critic's thunder.) Outright falsification of data in the *result* section is still relatively rare, but it is all too easy for some people to cheat in other ways, such as to come up with a reason to drop one or two subjects from a study who do not conform to the overall predicted pattern and thus lower the obtained alpha level just enough to obtain statistical significance. Finally, it is equally important to be truthful in the *discussion* section. For a not inconsequential number of researchers, the implications of their studies will be the same regardless of their empirical outcomes. For these people, the truth is known prior to conducting the study. (Theory X, for example, is correct, and any outcome can be explained in such a way that it constitutes conclusive evidence thereof.)

Any person with uncorrectable tendencies toward any of these practices should not conduct research. *Research is not a game.* It is a serious attempt on humanity's part to understand the universe and improve the human condition therein. We simply cannot afford cheating, falsification, or gamesmanship in this pursuit.

CHOOSING THE MEDIUM

The basic hierarchy for communicating research results, from most to least prestigious, is:

1. *A research monograph* published as an adjunct to a refereed journal (see below) or a prestigious publishing company (especially a university press). Such publications are normally current for longer periods of time than journal articles, although in many cases the*y* may actually be read by *fewer* people. This medium is appropriate only for large-scale studies that are perceived to be of major import. It is not normally an option available to a beginning researcher.

2. *A refereed research journal.* Academe is placing increasing importance on the refereeing process, which normally translates to an editor (perhaps after a gross screening to make sure that a manuscript is generally appropriate for his or her journal) sending a paper out to several reviewers judged to be conversant with the represented research area. These reviewers, who normally aren't told either the author's name or institutional affiliation (called blind review), are asked to do two things:

   (a) Make a judgment as to whether or not the manuscript should be accepted outright, accepted pending minor revisions, revised and reviewed again, or rejected outright.

   (b) Supply comments regarding suggestions, revisions, or a rationale for why the paper was either accepted or rejected.

   Given the selection of good reviewers, this process works very well in weeding out trivial research and in discovering methodological flaws. It also serves as a good instructional medium for beginning researchers, who are able to receive expert critiques and advice free of charge.

   In my experience, the most prestigious research journals are in fact the journals with the more competent and conscientious reviewers, hence it is often a good idea to start at the top when submitting a research article. (There is a definite hierarchy among research journals, with those possessing the larger circulations and being affiliated with major professional organizations generally being the more prestigious.)

3. *A national professional convention.* Each discipline normally has one chief convention given over primarily to the delivery of scholarly papers. Some are exclusively research oriented, although many allow for a combination of research, theoretical, and applied topics. These, like most research journals, are normally refereed. The medium of delivery here, of course, is oral, often limited to 15- or 20-minute presentations supplemented by a written paper (which is either handed out or available from the author on request) or audiovisual aids of some sort.

An oral presentation is really not an optimal medium to communicate research results, thus many associations publish abstracts of their proceedings. The more ambitious researchers also submit their papers to refereed journals following the convention, often with a note to the effect that the manuscript is based on a paper presented at the Annual Meeting of the Society for. . . . As with journals, there is a definite hierarchy among conventions with respect to attendant prestige. Some of the larger conferences accept so many papers (sometimes over a thousand as in the case of the American Educational Research Association or the American Psychological Association) that the quality and significance of many of the studies are almost invariably less than those published in some of the better journals (which may publish fewer than 40 manuscripts per year).

There are distinct advantages to presenting a research report to a live audience, not the least of which is the opportunity to meet other researchers working along the same lines of inquiry. Therefore, I recommend the oral presentation of research findings, but the beginning researcher should be aware that somewhat less credit is normally afforded such efforts.

4. *Other outlets for empirical research results.* Although the above three outlets are the media of choice for most researchers, there are several additional ways to disseminate research results. Briefly, they are:

   (a) *Nonrefereed journals, research and otherwise.* Although such journals are looked on somewhat dubiously by many professionals (whether rightly or wrongly), these outlets do constitute a definite option for research that cannot be published elsewhere. I recommend that refereed journals be tried first.

   (b) *Regional or local research conferences.* These are similar to item 3 above, but are often scaled down in terms of size, attendance, and prestige. They can serve as a nonthreatening platform for the beginning researcher to start out with.

   (c) *Descriptive articles in nonresearch journals.* Many of the most widely read publications, even among professionals, do not publish empirical research per se. Instead, they often contain some articles describing particularly interesting studies, thus affording a researcher a much wider audience than he or she would normally have. Increasingly, some researchers are going directly to the press with their results, although I recommend that research first be submitted to peer review before that step is taken.

Publishing the Same Study Several Times

A growing phenomenon in recent years involves the practice of breaking up a single study into what is referred to as least-publishable units. It represents a sort of gamesmanship designed to maximize one's mileage from any given effort, thus the same study may appear in various guises in several different journals (often spanning diverse disciplines to avoid notice). The effect of the practice is to trivialize the research effort and I definitely recommend against it, both professionally and personally (since I believe that far more mileage is obtained from one important study than any number of trivial ones).

Multiple Authorships

Another game often played by individuals interested chiefly in quantity rather than quality is to include large numbers of coauthors who may be related only tangentially to the study at hand. These coauthors then reciprocate when they publish, thus providing everyone with an impressive curriculum vitae. This is basically an unethical practice and a form of gamesmanship that has no place in research. Research is simply too important an endeavor for games of any sort.*

WRITING THE RESEARCH REPORT

The first step in preparing a research report is deciding on the medium through which it will be disseminated. I unhesitatingly recommend that a specific refereed journal be selected for this purpose if the study was performed well enough and makes a sufficient contribution (assuming that a research monograph is not an option). Journal articles generally receive wider (and more sustained) attention than papers presented at conferences (although there is seldom any restriction on both presenting and publishing a paper, as long as the former occurs first).

Choosing the specific journal to which a manuscript will be submitted requires both knowledge of the publications in a field (with respect to both the types of research each publishes and their relative hierarchy) and the ability to evaluate one's work objectively. The more prestigious the journal, the higher will be its rejection rate. Since it may take three months or more for some journals to reject a manuscript, the probability of failure must be taken into consideration. (It is not permissible to submit a manuscript to more than one refereed research journal at a time.) Advice from well-published colleagues

---

* This should not be interpreted as advising against the use of coauthors. Credit should be given where credit is due. It is even better to err on the side of generosity. In some disciplines (such as medicine), however, 15 or more coauthors are not that uncommon for a single empirical study. This, in my opinion, borders on the ridiculous.

regarding a good outlet for a particular study can be quite helpful for researchers relatively new to this process.

In general, I would recommend aiming high (at least within the realm of reality). Even when a manuscript is rejected, reviews from good journals often contain constructive suggestions for improvement. As an example, I once conducted a study as a graduate student that neither I nor anyone in my institution knew how to analyze statistically. On the advice of a mentor, I submitted the manuscript to the most prestigious journal in the field (even though its analysis was obviously inappropriate) on the theory that, even though it was likely to be rejected, the reviewers would probably mention how the data should have been analyzed. Sure enough, the manuscript was returned with a detailed description of what the appropriate analysis should have been along with an invitation to resubmit once this analysis had been effected. (The manuscript was subsequently published by the journal.)

I recommend that the specific journal to which a manuscript will be submitted be identified *prior* to writing the research report, simply because individual journals normally have idiosyncratic requirements. Journals differ from one another in the headings they use, the ways in which tables are laid out and labeled, reference and citation formats, and so forth. (These are normally described on a page somewhere in the journal or are available from the journal's editorial office.) Such requirements should be strictly adhered to, which means that a manuscript must be tailored for the journal to which it is to be submitted. Should it be resubmitted to another journal following rejection, appropriate sections should be retyped.

Once the specific journal format has been assimilated, the most important task is actually to begin writing. Undoubtedly, *beginning* is the most difficult part of preparing a research report. It is so difficult, in fact, that a surprising number of professionals never manage it. One way to approach the task is to visualize it as writing four small papers instead of one longer one. These four papers comprise the four sections of a research report, of course, and since, with the exception of the last one, they are relatively discrete, the researcher can begin with the one he or she finds the easiest to write. Some researchers prefer to write the *methods* section (see Part Two) first, since in some ways an empirical study's procedures are its heart. Regardless of where one begins, however, some very *general* suggestions follow for preparing each of the constituent parts of the research report.

PART ONE: THE INTRODUCTION

This section normally contains a case for the importance of the general problem under investigation, a literature review of related research, and an explicit statement of the hypotheses or relationships being tested. Some journals use a subheading such as *introduction* (in which the general problem area is laid out), *review of related literature,* and *hypotheses* (in which the hypotheses or specific research questions are formally stated). Others use no subheadings at all; some journals do not even encourage a formal statement of the hypotheses, relying instead on a statement of the study's purpose. There is no right or wrong format for a research report; the only rule is the pragmatic suggestion to use whatever conventions the medium and its readers are accustomed to.

The introduction to a research report should be visualized as possessing a dual purpose: communicating the exact purpose that the study was designed to serve (or, said another way, the questions it was designed to answer) and building a case for the importance of these purposes or questions. These are both important components; obviously, the readers need to know exactly what the study was designed to address, but it is equally important that they be apprised of the significance of what is being so addressed. What may seem perfectly obvious in these regards to someone who has been working on a study for six months may be far from obvious to someone who has not. Viewed from another perspective, there are far more research articles than anyone can, or cares to, read. Part of the function of a research report's introduction is to lay out the case for the study's importance to enable readers to decide whether or not they wish to proceed.

Both of these objectives can be accomplished in a few brief paragraphs as a lead-in to the literature review. In a sense, the literature review is nothing more than a continuation of the process of selling the importance of a study. It tells the reader how the study at hand fits into previous research, while subtly demonstrating that other investigators have found the topic important enough to study (and by implication, that other journals have found such studies important enough to accept for publication). It demonstrates that the specific study at hand is a natural outgrowth (and, one hopes, an extension) of this previous research, which may well constitute the most cogent and persuasive case that can be made for a study's importance.

The literature review is so important in this regard that (coupled with the general introduction to the topic) it may be the single most important determinant of a study's ultimate acceptance or rejection. The review of literature should not be too long, too detailed, too cursory, or too brief. Its purpose, outside of doctoral dissertations, is not to demonstrate how much its author knows about the research in a particular area, but how well he or she has brought previous knowledge to bear on the present research objective. In general, references should be directly related to the variables and hypotheses under study. These references should also be primarily empirical in nature, unless a well-known theoretician in the area has posited a relationship directly relevant to the hypothesis being tested.

The manner in which references are integrated and used to justify and clarify the problem under investigation is far more important than the sheer number of such references used. Statements with long lists of unexplained references [such as "many investigators have studied this topic (e.g., Stokes, 1972; Smith; Williams & Jones, 1983. . .)"] are patently worthless. If a study is important enough to cite, its results are important enough to describe at least briefly. The opposite extreme is just as bad, such as a statement beloved by student researchers: "A review of the literature over the past 10 years revealed no pertinent research in the area." It is difficult to imagine any topic important enough to research that *someone* hasn't investigated it over the past 10 years. A statement such as this, therefore, will almost certainly be fatal to the author's credibility, especially if it is seen by a reviewer who has either conducted research in the area or knows of some research so conducted.

Journals differ with respect to the amount of background information they require (or even permit) to introduce their studies, thus, specific recommendations regarding length and number of references are difficult to make. Generally speaking, the entire introductory section seldom exceeds five or six typed pages. Prospective authors should always check typical practices in the journal to which they are submitting, although this is not to say that most editors will not grant exceptions to their norms for compelling reasons.

Purposes/Hypotheses

Following the general introduction to the problem and a thorough, integrated review of the literature, the specific purpose of the study at hand is normally stated. The reader, of course, already has an excellent idea of what the study will be about, but now the time has come to state it explicitly. Everything written previously should lead directly and logically to this point. The author, in fact, should actually be able to write (if he or she chooses): "The purpose of the present study, *therefore,* was to assess. . . ." Alternatively, the study's hypothesis(es) can be formally stated (via a list, if there are more than one).

The transitions from general introductory remarks to literature review to the explicit statement of the study's objectives should be as smooth as possible. The major function of this entire section is to communicate to the reviewers (and later the readers) the importance of the study, where it fits into previous research in the area, and exactly what is to be studied. If these objectives are not met, then the chances are excellent that the study will not be published.

PART TWO: METHODS

This section tells the reader exactly *how* the study was conducted (or how the hypotheses were tested). It is also the section that permits the reviewer and the reader to evaluate the appropriateness of the procedures employed and of the study itself. It is the section that will permit another researcher to replicate the study if so desired, thus absolute honesty and explicitness are essential. (Toward this end, it is a good idea to take copious notes, perhaps in log form, as the study is being conducted to ensure later accuracy in reporting exactly what transpired, especially if any length of time is to elapse between the conduct of the study and the actual writing of the report.) Many journals employ subheads such as *subjects* (or sample), *procedure,* and perhaps *instrumentation* (or instruments). For ease of explication, these headings will be assumed here, although, as always, prospective authors should consult the medium's guidelines to which they plan to submit their manuscript.

Subjects

This section provides pertinent detail about the study's sample including: the population from which they were selected, how they were selected, how many were selected, the proportion that declined participation or were lost during the course of the study, the reasons for this loss, and *possibly* some summary statistics regarding especially germane demographic characteristics (such as the percentage of males and females, the average age of the subjects, and so forth). All of this information should be communicable in no more than two or three paragraphs. Lengthy tables containing summary information with respect to a plethora of demographic variables are not usually welcomed anywhere outside of a dissertation or thesis because of (1) space restrictions and (2) the fact that they seldom help the reader that much in evaluating the study. Since the chief purpose of the methods section is to facilitate this evaluative process, any characteristic that might make the sample atypical to the population to which the results would normally be generalized *should* be mentioned.

Procedure

This section should be written to enable the reader to replicate the study if he or she so desired. Everything that transpired in the study should be described in sufficient detail to allow the reader to understand exactly what was done to the subjects, including:

1. How subjects were assigned to groups (for example, random assignment, the use of intact groups).
2. Instructions given to subjects (including procedures taken for guarding their rights).
3. A detailed description of all treatment and control conditions (when relevant).
4. How, when, and on what subjects were measured.

Since the chief purpose of this section is to help the reader evaluate the study's internal validity, any mistakes or unforeseen events occurring during the course of the study that could *possibly* affect it should be candidly mentioned. This can be painful, but full disclosure of this sort is the hallmark of a true researcher. It may help to remind oneself that few studies are conducted perfectly. If the temptation to gloss over such difficulties is just too great to resist, I seriousy recommend finding another field of endeavor.

Instrumentation

Unless the measures employed are extremely familiar to the research report's audience (such as the use of WISC-R for a psychology journal), the data-collection instruments should be described in as much detail as possible. At a minimum, relevant psychometric (for example, reliability, item format, and any other information bearing on the instrument's utility) should be supplied. For scales developed specifically for the study by its author, some detail about the construction process must be included. When possible, sample items are also often helpful in allowing the reader to visualize new or seldom-used measures as well. However, this subsection should be kept as brief as possible.

PART THREE: RESULTS

This is undoubtedly the easiest section of the report to write, although often the most dreaded. The section often begins by briefly mentioning the statistical procedures used to address the study's hypotheses. Unless an especially esoteric procedure is employed for this purpose (and none of the ones mentioned in this book so qualify), the statistic itself does not need to be explained. It is important, however, for the reader to understand on what the analyses were performed. In a procedure such as multiple regression, for example, the reader should understand exactly what the independent and dependent variables were and how they were defined (for example, if a categorical variable such as marital status is used, the reader should be told exactly what categories were employed and if they were dummy coded). With an analysis of covariance, the reader should be told how the groups were defined, what the covariate was, and, of course, what constituted the dependent variable.

A probability level should be reported for each hypothesis test as well as the statistic itself (for example, F, R, t) and its attendant degrees of freedom. When possible, an indicator of the relationship's strength (such as r^2 or R^2) should also be presented. Only one analysis per hypothesis should be reported. Some researchers like to analyze their data several ways, but this is simple redundancy. One analytic scheme should be selected and adhered to. Finally, the reader should be given some means of visualizing the results. For experimental and quasi-experimental studies, this translates to group means and standard deviations. For correlational studies, it might simply translate to a tabled list of the individual contributions to R^2 made by each independent variable.

Most researchers are guilty of overanalyzing their data, of testing every conceivable relationship between the variables employed. While there is nothing wrong with explanatory analyses of this sort per se, some tests may reach statistical significance simply as a function of chance. (For example, if 20 correlation coefficients are performed on sets of random numbers, one coefficient is likely to achieve statistical significance at the .05 level by chance alone.) The researcher should be wary, therefore, of placing too much credence in secondary analyses (that is, analyses not specifically targeted by an a priori prediction). I would instead counsel limiting the reporting of secondary analyses to a relatively small number of relationships whose testing possess some theoretical or empirical rationale.* Such analyses may be placed under a subheading (for example, *secondary analyses, subsidiary findings*) and should be

---

* This does not mean that secondary analyses should not be *performed*. Such analyses often suggest profitable directions for additional research.

discussed regardless of their statistical significance or nonsignificance. In other words, the decision to report an analysis should be made prior to its computation; if this computation yields a nonsignificant result, then that nonsignificant result should be reported.

In general, the results section should be clear and succinct. Some technical jargon is unavoidable, but it should not be pursued for its own sake. It should be obvious, even to the statistically unsophisticated reader, which hypotheses were and were not supported and exactly what the subsidiary findings, if any, were. Tables and figures should be used sparingly and with the reader's elucidation in mind rather than for cosmetic or false erudition purposes. They should be understandable with a minimum of study and not overly cluttered.

PART FOUR: THE DISCUSSION

This may well be both the briefest and most difficult part of the report to write. Although it may contain elements of summarization, it should be more than that.* The discussion section should review the original purposes of the study, discuss how these purposes were met, and attempt to explain why the obtained results occurred. (This latter task naturally invites a degree of subjectivity, thus the researcher should attempt to be as evenhanded as possible, discussing alternative explanations.) Perhaps most important, this section must present the author's *conclusions* for practice, theory, and future research.

An integral element of the final conclusions that can be legitimately drawn from a study is a frank discussion of its limitations, namely, the extent to which *the results can be believed.* Another element of these conclusions should be a brief, realistic evaluation of the contribution the study at hand makes to the literature cited in the introductory section.

I counsel against concluding a study with statements such as "these findings can only be generalized to the actual setting and sample employed" or "these findings indicate the need for additional research." Such statements unnecessarily brand their authors as beginning researchers; they also end any report with a whimper. Admittedly, it is a difficult line to walk, but the researcher should strive for *professionalism* rather than too much modesty or too much hype. The study should be evaluated fairly as a disinterested, highly professional reviewer might evaluate it. The researcher should not be afraid to mention both strengths and weaknesses, which is in itself a triumph of *confidence* over timidity.

THE ABSTRACT AND TITLE

Logic would appear to dictate that the abstract and title of a manuscript should be prepared first; in reality they are usually held for the end. There is nothing at

---

* Some journals require a formal *summary* or *summary and conclusions* subheading within this section.

all wrong with this, as long as the researcher saves enough time and energy to do these two very important constituents justice.

The Title

In this age of computerized retrieval systems, key words in the title can be prime determinants of how easily an article can be accessed. The author would be wise, therefore, to consider what key words best describe the study and include them, even if this precludes the possibility of a short, catchy title. Of equal importance, the title should communicate what the study is all about as accurately as possible. Of special importance, the title should not contain misleading or inaccurate information, such as specifying an effect for a variable when the study was correlational in nature.

The Abstract

Journals vary widely with respect to how long they allow abstracts to be. Usually, the preferred length is in the 100 to 200 word range, which is not a great deal of space to sum up one's intensive labors over the past six months. How well the abstract is written, and how interesting it makes the accompanying study appear, will have a large part in determining how many people actually read the full article. Many people scan the abstracts in a journal issue just to select the one or two offerings that they will actually read. Even with this in mind, it is very difficult to list rules for writing a good abstract. Word limitations, rather than being a drawback, are actually a boon in this regard, since they force authors to choose those words carefully.

The abstract contains elements from all four sections of the research report, including:

1. A brief two- or three-sentence case for the importance of the study (sans references of any kind) is a good beginning, followed by a succinct statement of the study's chief purpose.
2. The methods section is equally brief, seldom including more than the number of subjects, whether or not they were randomly assigned (in experimental and quasi-experimental models), and a *cursory* definition of the treatments (or variable sets in correlational models).
3. Results are presented, sans numbers (except perhaps probability levels), as they relate to the primary purpose of the study.
4. The conclusions, in one or two sentences, that best sum up the primary contribution of the study end the little piece.

There is seldom room for more than this, nor is it needed. There is room for exceptions, however, since anything that adds to a study (and might influence people to read it), such as an innovative design or an especially provocative subsidiary finding, *should* be included.

EVALUATING THE MANUSCRIPT

Let us now assume that the manuscript has been written, revised, and, one hopes, typed in rough form. After all the work that has gone into this effort, it is natural to experience an overwhelming desire to get the manuscript out and forget about it. This is not wise. *Because* of all the effort expended, the researcher owes it to himself or herself to give the report the best possible chance of being accepted in a high-quality journal.

To do this, the manuscript should be evaluated as thoroughly and dispassionately as possible, since that is exactly what is in store for it as soon as it is submitted to a journal. If possible, this evaluation should be accomplished on two levels. First, knowledgeable colleagues (who themselves have published research) should be given the manuscript to critique. (If the paper has coauthors, both they and colleagues of their choosing should be among the reviewers.) Certainly, critiquing other people's research reports is not a very rewarding activity, but it is a professional courtesy that can be returned.

The second, and more important, phase of the evaluation involves the paper's primary author. This personal evaluation is best accomplished a few days after the final version has been prepared to provide a little extra perspective. I have always found it helpful to try to effect this critique as though I were a reviewer for the journal to which the manuscript is targeted. Usually such reviewers are asked to concentrate on *two* primary dimensions: the contribution that the study makes to the professional literature *and* the methodological cleanliness with which the study was carried out. What this means, therefore, is that the introductory sections should make an especially cogent case for the study's importance. This case includes a logically developed prose argument, a thorough and up-to-date literature review, and a clear concise statement of the problem or question at hand.

I suggest that researchers ask themselves (and any other reviewers at their disposal) the following questions:

1. Is a *logical,* coherent case made for the study's importance?
2. Is there any way that this case could be improved, either logically or stylistically?
3. Does the literature review blend in smoothly with this case?
4. Is the literature review *relevant* to both the case for the study's importance and the research problem?
5. Is the literature review thorough?
6. Have the area's most important (and best known) studies been cited?
7. Does the literature review contain relevant recent citations (that is, that have been published within a year or so)?
8. Does the statement of the study's purpose (or research question, problem, or hypothesis) flow smoothly and logically from everything that precedes it?
9. Is this statement extremely clear and concise? (It should almost jump out at the reader.)

The presentation of the study's methodology (which includes the appropriateness of the data analyses performed) should be evaluated in three ways: (1)

clarity, (2) completeness, and (3) *honesty*. Everything of importance that occurred during the course of the study should be described. This includes the way in which subjects were selected, how many were selected, how many refused to be selected, and how many were lost over the course of the study (and in what groups, if relevant, this loss primarily occurred). If something went wrong during the course of the study, the reader should be told about it. If the study had a built-in flaw, this flaw should be mentioned up front. The method by which subjects were assigned to groups, measured, and what was done to them (including *both* experimental and control conditions, where applicable) should be described clearly, consisely, and in sufficient detail to enable the reader both to understand and evaluate the study. Measuring instruments should be described in sufficient detail to enable the reader to visualize them (if sample items are not included). Relevant psychometric details on each should be included, such as item format, internal consistency, validation attempts (if any), and so forth. The data analysis section should be equally clear and complete. All independent and dependent variables should be listed, along with the levels or groups constituting them when appropriate. Finally, all of this information should flow logically and smoothly.

By the end of the data analysis section, the reader should know exactly the extent to which the study met its earlier, stated purposes. He or she should also know which hypotheses were accepted and which were rejected, as well as have a good feel for the strength of any statistically significant relationships obtained. (If statistical significance was not obtained, the reader should be apprised of the amount of statistical power present.) The discussion section should underline all these findings and tie them back to both the original logical case made for the study's importance and the relevant previous research findings cited in the first section. More than that, however, the appropriateness of the methodology should be explicitly evaluated with respect to the findings. If a methodological flaw was mentioned in the procedure section, it should be mentioned again here with respect to its potential and probable impact upon the study's findings. In addition to these points, the following questions are helpful in evaluating the discussion section:

1. Does it sound professional? (It should sound as though it were written by an experienced researcher, not an experienced public relations executive.)
2. Does it contain appropriate evaluative elements (either positive or negative)?
3. Does it attempt to explain the findings (perhaps by offering alternative explanations)?
4. Do these alternative explanations possess any kind of empirical substantiation (either from the present data or past research)?
5. Are any weaknesses in the study mentioned (all studies have *some* weaknesses)?
6. Is the discussion section itself *honest?* Do the conclusions fit the findings?

Finally, after all the above points have been addressed, the study's title and abstract should be reread. The primary criteria by which they should be judged are: (1) the accuracy and thoroughness with which they describe the study, (2) succinctness, and (3) clarity.

PREPARING THE MANUSCRIPT

By the time a research report is ready to be typed and duplicated, it represents an enormous amount of labor (not to mention ego and aspirations). Therefore, I believe that it is ridiculous not to invest the additional amount of time and effort necessary to produce a cosmetically appealing document. As a journal editor for many years, I know for a fact that a manuscript submitted looking like something the cat dragged in can bias reviewers against a study. It may not result in an excellent manuscript being rejected, but it may well influence a borderline decision. With this in mind, the following suggestions are tendered:

1. Have a preliminary (preferably typed) draft reviewed/copyedited by colleagues.
2. Once reviewed, have the final version typed by a competent typist using a high-quality typewriter.
3. Make sure that the journal's guidelines have been followed.
4. Use sufficiently wide margins.
5. If the journal requires camera-ready copies of figures (and most do), have them prepared professionally. (Most institutions of any size have a graphics department that can do this at a reasonable cost.)
6. Proofread the final copy carefully. Have corrections made neatly. Retype when necessary.
7. Have the prescribed number of copies (most refereed journals require at least three) run off on a high-quality duplicating machine.

HANDLING REJECTION (IF IT COMES)

It is possible that all the suggestions presented in this book may be followed and the manuscript may still be rejected. There are any number of ways this can happen, including the fact that one of its reviewers may have simply gotten up on the wrong side of the bed on the wrong day. In the event of rejection, I suggest the following sequence of steps:

1. Complain bitterly to everyone within earshot.
2. Write the editor a devastating letter questioning his or her motives or competence.
3. Wait a day, tear up the letter, read the reviewers' comments closely and dispassionately for any suggestions that could result in a stronger manuscript.
4. Reevaluate the manuscript yourself.

If you now question its contribution to the literature or its worth, wait a week and see if your opinion changes. If it doesn't, design a better study and start again. If it does, incorporate those reviewer comments that seem reasonable and *resubmit to another journal immediately.* Next to quality, persistence is probably the single most important key to publishing research.

Having a manuscript accepted in a refereed journal, after all, is a matter of getting three individual opinions to concur. Resubmitting to another journal will result in three different opinions that may be more positive. Admittedly, one needs a thick skin, but the refereed process is usually blind, so rejections are seldom personal.

MOVING ONWARD

Prior to finding out whether one's manuscript is accepted or rejected (a process that often takes as long as three months), a true researcher will have already begun a follow-up study. Despite the early admonition that no single study will solve all the problems in a particular line of inquiry, everyone believes that his or her study is the single exception to this rule while he or she is conducting it. Since this particular admonition has no exceptions, however, anyone who has just completed a study will immediately see a dozen ways that the study could have been improved and at least a dozen additional questions in dire need of answering. I sincerely hope that the majority of my readers will someday find themselves in this particular situation, for it will mean that they have become *researchers.*

REFERENCES

A Manual of Style, 13th edition. Chicago: University of Chicago Press, 1982.

Isaac, S. and Michael, W. B. *Handbook in Research and Evaluation.* San Diego, Calif.: Edits Publishers, 1977.

Publication Manual of the American Psychological Association, 3rd edition. Washington, D.C., 1983.

Strunk, W. and White, E. *The Elements of Style,* 3rd edition. New York: Macmillan, 1978.

Zinsser, W. *On Writing Well,* 3rd edition. New York: Harper & Row, 1985.

Index